HOW TO CREATE A
WILDLIFE
GARDEN

HOW TO CREATE A

Christine & Michael Lavelle

WILDLIFE
GARDEN

Complete instructions for designing and planting wildlife habitats, with over 40 practical projects, a directory of 70 wildlife species and 960 photographs

Photography by Peter Anderson
Special wildlife photography by Robert Pickett

LORENZ BOOKS

639.9209
Law

DEDICATION

This book is dedicated to our son Richard,
the light of our lives.

This edition is published by Lorenz Books
an imprint of Anness Publishing Ltd
Hermes House, 88–89 Blackfriars Road
London SE1 8HA; tel. 020 7401 2077; fax 020 7633 9499

www.lorenzbooks.com; www.annesspublishing.com

If you like the images in this book and would like to investigate
using them for publishing, promotions or advertising, please visit
our website www.practicalpictures.com for more information.

UK agent: The Manning Partnership Ltd;
tel. 01225 478444; fax 01225 478440;
sales@manning-partnership.co.uk

UK distributor: Grantham Book Services Ltd;
tel. 01476 541080; fax 01476 541061; orders@gbs.tbs-ltd.co.uk

North American agent/distributor: National Book Network;
tel. 301 459 3366; fax 301 429 5746; www.nbnbooks.com

Australian agent/distributor: Pan Macmillan Australia;
tel. 1300 135 113; fax 1300 135 103;
customer.service@macmillan.com.au

New Zealand agent/distributor: David Bateman Ltd;
tel. (09) 415 7664; fax (09) 415 8892

Publisher: Joanna Lorenz
Senior Managing Editor: Conor Kilgallon
Senior Editor: Felicity Forster
Photography: Peter Anderson
Special Wildlife Photography: Robert Pickett
Illustrator: Liz Pepperell
Copy Editor: Richard Rosenfeld
Jacket Design: Jonathan Davison
Designer: Lisa Tai
Editorial Reader: Penelope Goodare
Production Controller: Wendy Lawson

ETHICAL TRADING POLICY

At Anness Publishing we believe that business should be conducted
in an ethical and ecologically sustainable way, with respect for the
environment and a proper regard to the replacement of the natural
resources we employ.

As a publisher, we use a lot of wood pulp to make high-quality
paper for printing, and that wood commonly comes from spruce
trees. We are therefore currently growing more than 500,000 trees
in two Scottish forest plantations near Aberdeen – Berrymoss
(130 hectares/320 acres) and West Touxhill (125 hectares/
305 acres). The forests we manage contain twice the number
of trees employed each year in paper-making for our books.

Because of this ongoing ecological investment programme,
you, as our customer, can have the pleasure and reassurance of
knowing that a tree is being cultivated on your behalf to naturally
replace the materials used to make the book you are holding.

Our forestry programme is run in accordance with the UK
Woodland Assurance Scheme (UKWAS) and will be certified by
the internationally recognized Forest Stewardship Council (FSC).
The FSC is a non-government organization dedicated to promoting
responsible management of the world's forests. Certification ensures
forests are managed in an environmentally sustainable and socially
responsible way. For further information about this scheme, go to
www.annesspublishing.com/trees.

© Anness Publishing Ltd 2007

All rights reserved. No part of this publication
may be reproduced, stored in a retrieval system,
or transmitted in any way or by any means,
electronic, mechanical, photocopying, recording
or otherwise, without the prior written permission
of the copyright holder.

A CIP catalogue record for this book
is available from the British Library.

NOTE

In the United States, throughout the Sun Belt states,
from Florida, across the Gulf Coast, south Texas, southern
deserts to southern California and coastal regions, annuals
are planted in the autumn, bloom in the winter and spring,
and die at the beginning of the summer.

12/07
Bist

CONTENTS

INTRODUCTION

The aim of this book is to show how gardeners and wildlife can share the same space without conflict and to mutual benefit. Many gardeners want to see wildlife in the garden but fear that it might damage their plants or be a thorough nuisance, so it's important to stress that the vast majority of garden creatures will never cause any trouble, and those that can, often make a meal for larger creatures. Over time, you will learn to recognize them, and if unsure, you can consult a local expert for advice.

Above: *Birds are probably the most popular and engaging visitors to gardens, where they find food, shelter and nesting sites.*

WHY HELP WILDLIFE?

This book is concerned, as are many gardeners, with the state of the environment and the effect we have on the natural world. Increasingly, people are realizing that plants and animals that were once common are now threatened as modern living and developments ruin their homes and habitats. Gardeners are particularly aware that we must share our outdoor living space with other creatures, and this book is a guide for both beginners and the more experienced who want to encourage nature back into the garden.

The book is structured in a simple, down-to-earth way, with easy-to-follow explanations that demystify this exciting aspect of gardening. The language is largely non-technical, although many of the techniques described are based on sound scientific principles. An explanation of the underlying principles of the natural sciences is followed by clear advice on how best to design, plant out and maintain areas that are suitable for wildlife.

Gardens can be visited by a wide range of creatures, and consequently the descriptions and explanations cover a wide range of topics and do not simply focus on the narrower requirements of one single geographic region. Despite different climates and surroundings, many of the techniques remain the same across the continents and are easily adapted.

THE WILDLIFE AGENDA

Wherever possible, ideas and design solutions are included to illustrate how you can create all kinds of habitats within a garden. Planting plans are included for specific projects, and to inspire your own ideas for making wildlife-friendly features. The text is lavishly supported with illustrations and photographs that bring the ideas to life.

The approach is packed with common sense, and is centred on the creation of outdoor living spaces that are attractive, functional and fun, while simultaneously being great for wildlife. Clear step-by-step guides show how different tasks can be realized, and many important tips are

Left: *Wildlife gardens need not look unkempt – they can be just as neatly designed and ornamental as any other type of garden.*

Below: *Many different insect species, such as this bee, depend upon bright and colourful flowers for their food.*

specially included. The aim is to make the functionality of your garden space, the needs of wildlife and a beautiful design completely gel, and dispel the myth that a wildlife-friendly garden must resemble a neglected, unsightly and overgrown patch of wilderness.

TOPICS COVERED

Starting with an explanation of what wildlife gardening is, the text clearly outlines the main principles and natural cycles that work both on a global scale and, most importantly, in your own garden. It shows how a wildlife garden works in harmony with all nature's rhythms and cycles, and spells out how all the wildlife in your garden has a part to play.

Once the basics are understood, the section dealing with planning and design explains how to take stock of what you already have, while giving detailed advice on how to assess your own needs, as well as those of the wildlife, and produce the best possible design for your garden. Sample designs show how the basic design principles can be applied to a range of garden sizes and settings.

The major habitat types are also clearly described, focusing on their relevance to the garden, and the section on creating new habitats gives clear and simple advice and instructions on how to recreate these features in a garden. Considerable emphasis is placed on the importance of getting out there and enjoying the garden. Maintenance should never be a chore, and

Above: *Carnivorous mammals such as this stoat are rare visitors to gardens as they need larger hunting territories.*

Above: *Adult ladybirds are small and highly visible beetles that eat aphids and help to control these pests.*

the wildlife garden ought to be a unique place for you and your family to relax and experience a closeness to nature.

Ideas for helping some of your favourite species, including birds and butterflies, are also outlined, with practical advice on feeding and helping all kinds of garden creatures. The aim is to create a super, all-inclusive habitat. You'll find advice on making hibernation sites and providing shelter and cover, and on helping some creatures that, in turn, will actually improve the health of your plants. Practical, effective horticultural practices and advice on watching, recording and enjoying the wildlife in the garden make sure that nothing is left to chance.

Finally, the directory gives clear descriptions of some of the commoner creatures that you'll see in a garden, complete with notes on recognition, how to attract them into the garden and what habitats they need. Understanding why they

Left: *Caterpillars are eaten by many animals, and these cinnabar moth caterpillars advertise that they are poisonous with their striking black and yellow colouring.*

Right: *Vegetarian mammals such as this mouse are common in gardens and are an important food source for larger carnivores that may occasionally visit the garden.*

visit and their needs are key aspects to the success of a wildlife garden, and the directory provides a firm basis, helping you to help your garden wildlife. There is also an extensive section covering some of the best wildlife-friendly plants, and how to grow them.

Whether you want your garden to be an outdoor living space, a dazzling array of colour or a place to grow food for the kitchen, the application of the following design principles will help you achieve this, and create a rewarding wildlife sanctuary.

WILDLIFE IN YOUR GARDEN

There can be few gardeners who have not experienced the thrill of a close encounter with some form of wildlife in their garden. Birds and butterflies are an obvious joy to watch flying among the trees and flowers, but there are many creatures that scurry and slide underneath the plants and into dark crevices that are less well understood and sometimes less welcome. Yet these crawling mini-beasts are actually the unsung heroes of the garden, and knowing why they are important and what they do is a vital first step in becoming a wildlife gardener.

Left: *Birds feeding at a bird table are a familiar sight in many gardens, adding movement as well as colour.*

Above: *Bees are commonly found in the garden and perform a valuable role in pollinating ornamental flowers.*

Above: *Butterflies are among the most colourful and best loved of all garden insects that visit to feed on nectar.*

Above: *Hedgehogs are frequent visitors to European gardens, where they eat a large range of garden pests, including slugs.*

WHAT IS WILDLIFE GARDENING?

The idea of gardening for wildlife has become popular, even fashionable, in recent years with many high-profile gardeners and organizations hailing it as a new approach. The simple truth, though, is that there has always been a huge variety of wildlife living in, or visiting, our gardens although conventional gardening techniques and materials have led to a decline in their numbers.

Above: *Gardens and wildlife have always enjoyed a strong association for many of us, as this garden sculpture shows.*

A NATURAL PARTNERSHIP

Gardens and wildlife have always shared the same space. The ants that forage, the worms that mix the soil and the bees that pollinate flowers are the most obvious examples. But some gardeners with an overly fastidious view of nature don't want to know about anything else, purging homes and gardens of anything verging on the "unclean" or "unhealthy".

While the idea of cleanliness is fine indoors, outdoors it causes a problem. The outside world is a living, functioning system, rich in many types of organism that depend on diversity and balance. In the quest for a sanitized environment, many gardeners have targeted some wildlife species on the grounds of plant health or simply because they don't want to share their space with them. A war began against creepy crawlies involving an array of noxious chemical agents whose effects were – and indeed still are – felt well beyond the confines of the garden. In addition, the combined forces of urbanization and industrial-scale agriculture have diminished the numbers of many other once common creatures.

It is only when the likes of birds and butterflies cease to visit the garden that the damage is noticed by the many, though surprisingly few regard their diminishing numbers as a problem. Fortunately, some gardeners realize that not only are we in danger of losing considerable natural diversity from our gardens, towns and cities, but that gardens are actually an ideal place for solving the problem. Domestic gardeners have a huge role to play in the future of many species of wildlife, especially now, as the traditional countryside in so many continents is under threat from the pressures of modern living.

Below: *Even a relatively small space can accommodate a variety of ornamental plants that, if chosen carefully, will provide a food supply, shelter or even a permanent home for a large range of garden wildlife.*

THE LOOK OF A WILDLIFE GARDEN

To some, the idea of being wildlife-friendly might mean forsaking the perfect lawn, trimmed borders and rose beds. Others might even assume that a wildlife garden means a disordered, untidy eyesore. Nothing could be further from the truth. True, some of the early wildlife gardeners did look to the countryside for ideas, attempting to make tiny, overgrown pockets of "wilderness" in their backyards. Increasingly, though, wildlife gardeners have taken a more fundamental approach, applying the model of nature – a dynamic, self-balancing and regulating system – when designing their own gardens. So, with a bit of know-how, every garden, however small, can act as a private nature reserve with its hedges, trees, flower beds and even sheds, walls and paths providing wildlife habitats. In fact, many gardens need only a little adjustment to vastly improve their wildlife credentials. Whether your passion is for herbs, flowers or vegetables, your garden has the potential to provide a habitat for many different wildlife species.

The most important requirements in a wildlife garden include providing creatures with shelter from the elements and a

Above: *Where space is limited, even a window box can provide a place for wildlife to visit and feed on the nectar-rich flowers.*

measure of protection from predators, while also providing food, water and nesting materials and, ideally, an environment in which to conduct their day-to-day lives, including mating and raising their young. Even those without a garden can help. Pots, window boxes and hanging baskets can all provide excellent feeding sites.

Left: *Spiders cause fear and revulsion for some people, but the majority are harmless to humans, and their tireless feeding activities help to balance the number of flying insect species in the garden.*

Below: *Dragonflies will visit a garden to feed, and if a suitable pond is present, they will readily lay eggs in it. They are superbly agile fliers with excellent eyesight, and are able to capture insects on the wing – a truly spectacular sight.*

Above: *Knowing which particular flowers provide food for which creatures is an important aspect of wildlife gardening.*

In most cases the types of plant used are an extremely important part of making your garden wildlife-friendly. Animals feed in a variety of ways and so ensuring that you have a range of plants, chosen to suit these varying needs, will help to maintain a healthy, thriving population of different animals. These in turn will attract carnivorous species, many of which may take up residence in your garden.

Below: *Many species, such as this robin, require not only food but also nesting sites where they can raise their young in safety.*

THE IMPORTANCE OF WILDLIFE

For many traditional gardeners, the idea of sharing the garden with wildlife sounds like a recipe for letting in a whole host of garden pests bent upon devouring their precious plants. It is worth remembering, though, that nature exists as a balance, and with these pests come a whole host of "beneficial" species. These eat the pests and help to reduce their numbers naturally and permanently.

Above: *Roses are often attacked by aphids, and brightly coloured daisy flowers attract beneficial insects that eat the aphids.*

ENCOURAGING WILDLIFE
On the whole, gardeners are understandably suspicious of techniques that appear to attract pests such as slugs and snails into the garden, but what you're really doing is creating a food chain, with aphids attracting hungry ladybirds, and slugs and snails attracting hedgehogs, frogs, toads and birds. In a well-managed wildlife garden, both plants and beneficial creatures flourish while more harmful creatures can be kept at bay.

THE WIDER BENEFITS
Creating wildlife-friendly gardens can not only benefit the health and well-being of your own garden, but create benefits felt well beyond the confines of your own plot. Many species depend upon habitats that are increasingly rare in nature. Gardens

Above: *Ladybird larvae will consume large numbers of aphids, reducing the damage done to plants on a daily basis.*

Below: *Butterflies are important pollinators for many plants and are often eaten by other wildlife species, particularly birds.*

form an important mosaic of green space and can link large, natural green areas either side of a town, for example, making it easier for the wildlife to travel between them. One garden may provide only a limited space for a few species to live but, collectively, such gardens often amount to a huge and important habitat capable of supporting large and significant populations of rare species. On top of that, of course, having wildlife in the garden can provide a huge amount of fun.

HOW MUCH SPACE DO I NEED?
Obviously, the bigger the space the more wildlife you can attract, but you can still create a wildlife haven in a very small area. Even a window box or a patio full of bright, scented potted plants will attract butterflies, moths and a whole host of flying visitors. If

Above: *Wildlife gardens are wonderful and exciting places for children to experience and learn more about nature.*

Above: *Flowers are an extremely important part of many wildlife gardens and give a stunning display, as well as being functional.*

THE BENEFITS OF A WILDLIFE GARDEN

Here are just a few of the positive benefits that a wildlife garden may bring to you and your environment.

• Provides a refuge for wildlife that is otherwise becoming rare as cities and farmland engulf habitats.
• Wildlife gardens can be very attractive and extremely interesting places to spend time in.
• As the variety of species increases, this acts as a biological control and helps to keep pest numbers low.
• Organic matter is recycled by many species and returned to the soil as vital plant nutrients.
• A garden that is rich in wildlife can ultimately prove very educational, especially for children.

you are passionate about growing your own food, then try edging your vegetable plot with herbs for the same reason.

When it comes to feeding birds, space isn't an issue. Packets of mixed seed are now widely sold, and there is a wide range of feeders in garden centres and pet shops. Birds aren't just beautiful in their own right, but can devour garden pests such as aphids. Your next step is to make sure that you eliminate insecticides, and grow flowers that attract insects that will help feed breeding birds. As a general rule, concentrate on "simple" flowers and not the gaudy, double types. They also tend to be more beneficial to bees, moths, butterflies and other insects.

In addition, composting your garden and kitchen waste and creating habitats such as log or rock piles will provide extra places for wildlife to feed and shelter. In time, even the smallest garden can become a thriving wildlife haven, albeit for smaller creatures.

Wildlife gardens are also wonderful places for the whole family to experience nature, first hand but in relative safety. A well-designed wildlife garden can combine an outdoor living space with what is essentially your own mini-safari park. Watching how these animals live can be inspirational and give tremendous satisfaction when you consider that your own efforts are actually helping to improve the wider environment for everyone. By

Above: *Birds are important creatures in many habitats, where they exploit almost every imaginable food source. Their feeding often helps to disperse seeds.*

Right: *Frogs are important in controlling the populations of slugs and many types of insect, and are common in gardens.*

helping nature you can ultimately start to redress some of the impact that our modern lives have upon the world around us.

ENVIRONMENTAL CYCLES

For gardeners, the constantly changing seasons remind us that nature is composed of many rhythmic cycles. Some of these are easy to see but others are less evident, although no less important. Chemical and nutrient cycles are extremely important for all plant growth and although they may be difficult to observe in some cases, knowing how they work can actually allow you to harness them and grow better plants.

Above: *Plants in the pea family, such as this clover, use the bacteria that live in special nodules on their roots to capture nitrogen.*

BIOGEOCHEMICAL CYCLES

The elements that combine to form the stuff of life are constantly being broken down, recycled and built up into new life in a series of processes that scientists refer to as biogeochemical cycles. (Gardeners are mostly concerned with how "nutrient cycling" affects plant growth, but they shouldn't ignore this aspect.)

Around 30 of the 100 or so elements in the Earth's crust are essential to life, but they are often in short supply. Initially they come from inorganic sources, such as rocks (through weathering), or the atmosphere, and once incorporated into living things many can only usually be released through biological processes, including decomposition.

WATER CYCLE

The water cycle is often referred to as an elemental cycle. This means that the amount of water on the planet remains more or less constant, although it may be combined with other substances or held within the bodies of living organisms. Water in a plant or animal body has been part of many other living things in the past as well as other naturally occurring things such as lakes, rivers, glaciers and the sea.

NITROGEN CYCLE

The nitrogen cycle is also an elemental cycle that involves the most abundant element in the air around us. Nitrogen is essential to life and especially plant growth. It constitutes around 78 per cent of the air

but is unobtainable to plants in this form. It must be "captured" and processed by bacteria in the soil before it is available to plants. Some plants, such as legumes (the "pea family"), use these bacteria to capture nitrogen for them in special root nodules. Humans have long known this, and for many years artificially "captured" nitrogen has been applied to the soil. In some cases this has led to a chemical imbalance, often with natural habitats suffering. An understanding of how to keep the soil healthy is often the best way to ensure good plant growth, and maintain a natural balance within (and indeed beyond) your own garden.

CARBON CYCLE

All life on Earth is based on carbon, and the chemistry of the carbon atom and its derived substances is called organic

Left: *Leaves falling in the autumn naturally decay and recycle nutrients ready for the next growing season.*

Below: *Composting garden waste is a way of working with the natural cycles of decay and nutrient release. The compost that is produced helps to enrich the soil and boosts plant growth.*

chemistry. Carbon has many sources, some living and some dead. When carbon is released into the air, the origin is called a source. All living things release some carbon and are sources, but there are other sources including volcanoes and activities such as burning wood and fossil fuels.

When carbon becomes part of a living organism, or is locked up in sediments or rocks, it is said to have entered a sink. The balance between carbon that has been liberated from a source and that entering a sink is extremely important for the health of the planet, and is best known for its effect on the global temperature.

OXYGEN CYCLE

The oxygen cycle describes the movement of oxygen within and between its three main reservoirs – the atmosphere; living things; and rocks, lakes, rivers and oceans. The main driving force for this cycle is plant life and its production of food through photosynthesis. When plants make food they release a lot of oxygen, and it is for this reason alone that the atmosphere on Earth contains around 21 per cent of it. We – and all other living things – breathe in oxygen and use it to release the energy contained in food. In this way, the carbon cycle and oxygen cycle combine and balance.

Nutrient cycles, then, are a matter of balance, having an important impact upon our daily lives and gardens; learning to work with them can actually improve the health of your garden.

Below: *Saving water after rain is an excellent way of making sure it is available in dry weather, when you need it the most.*

WATER CYCLE
Water is naturally recycled on a global scale and the water in a plant or even your own body has been through this cycle countless times.

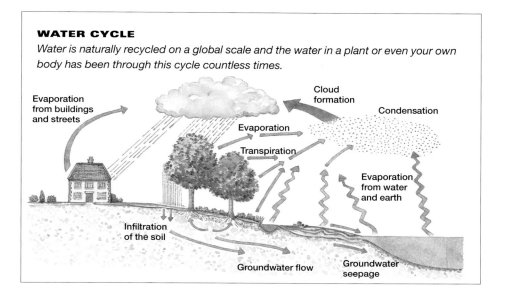

NITROGEN CYCLE
Most nitrogen is held in the atmosphere as an unusable gas. Through natural processes it is changed into a form that plants can use and ultimately returned to the atmosphere.

CARBON CYCLE
Carbon is contained in all living material. The natural cycles of growth and decay both consume and release carbon and achieve a balance that is essential to all life on Earth.

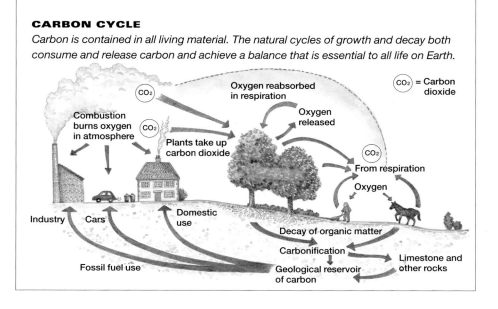

WORKING WITH NATURAL CYCLES

Many gardeners have an appreciation of the need to work within the constraints of the seasons. Understanding exactly how these natural cycles affect the plants and animals in our gardens is a key factor in successful wildlife gardening. Some cycles can be modified or adapted, whereas others are as inexorable as the passage of time itself, and our actions must fit in with them.

Above: *The changing seasons often bring cold periods and garden plants must be chosen to withstand these times.*

DAILY AND SEASONAL CYCLES

The simplest and most obvious cycle is that of a 24-hour period, marked by dark and light, which affects all life in the garden. Increasing warmth and day length, among other factors, speed up the growing process while lengthening nights signal the need for some animals to hibernate. It is the easiest natural cycle for us to measure, observe and understand.

The gradual passage of the seasons is something that humans have long sought to measure, and it's thought that some of the most ancient artefacts left by our ancestors were designed to help them do this. When it comes to deciding the best time for sowing seed, hedge cutting and pruning, for example, always be guided by the seasons but pay particular attention to the climate in your area. Spring can arrive early or late, and you need to be responsive. Always keep a record of what you did and when, and what the conditions were like, using this as a guide in future years.

WHEN TO PLANT

Much has been written about the best time to sow or plant in the garden. The accuracy of this depends upon where you live and the prevailing conditions. There's no point in sowing seed outdoors until the soil has warmed up and you're sure there will be no more frosts. Autumn, in temperate regions, is generally considered the best time for moving some plants and planting bare-root trees, since it causes them less of a shock when they're not in active growth. Again, though, the exact timing depends on local conditions. Warmth and moisture are vital.

NEW LIFE FROM OLD

Life, death and decay are all part of the wider environmental cycle. The gardener must keep in tune with this by composting, for example, and attempting to keep the garden habitat healthy.

Composting waste matter ensures that valuable nutrients are not lost and can be returned to the soil in a useful form. Organic matter is the food that many nutrient-cycling organisms depend upon, and this (with air and water) provides them with an

Left: *Autumn brings the end of the growing season and is often marked by spectacular displays of changing leaf colour.*

Below: *Spring brings warmth and an increase in light levels, and is when most plant growth commences.*

Left: *Warmer weather and an increasing abundance of food makes spring the start of the nesting season for birds, which must work hard to gather enough insects for their newly hatched chicks.*

Above: *Old leaves and stems naturally decay and release nutrients back into the soil. Mulching has the same effect.*

ideal environment. The more you return organic waste to the soil, the more self-supporting it will be, the healthier the plants, and the greater the range of wildlife.

HARNESSING NUTRIENT CYCLES

Cultivation is an ancient technique that helps to cycle nutrients. Freshly dug ground receives oxygen that encourages soil organisms, and helps them to break down organic matter. It also benefits many micro-organisms that process inorganic elements into a useful form for plants because they too need oxygen to breathe.

Keeping a healthy habitat, free of pesticides and the imbalances that can be caused by the excessive use of artificial fertilizers, is the best way to manage these cycles and benefit your own garden and the wider environment.

WORKING WITH NATURE

One thing that all gardeners have in common is that it is almost impossible to see exactly what the coming growing season will bring. Drought, heatwaves, floods or cold spells can all be features of an average summer and in some cases, the growing season may contain elements of them all at different times. A golden rule for any wildlife gardener should be to work with nature and never against it.

You will of course be able to anticipate some of these problems and if you are in a drier area, you will naturally need to plant drought-tolerant plants. Gardeners in wetter climes or on naturally wet ground will need species adapted to boggier

conditions. The biggest problem, however, will always be predicting what the prevailing weather conditions will be, and it is not uncommon for a long hot summer of drought to be followed by a cool summer with heavy rainfall. Reacting immediately to the summer conditions and changing your garden design accordingly may be rather short-sighted and may not always pay dividends in the long run.

NATURAL UNCERTAINTIES

The weather is naturally variable, but in the wake of predicted changes to the global climate – mostly referred to as "global warming" – it may yet become ever more complex and unpredictable. For us as gardeners, we cannot be certain whether global warming will mean drought or flood and so for now the best description would be "climatic uncertainty". Make sure that you don't ever act too rashly and try to remember that we never could accurately predict what the coming season holds – that is all part of the fun of gardening.

When things don't turn out as expected, remember that mistakes are simply part of gardening and that careful and patient observation of these can ultimately teach you as much about your garden as all the successes do. If particular plants have done well, you'll be on safe ground if you

decide to make more of a feature of them or closely related species, and if a particular feature is flourishing like never before, you might do well to expand it. Always look on your garden as separate areas that might be affected in different ways by the changes in weather patterns. While the majority of your garden remains unaffected, there might be some areas that become drier or wetter. If this trend is borne out over several seasons you might wish to redesign it in accordance with your ever "uncertain" weather.

Right: *Some birds, such as these barn swallows, travel vast distances to take advantage of the glut of summer insects in different latitudes.*

PREDATORS AND PREY

While some creatures eat only plants, many others rely on hunting and eating other creatures. These animals are called predators. A garden rich in plants will attract many plant eaters, and it doesn't take long before these attract the attention of other, mostly larger animals that want to make a meal of them. These in turn attract yet larger creatures that will eat them, and a complex cycle of "kill or be killed" gradually unfolds that is every bit as exciting as any big game safari.

Above: *Birds, such as this song thrush, are often some of the most important predators of garden pests, including snails.*

ENERGY AND FOOD SOURCES

When ancient peoples worshipped the sun, they were recognizing one inalienable truth. In order for life to continue, it needs a source of energy to power it. Sunlight cannot be eaten as food but certain organisms, principally plants, have evolved ways of capturing it and turning it into energy-rich molecules of sugar through photosynthesis. This food provides the basis of almost all life on Earth and, as a result, plants are described in an ecological sense as "producers".

The vast remainder of living species (or consumers) on the planet are not able to produce their own food and rely, instead, on eating other organisms. Some consumers (the herbivores) eat the plants directly, while others (carnivores) gain their energy by eating another consumer. Creatures such as humans, which eat a combination of producers and consumers, are omnivores.

Those that eat material from organisms that have died are "decomposers". These strategies provide organisms with the energy they need to live.

ENERGY USE AND LOSS

The First Law of Thermodynamics states that "energy cannot be created or destroyed, it merely changes form." To put this into context, remember that the energy of the sun is used to power life and, in doing so, the energy changes form. The energy contained in the sunlight is changed into food and used to assemble living tissue. The process is rather inefficient, with around 90 per cent of sunlight energy being lost. The remaining 10 per cent of the energy that is stored in the food suffers a similar fate each time it is used, so when the food is used to power growth and development around 90 per cent of it may be lost. This then means that there must always be

more food than consumers because the conversion of food is so inefficient.

Scientists use a diagram – the Pyramid of Biomass – to explain this. Biomass is the term used to describe the amount of living tissue minus the water content, and each layer in the pyramid can only have 10 per cent of the biomass of the layer below it. If the 10 per cent ratio is exceeded, the consumer quickly begins to run short of food and may starve.

FOOD CHAINS

A food chain is a simplistic but useful way of illustrating the relationship between predators and prey. The chain starts with the producer – a plant – and moves on to a primary consumer that eats the plant. In the example shown, the producer is grass and the primary consumer is a rabbit. The chain then moves on to show how a fox might eat the rabbit, and because few things found in a garden prey upon foxes, the fox is said to be at the "top of the food chain". While this is a good way of illustrating the basic principles of predation, the story is rarely as simple as this. Foxes, of course, feed on a wide variety of prey, and it is not only foxes that eat rabbits. In order to consider the complexity of natural systems, then, we would normally construct a food web.

FOOD WEBS

These help us to understand complex relationships between predators and prey. Their main drawback is that to be fully accurate, they would have to be extremely complex and almost impossible to follow. Nonetheless, they do draw attention to complex interdependences that form the basis of natural habitats. It is not always necessary to be able to construct one of these to understand that the more complex a system is, the more stable it tends to become.

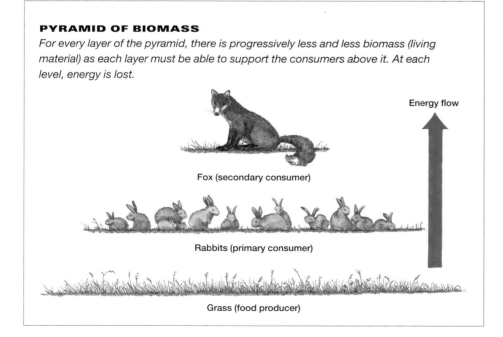

PYRAMID OF BIOMASS

For every layer of the pyramid, there is progressively less and less biomass (living material) as each layer must be able to support the consumers above it. At each level, energy is lost.

Energy flow

Fox (secondary consumer)

Rabbits (primary consumer)

Grass (food producer)

FOOD WEB

The complexity of nature can be shown in a food web. The direction of the arrows shows the flow of energy from one living organism to another, revealing a range of interdependencies typical in natural habitats.

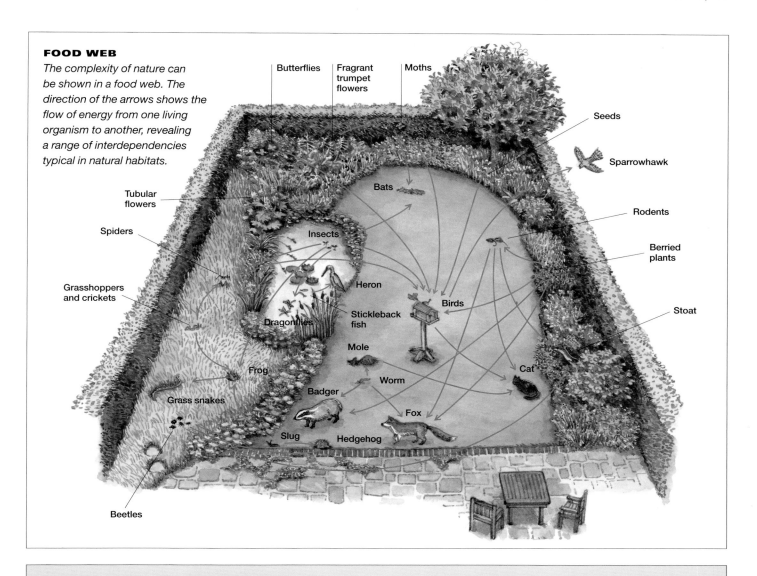

BENEFICIAL PREDATORS IN THE GARDEN

The average garden can play host to a whole range of common species, and some of them are voracious predators. Many offer a useful service in seeking out and eating a range of garden pests that would otherwise damage garden plants.

PREDATOR	WHAT IT EATS
Bat	Bats are mostly night-flying insectivores that locate their prey in darkness using a complex echolocation system consisting of high-pitched squeaks and clicks.
Blue tit	One of many birds that capture and eat garden pests, they are known for their agility, often picking aphids and caterpillars off in flight to feed their young.
Dragonfly	Larvae live an aquatic existence feeding upon various creatures. The adults are extremely agile fliers, capturing and consuming a wide range of mostly flying insects.
Frog and toad	The adults of both frogs and toads are carnivorous and capture a range of mostly invertebrate prey, such as slugs, using their long and sticky tongue.

PREDATOR	WHAT IT EATS
Hedgehog	Mainly insectivorous, although the hedgehog will eat quite a wide range of animal pests, such as slugs, depending on their availability. Long known as a friend to the gardener.
Hoverfly	Eats aphids. The hoverfly adults feed mainly upon pollen and are attracted to daisy-like flowers. Their larvae are voracious predators of many aphid species.
Ladybird	Eats aphids. Both adults and young of the common garden beetle are voracious predators of these troublesome garden pests.
Shrew	One of the smallest mammals, the shrew must capture and eat around two-thirds of its own body weight in food each day to survive. Captures mainly invertebrate prey.

Bat

Blue tit

Frog

Hedgehog

Hoverfly

Ladybird

PLANNING AND DESIGNING A WILDLIFE GARDEN

The real secret of success with any type of garden lies in how well it is planned. Good design leads to a garden that is both functional and pleasing to look at. Clearly this is less of a problem when starting from scratch, but redesigning your whole garden can be daunting, and it may be best to tackle the job in stages. Measuring the garden and assessing the soil and growing conditions is the first stage. Once you have done this you can think about the design elements that will help shape the perfect garden for wildlife.

Left: *A properly executed design will enable you to build the successful garden you always dreamed of.*

Above: *Garden plans should be drawn carefully and to scale to enable you to build the features and borders accurately.*

Above: *A well-drawn plan can form the basis of a wonderful garden, and is well worth the time and effort it takes to produce.*

Above: *For the more artistically minded, a sketch projection of a garden plan helps you to visualize the finished effect.*

THE ROLE OF GARDENS FOR WILDLIFE

Domestic gardens increasingly represent a direct link with the countryside. Many species, once seen as purely rural in their distribution, have started to move into towns and cities, where they find refuge in parks and gardens. This is often due to the loss of their traditional haunts through changes in land use or agricultural practices. The more suitable we make our gardens for wildlife, the more species are likely to follow.

Above: *Spiders' webs are a common sight in many gardens, and their presence is a sign of a healthy environment.*

HABITAT VARIETY

In nature, habitats, even when they are extensive, are rarely particularly uniform. Even slight variations in the soil and topography, for example, affect the microclimate and suitability for plant and animal species. In such cases a habitat is called a "mosaic", meaning that the total area is generally uniform even though it is variable when viewed in more detail. Suburban gardens may superficially resemble each other but, together, they create a mosaic because of their many differences. In this way they represent the maximum opportunities for species that are either present or are waiting to move in when conditions become more favourable.

Each garden's microhabitat is capable of supporting a particular combination of species (plants, animals, fungi and other organisms) that interact with one another and form a community. Across many gardens, then, the total diversity of species is greater than in any one part, although

Below: *To many creatures the underground layer is the most important place as they spend part or the whole of their life there.*

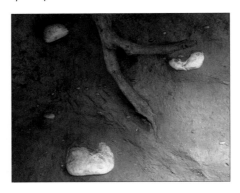

there is always the chance that an occupant of another part may visit your garden once in a while. Of course, the more opportunities there are for species, the more of them will visit and take up residence and, in time, your garden habitat may become a hotspot for species diversity.

BIODIVERSITY

In recent years, the term biodiversity has increasingly cropped up but few gardeners are aware of what it actually means, or why it is important. Put simply, biodiversity is an all-encompassing word that scientists have coined to describe the variety of life on Earth, and that includes plants, animals, fungi and micro-organisms. But biodiversity doesn't just refer to diversity at the species level, but to the genetic variation that contributes to the differences between individuals, and, at the other end of the scale, to the combinations of organisms, climate and soils that make up various habitats, including your garden.

SHELTER AND FOOD

In order to attract wild creatures, your garden must meet their basic needs, i.e. food, water, shelter and breeding sites. The first three are the easiest to supply in the form of supplementary food and artificial shelters, or preferably by planting the appropriate plant species that they need. If the first three are present, then some creatures may choose to breed, but this is not always the case because they may have very specific needs. This does not mean

Left: *For the insects that fly into our gardens to visit flowers, there is a constant danger. Spiders are important predators of flying insects and help regulate their number, thereby achieving a state of natural balance.*

that they won't visit your garden, though, and many species may appear merely to feed and drink before returning to a home elsewhere in the mosaic. But your garden still has an important part to play.

WILDLIFE CORRIDORS

Birds often fly long distances in search of a winter refuge or summer breeding site, and a garden may provide an ideal spot in which to rest, refuel and have a much-needed drink. Indeed, many modern cities are like deserts to migrating species, offering little comfort were it not for parks and domestic gardens. They often act as oases for both passers-by and residents, and if enough suitable sites are made, creating a continuous "super-habitat", they'll double as wildlife corridors for "through traffic", while also enabling less mobile species to enter from the surrounding countryside. Hedges, street trees and roadside verges are all part of this effect and offer shelter and respite for a large range of species. The more diverse all of these are in respect of the plant species they contain and the less intensively tended they are, the better for wildlife they naturally become.

Gardens are an essential part in this story, and the species that they contain today are increasingly refugees from the countryside, fleeing intensive farming practices and the loss of traditional habitats. It is within the grasp of the gardener to help such species and make our cities both greener and more diverse.

Above: *Many birds, such as this house martin, happily live alongside humans throughout much of their lives.*

Right: *Rodents are just one example of a mammal that quickly adapts to the changes wrought by human settlement.*

Below left: *Many species of birds were once exclusively rural, but as their habitats have been changed by human activities, they often find refuge in urban gardens.*

Below: *Ants mostly go unnoticed until they invade our houses or picnics. They have intricate and complex lives, even farming and protecting aphids to obtain their sweet honeydew secretions.*

THE WEATHER IN YOUR GARDEN

Each garden has its own microclimate, or even several within it. This will be mainly created by the prevailing weather, but will also be affected by factors such as altitude and the amount of available shelter from the wind and shade from the sun. To grow plants successfully, you need to know what kind of weather they will be subjected to, and make sure you choose species that can tolerate these conditions.

Above: *Sunny walls and fences help to capture heat and so make ideal settings to help ripen fruit such as these pears.*

PREVAILING CLIMATE

The prevailing climate for your area could best be described as the average of the weather on a yearly basis. Most places see a degree of seasonal variation and this, combined with a number of climatic influences – principally temperature, precipitation, humidity, light and wind – characterizes the prevailing climate for a particular area. Any and all of these influences can have a dramatic effect on plant growth and development, especially when taken to extremes.

RAINFALL

Water is vital for food production and growth in plants, and for the optimum growth of most plants a steady supply of water is essential. In reality rainfall is very variable in both its regularity and quantity, and the best plants for your garden are those that thrive in such conditions.

HUMIDITY

The level of humidity is the quantity of water vapour in the atmosphere at any one time. It is normally referred to as the relative humidity, and is measured as a percentage of the saturation point (100 per cent humidity). In places that receive heavy rainfall, relative humidity also tends to be high. Plants such as ferns thrive in damp conditions, although high relative humidity can have undesirable effects on plants, facilitating diseases such as grey mould (*Botrytis cinerea*) and exacerbating heat stresses because water cannot evaporate from the leaves to cool them.

LIGHT

The light from the sun is a vital constituent of plant food production – or photosynthesis – and sustains existing plants and generates new growth.

The duration of light in a day, determined by latitude and season, is known as day length, and is characterized by the number of hours. Changes in day length often trigger reactions in plants: chrysanthemums, for example, produce flowers in response to shortening days in autumn. The most important factor, though, is the overall amount of light available to plants. Some will only thrive in bright light, while others, such as ferns and rhododendrons, have evolved to live under trees and do well in shade. Also note that strong sunlight can damage the foliage of

Left: *Cool shady areas such as this enable you to grow a range of "woodland" plant species that in turn provide a habitat for shade-loving creatures.*

Above: *Dry, sunny areas can allow you to plant a range of sun-loving and drought-tolerant species, such as this Mediterranean-style border.*

Right: *This drystone wall provides excellent cover as well as a range of habitats for both plants and animals, and is an excellent feature to include in a wildlife garden.*

some plants, with the leaves being scorched, especially if wet, the light being magnified by water droplets on the leaf surface.

WIND

This can easily damage plants, especially woody trees and shrubs. The stronger the wind, the more damage is likely to occur and, in windy gardens, the plants must be chosen in accordance with their ability to resist such conditions. Even quite moderate winds may cause desiccation of leaves when combined with cold or dry conditions, although a light wind often has beneficial effects by cooling the plant's foliage and alleviating a possible stagnant atmosphere that might promote disease.

TEMPERATURE

The plant's growth and life processes are affected by temperature, with all plant species having their own maximum and minimum temperatures at which they can survive. As a general rule, the maximum temperature for most plants is around 35°C (95°F) while the minimum is highly variable. Plants may enter dormancy beyond these thresholds or, in more extreme cases, may

actually die. In some gardens, though, a sheltered site that benefits from the warming effects of the sun may be used for growing plants that are usually suited to warmer climates.

Soil temperature may also vary, with sandy soil warming up more quickly after a cold season than clay, mainly because sand is relatively free-draining and does not hold as much water. Sites facing, or with a slight incline towards, the direction of the sun, will also warm up more quickly than a shady one, enabling you to grow a range of sun-loving plants. Such local variations are termed microclimates.

MICROCLIMATE

Gardeners often exploit their microclimate by growing a wider range of plants than would be possible elsewhere in their region. This doesn't just benefit you, but the wildlife too, creating a greater range of habitats than would otherwise have been possible.

A south-facing garden in the northern hemisphere provides most sun, whereas in the southern hemisphere it is a north-facing site. Away from the tropics, the sun is also higher in summer than it is in winter, resulting in less shade in summer. Lastly, exposure to wind, frost, or shelter will greatly affect the type of plants you can grow.

GARDEN ASPECT

The aspect of a garden mainly relates to the movement of the sun through the day and how this alters the pattern of sunny areas in relation to shade, as this will affect the type of plants you can grow in any particular area. In the northern hemisphere a south-facing garden is the sunniest, whereas in the southern hemisphere they

will be sunniest if facing north. In higher latitudes, the summer sun sits higher in the sky, reducing the amount of shade, whilst winter sunlight arrives from a low angle, casting long shadows. Aspect also concerns whether the garden is exposed to wind or frost or is sheltered, as these conditions also affect the plants you can grow.

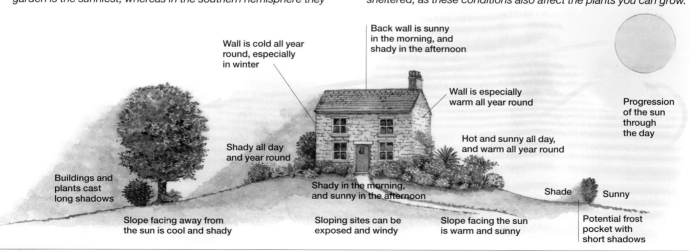

Wall is cold all year round, especially in winter

Back wall is sunny in the morning, and shady in the afternoon

Wall is especially warm all year round

Progression of the sun through the day

Shady all day and year round

Hot and sunny all day, and warm all year round

Buildings and plants cast long shadows

Shady in the morning, and sunny in the afternoon

Shade

Sunny

Slope facing away from the sun is cool and shady

Sloping sites can be exposed and windy

Slope facing the sun is warm and sunny

Potential frost pocket with short shadows

GARDEN SOILS

Understanding your garden soil and which plants it will support is a key aspect of successfully planning a wildlife garden. Soils vary according to the area in which they are found and also, in part, to how they have been treated in the past. Soil can be a complex subject but, by following a few simple rules, you can easily find out what type you have in your garden. Once you know this, you will be better able to choose plants that will rapidly establish, grow and ultimately thrive there.

Above: *Applying well-rotted mulch to a border helps add organic matter to an area and can result in a more open soil structure.*

DIFFERENT KINDS OF SOIL

Soil is made up of many ingredients but, in the main, the majority consist of small mineral fragments produced by the action of the weather on rocks. The fragments are classed according to their size and physical properties.

Clay is the smallest type of mineral particle found in soil, being less than 0.002mm (0.00008in) across. The particles bind tightly together, making the substance very sticky and water-retentive. Clay soils are heavy and can be hard to cultivate. On the plus side, though, they are very fertile.

Silt is larger than clay, being up to 0.02mm (0.0008in) across and, as such, shares some characteristics with both clay and sand. It is sticky when wet but does not form the same close bonds as clay, and may dry to a quite dusty soil in a drought. It makes fertile soil that, if well managed, can be an excellent growing medium for a wide variety of plants.

Sand is the largest particle, being up to 2mm (0.08in) across. While this is still quite a fine particle to our eyes, it is very large in respect of soils and, unlike the smaller clay and silt, is very poor at retaining nutrients. This is because the amount of air that is naturally present tends to rapidly break down any organic matter, and because the particles themselves are unable to hold on to nutrients. As a result, sandy soils tend to be free-draining and hungry, needing to be bulked up with organic matter.

ORGANIC MATTER

A normal part of topsoil, organic matter is derived from the dead parts of plants and, to a lesser degree, animals that live in or on the soil. Decaying plant matter is broken down by many soil organisms, especially fungi and bacteria, and consequently is not a constant quantity in the soil. If conditions are right, however, it can form a substance called humus that is relatively stable and is excellent at holding on to nutrients, especially when present in sand or silt. Organic matter is ultimately broken down and recycled by decomposers and plants, and needs to be replenished on a regular basis.

SOIL STRUCTURE

The constituents above are the building blocks of soil, but the properties of any garden soil also depend on how they are arranged. Imagine your home: it will have been specially constructed using a range of materials. This is its architecture or structure. Soil is much the same. In order to function, it must have areas of open space, called pores, that provide routes for water and air to move through. A well-structured soil has the right balance of air space to facilitate the drainage of excess water and air movement.

A good soil structure will ultimately help plant roots penetrate the soil and also

SOIL PROFILE

Made up of a number of layers, each soil section is distinct from the others and plays different roles.

Leaf litter layer This layer is composed of partly decayed plant remains and is home to a diverse range of insects.

Topsoil This can be 5–60cm (2–24in) deep. It is dark in colour and rich in organic matter. It contains the greatest number of soil life species.

Subsoil The topsoil finishes and there is a distinct colour change to the subsoil. Little organic matter is found.

Parent material On shallow soils you may see this layer. It may be found as rocky gravel, such as limestone, or other material.

TESTING SOIL TEXTURE

1 *This simple method is easy to do in a garden. Start with a ball of soil about the size of a golf ball and moisten it until it can be flattened into a ribbon shape.*

2 *Continue flattening out the ribbon, making it as long and thin as possible. The longer and thinner you can make it without it cracking or breaking, the more clay your soil contains.*

pH TESTING WITH AN ELECTRONIC METER

1 *After loosening an area of soil, moisten it using rainwater, and allow this to soak through the ground for a few minutes.*

2 *Using a trowel, take a sample of the wet soil and place it into a clean jar, adding a little more water if needed.*

3 *Always clean the probe on your pH meter using a sterilized cleaning solution to eliminate any risk of an incorrect reading.*

4 *Insert the probe into the soil solution and after a few moments the reading on the front panel will appear.*

encourage a myriad of tiny soil organisms, whose activities help to liberate nutrients for the growing plants.

WHY CULTIVATE SOIL?

The simple answer is to give nature a boost. Cultivation enhances the formation of pore spaces while often providing an ideal opportunity to add organic matter. This free flow of air both in and out of the soil allows oxygen to be replenished and toxic gases, that might otherwise build up, to escape. Adding organic matter also provides food for micro-organisms that, in turn, provide nutrients for the plant roots.

Left: *Digging is a good way of improving the structure of the soil by allowing air and water penetration. It also allows you to add organic matter at the same time.*

SOIL pH

A measure of the acidity of a soil, its pH is an important factor in deciding which plants will grow and thrive in your garden. It is expressed on a scale of 1–14 with 1 being highly acidic, 14 being extremely alkaline, and 7 being classed as neutral. Most commonly grown garden plants prefer, or tolerate, a specific pH range, i.e. acid, alkaline, or near neutral.

A low pH may cause nitrogen or phosphate deficiency for instance, may promote trace element toxicity or deficiency, and may cause a more general deterioration of the soil structure. Soils that maintain a pH of around 6.5, however, generally have the most nutrients available and are suitable for the widest range of plants.

ASSESSING SOIL TEXTURE BY HAND

The amount of mineral constituents present in the soil dictates, to a degree, what the soil will be like. They are often judged as a relative proportion of the total and, although measuring them can be a complex matter, there is an easy test.

Begin with a small amount of soil about the size of a golf ball. Moisten it and knead until it is like putty, and remove any hard lumps or large stones. Then mould the soil into a ball. If it does not readily form a ball, it is sand. If the ball is firm, try forming it

into a ribbon between thumb and crooked forefinger. If the ribbon breaks easily while being formed it is loamy sand. If it hangs freely, then the longer and thinner you can make it before it breaks, the more clay it has. The higher the clay content, the more it glistens when smoothed between thumb and forefinger.

SOIL pH AND PLANT SELECTION

All plants have their preferred pH at which they will grow best. Generally speaking, good results may be obtained from soils at the following pH levels.

Mineral soils (majority of plants)	pH 6.5
Mineral soils (turf)	pH 5.5-6.5
Container composts	pH 5.5-5.8
Peat/moss soils	pH 5.5 (or lower for specialist uses such as heather or bog gardens)

---

pH preferences of some common garden plants

Carnations	6.0–7.5
Chrysanthemums	5.7–7.0
Roses	5.5–7.0
Rhododendrons	4.5–5.5
Heathers	4.1–6.0
Hydrangeas (blue)	4.1–5.9
Hydrangeas (pink)	5.9–7.5
Coarse lawn grasses	5.5–7.0
Fine lawn grasses	4.5–7.0

DESIGN PRINCIPLES

Careful planning is the key to a successful garden, and this is often best done as a team effort involving the whole family. Planning the garden provides a real chance for everyone who uses it to have a say in what it should look like, making sure it caters for all their needs. The design should reflect the types of activity that you enjoy and should consider not just your current needs but also your longer-term aspirations and the time you can realistically devote to maintaining it.

Above: *Ideally, a wildlife garden combines an outdoor living space with a home and a visting place for a variety of creatures.*

FIRST STEPS

The first thing to remember about your garden is that it is fundamentally the same as any other living space. It needs to be organized around your activities. If the garden is predominantly for outdoor living and entertaining, then the design should reflect that. If you have children or pets, they must be considered, though of course their needs will change over the years. In addition to this list – which might well include play areas and a vegetable garden – you need a second one containing aesthetic features.

When you have made the list, consider how much space each ingredient requires and position them on a rough sketch. If you are limited for space, start making compromises, and be realistic. You might want to be self-sufficient in vegetables, but will you have the time to take care of them properly? When you have fine-tuned your design, check that each feature works in relation to adjacent areas and the garden as a whole. Remember that ponds, thorny and poisonous plants are best avoided if you have young children, and can be added later.

FORMULATING A CONCEPT

Finally, once everyone has had their say, you can think about a wildlife theme. A small courtyard in a city centre may be best geared towards birds, with feeders, a birdbath and hanging baskets and pots. If space permits, introduce more elements, but always be realistic about what you can achieve and whether particular species are likely to be in your neighbourhood. And remember to separate the areas being most heavily used from those where you want wildlife to shelter. While some species, such as sparrows and the European robin, might not mind close contact, other species are shyer and tend to shun busy areas.

Below: *With a little thought, even a relatively small garden space can provide variety and interest for both people and wildlife.*

CHOOSING PLANTS FOR THE DESIGN

Good garden design can be reinforced by good-looking plants but, for maximum usefulness in a wildlife garden, they must also provide food and shelter.

Form A plant offers a particular shape in three dimensions that is called its form. Use a variety of forms to complement both the surrounding plants and features.

Growth habit A term used to describe the overall branching pattern of a plant. Unlike form it only refers to the skeleton of growth. Note that a dense, twiggy habit offers good cover while an open habit offers perches for birds.

Colour An obvious reason for choosing plants is if they have attractive coloured leaves, stems, fruit or flowers. How you choose to use colour is subjective, but certain flower colours may attract particular insects.

Theme Within a wildlife garden, for instance devoted to butterflies or birds, choose certain plants because they favour particular species, either for food or breeding sites.

Seasonality Establish what time of year certain plants look at their best and are most useful for wildlife.

Food value Some plant species are better than others in providing food for wildlife, and choosing them can make your garden into a super habitat.

Above: *Strong, hot colours provide a very warm feeling when they are used in a garden, and are ideal for sunny borders.*

Below: *Blues and purples tend to give a garden a cooler feel, but they can also have a calming effect too.*

Above: *Strong, flowing lines are an important part of larger designs and look especially good near water.*

You might even want to make a few specialist areas where you can see particular species, planting a range of plants that will best favour their needs. Colour can also be an important element and by choosing carefully you can create subtle moods throughout your garden.

BASIC DESIGN PRINCIPLES

The key to any successful design is to apply a few basic principles. All of these are simple, and if applied consistently, will help you to produce a design that will meet the needs of both you and the wildlife in your garden, and it will look great when finished.

Unity This ties a design together. Avoid clashes and anything that appears out of place by using similar materials, patterns, shapes and colours throughout the design, and make them echo the house and even the wider surroundings.

Rhythm and line This applies to the flow of the design. Remember that strong lines are important, with flowing shapes looking good in larger, naturalistic gardens, and geometric shapes often working well in smaller or more formal courtyard settings.

Scale Simply refers to the relative size of each element, or part of the garden, in relation to the space in which it is placed. Features included should be neither too small and insignificant nor too large and overpowering for the whole scheme.

Balance Refers to the use of space in relation to other features in the garden. It is a matter of taste, of course, but too many features in too small a space can feel cluttered whereas too much open space can leave the occupants feeling exposed.

Variety and contrast They should not conflict with the need for unity. A certain amount of variety is, of course, vital for wildlife and relatively easy to achieve in large gardens, but it needs to be artfully juxtaposed in order to achieve a balance.

Functionality Even in a garden managed expressly for wildlife you still need space. Make sure that such areas don't conflict, for example with barbecues near flammable long grass, and items such as bins or storage areas are best hidden from view.

SURVEYING YOUR GARDEN

Once you have decided what you want from your garden in terms of its function, features and the types of wildlife you wish to attract, you can start planning. A thorough appraisal by surveying the site is the best way to start, and can be done quite easily using a few simple techniques. A survey involves nothing more than measuring the dimensions of the site, and making notes on what is already there.

Above: *If you have recently moved, talking to the neighbours will help you find out about your garden and its microclimate.*

WHY DO A SURVEY?

Before you attempt your design, surveying the existing garden site will help immeasurably, despite the fact that it isn't the most creative job. It'll certainly stop you from rushing blindly in, and can actually save you time in the long run. The survey also determines what plants you can grow because it will not only provide the measurements of the garden and details of existing features and views, but information about the microclimate and soil type.

WHAT INFORMATION IS NEEDED?

Find out as much as you can about what is already there. The more you understand your garden, the better the design will be. As you move around the garden taking measurements, make some notes about the following points.

The climate – that will greatly influence your new design. Check the direction of the prevailing wind, the annual and monthly rainfall, annual and monthly temperatures, and if and when frosts occur. All this information can be gathered from your local meteorological station.

The microclimate – measuring this can be more difficult, mostly because the slight differences might not be apparent at first glance. Often it is more a case of looking for the most likely variations caused by the permanent features or the lie of the land.

Sun and shade – extremely important

Left: *Unless you intend sitting out in your garden while you design it, photographs will be useful memory joggers when you draw up your survey at a later date.*

factors when selecting plants. Assess how much sun and shade your garden receives, and where it falls at different times of the day. Always note that even the sunniest garden may have shady pockets created by adjacent houses, fences, hedges or trees.

Site aspect – whether your garden faces the sun is important but a sloping site that faces either sun or shade will accentuate the importance of that factor. A sunny slope is often warmer and may also be more exposed or free-draining than an equivalent flat site. In addition to slope, walls and fences are also affected by their orientation. A wall facing the sun will retain heat, making it even warmer than a sunny fence, and it may be perfect for growing a more tender climber or shrubs that might benefit from this milder setting.

Exposure – an exposed site is often thought to be difficult due to high winds, but some species and seaside plants for instance might appreciate this more than others. Of course not all species of wildlife or plants will tolerate exposure and the type of features you include must either

TIPS FOR MEASURING YOUR GARDEN

Unless you are a trained surveyor, the prospect of measuring your garden might seem a little daunting. This need not be the case, though, as the techniques are relatively simple – it is just a case of being careful and methodical at all times.

Two's company Always work with a friend. It makes life easier, especially when trying to keep a tape straight to take measurements. One person should normally be in charge of measuring, the other recording the information.

Divide the site into triangles Since the time of the ancient Greeks, the value of the triangle as a shape for surveying land has been recognized. The most obvious way to apply it to a rectangular garden is to measure and plot the boundaries, and then measure from corner to corner.

Use two tapes to mark the position of a fixed point You will need to plot the positions of features such as trees and flower beds, which are best measured at right angles from a nearby straight edge such as a boundary line. Stretch a tape along this edge. Place the start of a second tape nearest the object you are measuring towards, and move the other end in an arc across the tape along the edge. The shortest distance you measure across this arc is the distance at a right angle from the first tape line. Note this measurement and how far along the first tape it occurs.

Take photographs They are invaluable when drawing up the initial ground plan, and particularly when you start to draw up the final design. Enlarge a few photographs and cover them with tracing paper, and then sketch on your ideas to get an idea what the finished garden will look like.

Photographs can be stuck around the edge of your drawing to act as a constant visual reminder of what the site looks like and help you envisage the space while you are not actually in the garden.

cater for those that will or be sheltered by a windbreak or hedge.

Soil type – check what you've got so that you know which plants will thrive there, and which ones won't. Also check what's growing well in your neighbours' gardens, and talk to them about their experiences.

Drainage – note any problems.

Existing features – both on, and near, the site including trees, garden beds, driveways and garden sheds. Decide which ones you

Left: *Take a soil sample to test later if you don't have time or the equipment to hand when you are measuring the site.*

want to retain. Also note the position of water and gas mains, sewers, meters, taps and power lines (underground and overhead).

Good views – from within the garden, and into it from without. Check which ones you want to retain, and the extent to which the garden should be private.

Once you have collected all this information, you can draw up a plan (see below) that will provide a detailed picture of the site, its features and other information relating to its suitability for growing plants. From this point on, you can begin to plan your wildlife garden.

RECORDING THE SITE DIMENSIONS

1 *The easy first stage is to make a rough sketch plan of what is already there. This forms the basis of your survey so that when you take measurements of the site, you can record them on the sketch plan. In many cases a freehand sketch is all that is needed, as long as you are not planning to undertake any detailed engineering or building work that needs precise dimensions.*

2 *Using two measuring tapes – one long and one shorter – start by establishing a base line along the house or boundary from which to build the survey. Establish the boundary dimensions, taking additional measurements between the corners as cross checks. Note the position and dimensions of other features, including the house and outbuildings.*

3 *Make notes about the microclimate, sunny areas, damp areas, soil, existing plants and the condition of any features. Put this series of observations on the survey drawing. Neatly draw your plan using the information contained in the sketch, the measurements and the notes, keeping it to a scale. Use graph paper, using one large square, for example, to represent 1m (1yd).*

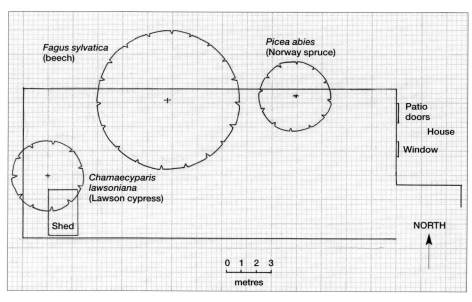

Fagus sylvatica (beech)

Picea abies (Norway spruce)

Chamaecyparis lawsoniana (Lawson cypress)

Patio doors

House

Window

Shed

NORTH

0 1 2 3
metres

4 *Once you have marked down the dimensions, add the location of doors and windows on buildings, and the position of drains, pipes, power lines and existing landscape features, such as the driveway, paths and trees, that are to remain. Where possible, add the name of each tree and plot the dimensions of the canopy. This information will help at the next stage of planning the garden. Also show the direction of the prevailing wind, the areas in shade or sun, and any other site particulars, including views which you would like to keep or to open up. Finally, it is extremely important to find where north is and chart this on the survey, as this will help determine the plants chosen to cope with sun or shade at the planning stage.*

DRAWING UP A PLAN

Garden plans range from complex designs to sketches, with most domestic settings requiring relatively simple drawings. Even if you find it difficult to come up with a design you really like, sketches and ideas are always useful. Alternatively, if you are prepared to pay for it, you can hire a professional garden designer. Whichever you opt for, it is important that you are absolutely clear as to what you want to get out of your garden for both you and the wildlife you intend to help.

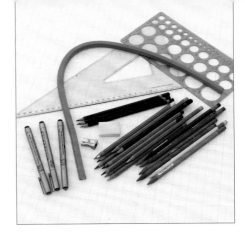

Above: *Drawing up a garden plan does not need anything more complex than simple drawing equipment and graph paper.*

INTERPRETING YOUR WISH LIST

Once you have drawn up the survey sketch plan, use it to create the design for your new garden. The first stage involves using tracing paper to draw the base plan. You need to trace over the garden boundary, and any features on the site (trees, shed, existing paths, etc.) that you intend to keep. This is preferably done using an ink or fine fibre-tip pen. Then place this over a piece of plain white paper. The result is your garden, minus all the features that you will be removing. In essence it is your blank canvas. Place another sheet of tracing paper over this and start to sketch your ideas.

SITING FEATURES

It is very important that you clarify the priorities at this early stage. Start with the basics, e.g. positioning the washing line, dustbins and storage areas. Remember that they will need to be accessible, perhaps even in the dark, while being screened from view. Then add a shed or compost area, and car parking space if required.

Once you have the basic needs, consider the rest of your wish list. Start with the most important items and work down the list. Remember to think very carefully how much space each will realistically need, and how often it will be used. Make sure you separate *real need* from *desire*. Cost is also a consideration, and there is not much sense in coming up with a complex design if you cannot afford it. Work out how much you are prepared to spend and investigate what materials are available. And never forget that the garden needs to look good as well as being a functional space.

Maintenance is also a key consideration at the design stage. The amount of money and/or effort and expertise needed to keep it in first-rate condition should be clearly thought through. Try to fit maintenance requirements around your own lifestyle, and avoid being too ambitious.

HOW DETAILED DO DRAWINGS NEED TO BE?

The amount of detail needed ultimately depends upon the complexity of the design and the types of features you use. Hard landscapes and constructions, such as walls, need to have accurate estimates of the amount of materials required. Ponds and other water features also need estimates for the amount of liner material and the quantity of excavated earth. If your drawings are simple but your ideas are complex, it can lead to problems. Equally, there is little point in making extensive and elaborate plans if you simply intend planting a few extra roses.

If you are wary of this design stage, you can always enlist the help of a professional designer. Check the fee, and while it may seem costly, note that a professional will often find solutions that you hadn't considered. Even if you do employ a designer, try to complete as much of the design stage as you can. If drawing is not your strong point, then survey the garden in note form and make your wish list. It will help the designer to understand your needs and, ultimately, result in a design that is tailored to your taste. Remember that even when someone else draws it for you, it is still your garden and so must always meet your own needs.

Left: *Employing a professional garden designer can be costly, but the results are often well worth the additional expense.*

MAKING A PLAN

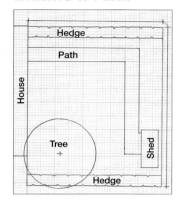

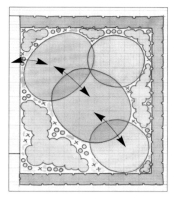

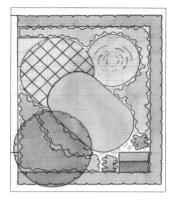

1 *Before beginning your plan, a survey of the area is required. The survey needs to be drawn to scale on graph paper, with all the important features included, for example paths, outbuildings, hedges and any tree with its dimensions shown in outline.*

2 *Redraw the boundary lines of the garden on new graph paper, omitting any feature not required. Divide the garden space into zones according to the list of essential and desirable features required. Movement around the garden is shown using arrows.*

3 *At this stage, the design progresses by working the different zones created into a formal sketch. The sketch shown here is of an informal garden displaying flowing lines and curves. Try out a few different sketch ideas.*

4 *This is an alternative sketch idea for the same area. Again, the different zones created here have been sharpened up into different areas, e.g. pond, grass. This sketch is very formal and uses straight lines and right angles to give this effect.*

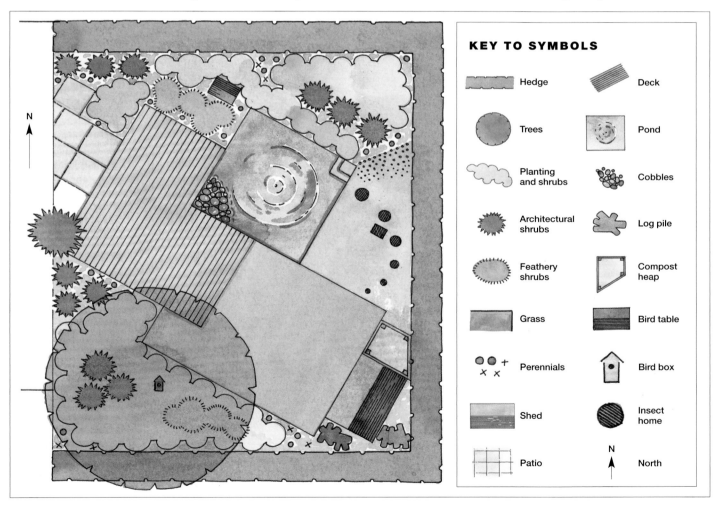

KEY TO SYMBOLS

	Hedge		Deck
	Trees		Pond
	Planting and shrubs		Cobbles
	Architectural shrubs		Log pile
	Feathery shrubs		Compost heap
	Grass		Bird table
	Perennials		Bird box
	Shed		Insect home
	Patio		North

5 *Once you have had a few attempts at sketching ideas using the zonal areas, place them side by side and try to envisage which would be the best use of the available space to meet your needs. Once you have chosen the final sketch, it can be drawn up neatly using recognized symbols to indicate what each part represents. Colouring the drawing is not essential, but it is very effective.*

A LARGE COUNTRY WILDLIFE GARDEN

Large country gardens offer a wealth of possibilities for wildlife, having plenty of space for both a range of features and a wide variety of species. While a large garden is not inherently more useful in terms of wildlife than a smaller one, it does enable you to mimic nature with a mosaic of different habitats. Many more species are likely to be resident in your garden rather than just paying a casual visit.

Above: *Larger country gardens can accommodate forest trees, such as this oak, which are fantastic wildlife habitats.*

USE OF SPACE

A large space also allows you to let your imagination run freely. The bigger the space, the less limit will be placed on the inclusion of sizeable features such as trees. This does not mean, however, that designing a large garden is simply a matter of including every possible feature and deliberately making it big. As with any living space, it should be carefully tailored to your needs. It is also vital that your own personal space for leisure, relaxation, socializing and play is clearly defined. Decide how much of the garden is for your own use, and if any areas are exclusively for wildlife.

Scale must be carefully considered, with each chosen element being designed in relation to the space in which it is placed.

Above: *Art and sculpture in the garden can create an extremely ornamental feel to an area without affecting the different types of wildlife species that are attracted.*

A wildlife pond, for instance, should be neither too small and insignificant – for the space or visiting wildlife – nor too large and overpowering for the whole scheme. Indeed, a series of smaller, linked ponds and bog gardens may work better than one large pool with its considerable maintenance requirements.

Remember, too, that open expanses will attract certain species, such as ground-feeding birds, but this must be balanced with more confined spaces for shyer creatures. Use the space wisely in relation to all the other features in the garden, and ensure that habitats are linked and merge to allow the maximum diversity and plenty of escape routes between different areas.

ATTRACTING WILDLIFE

Large gardens often attract and can support large numbers of individual animals, and understanding where they will congregate may affect your choice of where to site the different areas. By placing flower borders and feeding stations near the house you'll be able to watch wildlife from indoors, but don't forget to make more secluded areas both for feeding and shelter, particularly if you are likely to use the area near the house for your own purposes on a regular basis.

ORNAMENTAL FEATURES

Features such as sculpture and willow tunnels can be added to the wildlife garden to improve its aesthetic appeal. Another design tip is to repeat features. This can be seen in this design, where trees surrounded by woven grass seats are used throughout the garden and are linked by the eye to aligning habitat entrances.

Left: *Lawns create space in a garden and link areas together. Ground-feeding birds use lawns to forage for insects and grubs.*

LARGE COUNTRY WILDLIFE GARDEN

A design on this scale has the scope to contain some well-manicured ornamental borders, while still allowing room for a wilder, more secluded area. While smaller gardens may have to mix fruit and vegetables with ornamental plantings due to lack of space, separate fruit and vegetable gardens are featured here. This design has been divided into smaller areas, but they are all linked up by the use of hedges and interconnecting borders to provide continuous cover for the resident wildlife.

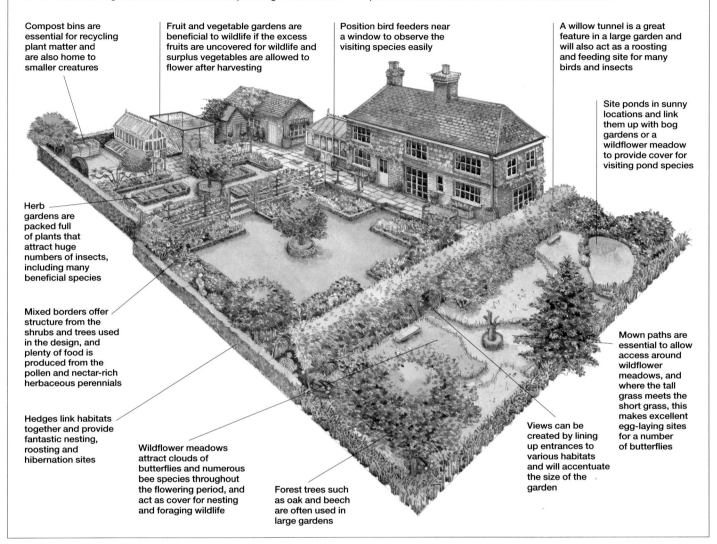

Compost bins are essential for recycling plant matter and are also home to smaller creatures

Fruit and vegetable gardens are beneficial to wildlife if the excess fruits are uncovered for wildlife and surplus vegetables are allowed to flower after harvesting

Position bird feeders near a window to observe the visiting species easily

A willow tunnel is a great feature in a large garden and will also act as a roosting and feeding site for many birds and insects

Site ponds in sunny locations and link them up with bog gardens or a wildflower meadow to provide cover for visiting pond species

Herb gardens are packed full of plants that attract huge numbers of insects, including many beneficial species

Mixed borders offer structure from the shrubs and trees used in the design, and plenty of food is produced from the pollen and nectar-rich herbaceous perennials

Hedges link habitats together and provide fantastic nesting, roosting and hibernation sites

Wildflower meadows attract clouds of butterflies and numerous bee species throughout the flowering period, and act as cover for nesting and foraging wildlife

Forest trees such as oak and beech are often used in large gardens

Views can be created by lining up entrances to various habitats and will accentuate the size of the garden

Mown paths are essential to allow access around wildflower meadows, and where the tall grass meets the short grass, this makes excellent egg-laying sites for a number of butterflies

Above: *Big gardens offer enough space for hedges to grow uncut for two years or more, therefore producing more flowers and fruit.*

Above: *In a large garden, a pond can be linked to a bog garden. Together, these habitats will support many amphibians and reptiles.*

AN URBAN WILDLIFE GARDEN

The main problem faced by wildlife in an urban setting is that it will always be in close proximity to people. Add to that the dangers posed by pets – dogs and especially cats – and the garden suddenly seems a precarious space for wildlife to survive in. Despite these hardships, clever design can overcome some of the dangers and many "urban" creatures become surprisingly habituated to the people who "share" their home.

Above: *Bird tables and feeders will attract birds into your garden from surrounding gardens and the neighbouring countryside.*

NEIGHBOURING INFLUENCES

Despite such drawbacks, domestic gardens are often rich in wildlife. This is usually because many adjoining gardens combine to create a larger super-habitat. Of course parts of this area will be more useful than others, and if you choose the right features for your own patch you can benefit your own wildlife while enjoying the visits of other creatures from the surrounding areas.

USE OF SPACE

As with any domestic space, the golden rule is to decide how much of the space is for your needs, and which areas are to be devoted to wildlife. In a smaller space, however, such lines become blurred and

Below: *A winding path in a narrow space makes a garden look wider than it really is. The dense borders provide valuable cover.*

you may need to compromise in order to find as near-perfect a solution as possible. Lawns are a prime example because most people use the space on the lawn for both play and relaxation. But there is no reason why such a space cannot also benefit wildlife, and a medium to short, clover-filled flowering lawn will instantly help wildlife without the need to keep off it. In addition, a corner of the lawn can always be left for naturalized bulbs and the grass allowed to grow long.

ATTRACTING WILDLIFE

Hedges and wildlife borders can also be included in most gardens, where they will provide valuable cover for many species

Left: *Hawthorn, sometimes classed as a small tree, is ideal to use as a large shrub in a restricted urban space. It provides both structure and food for wildlife.*

Above: *Water is vital for the survival of resident or visiting wildlife. Create drinking shallows for smaller creatures to drink from.*

and, if there is space, a small tree can even be included. Ponds and water features are often a big attraction for many species, and even a modest pool can make quite an impact. Not only will it act as a watering hole, but it will be a crucial breeding site for amphibians and aquatic insects.

Right: *Climbing roses provide excellent sites for roosting insects and birds feeding on pests such as aphids. Choose single-flowering cultivars because they produce copious amounts of pollen for insects, particularly bees.*

URBAN WILDLIFE GARDEN

Although they vary in size, nearly all urban gardens will be large enough to include a variety of different habitats. The resident and visiting wildlife found in a built-up area is strongly influenced by the surrounding gardens and habitats. Therefore, if your garden has neighbouring large trees or a pond, it may not be necessary for you to include these in your own design. Although the design pictured here looks like any well-designed ornamental garden, it contains all the vital ingredients for a classic wildlife garden.

A bog garden is a transitional area between the water and dry land, and is used by creatures that like damp places, such as amphibians

An ornamental pond with a slope ensures that wildlife can enter and exit the water

Pots and containers provide seasonal colour and good quantities of nectar and pollen for insects

Wall shrubs and climbers can be great sources of nectar and pollen for insects and fruit for birds; they are often used as nesting sites for birds and insect roosting areas

Mixed borders contain shrubs, trees and herbaceous plants; select species to flower and fruit all year round

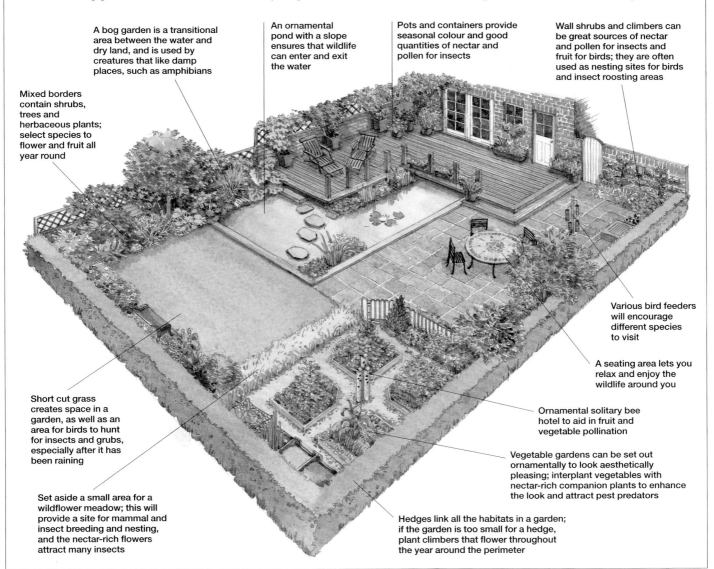

Various bird feeders will encourage different species to visit

A seating area lets you relax and enjoy the wildlife around you

Short cut grass creates space in a garden, as well as an area for birds to hunt for insects and grubs, especially after it has been raining

Ornamental solitary bee hotel to aid in fruit and vegetable pollination

Set aside a small area for a wildflower meadow; this will provide a site for mammal and insect breeding and nesting, and the nectar-rich flowers attract many insects

Vegetable gardens can be set out ornamentally to look aesthetically pleasing; interplant vegetables with nectar-rich companion plants to enhance the look and attract pest predators

Hedges link all the habitats in a garden; if the garden is too small for a hedge, plant climbers that flower throughout the year around the perimeter

A COURTYARD WILDLIFE GARDEN

Small gardens can be fantastic areas for wildlife. Courtyards are often devoid of birds and animals, but with the careful use of containers, hanging baskets and window boxes, you can easily grow a diverse range of plants, which in turn will attract a surprisingly large range of wildlife. While your garden may not be a permanent residence for all these creatures, it will prove to be a valuable and much appreciated food and drink stop.

Above: *Wildlife in a courtyard garden is easily observed due to the lack of space. Create seating areas to relax and enjoy this.*

USE OF SPACE

To ensure that a courtyard garden is fit for wildlife, tackle it in three dimensions. Avoid thinking exclusively about the space that is available on the ground. Many plants that are attractive to wildlife are perfectly at home in containers, and a little imagination can work wonders. Walls are relatively unattractive places for many species of wildlife, but can easily be improved by attaching a trellis and allowing climbers to grow up and over them. This will provide shelter for many species and, in the case of flowering and fruiting species, a valuable food source. Hanging baskets, wall and window boxes are also very useful ways of improving the appearance and wildlife value of the garden, while avoiding the need to use up too much of the ground space.

Above: *Water can be provided for birds in small gardens by hanging up bowls or attaching containers or troughs to a wall.*

PROVIDING WATER

Water is often in short supply in towns, and you may not have space for even a small wildlife pool, but you should endeavour to provide a constant source of fresh water for visiting creatures. This can be as simple as a shallow bowl or birdbath, or a small, raised, wildlife pool. A permanently planted water feature can be a mistake, however, if it is too small and shallow because it can easily become a breeding ground for mosquitoes. If this is likely to be a problem, add a small bubble fountain to keep the water moving.

DESIGN TIPS

Smaller gardens are harder to design as most of the space can be viewed at any one time. Vertical interest is needed to lead the eye away from the enclosed space, and will give the feeling of a larger area. This can be done with the use of trees or by installing a pergola and growing climbers up the frame to help draw the eye upwards. The pergola structure should be strong and the design simple so the area doesn't look too busy. Another tip is to avoid furniture that is bulky. Instead, select light and airy furniture such as wrought iron or teak as it will appear to take up less space.

Planting also plays a crucial part in giving the garden a larger look. Select cool colours such as blues and purples as this will give the illusion of the border being further away. Limit the number of different types of plants to avoid having the area look too busy. By incorporating these simple rules for gardening in a confined space your area will definitely give the illusion of being larger than it really is.

Left: *A small garden can become lush with vegetation in a short space of time, and can create a wonderful wildlife paradise.*

Above: *All the plants displayed here are selected for their excellent nectar and pollen production for visiting wildlife. Despite this courtyard garden's small size, it is still a spectacular ornamental display.*

Above: *A pergola in a courtyard garden creates an enclosed area. It also creates cool, shady areas within a garden if climbers and wall shrubs are grown up and around the structures.*

COURTYARD WILDLIFE GARDEN

Small courtyard gardens can be teeming with wildlife if a variety of different features are introduced. Much of the nectar and pollen production in a courtyard garden will be found in hanging baskets and containers. If you can remove an area of paving, a small mixed border can be created, otherwise plant up shrubs and trees in pots and arrange to create the same effect. Water can still be added in the form of a small fountain or a hanging saucer to tempt resident and visiting insects and birds.

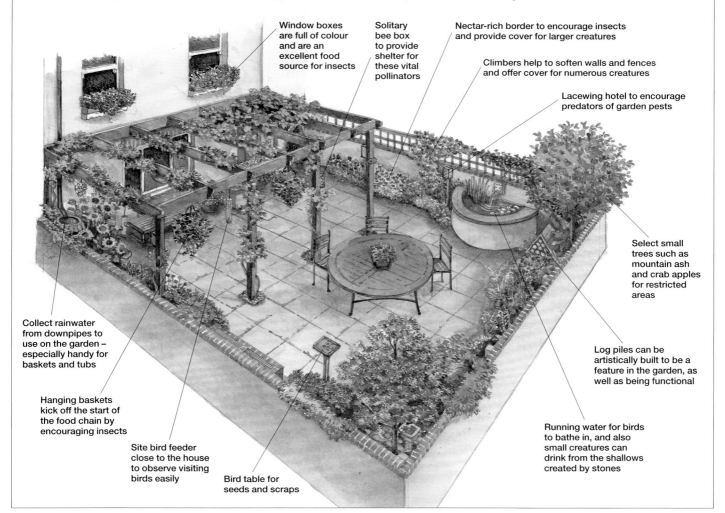

Window boxes are full of colour and are an excellent food source for insects

Solitary bee box to provide shelter for these vital pollinators

Nectar-rich border to encourage insects and provide cover for larger creatures

Climbers help to soften walls and fences and offer cover for numerous creatures

Lacewing hotel to encourage predators of garden pests

Select small trees such as mountain ash and crab apples for restricted areas

Log piles can be artistically built to be a feature in the garden, as well as being functional

Running water for birds to bathe in, and also small creatures can drink from the shallows created by stones

Collect rainwater from downpipes to use on the garden – especially handy for baskets and tubs

Hanging baskets kick off the start of the food chain by encouraging insects

Site bird feeder close to the house to observe visiting birds easily

Bird table for seeds and scraps

A WILD GARDEN

Wild gardens offer potentially the closest substitute to a natural habitat and, if designed properly, can be a wonderful place. However, the decision to build a wild garden should not be taken lightly, nor should it be thought of as a low-maintenance option, becoming completely disorderly and chaotic. It is still a garden, and the term "wild" could equally be replaced by "naturalistic". Regular maintenance is still required, especially in habitats such as the wildflower meadow.

Above: *In dappled shade areas, a mass of spring bulbs such as wild garlic offers a welcome early supply of nectar for insects.*

NATIVE OR EXOTIC PLANT?

Wild gardens differ from other styles of wildlife garden primarily because they use only plants that are native to the area. It is precisely because of this that more traditional gardeners sometimes deride them, regarding them as little more than weed patches. But many native plants are not only supremely beautiful, but are well adapted to the site and soil conditions of the area.

Thankfully, recent years have seen a reversal of the traditional form of gardening, with native plants now being commonly seen in an ornamental setting. With a little imagination they can form an immensely attractive display. Always avoid plants that are known to be invasive, however, because

there are always less troublesome, attractive alternatives. Native plants also offer certainty that they are excellent choices for the local wildlife in terms of their food value. Always choose a range of species to flower, and provide food, over as long a period as possible.

MAINTENANCE

When it comes to maintenance, most native plant species are no different from other garden plants. In fact your main focus should be on being untidy. Fallen plant debris harbours many overwintering

Above: *Wildflower areas are more accessible if paths are mown through following natural "desire lines". Several species of butterfly lay their eggs alongside the mown paths.*

insects, and those dead flowers in the borders are often a rich source of seed for birds in the winter. The only real difference in making a wild garden is that you will have created a refuge for a whole host of interesting creatures using a rich diversity of native plants, many of which are becoming increasingly rare in the wild.

Left: *This well-balanced pond is packed full of hidey holes by the use of wood, pots and plants for insects and amphibians to seek shelter, hide and hibernate in.*

Right: *Many species of butterflies are attracted to wild gardens, where they feed on nectar from flowers found in the wildflower meadows, and several lay their eggs in the edges of long grass areas.*

WILD GARDEN

A design for a wild garden has to be as well thought out as a formal design. Care should be taken to include as many different habitats as possible, especially wildflower meadows and deciduous trees *which are renowned for the number of creatures that are associated with each. Short cut grass areas are kept to a minimum and standing deadwood extends proudly in this type of garden.*

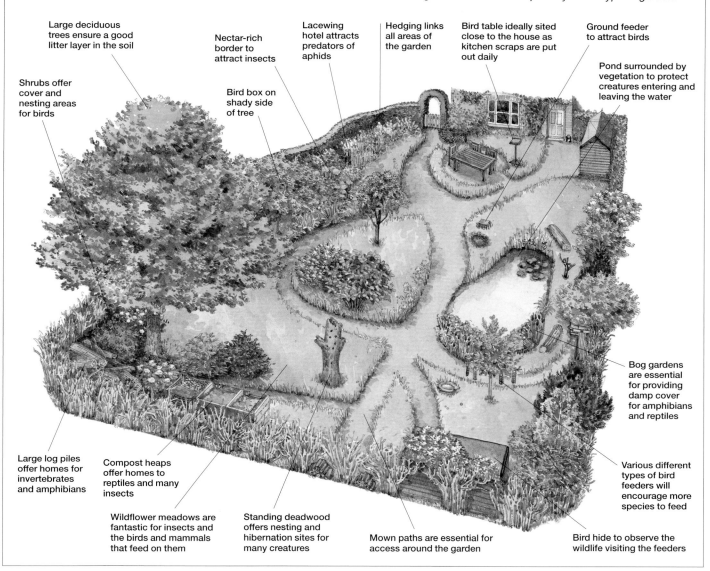

Large deciduous trees ensure a good litter layer in the soil

Shrubs offer cover and nesting areas for birds

Nectar-rich border to attract insects

Lacewing hotel attracts predators of aphids

Bird box on shady side of tree

Hedging links all areas of the garden

Bird table ideally sited close to the house as kitchen scraps are put out daily

Ground feeder to attract birds

Pond surrounded by vegetation to protect creatures entering and leaving the water

Bog gardens are essential for providing damp cover for amphibians and reptiles

Various different types of bird feeders will encourage more species to feed

Large log piles offer homes for invertebrates and amphibians

Compost heaps offer homes to reptiles and many insects

Wildflower meadows are fantastic for insects and the birds and mammals that feed on them

Standing deadwood offers nesting and hibernation sites for many creatures

Mown paths are essential for access around the garden

Bird hide to observe the wildlife visiting the feeders

Above: *Water lilies provide an ideal landing pad for damselflies, dragonflies and frogs to bask on.*

Right: *Allowing short grass to regenerate naturally can result in areas abundant with cow parsley.*

A BEE BORDER

Bees are one of nature's busiest creatures and superb pollinators, and without them many plant species would dwindle and, ultimately, become extinct. Fortunately, many very showy plant species will attract and serve bees well by providing nectar to make honey and pollen to feed developing grubs. Most gardens will have space for a bee border; it will be a great asset and, once you have one, you can enjoy the gentle hum of bees all summer long.

Above: *Bumblebees may have long or short tongues, and the shape of a flower dictates which type is able to access the nectar.*

WHY ARE BEES SO IMPORTANT?
The hum of bees visiting a border rich with flowers is one of the true delights of the summer. Plants are pollinated by bees when they gather nectar from the flowers, though wild bees and honeybees also collect pollen. Pollen is a vital food, used to feed the developing bee grubs, and is gathered with the nectar. To feed bees, then, you'll need a mixture of nectar- and pollen-rich plants.

DECLINE OF NATIVE SPECIES
Urbanization and changes to farming practices have resulted in the destruction of native flowers that provide both nectar and pollen, and consequently many wild species of bee have declined. This trend has to be reversed, and gardeners can help.

Bees – particularly species such as the long-tongued bumblebee – are choosy about which flowers they visit, most needing deep flowers with abundant nectar. Both the flowers and bees are reliant on

each other's continued existence, and the loss of one bee species often has wider consequences than many people realize, with several plant species being affected as a result. Gardeners are in an excellent position to slow, and even reverse, this decline by growing plants that are suitable for these important wild bee species.

FORAGING BEHAVIOUR
Bees forage for a wide range of flowers, and the main thing that you need to promote is a variety of flower shapes. Different bee species have favourite shapes according to their size, weight and mouthparts. In addition, many large, cultivated forms of flowers no longer resemble ancestral forms, and are inappropriate for bees because they have

Below: *Choose a range of flower shapes when designing a border, as different species of bee will prefer a certain size or weight of flower to land and forage on.*

trouble foraging from them. Old-fashioned cottage-garden varieties are usually the best option. In general, simple, unmodified flowers usually have most nectar, although the bees cannot easily distinguish between them and double flowers or cultivars that are poor in nectar.

DESIGNING THE BORDER
The trick is to plant a range of species, and mix them with attractive native wildflowers. Choose a range of plants to flower, and feed the bees, over a long period. This is especially important for bumblebee colonies, which generally only store a few days' worth of food and are much more vulnerable than honeybees to food

Below: *Bees such as the honeybee collect pollen in sacs on their rear legs. This activity not only pollinates the flowers but also makes an ideal food for their developing larvae.*

shortages caused by a scarcity of flowers or poor foraging weather. The bumblebees need constant access to nectar-rich plants throughout spring, summer and autumn.

Early season, nectar-rich plants are vital for newly emerging females. The female solitary bees often appear in mid- to late spring and, having mated, they then prepare the overwintering nest for next year's brood. Bumblebees, on the other hand, are social insects, and the females that emerge from hibernation in early spring are called queens. They must find and establish a nest – often a disused mouse burrow – and find enough food to mature the eggs and rear the first batch of workers. Consequently, early flowering plants play an extremely important role in ensuring the survival of these colonies and the species in general, so always include a few.

In the design shown here, the needs of both long- and short-tongued bees have been considered, as has the flowering season. From early to mid-spring,

short-tongued species can forage on the cotoneaster whereas the long-tongued species will be attracted to the flowering currant (*Ribes sanguineum*) and the gorse (*Ulex europaeus*). Later, in spring and early summer, the short-tongued bees will be helped by the roses and any remaining flowers on the cotoneaster, while the long-tongued bees will delight in the foxglove (*Digitalis purpurea*), the perennial pea (*Lathyrus latifolius*), columbine (*Aquilegia vulgaris*) and red clover (*Trifolium pratense*).

From midsummer until early autumn the short-tongued bees will continue to visit the climbing rose, *Rosa* 'Mermaid', borage (*Borago officinalis*), the Japanese angelica tree (*Aralia elata*) and traveller's joy (*Clematis vitalba*). The long-tongued bees will visit catmint (*Nepeta* x *faassenii*), the giant thistle-like *Echinops nitro*, and honeywort (*Cerinthe major*), with *Hebe salicifolia* and the bellflower (*Campanula latifolia*) feeding a wide range of species at this time.

Above: *The selection of single flowers for a border is vital in a bee garden as the many petals in the make-up of a double flower will hinder access to pollen and nectar. Old-fashioned cultivars and cottage-type plants are among the best flowers to do this.*

BEE BORDER

The plants selected in this design for a bee border are ornamental as well as rich in nectar and/or pollen. A range of annuals, bulbs, perennials, shrubs, climbers and trees have been selected to flower from spring right through until autumn, offering food throughout the seasons when bees are active.

1 *Trifolium pratense* – Red clover
2 *Salvia nemorosa* – Wood sage
3 *Cotoneaster horizontalis* – Herringbone cotoneaster
4 *Ceanothus impressus* – Santa Barbara lilac
5 *Digitalis purpurea* – Foxglove
6 *Lathyrus latifolius* – Perennial pea
7 *Hebe salicifolia* – Hebe
8 *Campanula latifolia* – Bellflower
9 *Aquilegia vulgaris* – Columbine

10 *Nepeta* x *faassenii* – Catmint
11 *Echinops nitro* – Globe thistle
12 *Cercis siliquastrum* – Judas tree
13 *Rosa* 'Mermaid' – Rose
14 *Ribes sanguineum* – Flowering currant
15 *Monarda didyma* – Bergamot
16 *Cerinthe major* 'Purpurascens' – Honeywort
17 *Sedum spectabile* – Ice plant
18 *Ulex europea* – Gorse
19 *Rosa canina* – Dog rose

20 *Clematis tangutica* – Clematis
21 *Aralia elata* – Japanese angelica tree
22 *Borago officinalis* – Borage
23 *Cirsium rivulare* – Plume thistle
24 *Eschscholzia californica* – California poppy
25 *Alcea rosea* – Hollyhock
26 *Allium giganteum* – Ornamental onion
27 *Perovskia atricifolia* – Russian sage
28 *Agastache foeniculum* – Anise hyssop
29 *Limnanthes douglasii* – Poached egg plant
30 *Phaseolus coccineus* – Scarlet runner bean

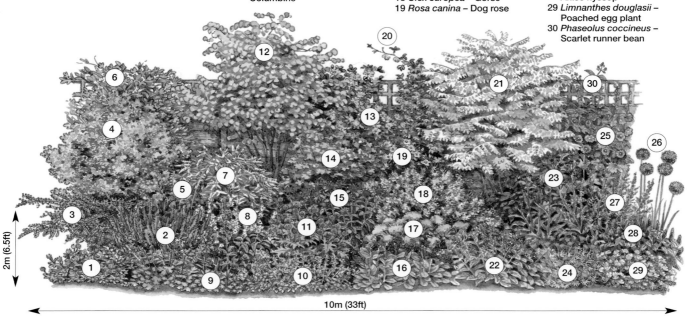

2m (6.5ft)

10m (33ft)

A BUTTERFLY BORDER

Butterflies are the true aristocrats of the insect world – they have inspired poets and are the epitome of a warm summer's afternoon. They are frequent visitors during the summer, attracted by the rich concentration of nectar offered by garden flowers. Attracting butterflies is generally quite easy, although it does require some planning. Find out which butterflies are native to your area and research their feeding preferences, the places where they prefer to see out bad weather, and what their larvae feed on.

Above: *Butterflies prefer single-flowering dahlias, such as the Collerette Group, rather than the showy blooms of other dahlia types.*

UNDERSTANDING LIFE CYCLES

Although showy adults are the prime attraction, the plants also need to support the larvae, or caterpillars. They are essentially a long, worm-like eating machine that must consume a prodigious amount of leaves, or other vegetation, to get enough energy to change (or metamorphose) into the adult butterfly. Unfortunately, the idea of a border full of tatty plants that have been munched by caterpillars is too much for most gardeners. The trick is therefore to grow a few of the more showy food plants, but so spread them out that if they are devoured by caterpillars they won't be so obvious. Also keep any clumps or patches of the less attractive food plants, such as nettles or brambles, in more out-of-the-way places, and remember that many species have caterpillars that feed on grasses. Making a long-grass area for wildflowers is a useful addition to your border.

Adult butterflies, on the other hand, are almost entirely nectar-feeding, although a few – depending on the species or season – may feed on fermenting fruit, manure and carrion. Most will also land on moist, muddy ground to get a drink of water and top up their mineral salt intake.

DESIGN AND PLANT SELECTION

Any site for a butterfly border must have good shelter and receive plenty of sun. The majority of flowers that attract butterflies are clump-forming or shrubby, make excellent subjects for a mixed border, and provide a striking display for you and the butterflies.

Adult butterflies need plenty of nectar to give them energy, and a good butterfly border should provide nectar from spring to autumn. Adult butterflies have mouthparts shaped into a long, coiled tube called a proboscis into which they force blood, straightening it out so that it can probe into flowers. They then suck up the nectar, and that's why good butterfly plant species often have narrow, tubular flowers.

The colour of the flowers can also be important, with most butterflies preferring blue, mauve, yellow and white. They do not see red as well as we do, but they can see ultraviolet light that is present on many flowers, guiding them to the nectar. Butterflies also seem to be attracted to areas with large masses of a single colour, or closely related colours, rather than to borders with many mixed colours. They also have a well-developed sense of smell from their antennae, which is why so many butterfly-attracting plants also have a sweet fragrance, increasing their appeal. If you visit a nearby garden where butterflies are plentiful, make a note of which butterflies are present, and which species visit which plants.

Make sure that any design for a butterfly border has a long flowering season to maximize its appeal to the greatest possible number of species. And provide a wide range of plants because all habitats thrive on diversity (stagger groups of wild and cultivated plants through the border). In the design shown here, spring-flowering species include holly (*Ilex aquifolium*), which

Below: Buddleja davidii *is aptly named the butterfly bush because the large panicles of its small tubular flowers are frequented by many butterflies.*

Below: *The monarch butterfly is a truly amazing insect that will migrate thousands of miles as part of its yearly life cycle.*

is also the food plant of the holly blue butterfly caterpillar, candytuft (*Iberis amara*) in mild areas, the alder buckthorn (*Rhamnus frangula*), which is also the food plant of the brimstone butterfly caterpillar, and, towards the end of spring, *Escallonia* 'Langleyensis'.

In summer – the prime time for many butterfly species – buddlejas, candytuft, sweet scabious (*Scabiosa atropurpurea*), *Verbena bonariensis*, red valerian (*Centranthus ruber*), hemp agrimony (*Eupatorium cannabinum*), heliotrope (*Heliotropium arborescens*) and *Escallonia* 'Langleyensis' all provide a feast of nectar. Autumn is also important for many species of butterfly that overwinter as hibernating adults. Nectar is provided by *Aster* x *frikartii*, ivy (*Hedera helix*), dahlias and the ice plant (*Sedum spectabile*).

Where space is limited, just grow a few nectar plants beside some woody ones to provide butterflies with shelter during bad weather and at night. And because butterflies bask in the sun, often early in the day, place a large, flat stone in full sun. Also note that adult butterflies cannot drink from

Above: *The caterpillars of some butterflies and moths store toxins. As a result, they have brightly coloured bodies or hairs to warn off any would-be predators.*

Above: *The meadow brown butterfly is a frequent visitor to garden flowers but requires an area of long grass to breed successfully.*

open water, so provide a patch or tray of wet sand or soil to which you have added a pinch of rock salt. Finally, a butterfly-feeding station is a useful border addition. If you have fruit trees, leave some produce to rot on a feeding table where late-emerging butterflies can feed.

BUTTERFLY BORDER

In order to attract butterflies, a border needs to contain a range of large or flat flowers for the insects to visit. In addition, it is vital that you choose plants so that some of them will be in flower for as long a period as possible. Spring and autumn are especially important times for overwintering species because nectar is often scarce then.

1 *Lotus corniculatas* – Bird's foot trefoil
2 *Aster* x *frikartii* 'Mönch' – Aster
3 *Ilex aquifolium* – Holly
4 *Colletia hystrix* – Crucifixion thorn or barbed wire bush
5 *Hedera helix* – Ivy
6 *Dahlia* Collerette Group – Dahlia
7 *Heliotropium arborescens* – Heliotrope
8 *Iberis amara* – Candytuft
9 *Scabiosa atropurpurea* – Scabious or mourning bride
10 *Buddleja* 'Lochinch' – Butterfly bush

11 *Humulus lupulus* – Hop
12 *Rhamnus frangula* – Alder buckthorn
13 *Verbena bonariensis* – Tall verbena
14 *Sedum spectabile* – Ice plant
15 *Origanum vulgare* – Oregano
16 *Centranthus ruber* – Red valerian
17 *Hedera helix* – Ivy
18 *Buddleja alternifolia* – Fountain butterfly bush
19 *Eupatorium cannabinum* – Hemp agrimony

20 *Escallonia* 'Langleyensis' – Escallonia
21 *Anchusa azurea* 'Dropmore' – Anchusa
22 *Zinnia elegans* – Zinnia
23 *Polygonum bistorta* 'Superbum' – Snakeweed
24 *Origanum majorana* – Marjoram
25 *Hebe* 'Great Orme' – Hebe
26 *Phlox paniculata* – Summer phlox
27 *Dianthus barbatus* – Sweet William

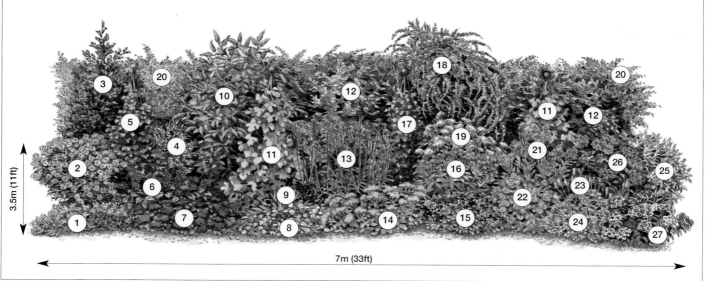

A BIRD BORDER

Birds are an absolute delight in the garden, both during summer for their sweet songs and useful habit of eating garden pests, and in winter when their bright plumage helps brighten up dull days. It's during this winter period that they most need our help, and a border, planted with birds in mind, can be a real lifeline, providing a diverse array of foods, including seeds, berries and even the odd overwintering insect hiding among the vegetation.

Above: *Blue tits are common garden birds in Europe. They rely on seeds and small fruits to see them through the winter.*

WHAT IS A BIRD BORDER?
A bird border doesn't have to be wild or overgrown, but can look attractive all year round. There are few absolute rights or wrongs when you plan one, and growing a wide variety of plants to attract wildlife in general will offer garden birds food and shelter, helping them both survive winter and feed their hungry fledglings the following spring. Think of your bird border as a roadside café, a place where birds can feed and rest before moving on.

CHOOSING A SITE
It is usually best to set aside a quiet area for a bird border because some species are much more sensitive to disturbance than others. The ideal backdrop might be a hedge or berrying shrubs. If planting against a fence or wall, clothing them with climbing plants and shrubs can turn them into a "living boundary", and might well provide

cover and nesting sites. Bird borders can be made on any scale with even a small one proving useful, although the more space and diversity you can devote to such a feature, the better.

CHOOSING THE RIGHT SPECIES
Depending on where you live, it is often best to include a range of native plants in your border, and you should try to include as many different kinds as possible. In the example shown here, a formal backdrop has been created by using a hedge made of yew (*Taxus baccata*), although beech (*Fagus sylvatica*), holly (*Ilex aquifolium*) and hornbeam (*Carpinus betulus*) are equally effective, all providing good shelter for birds.

Below: *Barberry is an ideal plant to include in a bird border, offering both spring protection from predators as well as a rich crop of autumn berries.*

If space permits, try a less formal hedge of native shrubs, pruned on only one side in alternate years to provide an excellent source of food and nectar, as well as nesting and shelter.

Trees are also extremely useful, although large forest species – such as oak (*Quercus*) – are often too large for most gardens. If choosing trees for a town garden, make sure you use smaller examples like the ones shown in this design. Mountain ash (*Sorbus aucuparia*), holly (*Ilex aquifolium*) and the crab apple (*Malus* 'Red Sentinel') provide perches and shelter, and an excellent food source when in fruit.

A range of shrubs will provide cover from predators and the worst of the weather. Native species might come top of the list, but more importantly consider a range of evergreen and deciduous types to give variety and hiding places in winter. The barberry (*Berberis thunbergii atropurpurea*)

Below: *The song thrush is an example of a bird species that is carnivorous in the summer but switches to berries and seed during the dormant winter months.*

is an attractive semi-evergreen whose thorny branches offer protection to smaller birds from the likes of cats. Firethorn (*Pyracantha coccinea*) offers similar protective cover for larger birds, and both have berries that can be eaten over winter. The Oregon grape (*Mahonia aquifolium*) is a slightly shorter, evergreen, prickly leaved shrub with berries that ripen in summer, while both elder (*Sambucus nigra*) and blackcurrant (*Ribes nigrum*) are deciduous species that attract many insects and bear summer berries.

Ideally, in addition to these woody plants, you should aim to plant a range of annual and herbaceous plants. Natives are very useful but, if you want a more ornamental look, choose a range of showier species that will attract insects in spring and summer, and later produce good seed heads to help feed small songbirds.

Lastly, you might want to leave some space in your border for a birdbath and feeders, providing food supplies when natural sources run low.

Above: *The shy jay is an occasional visitor to the urban garden. It will take a range of foods, including insects, seed and fruits.*

Above: *The greater spotted woodpecker usually feeds on wood grubs and other insects, but occasionally eats fruit in winter.*

BIRD BORDER

This type of border needs to provide a range of food throughout the seasons. The plants are chosen to either attract insects or bear fruit in the summer, or to be rich in seeds and/or fruit in the winter months. It also includes a range of trees, shrubs and smaller herbaceous plants.

1 *Polygonum bistorta* – Common bistort
2 *Artemisia vulgaris* – Mugwort
3 *Helianthus annuus* – Sunflower
4 *Sorbus aucuparia* – Rowan
5 *Berberis thunbergii atropurpurea* – Barberry
6 *Achillea millefolium* – Common yarrow
7 *Oenothera biennis* – Evening primrose

8 *Lavandula angustifolia* – English lavender
9 *Ribes nigrum* – Blackcurrant
10 *Sambucus nigra* – Elderberry
11 *Pyracantha coccinea* – Firethorn
12 *Ilex aquifolium* – Holly
13 *Angelica sylvestris* – Wild angelica
14 *Amaranthus caudatus* – Love-lies-bleeding

15 *Myosotis arvensis* – Field forget-me-not
16 *Mahonia aquifolium* – Oregon grape
17 *Malus* 'Red Sentinel' – Crab apple
18 *Taxus baccata* – Yew
19 *Dipsacus fullonum* – Teasel
20 *Solidago virgaurea* – Golden rod
21 *Lunaria annua* – Honesty
22 *Viburnum opulus* – Guelder rose
23 *Tanacetum vulgare* – Tansy
24 *Melissa officinalis* – Lemon balm
25 *Ribes uva-crispa* – Gooseberry
26 *Cotoneaster horizontalis* – Herringbone cotoneaster
27 *Fragaria vesca* – Wild strawberry

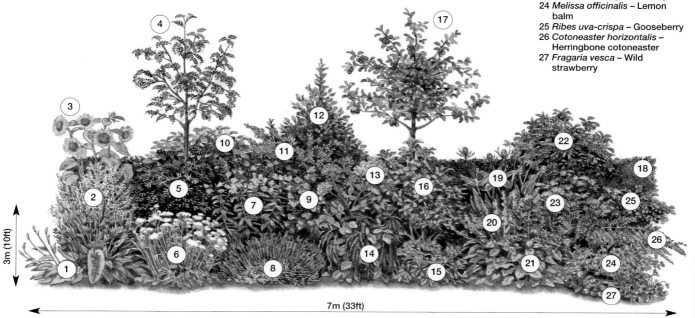

3m (10ft)

7m (33ft)

MAJOR HABITAT TYPES

To provide for the needs of wildlife in your garden, you must first understand where that wildlife lives. Major habitats may be extensive in the case of woodlands, while others may be as small as a piece of rotting wood within the same woodland, or can be found in the narrow space between two flat stones in a wall. All of these habitats are important and to support the widest range of wildlife your garden should aim to have as many of them as possible. Once you understand the nature of different habitats, large and small, you can start to replicate them in your own garden.

Left: *Flower-rich grasslands are a superb wildlife habitat and a wonderful garden feature during the summer months.*

Above: *Water is not only essential for wildlife but can also be a habitat in itself, supporting visiting and resident wildlife.*

Above: *Woodlands are extensive habitats that often contain many smaller habitats within, supporting a wide range of species.*

Above: *Even the narrow dark recesses of a drystone wall can provide a habitat for a range of creatures, such as hibernating newts.*

NICHES AND HABITATS

Animals, like humans, have basic living requirements. By providing these (for example, by establishing feeding and breeding areas), you enable creatures to make your garden their home – their habitat. Habitat can also refer to the entire environmental conditions that affect a whole range of species that live in an area, including soil, climate and interactions with other plants and animals. This second definition refers to a wider habitat, and is often called an ecosystem.

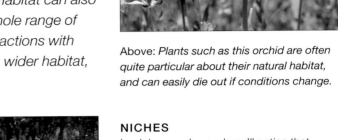

Above: *Plants such as this orchid are often quite particular about their natural habitat, and can easily die out if conditions change.*

WHAT ARE ECOSYSTEMS?

Ecosystems are complex and involve the interaction of all the different elements present, living and non-living. The word is a shorthand for "ecological system" – "ecology" being derived from the Greek *oikos* (meaning a house) and *logos* (to study). It is therefore the study of a house, and involves not only the study of a single occupant in an area but also considers how that occupant interacts with the surroundings and other occupants. Although we are going to stick to the term "habitat", the analogy of a house is useful.

Below: *Areas where two habitats meet, such as this pond and rock garden, offer the greatest diversity and are usually rich in different types of wildlife.*

NICHES

Look in a garden and you'll notice that many different animals live in the same general habitat, though not all have the same specific needs. Bats eat night-flying insects, while dragonflies eat flying insects by day. Blackbirds eat worms from above a lawn, whereas moles do so from below. The niche that each animal fills depends on a range of factors including body size and shape, its particular abilities and, of course, its behaviour.

If all the animals living in, say, a shrub border ate the same food and lived in the

Left: *Deadwood is a common part of any natural woodland habitat. It is essentially a mini or niche habitat that acts as shelter for some species and food for others.*

Right: *This varied waterside, with plants and shingle "beach", provides a diverse habitat for visiting animals. The "beach" is ideal for basking insects, reptiles and amphibians.*

same place, it would not take long before they ran out of space. The reason that a variety of animals can share a habitat is that there is no direct competition between species. They therefore exploit a different food source or feed in a different way, and may shelter in a different manner. Other potential competitors may avoid each other by having life cycles that do not overlap. The exact way that an animal occupies its habitat is said to be its niche.

GARDEN HABITATS

For some animals and plants, particularly the more attractive ones, we often have a reasonable idea of some of their requirements. Adult butterflies, for example, love feeding on the flowers of a buddleja. This is only part of the story, though, and without other food plants the caterpillars will not be able to breed in the garden. With many other garden residents you may know even less about their precise requirements, although much can be achieved by careful design.

In nature, both the greatest variety of species and the highest numbers of individuals are usually found where two

or more habitats meet. This is because their four basic needs – food, water, shelter and breeding sites – are more likely to be found in several habitats combined rather than in a single one. Gardens often meet these criteria and may have several habitats, for example providing hedges and shrubs, grasses, pond and flower beds in close proximity. So, a songbird might nest and take shelter in your shrubs, eat berries from bushes, feed on worms on the lawn, devour caterpillars in the flower beds and drink and bathe in the pond. These sites represent the naturally occurring habitats of a woodland,

with shrubs, woodland glade and open water. Even quite a formal design can be made to encompass the needs of wildlife. As gardeners, we have the opportunity to create an artificially high number of habitats within a garden, boosting its value for wildlife and creating an oasis for a rich variety of species that might otherwise have difficulty finding a home.

Below: *Different types of grassland can provide an excellent habitat for plants that in turn support many animal species by offering feeding, breeding and nesting sites.*

Below: *Even in a semi-natural setting, trees and shrubs can be pruned quite formally. This creates a complete contrast of styles, which is very striking and pleasing to the eye.*

GRASSLANDS

These windy, partly dry habitats are dominated by grasses, with trees and bushes few and far between. Almost a quarter of the Earth's land surface is grassland and, in many areas, grassland is the major habitat separating forests from deserts. In gardens, most grassland areas consist of lawns, and these often bear little resemblance to their wild counterparts. With just a few changes to the way we maintain our lawns, however, we can transform them into superb wildlife habitats.

Above: *Grasshoppers were once common but many are now threatened as their habitat is lost mainly due to grassland management.*

GRASSLAND OR LAWN?

The commonest use of grass in the domestic garden is on a lawn. These manicured features mimic grassland in certain respects but, in many ways, the traditional lawn is quite different from its wild counterpart. In its close-cropped, well-tended state, a lawn might look good to humans but as wildlife habitat it doesn't offer much. Changing a lawn from what is effectively a green desert to a thriving wildlife habitat often involves little more than reducing the amount of mowing, and outlawing the use of fertilizers, pesticides and weedkillers. This will have an almost immediate benefit for wildlife, but it may take some years before the full effects appear. And the time saved maintaining it can be spent more usefully elsewhere in the garden.

Above: *Spring and summer are the most spectacular time for meadows. Flowering reaches its peak at this time and the sight is truly stunning.*

THE IMPORTANCE OF LONG GRASS AREAS

There is a simple truth where grass in your garden is concerned. If a lawn is less frequently mown and not walked on wherever possible, it soon becomes richer for wildlife. Indeed, long grass habitats are some of the most useful undisturbed areas in the garden and are very simple to provide. Where space is limited they may be restricted to strips of uncut grass alongside a hedge, or around the base of a tree, or if space allows they can form more extensive areas.

Whatever the size of a long grass area, they are an important, sheltered habitat and may provide respite or even residence for a range of creatures. Insects such as bumblebees or other wild bees often like to nest in longer grass, while grasshoppers or the caterpillars of moths will feed on the grass leaves and other creatures such as spiders and beetles move in to eat them. Small mammals including shrews make good use of these areas, both to hunt for food and to hide from predators, and many birds such as finches and sparrows may search the area for seeds to eat.

FLOWER-RICH GRASSLAND

Lawns that are converted into a wildflower meadow can be an important refuge for declining wildflowers, and are an excellent habitat for many insects and spiders. Lawns facing the sun are especially useful, attracting solitary bees and butterflies, and plants

Above: *The combination of dazzling flowers and brightly coloured insects makes a grassland a wonderful place to visit.*

Above: *Buttercups, once a common sight in pastureland, have become rarer with the intensification of modern-day agriculture.*

Left: *Traditionally, garden lawns were kept short by mowing and although this keeps the grass healthy, it results in a poor wildlife habitat.*

Right: *Even when you intend to let the grass grow, short cut paths allow access and create a contrast that is useful to butterflies. Some species lay their eggs alongside the paths.*

such as clover (*Trifolium*), knapweed (*Centaurea*), trefoil (*Lotus*), and vetches (*Anthyllis, Coronilla* and *Hippocrepis*) are excellent food plants that provide nectar for long-tongued bumblebees.

TYPES OF WILDFLOWER LAWN

In nature, grassland is a rich and varied habitat that is moulded by the effects of geography, climate, soil and, in many cases, human intervention. Choosing the right type of grassland for your needs will depend on all these factors. Where you live will automatically decide the first three, but the last factor is mostly your choice, and depends on what you want in the garden.

Short grass or downland turf is most commonly seen in temperate regions. It is usually the result of grazing sheep, and the consequent short-cropped turf contains a multitude of flower species. It is the closest model to the modern garden lawn, and can be maintained by regular (if infrequent) cutting by a mower on a high setting.

Hay meadows are a traditional way of managing grassland for the hay that is cut in the summer months and stored for animal fodder. The long grass frequently harbours many species of wildflower during spring and early summer, creating an extremely pretty artificial habitat. Traditional forms of management often resulted in poor soil that reduced the vigour of the grasses and favoured the growth of wildflowers. Sadly, modern intensive agriculture has seen a severe decline in these habitats and

consequently in many wildflower species. Wet meadows or flood meadows are largely similar to hay meadows, except that they are subject to seasonal flooding, usually in winter, and consequently harbour different species. All types of meadow can be established in gardens, but they need to be situated carefully and cut during the summer months, when they are not that attractive. Also note, they can be hard to establish on lawns that have been previously well fertilized.

Prairie is a term used to describe the vast areas of flower-rich grassland that once clothed North America, and is similar to the European steppe. The soils are often richer than those found in artificial meadows, and they are often full of wildlife and colourful flowers, many of which have become familiar plants. The effect is potentially much easier to establish in most gardens because it depends on rich soil, with similar mowing regimes to those used in meadows.

Marginal grassland is often used to describe remnants of grassland plant communities that occur on field margins, roadsides or waste ground, and which have been marginalized. They are often a last, vital refuge for native flower species and their dependent wildlife that were formerly common in that area. The effect can be duplicated in a garden at the base of a hedge, or by leaving an occasional space. All you need do is cut it back every year or two in late winter.

TYPES OF GRASSLAND

With such a wide distribution, grassland occurs in many different forms. The commonest types can be mimicked in a garden and provide excellent wildlife refuges.

Wildflower meadow These rich flower habitats are the result of traditional management of grassland to gather hay crops. The constant removal of hay creates a poor soil.

Pasture or downland Grassland was often maintained by the constant grazing of livestock. This results in short grass that is rich in low-growing herbs.

Water meadow Sometimes called flood meadow, these are very similar to hay meadows but are flooded on a seasonal basis and so harbour different plant species.

Prairie and steppe These vast swathes of grassland formerly covered large areas of the USA and Eurasia. Their rich soil supports many species of plants and animals.

Marginal grassland This simply refers to remnants of formerly extensive natural grassland and is often seen in field margins or roadsides.

WETLANDS, PONDS AND BOGS

A wildlife garden would not be complete without a pond because it provides a habitat for some species and a much-needed drink for other residents and visitors. This, with its aesthetic appeal, makes it a worthy addition to any design. Even where space is too limited for a pond, the smallest patch of water can be useful and a damp corner of the garden can provide a habitat for wetland flowers.

Above: *Amphibians such as toads spend much of their life on land in damp areas, but they always return to water to breed.*

WETLANDS

This general term is applied to areas that are wet or marshy. The term includes both seasonally and permanently wet areas often existing as a complex mosaic of wet ground and open water, including rivers, streams and natural ponds. The natural fertility of these areas means that they are often drained for agriculture or dwellings,

Below: *Even a relatively small area of water can be an attractive garden feature, which results in a surprisingly diverse habitat for numerous species of plants and animals.*

and the rich variety of plants and wildlife, as well as a range of surrounding creatures, are often critically endangered as a result.

WHAT IS A POND?

The term is surprisingly vague, and there is no clear distinction between a large pond and a small lake. The average garden pond is relatively small, often supporting a wide range of wildlife. In fact a well-designed pond can attract more variety of wildlife than any other single feature in the garden. It provides a breeding space for amphibians, such as frogs and toads,

and a whole host of insects, such as dragonflies, that spend part of their life here. In addition, it is the sole habitat for a range of other creatures, from water snails that spend their life beneath the water to pond skaters that spend most of their life on the water surface.

Ponds should be shallow at one end to provide a bathing area for birds and a watering hole for small mammals, and have wet, muddy margins to attract insects needing a drink. Ponds also provide a unique visual focus, and have a restful quality that is hard to match.

Above: *Ponds are full of interest, often revealing curiosities such as this empty dragonfly larva case in the summer.*

Above: *Pond dipping is a good way to assess what wildlife you have in a pond. It is a great way to interest children in wildlife.*

POND PLANTS

Plants are essential to the health of any small area of water, enabling the habitat to achieve a correct water balance and provide surface cover on otherwise open water. Without them the water would, over time, probably start to resemble a thick pea soup, as algae – small, mostly microscopic plant-like organisms – will start to grow prolifically and ultimately colour the water the same as their own bodies. Plant leaves have the double action of absorbing both carbon dioxide and minerals from the water, which in turn starves the algae. Many natural bodies of still or slow-moving water have extensive cover of floating plants and their sides are also shaded by larger, bank-side or shallows vegetation. In a garden pond it is easy to recreate this by ensuring that there are plenty of submerged plants, about half of the water surface is covered with foliage and that the margins have plants in them that are capable of surviving immersion in shallow water in order to achieve this balance. This will keep water clear and will also make the pond attractive for a whole host of fascinating creatures that come to visit or live there.

BOG GARDENS

Usually specially constructed areas, bog gardens provide permanently waterlogged soil. They are often made in conjunction with a pond, and can support a range of fascinating plant species that would normally be found in wetland habitats. Bog gardens are an important element of any mosaic, and can be a vital refuge for many semi-aquatic species, such as amphibians, which will relish the cool, damp shelter.

PLANTS FOR WETLANDS

Wetlands naturally contain both open water and wet ground, and the plants that live in these places are often adapted to occupy a particular situation.

Marginal or emergent plants Plants that have roots and sometimes stems that grow in shallow water but with shoots, leaves and flowers above the water surface.

Oxygenators Plants that have adapted to live beneath the surface are called oxygenators, due to their role in enriching the water with oxygen.

Water lilies and deep-water aquatics The roots of these plants are submerged, the leaves are on the surface of the water and their flowers are either found on or above the water surface.

Free-floating plants The leaves and stems are free-floating and are found on the water surface. The roots are submerged and the flowers grow on or just above the water.

Bog plants Plants that prefer to grow in permanently wet or waterlogged ground. Some marginal species can also be grown as bog plants.

POND PLANTINGS

Ideally, a pond profile will include shallow areas as well as deeper areas of water. In the deeper reaches, the vegetation consists of plants that are capable of living permanently under water or those with roots that send up leaves which in turn float on the surface. Shallow water will support plants capable of tolerating waterlogged conditions and the remainder are free-floating on the surface.

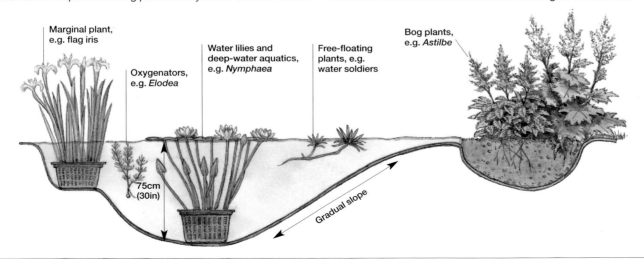

HEDGEROWS

Widely used as boundaries and dividing features in landscapes for centuries, hedges are important habitats for many creatures. Some hedges are relics of former habitats, meaning quite simply that they harbour species found in prior woodland cover, and may even be the oldest remaining feature in the area. Properly managed, they provide a great opportunity for wildlife to find shelter and food, and are home to many once common and often beautiful wildflower species.

Above: *Hedgerows are often rich in seed- and berry-producing shrubs that provide an ideal food source for overwintering birds.*

WHAT IS A HEDGE?

A hedge can be defined as a boundary of closely planted woody shrubs or trees. The earliest known use of the word dates back to the Anglo-Saxons (though hedges would have been grown before that), being derived from the Saxon *hæg* or *hag*. The Saxons used hedges as a way of defining ownership of land, but their hedges were not the same as those we know today, being more like a rough fence, only loosely clipped and often containing as much deadwood as living material. They used many species, such as hawthorn (*Crataegus monogyna*) – haw also means hedge in Old Saxon – and briar roses.

In centuries past, people exerted less pressure on wildlife and hedges were just another place for animals to shelter and forage. With increased land clearance, intensification of agriculture and a growing population, however, habitats dwindled and hedges became a refuge for many native species. In this way ancient agricultural hedges are a tangible link with the wildlife that once inhabited the woodland edge and open spaces across many areas, containing a rich variety of animal life and a multitude of plant species, both woody and herbaceous. Hedges are often a prime habitat in their own right.

THREATS TO TRADITIONAL HEDGEROWS

The intensification of agriculture in recent decades, coupled with the introduction of large machinery, has meant that many areas traditionally managed using hedgerows as part of the rural landscape have been transformed beyond recognition.

Machines work more efficiently in large fields, and hedges were seen as taking up valuable land that could produce crops. In addition, hedges in the United States contained a lot of barberry (*Berberis*), and this was identified as the alternative host species of the wheat rust *Puccinia graminis*, which is a serious fungal disease of wheat.

The net effect of this was that farmers on both sides of the Atlantic were encouraged to remove hedges and in doing so this rich and vital habitat was removed from these landscapes. In the case of European hedges, the rich legacy of over a thousand years was lost in some cases and it left wildlife in a precarious position. Gardens became one of the few places where hedges remained common and as such they are an invaluable wildlife resource.

Left: *Some hedgerow species, such as this hawthorn, have abundant spring blossom that is attractive to a wide variety of insects.*

Above: *Even where a more formal effect is required, you can choose a species well suited for wildlife, such as this hornbeam.*

Above: *The bases of hedgerows often provide a refuge for woodland flowers, and are rich in both animal and plant species that find refuge there.*

Above right: *Hedgerows often provide an excellent habitat for climbing plants, such as this ivy. Climbers add to the diversity of the habitat, attracting more species.*

GARDEN HEDGES AND WILDLIFE

The modern approach to hedges, especially in garden settings, has been to cultivate a tight-cropped and controlled shape with many closely planted specimens of the same species. But while highly decorative, they have limited appeal to wildlife. Some species are able to find shelter in the dense growth, but the range of species is limited, as is the likelihood of finding much food.

The answer often lies in planting a mixed, native hedge. Remember that a mosaic of plant species will favour a wider range of wildlife. Choose plants that provide food in the form of nectar-rich flowers and berries for overwintering birds. Hawthorn (*Crataegus*), wild roses (*Rosa*), holly (*Ilex*), hazel (*Corylus*) and elder (*Sambucus*) are good all-round choices. Also try barberry, cotoneaster and pyracantha, which produce lots of berries for the birds.

Resident birds may also appreciate the hedge for shelter, and even breeding, which is why wildlife hedges can't be trimmed in the nesting season, from early spring to late summer. Human impact can be further lessened by cutting back (not too tightly) only one side of the hedge on alternate years. Ideally, hedges should be pruned in late winter so that wildlife can take

advantage of the insects, fruits and buds during the cold months, and again in summer and autumn.

Hedgerows are especially important habitats because they share key characteristics with two other habitats – woodlands and open fields – providing corridors for wildlife, and allowing species to disperse and move from one habitat to another. Always allow the hedge bottom – the portion where the base of the hedge adjoins another habitat such as grassland – to become overgrown with grasses and flowers. The bottom is characteristically the dampest and most fertile area, and often proves to be the part richest in wildlife. Plants also find it difficult to spread across open fields, and "travelling" along the base of a hedge is their only realistic option.

Below: *Honeysuckle is a good example of a hedgerow climber that is both useful for wildlife, such as moths and birds, and is also ideal as an ornamental plant.*

TYPES OF HEDGE

Hedges are quite diverse in nature, partly as a result of what they are used for but also because of their maintenance.

Mixed hedges Quite simply, a mixed hedge is one where the intention is to grow a range of species and provide a habitat that has the maximum species diversity, and is most like a natural woodland edge.

Single-species hedges These hedges are common, especially in gardens, where their intention is to provide a consistent backdrop or feature. They can be useful for wildlife provided that a suitable species is chosen.

Formal hedges Found in highly manicured gardens and cut with a smooth face, the high frequency of their cutting and general absence of flowers or fruits mean that formal hedges are less useful for wildlife.

Informal hedges As the name suggests, these are hedges where the cutting regime does not entail frequent cuts or a smooth face or finish. They can be planted as single- or mixed-species hedges.

Dead hedges These are barriers that consist of dead branches and twigs that are firmly staked in place. Climbers are allowed to ramble through them and provide excellent shelter.

WOODLAND

An important feature of many landscapes, woodland provides a rich and varied habitat for an abundance of wildlife species. Woodland varies greatly, depending on where it grows and the tree species within it. In many cases, it is a product of the way in which it has been managed, due to the importance of timber to humans. In a few areas, however, natural undisturbed woodland still exists, and this is one of the most diverse habitats found anywhere on the surface of the earth.

Above: *Rodents, such as this wood mouse, are common and important in woodlands as food for larger predators, including owls.*

WHAT IS A WOODLAND?

There are still vast areas of the Earth's surface covered with trees. They are highly variable, although some generalizations are possible.

Almost all woodlands are structures with a number of layers of different plant species. The tallest and most dominant form the canopy. This can either be closed, in the case of dense woodland, or more open, with sunlight penetrating between the trees. Beneath the canopy is a layer of less dominant tree species, called the understorey, and beneath that is a layer of smaller, woody plants and immature trees called the shrub layer. The ground is covered to a greater or lesser extent with a layer of herbs. The soil is continuously enriched by the decomposing leaves, shed from the trees either throughout the year, in the case of evergreens, or in autumn with deciduous trees.

TYPES OF WOODLAND

Broadleaved woodland is dominated by trees with wide, flat leaves. There is considerable variation between such woodlands in different locations in respect of the wildlife and dominant plant species that they contain. The most obvious kind is the temperate, deciduous woodland found in cool, rainy areas with trees that lose their leaves in autumn in order to survive the cold, dark winter weather. They occur mostly in the northern hemisphere, in North America, Europe and Asia, with smaller areas in South America, Africa and Australia.

Above: *Fallen leaves and seed coats often naturally form dense layers on woodland floors. These slowly break down to release nutrients for trees and other plants.*

Coniferous woodland mostly grows in the northern parts of North America, Europe and Asia, and covers more of the Earth's surface than any other habitat – around 17 per cent of the Earth's land area. The trees are mostly adapted to a cold, harsh climate and a short growing season.

Temperate rainforest grows in areas with warm summers and cool winters, and can vary enormously in the kinds of plant life contained. In some, conifers dominate, while others are characterized by broadleaved evergreens. They are mostly restricted to coastal areas, with some coniferous woodlands having trees that reach massive proportions. They are mostly found in the north-west Pacific, south-western South America, New Zealand and Tasmania, with small, isolated pockets in Ireland, Scotland, Iceland, south-western Japan and the eastern Black Sea, and despite their relative rarity they are some of the most amazing natural habitats and home to some of the world's most massive trees.

Above: *Taking a long time to die, trees often become full of deadwood, which in turn provides a habitat for other creatures.*

Left: *Trees are very large, long-lived plants that form a dense shady habitat beneath them. Ground-cover plants only grow in spring before the trees form leaves again.*

Above: *Clearings in woodlands, such as this one alongside a path, are often the richest area in terms of wildlife and plant species.*

TRADITIONAL WOODLAND MANAGEMENT

In many areas where woodland once formed extensive cover, much has now been removed and the vast majority that remains has long been managed by people. Despite the loss of ancient "wildwoods" the remaining managed woodlands proved to be excellent habitats, whose exact nature depended upon the system of management employed.

Coppicing is one such traditional method of woodland management, by which young tree stems are cut down to 30cm (1ft) or

Below: *Branches and even whole trees naturally fall on to woodland floors and decompose over a long time, providing a rich habitat for many species.*

less from ground level to encourage the production of new shoots. This is done repeatedly through the life of the tree and results in a habitat that repeatedly transforms from a clearing into a woodland habitat. Many familiar woodland flowers and associated animals are well adapted to coppicing. Pollarding is a similar operation but involves cutting the branches from a tree stem 2m (6ft) or so above ground level. Pollarding was mostly practised in wood-pastures and grazing areas where cutting above head height protects the new shoots from being damaged by browsing animals.

THE BEST TYPES OF WOODLAND FOR WILDLIFE

The ability of woodland to support wildlife varies considerably. The age of a woodland and the variety of plant species it contains all have their part to play, as does the way in which it has been managed. Generally, open woodland, especially when deciduous, is more accessible than closed woodland to species that browse and graze, and it tends to be richer in ground-level plants.

The woodland floor is often rich in species that feed on decaying plant matter, and deadwood is also important for many insect species that live in rotting wood. Where the greatest concentrations of wildlife occur will vary greatly according to the type of woodland, but the richest areas always tend to be those that border other habitats, for example at the woodland margins. The latter is the easiest to recreate in a garden.

Below: *Deer browse and graze in woodland, and their activities create clearings among the trees. These clearings favour other smaller species of wildlife, such as invertebrates.*

SOIL HABITAT

To most of us, garden soil is simply a medium in which we grow plants. Indeed, the very word "soil" is often equated with dirt. It may come as a surprise, then, that the soil in your plot is one of the most diverse habitats you are ever likely to encounter. It is not only the place that plant roots must reside, but also home to a huge range of species, many of which, though invisible to us, are essential to all plant growth through their role in decomposition and nutrient cycling.

Above: *The earthworm is an essential recycler of nutrients, and it also aerates the soil in many different habitats.*

THE ULTIMATE HABITAT?

What do a worm, cow, human and daisy have in common? They are all soil organisms. Creatures that depend on the soil for their food or habitat can be defined as soil organisms or soil dwellers. While we do not live within its confines, our survival does depend on it.

WHICH ORGANISMS INHABIT THE SOIL?

The most obvious examples of soil life are those seen with the naked eye. Apart from plants, we often recognize some as being important – worms being taken as a sign of soil fertility, for example. But there are many others that are so tiny that, despite being just about visible, they often go unnoticed, with countless millions more microscopic creatures, arguably the most important ingredients of all garden life.

Below: *Centipedes, often overlooked in gardens, are voracious predators of many smaller soil organisms, and they help to provide a balance in the habitat. They are mostly harmless, although larger, warm-climate species can bite.*

MICRO-ORGANISMS

These organisms are extremely important to plants because they actually control the flow of nutrients. Some form a part of the nutrient cycling process for carbon, sulphur and nitrogen, all of which are essential elements in plant growth. Other micro-organisms are an important means of removing chemical pollutants that might otherwise build up in the soil. Microbes are also a food source for a vast array of larger soil organisms and form the start of many food chains. Their role in decaying dead material means that they can be seen as the driving force of the entire garden habitat.

Despite their huge importance, though, barely 1 per cent of the total soil volume is made up of microbes; compare this to the 5 per cent volume of plant roots and 10 per cent dead organic matter. The microbes make up for this, though, in sheer weight of numbers with around 90 million bacteria alone in just 1cm³ (0.4in³) of average, healthy, mineral soil. Bacteria also reproduce rapidly when compared to the larger organisms, and are generally concentrated where there is food (decaying matter), adequate water and, for most

species, oxygen. In general, this limits them to the top 30cm (1ft) of topsoil, where they live with tree and plant roots. This layer occurs naturally in all soils over time, and is familiar to gardeners through its darker colour and, often, quite different character to the subsoil immediately below.

In common with any habitat, soil is a complex community that takes a long time to develop. It is not static, and its balance often shifts to match a change in conditions. While it is resilient, it could lose the diversity of life contained if it is not cared for properly, causing problems for the larger plants and animals that ultimately depend upon it for their well-being.

SOIL LIFE AND PLANT ROOTS

Almost all plants must live with their roots in the soil and it is precisely because of this that we sometimes fail to understand the significance of this habitat. The most noticeable parts of the garden are what we see: the leaves, shoots, flowers and produce that our gardens provide for us. Roots, however, are just as vital, and the dark mysterious habitat they occupy is critically important for the whole plant.

Right: *The harvestman, often seen in gardens, appears spider-like but is actually more closely related to scorpions. It runs rapidly over the soil surface, preying upon any smaller creatures it encounters. Larger species such as this are often met with suspicion or even revulsion by gardeners, but they are essential creatures that help maintain a natural balance.*

Left: *Ground beetles are extremely important predators of many garden pests, such as slugs. They thrive in the litter layer that lies on top of undisturbed soil, and their numbers can often be severely reduced as a result of frequently cultivating the ground.*

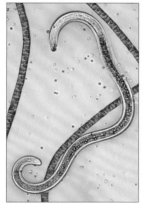

Plant roots have long exploited the soil and have struck up marvellous interactions with many other soil-dwelling life forms. Leguminous plants in the pea family, for example, make special nodules for a bacterium called *Rhizobia*, which collects nitrogen for the plant. Many forest trees also have roots that form close associations with fungi, called *Mycorrhizae*. The tree provides the fungus with sugars and in return for this food the fungus supplies vital mineral

Above left and above: *Slugs are often regarded as the scourge of gardens, but many species depend upon them as a food source. The slug (above) has been attacked by soil-living nematodes (above left) that naturally parasitize them. The actions of nematodes ultimately establish a balance.*

nutrients from the soil. This relationship is called a symbiosis and helps to show just how complex soil habitats are.

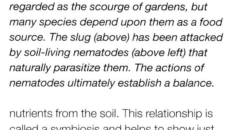

SOIL LIFE

Much of the life in the soil is unseen, either because it's so small or because it is buried. Microbes are an extremely important part of the soil, through which all essential life-giving elements must pass at some stage.

Bacteria, fungi and algae

Unicellular, and almost always invisible unless they are species that form extensive colonies, bacteria, fungi and algae are the most common organisms found in the soil, and there may be billions surrounding each plant. While a few may cause damage to plants, the vast majority are benign or even essential, by virtue of their ability to break down and cycle or recycle essential nutrients needed to support healthy plant growth.

Earthworms, spiders and insects

While these species are frequently large enough to be seen, they often remain out of sight unless disturbed during cultivation. Many such creatures are important in the early stages of recycling nutrients and, while some may attack plants, the vast majority are important in maintaining the balance within the complex soil food web. Pesticides that target some species often wreak havoc at this level.

Plants, trees, birds and mammals

With the exception of plants, it's all too easy to imagine that these have no direct link with the soil. In all cases, though, they depend on the soil either directly or indirectly as a source of essential nutrients, and their actions (whether feeding or otherwise) often modify the soil.

Far left: *Roots depend on a healthy soil habitat because good soil aids the release of nutrients that the plant needs, thus promoting its healthy growth.*

Left: *Many types of fungi are essential in the soil, not only because of their ability to decompose dead plant matter, but also because many species set up intimate associations with plant roots, supplying minerals to the plant in return for sugar.*

MINOR HABITATS

There are lots of habitats that you can easily build into your garden that will encourage a whole host of common animal species. Most are easy to create and can form decorative or unusual features. Essentially, by thinking about these smaller, less obvious living spaces, you can favour a wide range of species that might otherwise have difficulty finding a home. These creatures will add to the diversity of your garden and, in certain cases, might even return the favour by eating a few garden pests.

Above: *Fungi, so often neglected or forgotten in gardens, occur in many colours and forms, and can be very beautiful.*

NEW LIFE FROM OLD

Deadwood is an incredibly important part of a woodland ecosystem, and there is a whole host of species that are specialists in eating and decomposing it. A rather overly fastidious streak in many gardeners, however, often deprives species of this habitat. The easiest way to remedy the problem is by retaining and even making a feature of some deadwood.

Probably the easiest way of helping deadwood species is to make a small log pile, positioned in an out-of-the-way, shady and preferably damp part of the garden.

The thicker the logs the better and, unless you have a ready source to hand, you may have to buy them. Pile them up and add some thinner prunings and leaves from trees and old shrubs to avoid too many gaps. Then plant a few ferns, ivies and other plants to grow through and over the wood, thereby softening its appearance. Gradually, these rotting logs will attract many species, including fungi, insects and other invertebrates that, in turn, will attract small mammals, amphibians and possibly reptiles, who may also decide to take up residence in its dark recesses.

Left: *Deadwood is an important habitat for many species of insects and is naturally very common. It can be made more decorative by sculpting the top.*

Below: *A drystone wall can be a highly decorative feature in a garden, with small dark recesses that provide cover and hibernation places for small creatures.*

If you don't have the ideal spot for a woodpile, try making a dead hedge. This traditional feature dates back to the Middle Ages and involves driving two rows of stakes into the ground, and binding the sides with loosely woven hazel or willow to hold the structure together. Once the framework is made, the void is filled with deadwood. Start by putting the largest material at the base, with lighter material – brush and leaf litter or even lawn clippings – towards the top. You can easily make it more attractive by planting vigorous climbers, such as honeysuckle (*Lonicera*), to ramble through it, with more flowers being planted at the base on the sunny side, or ferns if it is shady. Dead hedges can be used as boundaries or garden divisions, and with luck will attract nesting birds. They can be surprisingly long-lived features, and if climbers become established they actually become more of a "live" feature than a "dead" one, combining the best features of both.

Right: *Dead hedges are made from pruned branch material which is woven between stakes that are driven into the ground. They provide good cover for many species.*

LITTER LAYERS

This refers to the loose layer of dead material that builds up on the soil, particularly in woodlands or around garden plants in the winter months. Traditionally, the litter was removed in early winter to prevent the spread of disease and, although there is some merit in this, it has the greater disadvantage of removing a valuable habitat for many predatory insects. Beetles, in particular, are very fond of a layer of decaying matter over the soil, and the litter can also help support several larger predators, such as shrews and hedgehogs. Adding a deep layer of well-rotted compost or bark will avoid most of the disease problems, while helping to create a useful habitat, and may also improve the soil.

WALLS

The two main kinds of wall are rock piles and drystone. Both are a valuable habitat for a range of species, and are especially useful features for hibernating reptiles and

Below: *Leaf litter naturally harbours a range of species, many of which perform a useful role as beneficial garden predators.*

Bottom: *Rock piles are an excellent refuge for many species, including reptiles and amphibians. It is best to site them in a cool shady area, under a hedge or shrub.*

amphibians needing a cool, shady retreat. The dark recesses between the stones are also ideal for beneficial creatures such as spiders, parasitic wasps, solitary bees, centipedes and ground beetles.

The rock pile is easily made, and is best constructed using rough-hewn, flattened pieces of stone. In many places drystone walls were a traditional way of utilizing local stone when making boundary walls. They offer the same benefits as a rock pile but are usually more aesthetically pleasing, and can be used in a more formal design. They look simple to make but can be tricky for the beginner, and are often best left to a specialist if you want a neat and tidy look in a more formal setting.

BURROWS

Many creatures make burrows, ranging from the tiny, in the case of some insect species, to larger excavations of mammals and other vertebrates. Bumblebees often occupy a disused mouse burrow, for instance, and a shortage of mice and voles can seriously hamper their nesting efforts. If you know that an area is being used by burrowing animals of any description, leave them undisturbed, as any attention might cause them to move elsewhere.

Below: *Many animals use burrows, including larger mammals such as badgers and rabbits. Bumblebees often colonize empty mouse burrows in long grassland.*

HABITAT LOSS

The loss of habitats is the single most important danger to wildlife, affecting not only single species of animal or plant but entire ecological communities. Every living creature needs a place to live, find food and reproduce. The loss of a habitat eliminates these possibilities, and many species now face a bleak outlook. Few parts of the world have not been altered, damaged or destroyed, mostly by human intervention as we occupy land for building, agriculture and extracting natural resources.

Above: *Leisure activities such as golf require playing areas that can result in the loss of habitats for wildlife.*

CAUSES

Humans have always altered their environment according to their needs, but modern technology has accelerated this process to unprecedented levels. Serious damage can now be inflicted very quickly.

There are so many demands on Earth for space; space to build roads and towns, to grow food, and for work and play. This problem is amplified by the huge increases in population over the last 200 years. Larger populations need ever more resources and, often, natural habitats suffer as a consequence.

WHICH HABITATS ARE MOST THREATENED?

Deforestation is the greatest concern, with over half the Earth's forests having disappeared already. The great European forest, which once spread from the west coast of Ireland to Siberia, has all but vanished, and many other forests are disappearing at an alarming rate thanks to agriculture and timber felling. Although forests can recover, and even be harvested in a sustainable way, the rate of loss is currently 10 times higher than the rate of re-growth.

In addition to deforestation, the drainage of wetlands, grubbing up of hedgerows and ploughing up of ancient meadows for agriculture contribute to habitat loss. Even the clearing of too much deadwood from managed woodland can affect the ecology, removing habitats for the grubs and beetles that form an important link in the food chain. No wonder many species are now classified as being under threat in terms of their long-term survival. It is likely that some were never particularly numerous in the first place, and extinction is a natural part of evolution – without it there would be no room for new species – but the current rates of extinction are far above those at which such species can be easily replaced.

HABITAT FRAGMENTATION

This process occurs when large, natural areas are broken up into smaller fragments or islands of habitat. Habitat fragmentation often happens in the course of urban development, oil and gas exploration and extraction, and the conversion of land to agricultural use. Habitats may be left intact, but they may be too small to support viable populations of some species, particularly those that occupy and defend territories. Inbreeding often results, and, without the influence of genetic diversity obtained by breeding with other populations, species may disappear even though their habitats remain.

Left: *Deforestation for timber has accelerated in the last century, and many habitats are now severely threatened as a result.*

CLIMATE CHANGE

Likely to have a considerable impact on most or all ecosystems in the 21st century, it is very likely that changes in climate patterns will alter the natural distribution range for many species or communities. If no physical barriers exist, it may be possible for species or communities to migrate. Forest or grassland, for instance, may move towards higher latitudes (i.e. nearer each of the respective poles) or to higher altitudes following changes in average temperatures. There is nothing new about this, and at the end of the last ice age (12,000–10,000 years ago) many plant communities moved quickly north in response to the rapid global warming that followed. The real danger to these habitats arises in most cases, however, where natural or artificial barriers prevent or limit this natural movement of species or communities. Many nature reserves and protected areas have been surrounded by urban and agricultural landscapes that will prevent the migration of species – especially plants – beyond their current artificial boundaries.

WILDLIFE CORRIDORS AND REFUGES

To help mitigate the effects of the loss of habitat, many scientists and conservationists urge the development and conservation of connecting patches of important wildlife habitat. These corridors, if planned correctly, allow wildlife to move between habitats, and also allow individual animals to move between groups. Often roads, urban developments, agricultural land and, of course, gardens can be designed in such a way that new wildlife habitats are created. It's always best to protect unspoilt habitats, but sympathetic design can help some of our most beautiful and vulnerable wildlife.

MAJOR CAUSES OF HABITAT LOSS

Without doubt, human activites have resulted in the most serious loss of habitats. While many of these are essential to our own well-being, they are not always done with wildlife in mind, this taking a "back seat" in favour of economic concerns.

CAUSE	EFFECT	CAUSE	EFFECT

Human population growth

This places incredible stress on ecosystems. Some estimates put the global population at around 10 billion by the end of the 21st century. More people means more development, a greater chance of "exotic" (non-native) plantings, more demand for energy, water and ultimately more pollution resulting from these and other activities. The more of us there are, and the greater level of development we achieve, the greater the demand is likely to be upon the already dwindling natural resources around us.

Water use

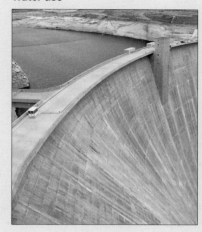

With population expansion comes increased demand for fresh water. For some, this is a basic need to survive, raise crops and livestock. Increased development, however, often means that water use per individual rises as water is needed for industry, domestic use, sewage and of course industrial-scale agriculture to support the population. Rivers being dammed to provide new lakes can have disastrous consequences for wildlife both downstream of the dam and by habitat loss in flooded valleys.

Agriculture

Agricultural development is a major threat to natural biodiversity (the total diversity of life), particularly the modern intensive agriculture that is now practised increasingly in both developed and developing nations around the world. In many developed countries, native grasslands have nearly disappeared beneath an onslaught of ploughing and grazing, and the development of water resources for both agriculture and urban use has also fragmented many freshwater habitats.

Road construction

An ever-increasing threat stemming from population growth is the increase in roads. More traffic means more collisions with wildlife, especially where new roads are built through habitats such as forests, where animals are unaccustomed to the dangers of vehicles. There is also an increased risk of toxic spills and air pollution, to say nothing of the resulting influx of people into formerly unoccupied areas, often resulting in new developments that might ultimately lead to the wholesale destruction of formerly pristine habitats.

Urbanization

Estimates predict that by the year 2032, more than 70 per cent of the Earth's land surface is likely to be destroyed, fragmented or disturbed by cities, roads, mines and other infrastructure of human civilization (a figure presently at around 50 per cent). Many wild animals are routinely poisoned in suburban situations, and still more are killed by traffic. The footprint of environmental damage often stretches far beyond the confines of the city itself, often having even international consequences in its demand for resources.

Pollution

Urban development brings a whole range of problems, most of which are inextricably linked with the ones described above. In cities, however, all of these problems invariably become more concentrated, particularly when development is rapid and areas become very over-crowded. The most immediate issue is that of habitat loss as land is developed for industry and habitation. The resultant vehicle and factory pollution, toxic waste and the problems of refuse and sewage disposal that inevitably follow such development all cause major harm.

CREATING NEW HABITATS

Nature is a mosaic of many different types of habitat that create a rich and varied tapestry across the landscape. Grassland gives way to woodland and wetland, and it is where these different habitats meet that we see the greatest diversity of wildlife. Gardens give the opportunity to help a wide range of wildlife for the same reason, since domestic gardens are also capable of supporting several habitat types, often in close proximity. By creating and managing garden features as potential habitats, gardens can become wonderfully rich in wildlife.

Left: *Naturalistic borders, rich in flowers, are excellent places for many species of wildlife to feed, breed and make their home.*

Above: *By adopting a new cutting regime in the lawn, you can incorporate bulbs, such as this cyclamen, as a food source.*

Above: *Water is an essential part of any wildlife garden, and can prove to be a highly ornamental feature visited by many species.*

Above: *Hedges provide dense cover for nesting birds and act as a corridor for wildlife that needs to seek food over a large area.*

ESTABLISHING A WILDFLOWER MEADOW

Any area of long grass is a valuable habitat, and by simply letting an area of existing lawn grow long, you will provide cover for many insects and small animals, as well as greatly enhancing both the look and diversity of the area. Wildflower meadows and flowery lawns are actually easier to make than you might think. You can add wildflowers by re-seeding an area or by planting pot-grown plants into existing grass.

Above: *Wildflower meadows offer both a habitat and a food source for bees, and are wonderfully ornamental in early summer.*

CHANGING AN EXISTING WILDFLOWER LAWN

The first step in transforming an existing lawn is to think about what you want it for, and how much you want to change. If it is important to keep the same amount of lawn, the simplest approach may be to change to wildlife-friendly maintenance. Alternatively, reduce the area of short cut lawn to a minimum, with wildflowers.

Assuming that you intend to keep some lawn, the simplest change is to let flowering plants colonize it. Reduce the frequency of cutting, and stop fertilizing, using pesticides and weedkillers, and watering it. The initial effect may be hard to see, but low-growing, broadleaved plants will soon begin to get a foothold. Even allowing areas on a clover-rich lawn to have a flowering break for a week or two will help the bees.

MAKING NEW WILDFLOWER LAWNS

Most grassland wildflowers grow best in full sun and open spaces with minimal root competition from trees, so choose your site accordingly. New lawns are best grown from seed that can either be bought ready mixed or you can mix your own. Ideally, the mix will produce about 60–80 per cent grass coverage, with the remainder being wildflower. The seed mix is sown sparingly –

PREPARING THE GROUND AND SOWING WILDFLOWER MEADOWS

1 *Start the project by marking out the area you intend to convert to a wildflower meadow. It is best to use a rope or hose to establish flowing lines and curves.*

2 *Once you have finalized where the edge of the meadow is to be, cut the line in the existing turf using a half-moon edging iron, following the line made by the rope.*

3 *Lift the existing turf, ensuring that you dig deep enough to remove all grass plants. Plants growing in wildflower meadows prefer nutrient-poor substrate and little topsoil.*

4 *Once the turf has been lifted and removed, lightly cultivate the whole area with a fork, before raking it to produce a light, crumbly seed bed ready for sowing.*

5 *Mix the wildflower seed into the grass seed prior to sowing. This will make it easier to distribute evenly. Lightly sow the mix at a rate of 15g/m² (½oz per sq yd).*

6 *The grass and wildlflower seedlings will soon emerge, and the light sowing rate ensures that the grass does not swamp the less vigorous wildflowers as they develop.*

PLANTING WILDFLOWERS INTO EXISTING GRASS

1 *Set out small wildflower plants grown in pots, and, once positioned, cut out and remove a plug of turf before planting.*

2 *The wildflower plants, once planted into the turf, have a head start and are able to compete with the surrounding grass plants.*

to avoid the grasses out-competing the wildflowers – at a rate of about 15g/m² (½oz per sq yd), or less.

You can also make an existing lawn richer in flowers by over-seeding in autumn with a mix of wildflower seed. To over-seed an area, cut the grass as low as possible and rake away the debris, leaving bare patches of soil. The seed is mixed with some fine, dry sand, particularly in the case of fine seed, and is thinly sown over the bare patches and then raked in lightly.

The results from over-seeding can be quite variable, and many gardeners prefer to plant out pot-grown wildflowers directly into an existing lawn. Mow the lawn early in the season and scrape or use bare patches for planting into. Arrange the young plants in groups of three to nine for the best effect and maximum chances of success. Once planted, the lawn can be mown on a high setting every two to three weeks in the first year to reduce the competition from grasses. The following year, the lawn can be mown less.

MAINTAINING A WILDFLOWER LAWN

The amount of time and effort a wildlife lawn needs will vary, depending on what you want. Shorter lawns need little change to their maintenance because the basic method of mowing remains the same, albeit less frequent.

Long grass is trickier, not least because it can be a fire hazard during dry weather. Always site an area of long grass at least 6m (20ft) away from buildings or other combustible items. A buffer zone of conventional lawn can be made more attractive by cutting the first strip of lawn next to the tall grass on the highest mower setting, and reducing this by one setting on each consecutive strip so that the longer grass blends in gradually.

Also, mowing a margin between long grass and features such as flower beds means that the grass will not collapse on to it following rain or storms. If you have a large lawn, mow a path through it so you can watch the wildlife without having to trample on the tall grass. Frequently mow areas you want to keep as paths, preventing long grass from developing and animals from sheltering there, and possibly getting killed by a lawnmower.

Hay and water meadows are usually best cut after they have stopped flowering, although if space allows you can try leaving some areas of long grass uncut until late winter to provide shelter and hibernation sites for insects and other grassland species. When you do cut the grass, remove all the clippings, usually after letting them lie for a day or two to let any wildlife escape, and then dispose of them elsewhere.

TOP PLANTS FOR A WILDFLOWER MEADOW

Choosing flowers for a wildflower lawn will depend on which species are native to, or will succeed best in, your area. The suggestions below give ideas for how some plants can be used; it is possible to substitute other species according to your local area.

SHORTER GRASS

Cowslip (*Primula veris*)
An ideal plant for areas of grass that are cut somewhat infrequently, it is suited for hedge bottoms and attracts a number of insects that feed on the abundant nectar in late spring.

Harebell (*Campanula rotundifolia*)
The diminutive harebell is extremely widespread in the wild, being found across much of the northern hemisphere. It is ideal for dry sites where its flowers attract bees.

Red clover (*Trifolium pratense*)
A pea family member with round, red flowerheads that are a real favourite with bees, due to the copious nectar that they produce. Often included in agricultural mixes of grass seed because of its ability to fix nitrogen in the soil and enhance grass growth.

LONG GRASS

Field scabious (*Knautia arvensis*)
One of the most nectar-rich of meadow flowers with pretty blue-mauve pincushions on branching stems throughout summer and well into autumn, when its seed is often eaten by birds.

Ox-eye daisy (*Leucanthemum vulgare*)
This quick-spreading, pretty perennial produces an abundance of yellow-centred, white daisy flowers in summer. Many daisy flowers – including coneflowers (*Echinacea*), tickseed (*Coreopsis*) and asters – are suited to long grass.

Wild carrot (*Daucus carota*)
This wild ancestor of the cultivated carrot has a delicate filigree head of dainty flowers that appear in summer, and are an excellent source of food for hoverflies, butterflies and a range of other species.

Cowslip   Red clover   Field scabious   Wild carrot

MAKING A WILDLIFE POND

Ponds are a real boost to wildlife gardens, being a watering hole for land-living animals as well as a complete habitat for others. They are relatively easy to construct, but need to be properly sited and designed for them to be useful habitats. A little care and attention at the planning stage can ultimately lead to a feature that will look good and boost the wildlife potential of your whole garden.

Above: *Frogs and other amphibians need water in order to breed, and they are highly dependent upon garden ponds for this.*

CHOOSING THE RIGHT SITE

Use an attractive, sunny place, sheltered from the prevailing wind. Try to avoid a site that is shaded by trees because they will not only cut out light, but their leaves will drop into the water, enriching it with mineral nutrients and organic debris. This promotes green water and blanket algae in the warmer, sunnier months.

In any garden where a water feature is planned, child safety is of paramount importance. If there is any risk that young children might fall in, consider delaying your plans until they are older. Children love water and the wildlife it attracts, but you should always weigh up the risks.

THE SHAPE AND SIZE OF A POND

As a general rule, 4m² (43sq ft) is the minimum area needed to create a balanced environment, with marginal shelves at least 25cm (10in) wide to support containers of emergent plants. Create the outline using sweeping curves with no sharp bends; a figure of eight or a kidney shape is often the best idea for smaller ponds. Then draw a rough cross-section of the pond to check how much depth you will get for your width. Aim to get at least 60cm (2ft) and ideally 90cm (3ft) or more in the deeper reaches to benefit a range of wildlife. The slopes should drop at a rate of one-third of the equivalent distance travelled across the top to assure stability.

CHOOSING A LINER

For small ponds, moulded or fibreglass pools can be used but they are limited in terms of design, and do not always look particularly natural. A flexible liner, such as butyl rubber, is generally considered the best (if most expensive) option, although UV stabilized PVC can be a cheaper alternative. Both these materials are prone to puncture, and particular care must be taken to line the hole with soft sand and/or an underlay, such as old carpet (made of natural fibres), to avoid this. The liners are easy to lay, and can also be used when creating bog gardens.

HIDING THE EDGE

Both flexible and rigid liners need to be hidden if you want to promote a natural effect. There are many ways of doing this.

A cobbled edge is easily achieved by setting some large stones or cobbles into a bed of sand/cement that has been laid on the liner, both below and above the eventual water surface on a shallow slope. The stones form a firm base, and other loose stones can be piled on and between them with the gaps providing sheltering space for small animals, while also providing a gently sloping "beach" for larger animals to approach the water and drink.

A drystone wall, or alternatively a loose rock pile set on a mortar base on the liner, just below the water, can act as a retaining wall for nearby planting, with the niches

---

CREATING DRINKING SHALLOWS

1 *The shallow areas of ponds are important to allow animals to drink, but they can become muddy traps for smaller creatures and offer little protection or shelter for visitors.*

2 *Start by placing some larger stones or rounded rocks both in the shallow water and on the bank, arranging them in small groups of varying sizes to create a natural-looking effect.*

3 *Once the larger stones have been placed, the spaces between them should be filled with round cobblestones to create both shallow stony pools and drier beach areas.*

4 *The finished effect is very ornamental, and the strong shoreline provides hiding places for smaller creatures as well as a basking area and safe drinking site for pond wildlife.*

between the stones providing excellent shelter for amphibians and reptiles. Walls or rock features are always best placed at the back of the pond so that they create a reflection on the water surface.

A planted edge is also an option with a "planting pocket" being built on the liner. This involves running the liner about 10cm (4in) above maximum water level, and then burying it in the soil around the edge. It provides a simple and natural effect, with the overhanging plants hiding the edge, but the liner will show when the water level drops, and there is always the added danger of damaging a flexible liner when mowing or gardening near the pond.

Concrete or stone slabs laid on a sand/cement bed over the edge of the liner are a somewhat formal solution, but are very practical if you want to view the water up close. Try to avoid this all the way around, though, as very small animals, such as young frogs, may have difficulty climbing in and out over the stone edge.

PUTTING IN A BUTYL LINER FOR A POND

1 *Start by marking out the outside edge of the pond using stakes or canes, and then mark out the locations of any shallow margins with spray paint.*

2 *Once marked out, begin digging the pond, starting with the deeper areas first, before digging out the margins and finalizing the edge of the pond.*

3 *Once you have excavated all of the pond to the required depth, establish the slopes on the side of the pond and the planting shelves within it.*

4 *To gain nicely smooth sides to the excavated pit, line the whole of the base and sloping sites with graded stone-free sand, fabric or old carpet.*

5 *Carefully lift the liner over the pit. Don't drag it because sharp stones may puncture it. Secure the corners using bricks or stones and start to fill the pond with water.*

6 *As the liner fills with water, it will mould to the shape you have excavated. Once the pond is nearly full, cut the edge of the liner, leaving a generous overlap.*

7 *As the water level continues to rise, fold the liner to create an even finish and avoid any unsightly creases across the pond bottom or sloping sides.*

8 *Once the water is almost up to the top, bury the edges of the liner by cutting and then lifting the turf edges of the pond and laying it under the cut turf.*

9 *The new pond can now be filled to the brim, then planted with various wetland species and drinking shallows created by using varying stone sizes.*

PLANTING PONDS AND WATER FEATURES

Naturally occurring ponds and wetlands are rich in plant life, much of which is specially adapted to grow in waterlogged ground, shallow water or even under the water surface, where it plays a vital role in the aquatic habitat. There are many forms of these plants, including some highly ornamental species, and by including a good range of them in your pond, you will improve both the look and habitat value of this essential garden feature.

Above: *Water lilies, such as this* Nymphaea alba, *are a beautiful addition to any garden pond. Frogs are often seen on the leaves.*

CHOOSING POND PLANTS

Surprisingly, new ponds can seem initially quite stark and lifeless. Plants provide the magic to bring them to life and, once surrounded by vegetation, the whole feature becomes more attractive to us and the wildlife.

To create a natural look, you could put a layer of soil on top of the liner for plants to root into, and creatures to hide in. This has the disadvantage, however, of introducing nutrients that can cause algal growth, and often means that you must be prepared to cull the plants regularly because aquatic plants can spread rapidly and choke the pond. Most people minimize the problem by using special aquatic plant containers that curtail excessive growth.

Most pond plants are perfectly happy in clay loam. Provided you ensure that the soil used is free of pesticides or pollutants most heavy types are fine, but the best idea is to buy a proprietary brand. The planting of most aquatic plants is the same as for other potted plants, but the soil needs to be

firmed down a little more than usual, and it is a good idea to spread gravel and/or cobbles on top of the soil to keep the pot stable and keep the soil in the pot. The best time for planting is late spring as the water warms up. Don't give plants a shock by plunging them into icy water.

There are three different types of plant that you need to attract wildlife. All are essential to a healthy pond because they constitute the range of habitats needed to support a diverse wildlife community.

Oxygenators spend the whole year submerged, and they supply a steady infusion of oxygen, which is needed by the aquatic creatures that breathe through their gills. Oxygenators often grow densely and serve as egg-laying sites, nurseries and cover for many aquatic animals.

Deep-water aquatics have roots and stems in the deeper reaches, but with floating leaves and flowers. They are especially important because they help to shade the water from too much sunlight in summer. Too much light entering the water

can cause algae to become a problem, and ideally you need to cover about half the surface of the pond with these plants. Water lilies (*Nymphaea*) are a big favourite, being very decorative, relatively easy to grow and available in a wide range of colours and sizes. Other plants are also available, and you must ensure that the species chosen are not too vigorous for your pond size. A few species are entirely free-floating and include duckweed (*Lemna*), water fern (*Azolla*) and water hyacinth (*Eichhornia crassipes*), but they can be very invasive and are best avoided.

Marginal or emergent plants grow in shallow water at the edge of the pond and offer shade and cover for animals, while greatly enhancing the visual appeal. They are used by dragonflies and nymphs to crawl out of the water and pupate. Many species of marginal plants are equally at home in a bog garden, and careful planting in such situations can help hide the division where the water stops and the bog garden starts, thereby enhancing its look.

FILLING A POND BASKET AND PLANTING IT UP

1 *Pond plants are best planted in specially made crates. These are lined on the base with gravel and filled with specially formulated compost.*

2 *Once the base is covered with stones and soil, put your plants in the crate and fill around the remaining gaps with more of the aquatic compost mix.*

3 *When the compost is up to the height of the top of your plant root ball, dress the compost surface with more gravel to help keep it in place.*

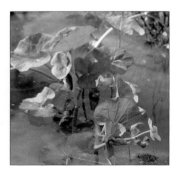

4 *The pond plants should quickly establish in their new surroundings and will soon send up new shoots and flowers above the water surface.*

RENOVATING A BOG GARDEN

1 *Thoroughly weed the bog garden, taking special care to remove all the roots of any persistent perennial weeds or unwanted plants.*

2 *Retain any useful specimens and dig in some organic matter to enrich the soil. Take a note of bare areas to calculate numbers of new plants needed.*

3 *Dig over the whole area to be planted, then set out the new plants and decide the best arrangement before planting them in their final positions.*

4 *Once the area is planted, give the garden a thorough watering to help the plants settle in. Take a note of all species planted in case replacements are needed.*

Above: *Small sections of oxygenating plants, such as this* Elodea, *can be tied with a stone and placed into the pond to grow and start to oxygenate the water.*

BOG GARDENS

Mimicking areas of marshy ground found in wetland areas, bog gardens are closely associated with ponds, lakes or streams. They are ideal cover for amphibians as the soil in these areas is permanently wet, and the plants that grow there have a great deal in common with marginal plants, with many species being equally at home in either as a result. This need for permanently wet ground means they are lined in a similar way to a garden pond. Bog gardens make an ideal accompaniment to a garden pond and are often constructed at the same time.

PLANTS USUALLY BEST AVOIDED

These plants can become invasive in a garden pond and, if they escape into the wild, can become a severe problem in natural ponds, lakes and waterways. Avoid using them in favour of native species or non-invasive plants.
Note: If these plants are already in the pond, dispose of them carefully to prevent their spread.

- Australian swamp stonecrop (*Crassula helmsii*)
- Fairy moss (*Azolla filiculoides*)
- Floating pennywort (*Hydrocotyle ranunculoides*)
- Parrot's feather (*Myriophyllum aquaticum*)
- Curly waterweed (*Lagarosiphon major*)
- Kariba weed (*Salvinia*)
- Water hyacinth (*Eichhornia crassipes*)
- Water lettuce (*Pistia stratiotes*)

TOP PLANTS FOR WILDLIFE PONDS

There are various types of wetland plants. They are split into categories to make it easy to select the correct plants for different areas of the pond or wetland.

MARGINAL/EMERGENT PLANTS
- Flowering rush (*Butomus umbellatus*)
- Water forget-me-not (*Myosotis palustris*)
- Marsh marigold (*Caltha palustris*)
- Yellow flag (*Iris pseudacorus*)
- Watermint (*Mentha aquatica*)

WATER LILIES/DEEP-WATER AQUATICS
- Water lily (*Nymphaea alba*)
- Water hawthorn (*Aponogeton distachyos*)
- Japanese pond lily (*Nuphar japonica*)
- Yellow floating heart (*Nymphoides peltata*)
- Golden club (*Orontium aquaticum*)

Flowering rush

Marsh marigold

Water lily

Golden club

OXYGENATORS
- Curled pondweed (*Potamogeton crispus*)
- Hornwort (*Ceratophyllum demersum*)
- Milfoil (*Myriophyllum spicatum*)
- Pondweed (*Elodea* spp.)
- Water starwort (*Callitriche stagnalis*)

FREE-FLOATING PLANTS
- Water soldier (*Stratiotes aloides*)
- Lesser duckweed (*Lemna minor*)
- Water lettuce (*Pistia stratiotes*)
- Water fern (*Azolla filiculoides*)
- Bladderwort (*Utricularia vulgaris*)

Hornwort

Pondweed

Water soldier

Water fern

PLANTING A WILDLIFE HEDGE

The best wildlife hedges usually consist of mixed species that provide nesting sites, year-round cover, flowers, berries, and areas at the base where wildflowers can flourish. Single-species hedges provide less variety, but may still be useful if managed properly. Wildlife hedges are a real boost to a wildlife garden providing cover for a range of animals whilst linking other habitats nearby.

Above: *Birds, such as this linnet, find cover and a food supply in a well-managed wildlife hedge that is not cut too frequently.*

CHOOSING A HEDGE

When deciding what sort of hedge will most benefit the wildlife in your garden, you must also consider your needs. If it has to double as a security hedge or barrier, or if you need a certain height, then check the plants' possible dimensions. Also note that a wildlife hedge will not be frequently pruned, and can grow both tall and wide in a single season.

The most wildlife-friendly hedge includes a range of four or five species in varying numbers. The exact species will vary considerably according to the conditions, but any plants chosen should always be compatible in their maintenance requirements when grown as a hedge. Start by walking around your neighbourhood, looking at the hedges and seeing what plants are growing well. Try to choose at least half of your plants from locally indigenous species because they'll often be most valuable to native wildlife, and if possible, when looking at other hedges growing locally, make some notes about the range and types of wildlife they attract.

A single-species hedge can be very useful, if only because all the plants will have similar maintenance requirements. For plants that flower and set fruit, you could try fuchsia, escallonia or barberry, all of which attract bees. Traditional agricultural hedges mainly consist of up to 80 per cent of one species, such as hawthorn (*Crataegus*), but will usually also have a diverse mixture of other trees and shrubs. This creates a variety of blossom, berries and scent with a range of niches that make such a hedge the best choice for wildlife. If you have a large garden, in the right setting, this type of hedge may be appropriate, but for a typical suburban semi-detached or terraced house, a single-species hedge may be more aesthetically pleasing.

PREPARATION AND PLANTING

When planting a wildlife hedge, prepare the soil properly beforehand. Dig a trench at least 50cm (20in) wide, and mix plenty of organic compost and a general fertilizer such as blood, fish and bone at around 50g (2oz) per m² (sq yd). Refill the trench and allow it to settle for a couple of weeks before planting.

Hedges are usually planted as either single rows of plants, about 30cm (1ft) apart, or as staggered, double rows with

SETTING OUT AND PLANTING A HEDGE

1 *Start by levelling your previously prepared ground, using a rake to ensure that there are no rises and dips along the length of the row.*

2 *Consolidate the ground to make sure there are no void spaces in the soil by lightly treading the area with a flat foot rather than a heel.*

3 *Rake the ground level, either with a rake or using the back of a fork, as shown here. It is best to start planting into level ground.*

4 *Using a spade to make a planting pit, slide the roots of the plant down into the hole, ensuring they are all covered.*

5 *Using a heel of a boot, make sure the young plant is firmly planted, with no air spaces around the stem.*

6 *To protect the stems from rabbits, place guards around them. These also shelter the young plants from wind.*

CUTTING A HEDGE

1 *Once the hedge begins to outgrow its setting, it must be cut. This is preferably carried out before or after the nesting season.*

2 *Set out a line of canes every couple of metres (7ft) or so to mark the line that you want to cut, thereby producing a good face.*

3 *Before cutting the top, set out a string line to mark the desired height and ensure that a straight line is maintained.*

4 *Even for neat wildlife hedges, the finished cut should not be too tight as it will still preserve a somewhat informal look.*

the same distance between the plants and rows. When planting, peg out a line of string to keep the hedge straight. Some species – beech (*Fagus*) and hawthorn (*Crataegus*), for example – are best planted at a 45-degree angle to encourage thick growth at the base. With other species this isn't necessary.

To stimulate dense, twiggy growth, trim off one-half to two-thirds of the total height of the hedge and then, for the first two or three years, remove at least half of the new growth during the winter period. Mulch the base of the rows annually, and apply an organic feed just before you do this.

MAINTAINING YOUR HEDGE

Once established, trim your hedge every second or third year, but avoid doing so when birds are nesting. The ideal time is in late winter, making nuts and berries available to birds and mammals for the longest possible period. Try cutting opposite faces of the hedge in alternate years where space is restricted, or if a slightly more formal shape is desired, because this will produce some flowers and fruit each year.

The best shape for a wildlife hedge is an "A" shape because the sloping sides allow light and rain to reach the bottom of the hedge. An established hedge, say four to five years old, can often be enhanced by planting climbers such as honeysuckle (*Lonicera*), roses (*Rosa*) and clematis. Take care, though, because planting climbers before the hedge is well established can easily result in the hedge being overwhelmed and strangled. You can also plant hedgerow wildflowers at the base to provide extra cover for birds and mammals, and additional food for other wildlife.

TOP HEDGE PLANTS FOR WILDLIFE

Any hedge has potential as a wildlife habitat, but the species described here are among the most useful to the widest range of creatures.

Alder buckthorn (*Rhamnus frangula*)
A thornless tree with five-petalled, green-white flowers, it's visited by many insects and is characteristic of hedges growing on damper soils, especially those on former marshes. The flowers are followed by pendulous red berries that turn black in autumn and are eaten by rodents.

Blackthorn (*Prunus spinosa*)
Also known as sloe, the flowers of this thorny plant attract early bees and butterflies, while the leaves support many moth and butterfly caterpillars. The whole plant supports over 150 species of wildlife. It doesn't like heavy shade but withstands strong winds, making it a good plant for coastal areas.

Hawthorn (*Crataegus monogyna*)
Frequently used for hedges in northern Europe, with several other species being used as small garden trees. Hawthorn is very important for wildlife, and can host at least 150 insect species with many songbirds and finches readily nesting in it, the berries being another attraction.

Hazel (*Corylus avellana*)
This well-known plant, also called hazelnut or cobnut, supports at least 70 insect species in addition to woodpeckers, squirrels and small rodents that are attracted to the nuts which ripen in late summer and early autumn. It is best left untrimmed for at least two seasons if you want to get any nuts.

Sweet briar (*Rosa rubiginosa*)
Also known as the eglantine rose, the leaves and stems of this European species have a brownish-red tint and the whole plant forms a dense mass. Bright pink flowers from late spring to early summer give way to bright red hips. The leaves have a fruity scent when rubbed because of the sticky, brownish glands on the underside.

Wayfaring tree (*Viburnum lantana*)
This small, attractive shrub is naturally found on chalk and limestone soils, and sports bright red berries in autumn that later turn black, preceded by clusters of scented white flowers in late spring and early summer. White, silky hairs coat the undersides of the leaves and young stems.

Blackthorn

Hawthorn

Hazel

Sweet briar

PLANTING TREES AND SHRUBS

Trees and shrubs form the essential framework of any garden, and provide cover for a wide range of animals, as well as nesting sites that are well above the ground and safe from ground-dwelling predators. The secret to success lies in careful ground preparation, stock selection and planting. Trees and shrubs are among the most rewarding plants you can grow, needing little or no maintenance once established.

Above: *Birds often rely on trees as nesting sites for their chicks. Holes in trunks are also used by insects, mammals and amphibians.*

SELECTING PLANTS

Always choose trees and shrubs that are vigorous, healthy and suitable for the site conditions or intended usage. They should always be free from any obvious signs of damage, pests or disease. If you are buying bare-rooted stock, make sure that the roots never dry out before planting, and keep them covered at all times – even a couple of minutes left exposed to cold or drying winds can cause a lot of damage. You should plant them as soon as possible; if the soil is frozen or waterlogged, plant them in a temporary bed of compost, at a 45-degree angle (heeling in), and keep them moist until you are able to plant them out.

PREPARING THE GROUND

Despite what is written in many books and guides, organic additives such as compost can be a mixed blessing if they are incorporated into soil at planting time. An enhanced soil mix does improve the soil but also causes the plants to become "lazy". Quite simply, the roots like it better than the

PLANTING AND STAKING TREES

1 *Container-grown trees should be thoroughly watered an hour before you intend to plant them or soak really dry ones overnight.*

2 *Clear any weeds and cut any suckers coming from the roots as these may slow the trees' top growth and root establishment.*

3 *Once you remove the pot, tease out any encircling roots to encourage root spread in the soil and to prevent root-balling.*

4 *Dig the planting pit and ensure that it is deep enough for the root-ball, checking this by lying down a spade or fork on its side.*

5 *Backfill the pit, firming the soil with a heel every 8cm (3in) to make sure it is well planted and contains no large air pockets.*

6 *Drive the stake in at an angle to avoid damaging the roots. Face the stake into the prevailing wind for stronger root growth.*

7 *Secure the stem of the tree using a tie, nailed on to prevent movement. Choose one with a spacer to stop the stem chafing.*

8 *The tree should remain staked for around one year, during which time the tie must be regularly checked and loosened.*

MULCHING A TREE

1 *Young trees growing in short or long grass are often slow to establish due to the competition from the surrounding plants.*

2 *Start by removing the turf around the tree. Create a cleared circle around the stem of the tree that is 1m (3ft) in diameter.*

3 *Thoroughly water the ground and then apply an even layer of mulch to a depth of about 5cm (2in) on the cleared circle.*

4 *The tree must be kept clear of weeds and competing vegetation for around 4 or 5 years. Water thoroughly in drought conditions.*

surrounding soil and circle round as if in a pot of compost resulting in an unstable "corkscrew" growth pattern known as girdling. Avoid this by applying organic matter across the surface after planting. This is much more like the natural situation and encourages many insects including ground beetles. Apply fertilizers only if really needed, after planting but before mulching.

WHEN TO PLANT

Plant deciduous species during early winter, when they are dormant. Evergreens, on the other hand, tend to do well if planted either in early autumn or late spring. Trees and shrubs growing in containers can be planted throughout most of the year, provided that the ground is kept sufficiently moist, although they too will generally establish best in the cooler months. Never plant when the soil is frozen, excessively dry or waterlogged, as this may damage the roots and lower stem. Make planting holes big enough, allowing a quarter to a third of the diameter again of the root spread. Check that the plant is at the same depth as it was before; placing a spade across the hole is the easiest way. As a rule of thumb, the topmost root should be about 1cm/½in below the soil level.

STAKING AND PROTECTION

Large shrubs and trees require staking, to prevent them blowing over in their first season. Smaller, more vulnerable stock is protected by putting it in a tree or shrub shelter that helps stems thicken, promotes rapid upward growth and protects plants from rodents and sometimes deer attack.

TOP TREES FOR WILDLIFE

If you have the space, trees are a valuable feature for wildlife, and by choosing the species carefully, you can greatly enhance the wildlife potential of a garden.

Apples and crab apples
(*Malus sylvestris*)
They are a familiar fixture in many gardens, and have enormous potential for wildlife. The older trees are best, supporting a diverse array of insects on the leaves and stems. The buds are eaten by some birds as is the fruit. The tree is of most use to wildlife if it is left largely unpruned.

Oak (*Quercus robur*)
While this long-lived tree has outstanding wildlife value, it is too large to grow in all but the largest garden. There are over 600 species, enjoying different climates, and some are the richest habitat trees available for insects, mammals, plants and birds.

Pine (*Pinus sylvestris*)
Pines are among the best conifers for wildlife, offering a source of seeds that are taken by birds and squirrels and dense crowns that are used by nesting birds such as owls. An excellent choice for dry soils, although they eventually grow quite tall.

Red mulberry (*Morus rubra*)
The mulberry produces berries throughout the summer that are eaten by at least 40 different bird species and makes an ideal tree for moist, fertile soils. Keep it clear of paths and patios as the fruit can be messy.

Rowan (*Sorbus aucuparia*)
A medium-sized tree that is well suited for the smaller garden, with numerous closely related species and cultivars. Rowan generally supports species that visit the tree, but don't make it their permanent habitat. Insects love the flowers, while birds (especially thrushes) often feed on the attractive, bright red berries.

Southern beech (*Nothofagus alpina*)
A fast-growing and, eventually, quite large forest tree, only worth growing in a big garden. In many places it supports large numbers of species that feed on the nuts and live in the tree, especially in the gnarled bark of older specimens.

Crab apple   **Oak**   **Pine**   **Southern beech**

CREATING WOODLAND EDGES

Woodland edges are found where forest gives way to another, more open area, and are potentially the most productive habitats for providing food for wildlife. In addition, such environments offer a whole host of shelter and breeding sites for species usually restricted to wooded areas, and while many gardens are too small for true woodland, the edge is much easier to recreate than you might think.

Above: *Squirrels often spend a great deal of time on woodland margins, searching for food in the trees and on land.*

VALUE OF THE WOODLAND EDGE

Woodland is most diverse at its edges, either at the tree-tops or adjoining another habitat. Here, species from both areas meet and share the space and its exact nature is largely dependent on the adjoining habitat.

Often this is grassland or cultivated land but, equally, it could be marsh or open water. Either way, the woodland produces an abundance of growth each year during the growing season. This leads to a rich organic layer deposited over the soil that produces very fertile ground, both within and just beyond its limits. Most gardens, even relatively large ones, do not have room for an area of naturalized woodland, but you might be able to accommodate a group of several small or medium-sized

Above: *Woodland edges are home to a great abundance of flowers, such as this blackberry, which thrive in dappled shade areas.*

Left: *Where trees and shrubs give way to grassland, the mosaic of different habitats is naturally rich in plant species and wildlife.*

REMOVING A TREE STAKE

1 *Start by removing any nails that were used to secure the tie to the stake, then unbuckle the tie. Do this carefully and avoid pulling at it as this may damage the bark of the tree.*

2 *Gently loosen the tie by feeding the belt through the spacer block that was used to prevent the stem from chafing on the stake. Check the stem for signs of damage.*

3 *Remove the stake by gently rocking it back and forth until it can be pulled upward. If it is too firmly in the ground it can be cut off with a saw, taking care to avoid the stem.*

TOP WOODLAND EDGE PLANTS FOR WILDLIFE

Woodland edges are naturally rich in flowering and fruit-bearing species, many of which provide a vital food resource for a rich variety of visiting wildlife species.

CANOPY PLANTS

Apples and crab apples (*Malus*) Deciduous, small, shrubby, spring-flowering tree with abundant round, fleshy, apple-like fruits that follow large, cup-shaped, white, pink-flushed flowers that attract bees. A food source for many insects and birds.

Rowan (*Sorbus*) Includes the familiar rowan or mountain ash *Sorbus aucuparia*, which becomes heavily laden with bright red berries in late summer and early autumn. A versatile genus that boasts many species and cultivars.

Box elder (*Acer negundo*) A small, usually fast-growing and fairly short-lived maple whose winged seeds are sometimes eaten by birds and other animals. Its sugary sap is sometimes eaten by squirrels and songbirds.

THE SHRUB LAYER

Rose (*Rosa*) Roses can be extremely attractive shrubs. If possible, plant a wild species and choose single flowers over double types as these are best for visiting insects. The hips that follow the flowers are often eaten by birds.

Rubus An important group of wildlife shrubs that includes the common blackberry (*R. fruticosus*). Care should be taken when choosing this as it can become very invasive. Many other species and cultivars are good garden specimens.

Viburnum An extremely varied group of plants that includes a wide range of species and hybrids, with good wildlife value and an attractive appearance. Choose varieties with berries, such as the guelder rose (*V. opulus*) to feed birds.

Crab apples

Rowan

Rose

Viburnum

PLANTING AND MAINTAINING A WOODLAND EDGE

You should plant a woodland edge so that there is a general increase in height from the front to the back of the area or border, thereby allowing light to reach all the plants. The tall plants at the back are called the "canopy edge" plants. In a narrow border, you will need around one canopy tree for about every 5m (17ft). Choose smallish, sun-loving woodland trees, particularly those that bear berries. The plants in front of this are the shrub layer, with the herbaceous layer forming the smallest layer at the front. Growing under the canopy trees, these layers can include both sun-loving and shade-tolerant plants because the canopy trees cast very little shade on the bed. There is always room for variety, though, and many smaller, more shade-loving plants, such as early perennials and bulbs, can easily be planted among the taller woody plant species.

Rather surprisingly, managing an area of your garden like a woodland edge takes far less time and work than you might imagine. Once planted, you just need to keep the area well watered until everything is established. You should also keep an eye on the border for the next few years, making sure that no one plant is dominating and smothering the others. Eventually, though, the area should need little or no maintenance.

trees, which will support many insect species and provide perches for birds. Even if space is limited, shrub borders fulfil some of the role of a woodland edge, and, if managed correctly, hedges can also attract woodland-edge species.

THE IDEAL SITE FOR A WOODLAND EDGE

Choose a strip along an edge of the garden facing the sunniest direction. This means you'll minimize shade on the rest of the garden while the woodland-edge bed gets the benefit of sunshine that will widen its appeal to a greater range of species. Alternatively, make it face the afternoon sun. This will, of course, cast shade on your garden in the morning, but this need not be a problem. The plants often benefit most from the warmer afternoon sun, especially in the cooler seasons. When choosing a site for your border, don't forget to discuss your plans with neighbours, whose gardens

may be affected by shade. A wall or a fence is the ideal back boundary for your woodland edge because it can provide support for some of the climbing plants.

Below: *Planting a mixture of trees and flowering shrubs in narrow strips mimics the edge of a woodland. You should remove tree stakes after one year.*

ESTABLISHING CLIMBING PLANTS

The vertical dimension of a garden is where many species – especially birds – make their nests, usually in the dense twiggy growth of a hedge. Climbers are an ideal way of providing some of the benefits of hedges where the space or setting does not permit hedge-planting. They are versatile and include some of the most beautiful flowering plants, many of which attract a wide range of wildlife.

Above: *Hoverflies are attracted to the nectar of flowering climbers, and their larvae are good for controlling aphids during summer.*

CLIMBERS AND WALL SHRUBS

One of the many reasons for planting climbers is that they can provide a way of screening or covering an unsightly object. In nature, climbers piggy-back, usually on woody species, to get up to the light. They often grow rapidly and some species are extremely ornamental. Wall shrubs are often used for the same purpose, although they are sprawling or scrambling species that do not actually climb, and must be trimmed and supported against a fence or wall to encourage vertical growth.

Climbers and wall shrubs are ideal where a hedge is not feasible. They can easily be trained up walls and fences, for example, and can even be grown in large pots on a patio. Climbers can also be used with hedge plants, where they can grow as they would in the wild, scrambling through the branches of a woody plant. Be sure to choose a good range of plants (where space permits) to provide plenty of flowers and berries.

TYPES OF CLIMBING PLANTS

Climbing plants are generally classified according to the way that they climb, which will affect the type of support required.

Self-clinging climbers can cling to sheer, vertical surfaces by attaching themselves to a support. They might use adhesive pads at the end of tendrils, like the Virginia creeper (*Parthenocissus quinquefolia*), or small adhesive rootlets on their stems, as in the case of ivy (*Hedera helix*).

Twining plants cannot climb up a flat surface and require wires, a trellis or the branches of another plant for support. Their tendrils (small, cord-like appendages) reach out and wind around narrow supports (a wire or slim branches) in the case of the pea family, whereas others, such as the clematis, curl specially adapted leaf-stalks around supports. Most species, however, are vines like the honeysuckle (*Lonicera periclymenum*), which twines its stems along and around supports.

Scandent, scrambling, rambling and trailing plants, on the other hand, are not strictly speaking climbers at all. They are usually referred to as wall shrubs, and all of them send out long stems that reach up to a support. Some, including climbing and rambling roses, have thorns or spurs that provide extra means of holding on to the support, though they usually need tying to a trellis or horizontal wires.

PLANTING CLIMBERS AND WALL SHRUBS

Once you know how your climber or wall shrub grows, you will need to fix a support. This should always be done before planting so that you don't damage the roots. Once you have done this, you can prepare the ground. Because the soil near walls or fences is often poorer than the surrounding garden, dig in plenty of organic matter, such as leaf mould, garden compost or well-rotted manure.

Left: *Even in a formal setting, such as this yew hedge (*Taxus baccata*), a climbing* Tropaeolum *adds variety, contrast and a nectar source for visiting species of wildlife.*

Above: *Climbers, particularly evergreens, make excellent screens and can both clothe and soften walls, sheds or other outbuildings in a relatively short space of time.*

Above: *A trellis uses very little space in the garden and makes a wonderful support for twining and flowering climbers.*

When planting climbers near walls, always remember that the foundations may extend out into the garden. In addition, many building walls can be very dry at the base, particularly if overhung by the roof, and if you intend growing a climber here plant it 45cm (18in) away from the wall, sloping the roots away from the house towards the open garden, where the roots can spread, drink and feed. Fences and lower walls tend to be less problematic, but you should never plant climbers right against the base of either. Climbers can also be grown in containers if they need winter protection or if they are grown on patio and roof gardens. In almost all cases, you will need to provide some initial support, even if you choose a self-clinging species.

TOP CLIMBING PLANTS FOR WILDLIFE

Climbers are mostly very quick and easy to grow, offering both the chance to help wildlife and a covering for unsightly or bland walls and fences in the garden.

Clematis A large and varied genus of woody-stemmed perennial climbers, often with beautiful flowers, followed by prominent, feathery seed heads that hang on through winter. Although some species are rather vigorous, they are easily controlled by pruning and make ideal garden plants. The seeds are eaten by birds, and the flowers are a good nectar source for moths, hoverflies and bees. The seed heads are used by breeding birds to line their nests.

Honeysuckle (*Lonicera* spp.) Naturally found in hedges and woodlands, this woody climber has clusters of highly scented yellow, tubular flowers flushed with purple and red, appearing from midsummer to early autumn, that attract moths. Twining stems are reddish when young but become brown and woody with age, climbing around stems and branches of other plants. Bright red berries form in clusters after flowering, and are attractive and long-lasting, provided they are not eaten by birds.

Ivy (*Hedera helix*) This vigorous evergreen climber, found in woodlands and hedges, on banks and walls, is an excellent wildlife plant, arguably one of the most important for a garden. Large specimens offer shelter, nesting sites and food for birds, and it is also the food plant for many species of moth. It flowers rather late in the season, and as a result can offer nectar to a huge range of insects late in the year when most other sources are becoming quite scarce.

Jasmine (*Jasminum officinalis*) Grown chiefly for its mass of highly scented white flowers that continue from midsummer to early autumn, this strong, twining shrub is a vigorous grower and needs plenty of room. It is usually best pruned annually to keep it tidy and mixes well with climbing roses (*Rosa*), honeysuckle (*Lonicera*) or clematis, although it looks equally good on its own. It is moth-pollinated and is most fragrant in the evening, when a single vine fills the whole garden with scent.

Clematis

Honeysuckle

Ivy

Jasmine

PLANTING A CLIMBING PLANT AGAINST A WALL

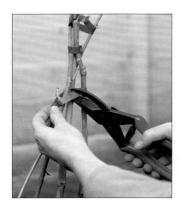

1 *Before planting, remove any ties or canes from the plant that would restrict growth, and remove any damaged growth with sharp secateurs or a knife.*

2 *Dig a hole 30cm (1ft) or more from the wall or fence to make sure that the roots will receive rainfall. Angle the shoots towards the climber supports.*

3 *Once properly positioned, backfill the hole, using the excavated topsoil, then firm the soil with your heel to ensure that the climber is well planted.*

4 *Use garden twine to tie the climber stems to the supports. Water the plant in well. Keep tying it in and water in dry spells until it is well established.*

CREATING FLOWER BORDERS

A flower border full of nectar-rich plants is an essential feeding station to a variety of insects that in turn attract other wildlife to feed on them. Although beautiful summer borders are very contrived features, they provide both homes and shelters to various wildlife species, and so your choice of plants can have a significant impact. Quite simply, the greater the variety of plants you grow, the better.

Above: *A good range of nectar-rich flowers is the best way to attract butterflies, bees and other insects into the garden.*

PLANT SELECTION

Nectar-rich borders, full of plants chosen to attract bees, butterflies or even nectar-feeding birds, need a sunny, sheltered position. Ideally, plant groups of the same species in small blocks to create a pleasing effect and ensure that insects can find them easily.

Also choose plants that flower at different times to ensure a continuous supply of nectar throughout the growing season. Include plants that flower late or early in the season, using lady's smock (*Cardamine pratensis*), chives (*Allium schoenoprasum*), golden rod (*Solidago*) and borage (*Borago officinalis*), to attract bees and butterflies from spring to autumn. Regularly deadheading (removing the old, dying flowers) will help generate more buds and therefore wildlife. And note that plants that have been highly bred to produce large or double flowers are often far less suitable

Below: *Flower-rich borders are wonderful for wildlife and provide a colourful summer spectacle and a winter retreat if left uncut.*

for wildlife, being poor in nectar, with bees in particular being unable to reach it in some highly cultivated forms. Concentrate on cottage garden plants or old varieties because they generally have flowers with simple structures, and their pollen and nectar is more readily available to foraging insects.

WILDLIFE VALUE

Once you start attracting insects into the garden, they will become food for other animals, including birds. The latter may be

carnivorous for some of the year, but will appreciate seed left on the plants through autumn and winter. Many ornamental grasses, such as the garden cultivars of millet (*Pennisetum glaucum*), and annuals, like the sunflower (*Helianthus*), provide valuable sources of energy-rich seed at the end of the season for both resident and migratory birds. The tobacco plant (*Nicotiana*) has the added advantage of providing nectar-rich, night-scented flowers for night-flying insects, such as moths, which in turn provide food for bats.

The plants you choose for your initial design may be less effective in attracting wildlife than you hoped, so be prepared to modify your border, either by including spaces for annuals, or by trying different plants. When visiting other gardens in your area, make a note of any plants that attract large numbers of insects.

Left: *The abundant nectar of flowers such as this* Centaurea macrocephala *is an essential food for both domestic and wild bees.*

Above: *Birds occasionally visit flowers to access nectar from blooms such as this red hot poker. The visitor is rewarded with a rich, sugary drink from the tubular flowers.*

PLANTING A HERBACEOUS BORDER

1 *Dig over the whole plot using a digging fork and remove stones and any weeds, paying particular attention to the roots of perennial weeds.*

2 *Break down the larger clods using the tines of the fork, and remove any remaining plant debris, large stone or rubble to leave a level surface.*

3 *Tread over the whole area using "flat-footed" steps to get rid of any large air pockets and to ensure an even consistency across the whole bed.*

4 *Rake over the surface to give a level finish and to remove any remaining debris or stones from the soil before commencing planting.*

5 *Wearing gloves, apply an organic fertilizer rich in phosphates, such as bonemeal, to enhance the root growth and the establishment of the plants.*

6 *Before planting, finish off the bed preparation by forming an edge with a half-moon cutter and make a gulley between this and the prepared soil.*

7 *Thoroughly water the plants at least an hour before you plant them to give the plants time to take up water and allow the excess moisture to drain.*

8 *Use sand or grit to mark out the bed according to your plan and set the groups of plants out before planting them in their final positions.*

TOP PLANTS FOR FLOWER BORDERS

Flower borders are a mainstay of many gardens, providing both colour and interest throughout the summer months. Choose your plants carefully to ensure a long flowering season, and include a range of types to suit different insect species.

Coneflower (*Echinacea purpurea*) Large, daisy flowers attract many insects, and its seeds will feed visiting finches.

Heliotrope (*Heliotropium arborescens*) A highly fragrant, tender perennial notable for its intense, rather vanilla-like fragrance.

Sea holly (*Eryngium planum*) A coarse, thistle-like plant with flowers that attract many bee species in summer.

Fern-leaved yarrow (*Achillea filipendula*) Easy-to-grow perennial that attracts bees and many other insects in summer.

Honeywort (*Cerinthe major* 'Purpurascens') Unusual blue-green plant with mauve-purple flowers. Immensely popular with bees.

Tall verbena (*Verbena bonariensis*) Possibly the best butterfly-attracting plant, even exceeding *Buddleja* in this respect.

Coneflower

Fern-leaved yarrow

Heliotrope

Honeywort

Sea holly

Tall verbena

NATURALISTIC PLANTING

Many of us lead busy lives and the idea of low-maintenance, self-sustaining landscapes is an attractive proposition. In nature, plants fend for themselves, and ultimately, plant communities become stable and self-sustaining. Naturalistic or wild planting styles are becoming increasingly popular with landscape architects and the general public. Like many simple ideas, however, good naturalistic design needs careful implementing.

Above: *Thistles provide good height in the garden, giving it a naturalistic look and attracting insects such as this burnet moth.*

WHAT IS NATURALISTIC PLANTING?

Planting described as naturalistic has the appearance of a natural area (e.g. a prairie, woodland or wetland) and obviously differs from more traditional, structured designs. The layout of the plants is inspired by the patterns and groupings in the wild. It should not be confused with ecological planting, though, when plants are allowed to spread and seed so as to create a changing or dynamic plant community. Naturalistic planting is more structured and permanent than that, despite the apparent lack of artifice.

There are several ways that naturalistic planting arrangements can be laid out, with block planting and drifts being two of the best. Block planting is the most commonly used, and involves planting similarly sized groups of each species in irregular, repeating patterns. The groups of plants are arranged according to height and aesthetic qualities, such as foliage colour and texture. Drifts are much more variable in respect of size and shape, and have no obvious repetitive pattern. Small groups may repeat again and again, with larger, more occasional groups providing contrast and variety.

Even though you are trying to create a random effect, you should divide your plants into general categories according to habit and form. As a guide, a balance is readily achieved with tall, solitary, architectural specimens occupying 10 per cent of the total area, lower-growing, clump-forming plants occupying 40–50 per cent of the space, scattered irregularly, and the remainder filled with ground cover. This will give the balance of height and space that is needed. Avoid a random assortment of plants. Even if they are all planted in the right conditions and grow well, they still need an overall structure.

Naturalistic should never mean haphazard or formless. Always remember that a collection of choice plants arranged without thought is no more a garden than a collection of choice words, spread randomly across a page, is a poem.

THE BENEFITS FOR WILDLIFE

The exact benefits of the naturalistic effect are debatable because many traditional garden features may already provide the same results. However, the naturalistic garden is prone to fewer disturbances, particularly at soil level, making a more

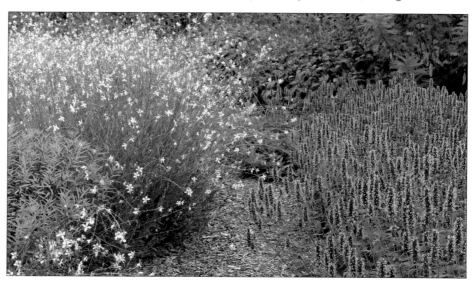

Left: *Dry areas can be planted using a range of drought-tolerant plants to give a stunning display, especially with focal points such as this* Agave.

Below: *Despite their lower maintenance needs, naturalistic borders can be just as beautiful as more formal gardens, as well as providing a refuge for wildlife.*

complete garden ecosystem possible. The mosaic of flowers and plants is also an enticing place for a range of insects and birds, and the dense, packed summer growth will harbour many larger creatures.

THE BEST PLANTS

As with any type of garden, you should choose plants that are suited to your conditions. Remember that the plants in a naturalistic garden are going to be left to fend for themselves, and must compete with the other plants. Don't include too many species that spread very rapidly either by seed or vegetatively because they'll quickly take over, and destroy the effect.

Decide which type of habitat you are mimicking and choose the plants accordingly. Visit a similar wild place and take notes on the best types and mix of plants. Use species that you know attract wildlife, giving careful consideration to which species they attract at any given time.

MAINTENANCE OF NATURALISTIC PLANTINGS

Although the planting style is borrowed from nature, it is a contrivance relying on conventional horticultural techniques. Herbaceous plants will need a measure of weeding, particularly in the first couple of years, while woody plants will need some pruning. You may wish to lift and revitalize certain areas from time to time but, on the whole, it is a case of a little work done often that will ensure the best results and allow the plants to form a stable and self-sustaining community.

TOP NATURALISTIC PLANTS FOR WILDLIFE

Plants for naturalistic plantings must be tough and able to thrive with a minimum of maintenance. They often self-seed and so help retain a natural effect in the border.

Bog sage (*Salvia uliginosa*) This striking, tall perennial has blue flowers and is covered in bloom during late summer and autumn. In its native habitat, it grows in bogs and can therefore grow aggressively in wet soils. A popular plant with bees.

Carrot (*Daucus carota*) The wild form of this biennial plant, also known as Queen Anne's lace, is related to domesticated carrots, but has small white roots. Excellent for attracting butterflies and hoverflies.

Coneflower (*Echinacea purpurea*) This popular ornamental plant is quite tolerant of drier soils and produces a multitude of large daisy flowers in the summer. It attracts butterflies and bees.

Fennel (*Foeniculum vulgare* 'Purpureum') This cultivated variety is an excellent foliage plant with feathery leaves that contrast well with other plants. The flowers attract butterflies and beneficial insects.

Field scabious (*Knautia arvensis*) This summer-flowering perennial can form a small to medium-sized plant that is equally at home in a flower border or meadow, and it will readily self-seed. The flowers are attractive to a wide variety of insects.

Plume thistle (*Cirsium rivulare* 'Atropurpureum') An excellent choice due to its reliability, which, although related to the thistle, is not invasive. Its flowers are long-lasting and attract many insects, including beetles, butterflies and bees.

Solidaster (X *Solidaster luteus* 'Lemore') A naturally occurring goldenrod-aster hybrid, discovered in France during the early 20th century. Its pale, buttery blooms fade to nearly white and attract numerous insects.

Tall verbena (*Verbena bonariensis*) This tall perennial has purple cymes of flowers borne on tough, wiry stems from midsummer onward. It readily self-seeds, and the tiny individual flowers are very rich in nectar.

Carrot   Coneflower   Fennel   Plume thistle

CREATING A NATURALISTIC PLANTING

1 *Choose a variety of plants to fill the space and arrange them within the bed, ensuring that more vigorous ones are not planted too close to slower growing ones.*

2 *Once you have finalized their positions, place the plants into the prepared ground and firm them in using a heel to knock out any air pockets trapped in the soil.*

3 *After planting is complete, water the area thoroughly. Subsequent watering should be infrequent but deep, especially during dry spells in the summer.*

ESTABLISHING A HERB GARDEN

Herbs – encompassing any plants or trees with leaves or flowers that are used for food or medicine – are a great addition to the garden. They attract a wide range of insects, with many having the added advantage of being drought-resistant. A herb garden can therefore include trees, shrubs, ground cover, perennials and annuals. With such a range of material, there will always be some herbs that will suit your garden.

Above: *When in bloom, herbs – especially this oregano – are often very attractive to bees and other pollinating insect species.*

PLANNING YOUR HERB GARDEN

First, make a list of all the herbs you use in the kitchen or home. If a few favourite plants are just used on an occasional basis, it may be simpler to grow them in a few well-placed containers or in gaps in a flower border. Also consider the plants' site and soil preferences, and the levels of maintenance required. Fresh herbs are very useful, but remember that most are plentiful in short seasons, and planting too many will be a waste of time and effort.

SELECTING A SITE

Most herb plants require a site with well-drained soil and full sun for at least six hours each day. If your garden soil is clay, or if you live in an area prone to prolonged wet spells, you may need to make a raised bed

---

TOP HERBS FOR WILDLIFE

Herbs are excellent plants to use in any garden, and are notable for their ability to attract wildlife and, in particular, beneficial insect species.

They can be grown in pots, herb borders or alternatively dotted in spaces among flower borders.

Basil (*Ocimum basilicum*) This annual herb is frost-tender and is usually planted out as a summer addition to the herb garden. It is highly aromatic and greatly valued by cooks; the flowers, borne later in the summer, attract bees, butterflies, and a few moths.

Bergamot (*Monarda didyma*) Perennial, more commonly known as bee balm because bees are so attracted to the scent of its vivid red flowers, it smells rather like the bergamot orange used to flavour Earl Grey tea. Bergamot's leaves can be used to make a refreshing herbal tea, and it is an attractive inclusion in any herb garden.

Chives (*Allium schoenoprasum*) This little perennial onion relative is arguably one of the best herbs for attracting bees when the flowers appear from early to midsummer. It is an adaptable and accommodating plant that is best grown in a sunny position, in moist, rich soil where it will rapidly form clumps and self-seed.

Hyssop (*Hyssopus officinalis*) A wonderful shrub for attracting butterflies, bees and hoverflies, and an ideal candidate for a low hedge in a herb garden. Can also be grown in stony areas where there is little soil. The flowers are violet-blue but also come in white and rose.

Lavender (*Lavandula angustifolia*) Very attractive shrub for bees, bumblebees and butterflies. It is often used to make low, informal hedges, and the seed is popular with many smaller birds, such as chaffinch, goldfinch and tits, during autumn and early winter.

Mint (*Mentha* spp.) Perennial mint is almost irresistible to bees, which are attracted to the lilac-pink flower spikes of many types, including peppermint, water mint and spearmint. It is one of the few herbs that likes moisture, but it can be very invasive so it is best grown in a bottomless pot sunk into the ground.

Oregano (*Origanum vulgare*) This perennial is popular with bees, small moths and a range of butterflies that take nectar from its small, whitish flowers. It makes an attractive groundcover plant, spreading rapidly without becoming too invasive, and grows best in full sun on well-drained soil.

Rosemary (*Rosmarinus officinalis*) This evergreen shrub likes a sunny, sheltered position and is especially good in a poor soil. Its clusters of mauve-white flowers are popular with bees, hoverflies and early flying butterflies. It is slow growing and ideal where space is limited.

Thyme (*Thymus* spp.) Despite its diminutive nature, shrubby thyme provides nectar for honeybees, bumblebees and butterflies, although golden and lemon-scented varieties are unpopular with butterflies. It is best when grown in large patches, and thrives in paths, walls and containers, or exposed or seaside gardens.

Basil

Bergamot

Chives

Lavender

Rosemary

Thyme

Right: *Herbs are often grown in specialist borders or gardens where their foliage and flowers create wonderful contrasts of both colour and fragrance.*

with good drainage or (more simply) plant the herbs in containers. If you do the latter, use a well-drained potting mix. A loam-based one is ideal, but can be expensive. Alternatively you can make your own potting mix, with one-third of well-rotted and friable organic matter (leaf mould or well-rotted compost is ideal) with one-third of grit, vermiculite or perlite, and a final third of sand or sandy loam if it's available.

Herbs grown in pots benefit from the free drainage, but will always need watering. Perennial herbs growing in the ground will become less prone to drought in their second and third seasons, but will need some water if it is dry in their first season. Annual crops will always be more drought-prone and need watering. When choosing a site, ensure that there is a reliable source of water close by.

PLANTING COMBINATIONS

Once you have decided what sort of herb garden you want, the next stage is to select the appropriate plants. Always ensure that those you select are suited to your soil type, climate and site conditions. If you are growing them in pots, for instance, group together plants that require the same conditions. Remember also that a herb garden should be as attractive as possible to complement the rest of the garden. Use plants that make pleasing contrasts of leaf texture or colour for the most striking effects, and include a diversity of species to ensure a wide range of flowering and fruiting times to create the maximum benefit for the wildlife.

HERBS IN THE REST OF THE GARDEN

Herbs are ideal candidates for existing flower beds, containers, or kitchen gardens where their abilities to deter pests and attract beneficial predator insects have long been recognized. Their ability to thrive in containers has led many gardeners to plant edible hanging gardens with fruit, vegetables and herbs in displays that are both attractive and delicious, and yet other herbs have gained merit as ornamental garden specimens in their own right, playing a central role in herbaceous or shrub beds.

PLANTING UP A HERB CONTAINER

1 *Start by choosing a large container and select a range of herbs of various sizes and habits, as well as a suitable potting mixture.*

2 *Cover the drainage holes at the pot's base with flat stones or crocks from a broken pot to stop the compost from leaking out.*

3 *Part-fill the pot until the largest specimen can sit on the surface with the root-ball about 2.5cm (1in) below the rim of the pot.*

4 *Put in more compost and place the smaller plants, checking they are similarly positioned below the rim. Remove pots before planting.*

5 *Fill the remaining gaps between the plants with compost, taking care not to over-firm it. Water the pot and top up with compost.*

6 *The finished decorative container can be placed on a patio along with other pots of herbs to create a mini patio herb garden.*

PLANTING VEGETABLE GARDENS

Offering an unusual alternative in wildlife gardens, vegetables can replace ornamental plants. They are often every bit as good as their ornamental counterparts for attracting wildlife, and have the added advantage of producing fresh food. Grow them in a kitchen garden or as elements among existing features, or if space is more limited, you could try growing them in hanging baskets or containers.

Above: *Try not to worry if caterpillars attack the green leaves of your vegetables, as visiting birds will soon pick them off.*

WHY GROW EDIBLE PLANTS IN A WILDLIFE GARDEN?

There can be few pleasures that compete with gathering your own fresh produce. Home-grown well-ripened fruit, and vegetables harvested when they are just right, are always more flavoursome than those you can buy. In addition, you know that they are free of pesticides and have not been produced at a cost to the environment. They also save on grocery bills, and you can grow unusual varieties not normally available to buy.

VEGETABLE GARDENS

Edible plants, particularly vegetables, grow best where they receive at least six hours of full sunlight a day, in a well-drained soil with a pH of 6–6.8. If part of your garden matches that description, then that is where you should put the vegetable garden.

Below: *A traditional vegetable garden is usually quite formal, with the crops planted in neat, ordered rows. Plant companion plants to enhance the aesthetics of an area and encourage beneficial insects.*

Growing vegetables is too big a subject to cover here in any depth, but there are a few things that you can do to improve a vegetable plot for wildlife. Avoid using pesticides, use companion plants (plants that encourage beneficial predators) to keep your plants pest-free, and always rotate your crops to prevent disease build-up. Herbs are a wonderful addition to the vegetable garden and help attract many wildlife species. In addition, the flowers of many vegetables are very attractive, so, if you have a few unused crops in the ground at the season's end, try leaving them for the wildlife.

POTAGERS

Also known as kitchen gardens, potagers gain their name from the French word for a soup of broth with vegetables (*potage*), and generally refer to a garden where vegetables are grown, along with herbs for cooking and medicine. The garden is usually made up of small geometric plots, each containing a variety of useful herbs, vegetables, and perhaps some flowers for daily use. The design is a hybrid of styles that rejects the need for neat rows of produce. The difference is that most, if not all, the plants contained are edible.

TOP VEGETABLES FOR WILDLIFE

Vegetables can attract a whole host of wildlife and, when included as a part of your summer displays, add contrast and interest to any border or container.

Blackcurrant (*Ribes nigrum*) This small to medium-sized shrub is not particularly attractive but has extremely good wildlife potential. The leaves attract many insects that feed on them and these in turn attract predators. Birds love the dark, sweet fruit that ripens in midsummer.

Carrot (*Daucus carota*) The familiar garden carrot may seem an unlikely candidate for attracting wildlife, but leaving the roots unharvested and allowing them to flower in the second year will attract a huge range of insects, including many beneficials, such as hoverflies, small wasps and a whole host of butterflies.

Globe artichoke (*Cynara scolymus*) The large flowers of this stately and unusual garden vegetable can be highly beneficial if you leave a few to mature, attracting a range of bees and beetles. The seed heads that follow are used as nesting and lining material by birds in late winter and are best left on the plant until spring.

Tomato (*Lycopersicon esculentum*) Attractive to a whole range of species, many of which we consider pests, although these in turn attract many predators. The yellow flower trusses are immensely popular with bumblebees, which are important pollinators, ensuring a good crop of fruit.

Blackcurrant

Carrot

Globe artichoke

Tomato

PLANTING UP A VEGETABLE HANGING BASKET

1 *Choose a large-sized basket and a range of herbs, vegetables, fruits or plants with edible blooms that will provide contrasting colours and shapes to one another.*

2 *Fill the basket to around two-thirds of its depth with compost, and incorporate a slow-release fertilizer, mixing it thoroughly before starting to plant.*

3 *Plant the upright specimens in the middle first and then place the trailing specimens around the outside of the container, angling them over the edge of the basket.*

4 *Space the plants evenly around the edge of the basket. Once you have finished the arrangement, fill up any remaining gaps between the root-balls with more compost.*

5 *The completed basket is now ready for hanging. However, do not water it until you have hung it up, because this will make it quite heavy and awkward to place.*

6 *Once the plants are settled in, they quickly grow, and the basket will become a striking feature, as full of contrast, colour and interest as any good floral display.*

MIXED PLANTING

If you don't want to devote all, or even a particular part, of your garden to edible plants, then the best way to start may be to consider a one-for-one substitution. This means replacing existing (non-edible) specimens with an edible counterpart. If you plan to plant a small ornamental tree, for instance, plant a fruit tree instead. When choosing a deciduous shrub, opt for a currant (*Ribes*) or hazelnut (*Corylus*), and replace herbaceous flowers with plants with edible blooms, such as daylilies (*Hemerocallis*) or chives (*Allium schoenoprasum*). Some plants, such as peppers (*Capsicum*), have very colourful varieties and can be grown beside flowers. Lettuces, radishes and other short-lived greens can also be tucked into gaps in the flower beds, and rainbow chard and ornamental cabbage are also excellent additions. You could also make a gooseberry hedge that, with its thorny stems, makes a secure barrier, and if you are building a pergola why not grow a grape over it?

Edible plants come in nearly all shapes and sizes, and can do the same job in your garden as ornamental plants.

CONTAINERS AND HANGING BASKETS

Try putting some pots of herbs on the patio, with basil and cherry tomatoes in a window box or hanging basket. The combinations are endless and, with a little imagination, even a small courtyard garden can become a fairly productive space.

Above: *Even a small patio can house an excellent range of edible plants in containers, and can look very attractive.*

PLANTING ROOF GARDENS AND PATIOS

Despite the limitations that the lack of open soil presents on roof gardens and patios, there are many ways of quickly planting up these spaces. Properly designed, roofs and paved areas can easily be transformed to provide a welcome oasis of calm and a source of shelter and food for many wildlife species, which would otherwise find these areas a harsh and unwelcoming place.

Above: *Hanging baskets are a good way of increasing the number of plants you can grow, especially when space is limited.*

WHAT IS A ROOF GARDEN?

Roof gardens are as varied as any other type of garden and, with a little imagination, can easily form an excellent wildlife-friendly space, largely helped by the exclusion of cats, dogs, foxes and rats. In their simplest form, they are described as a green roof. This refers to the roof of a building being partially or completely covered with vegetation and soil, or a growing medium that has been placed over a waterproof membrane. The greenery can be placed on both pitched and flat roofs, and many different designs and construction methods exist. They vary in their complexity, and the work is invariably best left to a specialist contractor. The plants are an alternative to tiles or other roof materials.

More complex designs can create a space for relaxation and leisure. They may simply involve planted containers, arranged to make a roof terrace (or sundeck) more pleasant. Others, however, may be far more elaborate, using feature plants that are quite

Left: *Perched high on top of a city building, this roof garden provides a welcome respite from the busy streets below.*

Above: *This garden chalet roof has been covered with sedum (stonecrop) to provide insulation and a good home for wildlife.*

PLANTING THYME THROUGH A PATIO

1 *This patio has been laid over an engineering membrane put in place to suppress weeds, and so needs scissors as well as a trowel to plant the thyme.*

2 *Clear the gravel mulch to the side to expose the fabric. Use scissors to cut a cross shape in the fabric, making a hole slightly larger than the plant.*

3 *Dig a hole using the trowel, and remove the soil. Place the thyme into the hole and backfill around the plant using some of the excavated soil.*

4 *Thoroughly water the thyme in using a watering can, doing this slowly in order to allow the water to soak into the soil beneath the membrane.*

tough because they must cope with the dry, windy conditions that often prevail. If you want a roof garden, the first priority is to get a structural engineer from a specialized firm to check that the structure can support it. Get a design drawn up by an expert.

PATIOS AND COURTYARDS

Unlike roofs, patios and courtyards are often very sheltered, and may be shaded by the surrounding buildings, which will influence your choice of plants. A sunny, sheltered area, on the other hand, will allow you to grow more tender plants than you could in the open garden.

Remember that the soil in a container drains more quickly than topsoil in the ground, and the plants you grow will require a rich potting mix to be at their best. You can mix your own blend but it is often easier to buy a proprietary brand specially mixed for the type of plants you intend to grow.

The new patio can seem rather stark in relation to the wider garden, but you can always link it to the rest of the design by using plants at the edge of the patio. Also try ageing the look of the patio by planting smaller, creeping plants, such as thyme (*Thymus*), in the cracks between the paving slabs.

If your outdoor space is especially limited, you can increase the number of plants by making use of the walls: mount hanging baskets and troughs on the walls, filled with trailing plants to create a third dimension. This will save ground space but doesn't compromise your wish to grow some plants.

PLANTING AN ALPINE TROUGH

1 Choose a shallow, preferably clay trough and some free-draining compost and grit. Water the plants 1 hour before planting.

2 Mix some grit into the compost and cover the base with old bits of pot and a thin layer of compost before putting the plants in.

3 Fill the gaps between the plants using more compost mixed with grit; this will help with drainage. Ensure no air pockets remain.

4 Finally, dress the surface of the compost with a 1cm (½in) layer of grit to ensure that no water lies on the surface, as this will rot the basal growth of the plant.

In addition to wall-mounted pots, you can also place a few annual or smaller perennial climbers in large pots near the wall. They will clothe the walls in greenery and flowers, and have the added advantage of providing food and shelter for many wildlife species. Try growing a twining plant, such as honeysuckle (*Lonicera*) or a jasmine (*Jasminum*), on a wall-mounted trellis, and watch the moths feeding there at night.

TOP PLANTS FOR CONTAINERS AND HANGING BASKETS

There are many plants that you can grow in containers that will attract wildlife to your garden. As a rule, smaller containers, and especially hanging baskets, are best when used for shorter term planting, and so generally suit annuals or tender plants best.

Bedding chrysanthemum (*Argyranthemum* spp.) This tender plant, covered in daisy-blooms all summer, attracts many insects.

English marigold (*Calendula officinalis*) The bright orange flowers attract a whole host of insects, including bees and hoverflies.

Indian cress (*Nasturtium majus*) Bees love the flowers. Prone to aphids, but these feed other predators. Make successive sowings.

Petunia (*Petunia* x *hybrida*) A good choice for attracting moths. Grow upright forms in summer tubs and trailing varieties in hanging baskets.

Tobacco plant (*Nicotiana sylvestris*) Attracts moths, and is richly fragrant from dusk onwards. Grow it in pots near the house.

Trailing lobelia (*Lobelia erinus*) The tender, trailing half-hardy types are ideal in summer baskets, where they attract many insects.

Chrysanthemum

English marigold

Indian cress

Petunia

Tobacco plant

Trailing lobelia

WORKING IN YOUR WILDLIFE GARDEN

A wildlife garden should always be enjoyed, and there are few

better ways of doing that than by getting out and working in it.

There is never really an "off season", and there is always

something that needs tackling. The dormant season is the best

time to design new areas and prune deciduous shrubs and trees,

spring is the time to sow seed and realize your plans, summer is

the time to check how the wildlife is responding, and autumn

is the time for assessment and making plans for the future,

so that next year's wildlife garden will be even better.

Left: *This ornamental compost bin provides a welcome view from the house, while still fulfilling the function of a traditional bin.*

Above: *A well-balanced garden can be a superb place to watch wildlife. A pair of binoculars will help you spot any shy species.*

Above: *Wildlife, such as this fox, will sometimes turn up when most unexpected, and can result in memorable encounters.*

Above: *A wildlife pond can be a source of wonder for children and adults alike, filled with fascinating wetland creatures.*

WATERING AND FEEDING

In order to keep your plants healthy, they will need both nutrients and sufficient water in the soil, and a lack of either may limit their growth. With a little careful thought and planning, though, you'll keep your garden plants healthy all year round. Knowing when and how much to water and feed your plants is an essential part of maintaining healthy plant growth throughout the whole season.

Above: *Plants growing in containers can be especially vulnerable to shortages of water and nutrients. Always make regular checks.*

TO WATER OR NOT TO WATER?

Using water wisely pays dividends for you, your garden and the wildlife. The simplest way to help conserve mains water is to install a water butt to catch the rainwater from your roof. It's much better than chlorinated tap water, and can be used to give plants a drink and top up the pond. Remember that it is no good having a garden rich in wildlife if this is achieved at the expense of other habitats, for example where dams have to be built.

Collecting rainwater can have its limitations, though, especially in drier locations, and it may be better if you use plants and features adapted to the local conditions. If you are planning a new garden or revamping an existing feature, check to see if the plants are drought-tolerant. Summer-bedding plants, for example, require a lot of water because they do not get sufficient opportunity to establish extensive root systems. Herbaceous plants can have the same problem in their first year but soon root deeper, and are more tolerant in subsequent years. Shrubs and trees may

Above: *Hanging baskets and wall baskets need regular and careful watering to ensure they don't dry out, especially in summer.*

also be vulnerable in their early years but rapidly become better at surviving drought.

The rule of thumb, then, is only to water new plants and always avoid watering established plants unless they show signs of stress. Indeed, watering plants on a frequent basis encourages shallow root growth and actually weakens a plant's resistance to dry periods. If you must water, do so when it is cooler – during early morning or evening – to reduce evaporation, and avoid watering when it is windy for the same reason. Using mulches can also help.

Choosing large containers for patio plants will also help reduce water use because they retain moisture better than small pots. Furthermore, in order to reduce the rate at which water is lost, it helps to group pot plants together.

Left: *Rainwater butts are an ideal way to collect winter rain from glasshouses and sheds, ready for use in the summer months.*

Right: *Fertilizer applied early in the growing season can give a real boost to garden plants, which quickly take up the nutrients as the roots are very active at this time.*

Lastly, resist the temptation to water lawns in dry spells. Leaving a sprinkler on for an hour can actually use the same amount of water as a family of four uses in two days. Grass will slow its growth if left to grow a little longer and water demand will drop as a result. Longer grass also traps dew and reduces evaporation from the soil, making it more drought-tolerant, and the bonus for wildlife from flowers left in such a lawn, as well as the additional cover it provides, more than compensates for the loss of a green manicured sward.

FEEDING YOUR PLANTS

Plants require nutrients that are extracted from the air and soil, and if they suffer a shortage, there are generally two possible reasons. Either the nutrients are not available to the plant, invariably because of pH problems (in future, choose plants appropriate to the site), or there are few or no nutrients present. If that's the case, the problem is easily solved by applying a soil feed in a granular or liquid form. Alternatively, a natural source can be used to enrich the soil and encourage natural cycling of nutrients over a longer term. While the latter method should always be the preferred option, it does take time to work and, if your plants need an instant application, the quickest and easiest way is to use a liquid feed.

MAKING NETTLE TEA FOR YOUR PLANTS

1 *Cut some nettles from your nettle patch, choosing good, strong, young leafy stems. You may need gloves to protect your arms from the stings.*

2 *Place the nettles in a large container, packing them in tightly, then weigh the cut stems down with bricks. Fill the container with water.*

3 *Cover the container with a sack or old carpet to prevent evaporation and keep the smell in as the organic material starts to decompose and break down.*

4 *After 2–3 weeks, the resulting liquid feed is ready for use. It should always be diluted 10:1 with fresh water or mixed to the colour of tea before using.*

WATER-WISE GARDENING

Water is a valuable commodity and should be used wisely. To make best use of it, here are four quick tips.

Install a water butt This will collect the rainwater running off your roof to save water and money. It can be used instead of treated mains water, has the advantage of being naturally soft, is free of chemical additives and is ideal for topping up garden ponds.

Grey water This is waste water from household use that can be used in the garden. The most likely and least polluted source is bath water. Water from a washing machine or kitchen sink often contains grease, oils and chemicals that can adversely affect both your plants and wildlife.

Avoid using hosepipes and lawn sprinklers This particularly applies to those using mains water, and beware of using a fine spray because a lot of water is wasted – not all reaches the plants. Use a watering can instead, or attach your hosepipe to a water butt.

Don't water your plants too often Abstinence encourages them to make deeper roots and become more self-sufficient. Instead of watering a lawn, cut it longer than usual in dry periods. It may go brown for a while, but will recover as soon as it receives some rain.

PLANT NUTRIENTS AND FERTILIZERS

Plant nutrients are divided into two groups, depending on whether they are found in high or low concentrations. Those found in high concentrations, needed in large amounts, are known as macro or major nutrients; low concentrations, needed in relatively small amounts, are micro or trace elements.

MACRO OR MAJOR NUTRIENTS

NUTRIENT	SOURCES IN THE GARDEN
Nitrogen (N)	Abundant in the atmosphere but unavailable until "fixed" as nitrates by bacteria. Encourage availability by applying compost to soils or by applying a long-term feed, such as pelleted chicken manure, or fish, blood and bone.
Phosphorus (P)	Naturally occurs as mineral phosphates in soils but often with low availability in sandy, acidic and chalky ground. Present in bone meal, comfrey, horse manure and, to a lesser extent, pelleted chicken manure.
Potassium (K)	Often available in large amounts in the soil, although not all plants are good at taking it. Comfrey, horse manure and wood ash are good sources; nettles are especially good at taking up and storing potassium.

MICRO NUTRIENTS OR TRACE ELEMENTS

NUTRIENT	SOURCES IN THE GARDEN
Calcium (Ca)	Naturally abundant in the Earth's surface, although it is easily lost by leaching on certain soils, which tend to become acidic. Easily re-applied using ground limestone, comfrey, horse manure or bone meal.
Magnesium (Mg)	Magnesium is freely available in most soils but may be lost through leaching, or be unavailable in waterlogged or very limy soils. Apply a mulch of compost or Epsom salts if the deficiency is severe.
Sulphur (S)	Normally available in the soil, and replenished from rainwater or other atmospheric sources. A base dressing or a light dusting of flowers of sulphur can be applied if a severe shortage occurs.
Iron (Fe)	Iron shortage in chalky soils is due to lock-up by calcium and is difficult to avoid. Stinging nettles, compost, horse manure and blood and bone are good sources.
Manganese (Mc)	Tends only to affect plants growing in acidic soils, especially those in the cabbage family. Apply lime and top dress with compost, made from grass clippings.
Boron (B)	Can sometimes be lacking from sandy soil. Horse manure, compost and untreated sawdust are all good sources, although you can also apply borax in severe cases.
Copper (Cu)	Normally available in the soil, although sandy soils can become deficient. Stinging nettles, chickweed, horse manure, garden compost and untreated sawdust are all good sources.
Zinc (Zn)	Normally available in all but very sandy soils. Horse manure is possibly the best source, followed by compost and untreated sawdust.
Molybdenum (Mo)	Acidic soils can become short of molybdenum, and the cure is normally to apply lime and compost rich in grass clippings.

COMPOSTING

Turning your garden and kitchen waste into a compost heap is not only a great way to recycle these materials into the nutrients your plants need, but can also provide a miniature, frost-free wildlife refuge. Many creatures like to overwinter in the cool, dark safety of the decaying vegetation, and yet more find a rich source of food in its damp recesses. A compost heap also means you don't need to buy expensive soil conditioners, saving you both time and money, as well as helping wildlife.

Above: *A compost heap needs to be turned periodically to ensure all the plant material decomposes properly. Special turning tools can be bought for tall, narrow heaps.*

WHY RECYCLE WASTE?

The environmental impact of sending waste to landfill sites can be huge. Domestic gardens often generate huge amounts of waste that, if disposed of as landfill, does not rot but ferments, producing environmentally harmful substances such as methane (a greenhouse gas), and a toxic slimy substance called leachates. This is a pointless waste of one of the best resources your garden can generate.

Compost, made from plant waste, will reward you with rich, fertile humus to add to your garden soil or to use in pots. In addition, compost is full of mini-beasts that will provide a great feast for thrushes, robins and blackbirds, as well as predators of soil-borne pests. Furthermore, over winter, a compost heap is an extremely important feature of a wildlife garden, acting as a mini-wildlife refuge where insects, bacteria and fungi carry on the decomposition process, while providing a hibernation site for amphibians and hedgehogs.

WHAT TO COMPOST

Simply piling all your organic waste in a heap would ultimately result in compost, but the process might be inefficient and the results variable. Some gardeners take quite a scientific view of their composting, and construct heaps that generate heat and rot down very quickly (called "hot piles"). Wildlife gardeners, on the other hand, might take a more leisurely approach and allow the process to continue quite slowly, while providing a habitat for animals, using a method called the "cold pile".

Even if you take a slower approach, it is important to get roughly the right proportions of different materials to make the end product usable in the garden. In terms of composting there are basically two types of materials, referred to as "greens" and "browns". Green materials are mostly wet, soft, green and high in nitrogen. Brown materials are dry, harder, absorbent and high in carbon. You should aim for roughly

---

HOT PILE COMPOST BIN

A hot pile compost bin is the best method to use if you want compost in a hurry. A good mix of green and brown material is best for nutritional balance for microbes. Twigs at the bottom improve aeration. You should water underneath the pile before placing the twigs, and water brown layers as you add them. Nettles are included as a good natural compost activator, and old compost or soil will introduce natural decomposers to the new heap. A lid on top will keep out the rain and conserve heat.

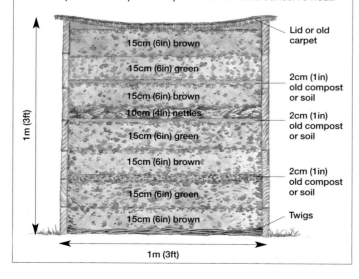

- 15cm (6in) brown
- 15cm (6in) green — Lid or old carpet
- 15cm (6in) brown — 2cm (1in) old compost or soil
- 10cm (4in) nettles — 2cm (1in) old compost or soil
- 15cm (6in) green
- 15cm (6in) brown — 2cm (1in) old compost or soil
- 15cm (6in) green
- 15cm (6in) brown — Twigs

1m (3ft) [height]

1m (3ft) [width]

WHAT TO COMPOST, AND WHAT TO AVOID

You can compost almost anything that was once alive or part of a living organism, although not everything is necessarily ideal for handling. Adding a lot of coarse, woody material will significantly slow down the composting process, although it can be shredded first. Be sure to add around equal amounts of green and brown, and reject all items in the "Avoid" list.

GREENS
- Fresh plants
- Grass cuttings
- Raw fruit and vegetables
- Seaweed, algae and garden pond cleanings
- Tea leaves
- Urine and manure
- Weeds/nettles (avoid perennial weed roots)
- Wood/peat ash

BROWNS
- Coffee grounds
- Dry plant stems and twigs
- Egg shells
- Pet and human hair (takes a little time)
- Scrunched-up paper
- Straw and hay
- Torn-up cardboard (e.g. cereal and egg boxes, toilet-roll centres)

AVOID
- Barbecue or coal ash
- Grease, oil, cooked food scraps
- Meat or fish scraps
- Dog or cat faeces (they can contain dangerous pathogens)

BUILDING A BEEHIVE COMPOST BIN

1 *Take two square timber batons and lay them with the closest ends about three-quarters of the distance of the other. Lay some thin planks on top.*

2 *Use a workbench to screw the boards in place on the batons, then saw off the overlap. Repeat this process for the opposite side of the compost bin.*

3 *Attach a base and top board to the two prepared sides so that the open sides have the same proportions as the other two sides of the bin.*

4 *Fix more boards to the open sides so that the box is fully formed, but leave the bottom two from one of the sides to form a hatch to empty the bin.*

5 *Saw off any overlap from the boards to give a good even edge, and ensure all the screws are tight. Sand off any rough splinters from the sawn edges.*

6 *Make the roof using two "A"-shaped pieces (as shown), ensuring that the bottom edge is just narrower than the sides. Fix more boards to this.*

7 *Fix two hinges to the board above the open side and attach a door that will allow access to empty the bin. This is made of two more wooden boards.*

8 *The finished compost bin can now be placed in the garden and used to make compost. It can be painted to ensure it lasts longer and looks good.*

---

equal amounts of browns and greens set in layers to keep the compost moist but not too wet, and supply the decomposing organisms with essential nitrogen and carbon.

EQUIPMENT

There are many different composting methods and containers, and the type you choose will vary depending on the amount and type of organic waste you will be composting. For most people, the choice is a relatively simple one between a composting container – such as a cone – or an open heap.

At its simplest, a compost heap is made by piling up your organic waste in the garden. The urge for tidiness means that most build a container for the material or purchase a commercially made container, the cone shape being a popular choice because it's compact and ideal for small gardens. It's usually made of plastic and has a long life; the manufacturers often claim that the contents don't need to be turned although the tumbler bin, like a barrel, is

supported by a metal frame, making it vermin-proof, and can be easily swung over. The only drawback is that such kinds only deal with small amounts of waste and almost never heat up. What is more they are less accessible or even completely inaccessible to some wild creatures.

Compost heaps, on the other hand, can deal with large volumes of waste. They can also be made large enough to generate heat, although not all will, and this helps the composting process and attracts some wildlife that will shelter here in the cooler months. The bottom of the pile must have contact with the soil so that creatures can gain access. Note that heaps work best when turned. If you bag your compost after about a year, it will continue to decompose in the bag and become finer and drier. When you do bag it up, put anything too coarse back in the heap for further decomposition, as the in-bag maturation tends to be rather slow and will not easily deal with larger items. Once mature, it can be used as a wonderful soil conditioner.

WON'T A COMPOST HEAP SMELL?

If you are adding the right things in roughly the right proportions, there shouldn't be any problem. Most compost heaps that smell are either lacking air or are too wet. In either case, the answer is to aerate the heap by turning and loosening it with a fork and, preferably, by adding some dry material at the same time.

Above: Sieving compost is the best way to remove larger pieces that have not fully decomposed. These can be returned to the heap to break down further.

WEEDING
AND WEED CONTROL

The term weed may seem peculiar in the context of a wildlife garden, where so many plants might be native wildflowers. It is important to remember, though, that the term does not automatically refer to a native plant and, indeed, many of the most notorious weeds in towns and the countryside are imports. Removing these plants is as essential in a wildlife garden as in any other, and may even improve the habitat as a result.

Above: *Buttercups are regarded as weeds by many gardeners, but their cheerful yellow flowers are much loved by many insects.*

WHAT IS A WEED?

Answer: A plant (often unsightly) that establishes itself in a garden, with no help from us, and which proceeds to compete with those that we have planted. Weeds are highly competitive species that rob cultivated specimens of nutrients, light and, most important, water. In fact uncontrolled weed growth may ultimately kill ornamental plants, which are often much less vigorous, and will often seriously inhibit their development. For most of us, a weed's "unwantedness" is its major crime.

Weeds are able to take control because they are species that have evolved to colonize, compete and become dominant. Most of them specialize in getting established on disturbed ground – often found in a garden – and usually have rapid growth rates when compared to cultivated plants. In natural habitats their competitive capabilities are held in check by the equal demands of neighbouring plants, but such equilibrium is very rare in the average garden.

While many common weeds are native plants and owe their competitive edge to this fact alone, many others are introduced plants that become weeds because they do not have the constraints of their natural habitat. They are often the most serious weeds in a garden, and can sometimes become so troublesome that they become a national problem. Don't make the mistake of thinking that a pretty plant can't become a weed. It can. Choose your plants carefully to avoid introducing problems.

Finally, note that a few plants, such as Japanese knotweed, no matter how tolerant you may be, are simply weeds that must be removed for the well-being of your garden. They will resist all efforts to eradicate them and, as any gardener knows, the only really successful strategy for weed control is persistent weeding.

COMMON TYPES OF WEEDS

There are many plants that can become weeds if they get out of control or grow where you don't want them to. Often they are native plant species that are able to take advantage of the conditions within your garden, and can be quite persistent.

Annual meadow grass A very common annual weed thriving in just about every situation in a garden. Very variable and adaptable, and able to grow and set seed all year round if the winter is mild.

Bittercress This diminutive plant is very common in container-grown plants, and often grows in mild periods in winter. Sheds abundant seed and can become invasive.

Chickweed Commonly found on soil that is well-cultivated and rich in organic matter. Spreads to make a large mat and produces seed prolifically. Seed lies dormant for years.

Couch grass This perennial grass spreads via underground rhizomes that often form thick masses in the soil over time. Very difficult to eradicate from borders, but can be tamed and weakened by constant cutting.

Dandelion The dandelion is quite a showy plant, often appearing in lawns, with a strong tap root. Readily regenerates by seed and by root unless the whole plant is removed.

Dock A persistent perennial that is difficult to dig out, with very tough roots that can regenerate from even a small section left in the ground. Seeds prolifically if not controlled.

Ground elder A spreading and smothering weed that is happiest in a loamy soil, which it can rapidly colonize. The white, spreading roots often go down deep, and it resists efforts to dig it up.

Horsetail Non-flowering plants that mainly spread via the thin, black roots. Often covers large areas, and is very difficult to dig out as the brittle stems and roots break easily when pulled, and regenerate.

Nettle Extremely common weed in gardens, primarily because it needs high fertility and disturbed ground.

Bittercress

Chickweed

Couch grass

Ground elder

Horsetail

Nettle

CHEMICALS

As a rule of thumb, don't use them. The majority of herbicides (or weedkillers) are toxic compounds that can affect the flora and fauna in your garden. The exception is where highly persistent weeds cannot be effectively controlled by hand weeding or mulches. While this situation is mercifully rare, plants such as Japanese knotweed have become a real problem in recent years, and threaten both garden and natural habitats in parts of Western Europe.

HAND WEEDING

Simply pulling out weeds, digging them up or using a cultivator, such as a hoe, is usually the least detrimental method of weed control. There is little skill in using most hand-weeding implements and, provided that you are careful, little and often is all that is required. The real trick is to be able to recognize weeds when they are very young, even when they are just seedlings, and remove them then.

MULCHING

A mulch is a layer of material that is laid over the soil, or other growing medium. It should be laid on a bare soil surface that is warm and moist, with autumn being the ideal time, although it can also be applied in the spring after the soil has warmed up. Many types of mulch will suppress the germination of weed seeds, and some will also benefit wildlife by introducing organic matter.

Below: *Dandelions can become troublesome as they spread quickly by means of the plumed seeds that follow the bright yellow flowers in late spring.*

Mulching an established border will help keep the plants' roots warm in winter and cool in summer. It also reduces soil water loss through evaporation, partly by shading the soil surface. The weed control benefits are mostly due to the mulch preventing the germinating weed seedlings from reaching the sunlight, or by "drawing" the weed up so that it is spindly and can be easily removed. It will not, however, inhibit established weeds, especially vigorous perennial ones, which must be removed by hand the moment they appear.

If a mulch is laid to a sufficient, even depth – 5cm (2in) or more – it will develop a dry, dusty surface that will deter the germination of weed seeds that land on it. While this is only a temporary measure, it can help reduce the need for weeding at the busiest times of year. Synthetic materials are unattractive, but can be useful if you choose the permeable types, which allow the passage of air and water. Indeed, some organic materials, such as grass clippings, can pack down on the surface and form a water-resistant layer. Finally, note that mulches encourage surface rooting, and that the mulching must be continued if the plants are not to suffer in the future.

Mulching also aids plant development by gradually raising soil fertility and encouraging nutrient cycling. Furthermore, natural, organic mulches will actually harbour many beneficial insects, such as carnivorous beetles, which will help keep the plants healthy by eating pests, including slugs and caterpillars.

MULCH TYPES AND THEIR BENEFITS TO WILDLIFE

The materials that can be used for mulching are varied in their composition and effects. They are generally classified into organic and inorganic types. Organic mulches are mainly bulky materials of living origin. Inorganic mulches, on the other hand, include some naturally occurring but non-living materials such as pebbles and gravel, as well as synthetic materials of artificial origin. In the inorganic category, the materials may be further subdivided into loose fill and sheet materials. The six main kinds are:

Bark and composted woodchip Makes an excellent material because it is recycled, and will gradually break down and yield organic matter to the soil below. It also lowers the chance of weeds germinating, and is possibly the best material for encouraging beetles due to its open nature.

Garden compost Often makes a first-rate mulch, increasing soil fertility and encouraging beneficial insects, but it can also be an excellent place for germinating weeds to become established, and large quantities can be difficult to produce.

Straw A moderately good material to use around the base of plants in the summer, particularly under fruiting strawberries. While surprisingly durable, it eventually rots down. It should be chopped into short lengths prior to use.

Black polythene Quick and easy to lay, and a common material that can be readily obtained from many suppliers. It does not allow for water penetration into the soil though, and is generally best restricted to uses under paths or for temporary coverage.

Woven plastic sheet An improvement on black polythene, although it also has the disadvantage of denuding the organic content from the soil below by preventing it reaching there. Use in similar places to polythene as a water-permeable substitute.

Grit, pebbles, gravel or sand These inorganic materials are very durable, although they often become incorporated into the topsoil layer because of the actions of worms and other organisms. They are ideal in dry gardens, around alpine plants, and as a topping around potted plants.

Bark

Straw

Black polythene

Gravel

PESTS, DISEASES AND DISORDERS

While the vast majority of the creatures and other organisms in the garden don't cause any harm, a small number can sometimes become your worst enemies, seemingly intent on devouring crops and damaging the appearance and overall vigour of other plants, possibly shortening their lifespan. Controlling them might be easier than you think, though, and wildlife gardens have a whole "army" of helpers to help you do this.

Above: *Snails and slugs are a problem in any garden if their number gets too high. Beer traps can help to control them.*

DEFINING A PEST

In the simplest terms, a pest is a creature that eats a plant. Many culprits are visible – although a few are very small and may even be microscopic – and they are usually present in large numbers. That is not always the case, however, and a single large pest, such as a deer, may affect many plants in quite a short time, often in a single visit. Pests may be host specific or more general in their feeding habits.

WHAT IS A DISEASE?

A disease describes the symptoms caused by a small (usually microscopic) parasite that attacks the plant's cells, possibly causing extensive harm before any obvious symptoms appear. Plant diseases are usually caused by fungi, bacteria or viruses.

A fungus is a small unicellular or colonial mass of cells, often with complex life cycles. Most are beneficial or benign to plants. The vast majority are only evident at the reproductive phase, and they may go unnoticed unless serious harm occurs.

Bacteria, on the other hand, are very simple (unicellular) organisms, only some of which are capable of life outside their host (victim) species. They too usually parasitize individual cells, and often reproduce and spread rapidly once an infection occurs. The most common source of harm occurs when they release poisons into the cell. Bacteria can be very hard to treat because they live inside the plant cells.

A virus is quite unlike the other two disease-causing agents. All viruses are incapable of functioning outside the host cell, and they consist of a shell that contains a small amount of very basic genetic material. This is used (once inside the cell) to cause the host cell to produce copies of the virus. The host cell then usually dies, and damage often spreads through the copies.

DISORDERS

A disorder is a condition whereby the growth or internal functioning of the plant physically deviates from the norm. The most common cause is an environmental stress – such as nutrient imbalance or lack of light. Disorders differ from temporary stresses (e.g. wilting) because they cannot be readily reversed, even if the cause is promptly removed. Plants suffering a disorder often resemble diseased or pest-stricken plants, and may become sicker than if they had been attacked by a pest or disease-causing organism.

Left: *A scarecrow was a traditional way of discouraging birds, although in truth, they are often more ornamental than useful.*

RECOGNIZING THE SYMPTOMS

Knowing what is likely to harm the plants you intend growing is the best starting point. Only a few insects are actually harmful, and learning which are pests and which are not is vital. In addition you will be well advised to find out which plants are susceptible to particular pests, and learn what are the signs. In many cases, the pest or disease will be visibly present, allowing an easy diagnosis. Get into the habit of looking closely at all your plants and checking for early symptoms of attack. Disease symptoms can be tricky to diagnose, but a few of the commoner ones are outlined here.

Blight is usually noticed as a softening and death of tissue in patches, whereas damping off is a localized blight of the stem near the soil. Wilt is sudden wilting, usually of the stem tip, whereas foot rot (affecting the lower stem) and root rot are often less visible without close examination.

Anthracnose usually refers to any skin tissue where black lesions appear, with leaf spots specifically affecting that area. Scab also affects the skin, being a hard, corky layer on the stems, leaves and fruit. Canker is an area of flaking or bleeding bark tissue, whereas yellowing and mosaics are often disease-related.

A few other disease-like conditions can be less threatening, and are actually an interesting addition to the diversity in your garden. Galls – and there are many of them – are a hyperplasic deformation of the plant tissue, and are often caused by tiny mites, midges or wasps. They are mostly harmless and can occasionally be extremely curious shapes. Other deformations also occur, such as "Witch's Broom", and they can have a variety of causes including bacteria, fungi, mites, aphids, and even mistletoe. On the other hand, a plant may simply be showing a genetic abnormality, such as fasciation, where a normally round stem is flattened, looking as if many stems have fused together.

PREVENTION IS BETTER THAN CURE

The best way to control problems is to ensure that your plants are healthy by giving them the right conditions. Healthy plants are often more resistant to diseases and stresses, and a healthy, balanced garden, full of the appropriate plants, is also the ideal environment for beneficial organisms. Traps, barriers, scaring devices and repellents can all be effective methods of dissuading pests, provided they do not prove too tempting or disruptive to the more desirable creatures.

BENEFICIAL ORGANISMS

By attracting beneficial organisms, you'll be well on the way to balancing the ecology of the garden and removing the majority of threats posed by pests.

All pests tend to become numerous and, as such, they are almost always a food source for a whole array of predators (species that eat them), parasitoids (creatures that lay eggs that hatch and eat them), and parasites (diseases of the pest). You can actually buy all three for use in the greenhouse, but they are often less effective outdoors. In the latter case, it is often better to enlist the help of a local volunteer force. Your garden can easily become a haven for many beneficial insects that are attracted by the plants or the habitat, and they'll reward you by eating as many of the offending

insects as possible. With an army of natural pest killers on your side, matters will improve as their tireless efforts to devour the pests will keep their number in check.

Below: *The larvae of ladybirds are particularly voracious predators of a range of insects, and are especially fond of aphids.*

BENEFICIAL PREDATORS

Many familiar creatures that visit or inhabit gardens are voracious predators, and help control the numbers of pests. Some are very common and, by encouraging them, you can help restore a natural balance in the garden.

Frog, toad and newt All amphibians are carnivores and eat an array of garden pests. Toads tend to be particularly good in this respect, and all amphibians can be attracted by a pond to breed in and cover such as rock piles and long vegetation.

Ground beetle A fierce-looking beetle living among the litter layer, just above the soil, where it hunts its favourite prey – the slug. The beetle is common everywhere, and can be encouraged by mulching and leaving areas untouched.

Hedgehog It eats a variety of garden pests. Encourage it by providing brush piles or a nesting box, and dense growth next to hedge bottoms.

Hoverfly Though the adults are vegetarian, feeding on pollen and nectar, the larvae are voracious predators of aphids. Encourage the adults into the garden by planting flat umbelled plants, and those with daisy flowers.

Lacewing A strange, graceful, night-flying insect; the larvae are among the best of all garden predators. They attack and eat a whole range of insects, favouring aphids.

Ladybird Though inconspicuous, the larva is the most voracious predator of aphids.

Robin Carnivorous bird that normally catches its prey on the ground after seeing movement from a perch above. Often follows gardeners digging the soil to catch unearthed grubs.

Slow worm Not a worm but a legless lizard, feeding on slugs and earthworms, but will also eat insects. Prefers damp and warm habitats, and hibernates under piles of leaves in winter.

Spider Probably the most important predator in the garden. Catches mostly flying insects in webs, although some species are specialists at ambushing prey. Spiders vary considerably in size and can be found in every type of habitat.

Wasp Renowned for its sting and reviled for this reason. An incredible hunter, particularly of caterpillars in early summer. Can be a problem if they nest in or near houses and other buildings.

Frog

Ground beetle

Hedgehog

Hoverfly

Lacewing

Ladybird

Robin

Slow worm

Spider

Wasp

PRUNING

Pruning is a necessary activity in the garden, especially when plants become too big and unmanageable, or perhaps to try to encourage better flowering or rejuvenate older specimens. While sometimes a little confusing to the beginner, there is no great mystery surrounding pruning and, like most jobs in the garden, it merely involves the application of simple and straightforward principles. Follow these guidelines and in no time at all you'll be pruning with confidence.

Above: *A garden shredder is an ideal way of recycling prunings, as the shredded material can be used in making mulch for the garden.*

WHY PRUNE?

The main reason to prune is to control a plant's growth. It may outgrow its space or need to be shaped for aesthetic reasons. But pruning can also improve the flower size of some shrubs and climbers, and maintain a regular supply of new growth valued for its attractive colours (e.g. dogwoods).

CHOOSING THE RIGHT TOOLS

Secateurs are used to snip through thinner growth, up to about 15mm (½in) in diameter. For thicker growth you will need a pair of loppers that are used on branches up to 2.5cm (1in) thick. Use them when you can't reach in with secateurs, for instance in dense, tangled shrubs. Normally, loppers should not be used for very thick branches because they may easily be damaged, although several models of ratchet-operated loppers can cut through growth of up to 5cm (2in).

Above these thicknesses you will need a pruning saw. Again many designs exist, but the most useful is the curved or Grecian type, and a bow saw for really thick wood. Always make sure you have the right tools for the job. If you don't, it will make the job harder, and you may actually end up causing more harm than good by either breaking the tool itself or by making untidy or ragged cuts that increase the chances of disease.

DECIDING WHAT TO DO

The first and simplest thing that you can do is to remove all dead, dying, damaged or diseased wood. Remember, though, that deadwood is very important to some wildlife, especially what is called "standing deadwood" in a tree. This is often removed to ensure that dead branches do not fall suddenly, and should be left on the ground for wildlife and not removed and burned as is often recommended. Diseased material, on

---

DOS AND DON'TS OF PRUNING FOR WILDLIFE

Whilst pruning always employs the same basic methods, the choice of how and when to prune can have serious implications for wildlife.

- **Do** identify the shrub or tree, and check its pruning requirements.

- **Do** leave piles of thicker branches on the ground for wildlife. Log and brush piles can provide escape cover, nesting and den sites for many species and, if placed along the edge of water, can be an important habitat for amphibians and reptiles.

- **Do** thin shrubs over a two- to three-year period in preference to one hard pruning session to allow them to make new growth while still producing fruit and flowers.

- **Do** leave "standing deadwood" where possible, especially stumps and boles of dead trees for wildlife.

- **Don't** prune and deadhead shrubs until late winter to allow the birds to feed on berries and seed heads.

- **Don't** prune in spring because this will disturb nesting birds.

- **Don't** compost diseased material as this will infect other plants. Remove and burn it to avoid re-infection.

- **Don't** worry if you see fungus growing on deadwood because it cannot infect live material.

GOOD AND BAD PRUNING

Above: *Cuts should be made like this one, just above a bud or pair of buds. Make sure the cut does not get too close so that you don't damage the delicate buds.*

Above: *Leaving too long a stub above the buds will result in a piece of deadwood that can act as an entry point for fungal diseases. This can affect the rest of the branch.*

USING PRUNINGS TO CREATE A HABITAT

1 *Collect prunings from a variety of healthy plants, and drive some short stakes into the ground, ensuring they are firmly in place.*

2 *Lay down bundles of long, straight branches horizontally behind the stakes. Pack them together tightly to make narrow spaces, which will provide excellent cover for insects in all seasons.*

3 *Cover the packed pile with loose material and add a layer of leaves. Place larger logs in front to help secure the prunings and to create an even more diverse habitat, attracting more species.*

the other hand, should be removed and burned, especially if there is a chance that it will spread and affect other plants.

Criss-crossing branches and crowded growth should also be cleared, with their removal prompting the appearance of new growth in many species. This is normally then followed by the removal of any unwanted growth that is obstructing paths or crowding out adjacent specimens. Always take care when doing such pruning because removing large amounts of plant material may cause the plant to assume an unbalanced form that is difficult (if not impossible) to counter with further pruning.

Once you have cleared this material, it is possible to see what further work needs to be done. Creating balance, form and a pleasing shape requires a keen eye, and it is worth taking your time, intermittently viewing your work from a distance.

Finally, note that the real results of pruning may not always be apparent for months and, in the case of trees, years.

PRUNING CUTS

The two basic pruning cuts are heading (the removal of a part of a shoot or limb) and thinning (the removal of the entire shoot or limb). Heading stimulates re-growth near the cut and is the most invigorating type of pruning cut, resulting in thick, compact growth and a loss of natural form, as found in a formally pruned hedge. Thinning, on the other hand, generally provides a more natural look, with only around one-third of the growth being thinned at any one time, leaving the natural flowering and fruiting cycle to continue. Thinning is often the best type of pruning to favour wildlife, although the dense growth promoted by heading does provide good dense cover for some species, such as nesting birds.

Pruning cuts should always be cleanly done using sharp cutters or a saw, and always avoid tearing. When removing a whole limb, try to leave as short a stub as possible. If you are heading (i.e. shortening) a branch, make your cut 3mm (⅛in), or just less, above a bud and always ensure that the bud is not damaged while cutting. And remember, if you cut the wrong stem or branch, that's it. Always check that you know what effect its removal will have before cutting.

TIMING OF PRUNING

Many woody ornamentals are pruned according to their date of flowering. Spring-flowering plants, such as forsythia, are normally pruned only after they bloom because pruning them during the dormant season will remove the flower buds formed the previous autumn. Summer-flowering plants, on the other hand, are generally pruned during the dormant winter season. As a rule of thumb, avoid heavy pruning during late summer and autumn because this can remove berries and seed needed by wildlife, and in spring to avoid disturbing nesting birds.

CUTTING A HERBACEOUS BORDER

1 *Herbaceous borders will always look better after a tidy-up, and this will also allow light to get to the crowns and encourage strong, healthy new growth in spring.*

2 *Try to leave cutting back herbaceous stems until the early spring, if possible, as old stems often act as a vital refuge for insects, including many beneficials in winter.*

RAISING NATIVE PLANTS FROM SEED

Seed is the principal way in which flowering plants produce a new generation. It is also the way that they ensure genetic diversity in a population and so collecting and sowing seed of trees, shrubs, grasses and flowers is extremely worthwhile. Native plants are often best for wildlife, and those that are native to your particular locality will be the best of all for attracting the local wildlife.

Above: *A field of cowslips is a good feeding place for early emerging bees and long-tongued flies that will in turn pollinate them.*

WHY DO IT?

The two advantages of collecting seed and raising your own plants are, first, saving money and, second, helping the local environment.

Native plants may be quite variable across their range, and the slight difference between local populations is called their provenance. If these plants occur naturally without being planted, they are called indigenous plants. Commercial supplies of seed usually come from seed or plant material from a different area or, in some cases, from another country. Therefore, though the plants are often genetically very similar, they may not always be best suited to the conditions in your area. By gathering and propagating local seed, then, you are helping to maintain the natural variety of native plants across a wide range.

WHAT TYPE OF SEED TO COLLECT

This depends on what kind of garden you want. Diversifying your lawn, for instance, will need different plants to those for creating a woodland edge. Once you have a clear plan, you can decide where to collect the seed.

Above: *The seed of a cowslip is very easy to harvest. Simply gather the ripe seed heads and gently rub them to release the seed. It is best sown fresh, or store in a paper bag.*

THE BEST PLACE TO GATHER IT

Your own garden is obviously the easiest place to collect seed. The best policy before you collect any seed from land that is not your own is to first ask for permission from the landowner. Remember to check whether the plants you intend collecting from are rare or endangered because some species might be protected, making it illegal even for the landowner to take seed, and collecting seed of any wild plants should be limited to small amounts.

When you visit the site, you must be able to make a clear distinction between plants that have become naturalized and those that have always grown there. A good place to look may be land earmarked for building because new developments are often built on land with native plants.

HOW TO HARVEST SEED

There are three main kinds of seed. The commonest and easiest type is that which can be collected, dried and stored prior to sowing. Berries and softer fruit are slightly more difficult, and often need the soft flesh removed before they can be sown. The seed is usually short-lived and must be sown at once to retain its viability. Nuts, and many larger kinds of seed, are also difficult to store because they will only germinate when fresh. Berries and nuts should only be collected after they have fully ripened, usually once they begin to fall off the branch.

Whichever type you are collecting, you must remove only a small or modest amount from the plant. Unless you need a very large number of plants, you will need only a small amount of seed. Remember to

---

MACERATING AND FLOATING BERRIES

1 *Lay the ripe berries on a firm surface and cover with a large plastic sheet. Squash the berries by pressing them underfoot.*

2 *Pour the squashed berries into a bucket full of water and leave for several hours. The soft parts of the fruit will separate from the seed.*

3 *The seed will sink to the bottom and the fruit and skins will float. These can be poured off. Wash the seed and it is then ready to sow.*

collect from more than one plant to get as much diversity as possible. If the seed pods are not quite ripe, you can always put them in paper bags and allow them to dry and burst open.

THE FIRST STAGE

Germination is the growth of the embryonic plant inside the seed. This embryo lies in a dormant state, only barely alive until this time; some seed, such as poppy, can survive successfully in this dormant state for 50 years or more. Most seed, however, is capable of lasting for only a few years before the embryo dies and the seed becomes unviable. The term "viable seed" is used to describe seed that is alive and in a healthy state, thereby allowing germination. As time passes, the amount of viable seed usually decreases under normal storage conditions, and seed is best sown fresh.

To germinate, seed requires moisture, warmth and oxygen. Most seed germinates best at 18–24°C (65–75°F) and, although most seed will happily germinate in light, some – such as periwinkle (*Vinca*), pansy (*Viola*) and verbena – germinates best in the dark.

While most seed is easy to grow, a few species have specific germination requirements. Bought seed has specific instructions on the packaging, but collected seed might require a bit of guesswork. As a general rule, small dust-like seed such as thyme (*Thymus*), basil (*Ocimum basilicum*) and begonia needs light to germinate. Make sure that the seed is well pressed into the moist compost, but do not cover it. Larger seed, on the other hand, is most commonly covered to twice its thickness, preferably with finely sieved compost.

Some seed can be a little tricky to germinate, and the commonest problem is caused by a lack of cold-temperature dormancy. Cold dormancy is mostly required by plant species that originate from cooler climates. The solution is stratification. This simply involves covering the seed in damp material, such as compost, leafmould or sand, depending on the seed size. Large seed can be kept in organic matter, but smaller seed is best mixed with sand to make sowing easier later on. Keep it in a refrigerator at about 4°C (40°F) for up to three months, when it can be removed, being ready to germinate. Oak (*Quercus*) and hellebore (*Helleborus*) seed needs such treatment to break dormancy.

SOWING SEED

1 *Fill a seed tray with seed compost. Don't use general purpose compost as this is too rich in nutrients. Water well using a watering can with a fine rose, and allow to drain for around an hour.*

2 *Sow the seed carefully. With larger seed you can place a couple of seeds in each of the cells in a modular tray; smaller seed can be mixed with fine sand to make it easier to spread evenly.*

3 *Unless the seed is of a plant that needs light to stimulate germination, the seed must now be covered. Do this with sieved compost or vermiculite so that all the seed is just covered.*

NATIVES V EXOTICS

While gardens are usually full of imported plant species, native species are often considered to be the best option for the wildlife in your area and the surrounding habitats.

PROBLEMS WITH INTRODUCED PLANTS	**ADVANTAGES WITH NATIVE PLANTS**
• Many introduced species have short flowering seasons, many of which occur at the same time in high summer to benefit the retail garden trade.	• They tend to be the best for nurturing and supporting wildlife all year, and their flowering times often coincide with the life cycles of native animals.
• Cultivated plants often have flowers unsuited to native pollinators. This is usually because they have large, colourful or double flowers, or because they are native to other countries.	• Most native flowering plants are able to survive only in an area with the appropriate pollinating insects. Their flowers will therefore nearly always be suited to the local species.
• Introduced plants are often the result of intensive breeding programmes, and do not always offer the same advantages for native wildlife when they are used in landscape settings.	• Many native plants are becoming rare due to habitat loss and competition from introduced weeds. Incorporating native plants in landscaping is a small step towards reversing this trend.
• Garden plants can escape and become invasive because they have few species that eat them and control their numbers. This often reduces the biological diversity of surrounding natural areas, as they compete with native species.	• If they escape your garden they cannot become invasive weeds because they are usually kept in check by animals eating them, or through competition from other plant species.
• Cultivated plants often perform poorly away from their native environment, and must have intensive cultivation and care to ensure their survival.	• They are invariably well adapted to the local climatic conditions, having had many generations to shape them into the fittest possible race for the area, and once established, need less intensive care.

DIVISION, CUTTINGS AND LAYERS

Most new plants are reproduced from seed or spores. In certain circumstances, however, plants produce offspring in other ways, enabling you to grow new plants quickly and easily from existing stock, and often involving very little specialist equipment. Plants propagated in this way are said to have been propagated "vegetatively" or "asexually", and this is one of the most interesting and rewarding areas of gardening.

Above: *Bulbs, such as these tulips, naturally form offsets that can easily be divided to produce many more plants at no extra cost.*

VEGETATIVE PROPAGATION

The vegetative parts of the plant are the stems, roots and leaves. In certain circumstances all these parts can be used to produce a new plant, although the ease varies considerably between species. Most fruit trees, for instance, are propagated asexually, using a bud or a twig from a tree that produces exceptionally good fruit. When this bud or twig becomes an adult tree, it has the same qualities as the parent tree and is essentially an identical clone.

BEST PARTS FOR PROPAGATION

Plants may be propagated from many different parts and, in certain species, specialized roots, stems and leaves have a tendency to form new plants, and can be used for propagation.

Rhizomes usually grow underground and, although they appear root-like, are actually horizontal stems that often send out roots and shoots. Stolons are similar to rhizomes, but usually exist above ground level and sprout from an existing stem. Irises and bamboos are common examples

of plants propagated from rhizomes and stolons. Runners are similar to stolons but arise from a crown bud and creep over the ground. Good examples include strawberries and spider plants (*Chlorophytum comosum*).

Bulbs, such as tulips (*Tulipa*), onions and lilies (*Lilium*), consist of swollen leaves on a short stem. They are easily propagated from natural offsets that form next to the parent bulb, or from sections of the bulb itself. In some species, such as lilies, individual scales can be separated and propagated. Lilies also produce small bulbils in their leaf axils that will become bulbs if grown for 2–4 years in a rich, light soil. This procedure also applies to plants that form offsets from corms, such as gladioli (*Gladiolus*).

Corms are similar to bulbs and are often confused with them. Structurally, however, a corm is different, consisting of a stem that is swollen as a food store. It is shorter and broader than a bulb. The leaves of the stem are modified as dry, thin membranes that enclose the corm and protect it against injury and drying. Good examples include

the crocus and gladioli. True corms are usually propagated from offsets produced by the "parent" plant or from seed.

Tubers are underground swollen stems or roots that store food, such as the potato, used individually to produce new offspring, and generally sold as seed potatoes. Root tubers of the dahlia, cyclamen and anemone can be divided while dormant, provided that each new segment has a bud attached that will form new shoots.

ROOT CUTTINGS

Some plants can be propagated from roots. To produce a new plant from a root cutting, there must be a shoot bud present or it must be possible for the cutting to form one. The ability of root cuttings to form these buds depends on the time of year. The dormant season is usually best with phlox and euphorbia, two examples of plants that can readily be propagated from root cuttings.

The cuttings should be taken from newer root growth, making cuttings 3.5–10cm (1¼–4in) long from roots that are 1–1.5cm

MAKING DIVISIONS

1 *Lift the herbaceous plant as a whole clump and insert two forks into the clump. Prise the clump apart to divide it.*

2 *Work the ground using a fork, and incorporate organic matter at the same time to produce an ideal planting medium.*

3 *Place the divided sections in their final positions before planting them with a spade. Use your heel to firm them in.*

4 *The divided sections quickly establish and fill the space in between. Dividing rejuvenates the plant and encourages growth.*

TAKING CUTTINGS

1 *Fill a seed tray with seed and cutting compost and level this using a flat wooden board. This will ensure that the compost is filled all the way to the brim.*

2 *Prepare your cuttings by taking short sections of the tips and carefully removing the lower leaves as close to the stem as possible, using a sharp knife.*

3 *Insert the prepared cuttings into the compost, making a hole with a narrow stick. Make sure that the leaves do not touch the compost, or they may rot.*

4 *Water with a fine rose on a watering can to firm the cuttings in. Place them in a propagator or on a warm windowsill and cover with a plastic sheet.*

(⅜–½in) in diameter. Cut straight through the end of the root closest to the stem, but cut the other end at a slant. This helps you to remember which end is the top (the straight cut) and which is the bottom. Cuttings taken from dormant roots are placed in a moist rooting medium at 5°C (41°F) for around three weeks before they are planted in small pots. Thereafter, they are kept moist and warm in a bright location to encourage growth until ready to plant out.

STEM PROPAGATION

Many trees, shrubs and herbaceous plants are propagated from stem parts. The two commonest methods are layering and stem cuttings.

The main difficulty involved in producing new plants from stem cuttings is keeping the stems alive while they form new roots. Some stems root better when the wood is soft and growing, others root best from mature wood. Cuttings taken from plants that are actively growing are called softwood cuttings. They are taken from first-year growth that has not yet become woody. Many flowering shrubs are propagated by softwood cuttings, with late spring and early summer being the best times for the majority of species.

Take cuttings 5–10cm (2–4in) long. Larger cuttings produce larger plants sooner, but they are prone to more rapid water loss. Make cuts slightly below a leaf node (the point where the leaf meets the stem) and remove any leaves on the lower section. Insert the cuttings into the compost, making sure that no leaves are touching each other or the compost. Remove any cuttings immediately if they

die, and transfer individual, healthy cuttings to small pots once they start growing, following rooting.

Cuttings taken from mature growth are hardwood cuttings, and are taken when the plant is dormant. Cuttings can be taken two weeks after leaf fall but before new buds open next spring. Select healthy wood that was produced the previous summer, about pencil thick, and cut into sections of approximately 15–20cm (6–8in). Several cuttings can often be made from the same branch. The bottom cuts are made just below a node, and the upper cuts slightly above a bud (again, the upper cut should be slanted so that a cutting can't be inserted into the compost upside down).

Bury cuttings vertically in moist, sandy topsoil or sand, leaving 2.5–5cm (1–2in) showing, and put them in a cool, shady place, taking care not to let them freeze. In spring, remove the cuttings from storage and plant at the same depth in pots or open ground, in a sheltered position in dappled shade. Keep them moist until a root system forms, and transplant them the following spring while they are dormant.

LAYERING

Plants that are difficult to root from cuttings can often be propagated by layering. Bend a young, flexible branch down to the soil, peg it down and bend the tip back up, supporting it clear of the ground, and cover the bend with soil. At the point of the bend, roots will form as the bend interferes with the flow of sap. Sap flow can be further reduced by twisting the stem, or cutting a tongue in the lower side of the bark with a sharp knife. The bend will need extra

covering through the summer to encourage stem rooting. Species suited to this method include magnolia and hazel (*Corylus*).

DIVISION

Usually practised only on herbaceous plants, division involves cutting or breaking up a crown or clump of suckers into segments, creating new, vigorous plants. Each segment must have a bud and some roots. The clump is carefully dug up and split with two spades or forks, or is chopped up with a spade or large knife if the clump is firmly massed. Autumn-flowering perennials are commonly divided in spring, while those flowering in spring and summer are best done in autumn. Pot-grown plants can also be divided, with one pot giving rise to many offspring.

Below: *Choosing the right plants from a nursery can help increase your stock. To get value for money, choose crowded pots that are in need of dividing.*

FINDING HIDDEN TREASURES

Much of the wildlife in our gardens remains hidden from view, and the only evidence of its presence is often the small clues left behind. If you want to find out what lives in your garden, you must become a detective. Like any good sleuth, you will need to look for the slightest detail, often revealing a surprising amount about the animals in your garden. Taking a close look can help tell who is there and what they are doing.

Above: *Some creatures, such as this stick insect, escape detection by their close resemblance to the vegetation around them.*

CAMOUFLAGE AND MIMICRY

The main reason why so many creatures are difficult for us to spot, apart from the small size of a lot of them, is of course because they are camouflaged, having evolved all kinds of sophisticated ways of avoiding detection by predators or prey.

A creature's environment is often the most important factor in determining what the camouflage looks like, and the simplest kind involves matching the background. For most creatures, such blending in is the most effective approach, with deer, squirrels and hedgehogs, for example, having brownish, earth tones that match the vegetation and soil.

Other creatures have distinctive designs on their bodies to match their surroundings. Animals that inhabit areas with tall, vertical grass, for instance, often have long, vertical stripes. The designs may also obscure the body's contours, making it hard for a predator to get a clear sense of where the animal begins and ends.

Above: *Many night-flying moths escape predators in the daytime, with wing patterns that blend in perfectly with their surroundings.*

A related tactic is for a creature to take on the appearance of some object, one of the most obvious examples being the stick insect that resembles an ordinary twig.

Other creatures use mimicry, and some moth species have patterns on their wings to resemble the eyes of a larger animal.

Hawk moth caterpillars sometimes resemble a snake's head, and some stinging or poisonous insects develop a bright coloration to ward off predators. Over time, other non-poisonous species may develop the same coloration as a means of survival.

HIDING PLACES

In a wildlife garden, the most important features are hiding places for creatures. Even the best-camouflaged species will need to take shelter from the elements, make nests or hibernate. These places often contain a plethora of interesting species that are only rarely seen. Many reptiles or amphibians, for instance, will take shelter under an old corrugated metal sheet left lying on the ground, and often the only way to see these elusive creatures is to lift the sheet. Large stones are also helpful, but often for smaller species, such as beetles. If you do expose a hiding creature, take a quick look but then replace the cover. If you regularly disturb it, it will soon move.

LOOKING FOR WILDLIFE UNDER LOG SLICES

1 *A log slice makes an ideal cover for a hiding place for garden wildlife. This one has even had a handle fixed to the top.*

2 *A piece of Perspex placed beneath the log can allow you to see whether there is anything there without really disturbing it.*

3 *Many creatures, such as this female newt, will take temporary residence in such a place, and make fascinating encounters.*

BURROWS AND NESTS

Many creatures make underground burrows where they can escape the attention of predators and raise their young in relative safety. They may make their own burrows, while a few either share or use disused burrows belonging to other species. Often, the only evidence that there is something inside is the telltale entrance (or exit) hole. This will not tell you if the burrow is currently occupied, though, and often you'll need to wait and see what emerges. This can be doubly difficult if its inhabitant is nocturnal and slips out only under cover of night, so also look for evidence of fresh activity, such as tracks or recently excavated earth.

If you do come across a burrow in the garden, never dig into it. Although some burrows are only seasonal or temporary, the occupants may well be inside and, in the case of many insect species, the larvae overwinter in burrows as cocoons before emerging next year as adults to begin a new breeding cycle.

Nests are sometimes located above ground in rocky crevices, clefts or holes in trees as well as in dense vegetation. If you find one, leave it alone because its owner may only be temporarily away.

FOLLOWING TRAILS

Despite their secretive nature, many animals leave clear evidence – tracks, droppings or the remains of a meal – that they are in your garden. Their shy and secretive ways make them difficult to see, but if you know that they are there, your garden has become a success. Often these clues are the only tangible evidence of their presence but by finding them you experience a closeness to them and, in time, knowledge of their regular habits.

Above: *Birds' nests can sometimes be found in secluded spots, such as hedges or dense shrubs, and if seen, should be left undisturbed wherever possible.*

TRACKS AND TRAILS

Many animals are very secretive, and even an experienced wildlife observer may only see them occasionally. In such rare cases, the clues the creatures leave behind are essential ways to find out where they are and what they are doing there.

Badger tracks A badger footprint is very distinctive. It consists of a broad, kidney-shaped pad with five toes in front. The prints of the front feet are larger than those of the back feet, and the distance between the claws on the toes of the front feet is greater than that of the hind feet.

Deer tracks Deer hooves have two separate halves or cleats. If a deer walks over muddy or sandy ground, clear imprints are evident, and it may be possible to match these tracks to species of deer that are known to live in your area.

Fox tracks The prints of foxes show four toes and claws but, because the front of their feet are often covered with hair, the toes can be indistinct. Red foxes have hard pads on their toes that sometimes show up in the prints. There is also a V-shaped callus pad on the heel. No other canine has this.

Owl pellet The acid in the owl's gut is rather weak, so it can only digest soft tissue. The bones (including intact skulls), fur and feathers of its prey remain virtually intact, and this is regurgitated in a small pellet which, if carefully prised apart, shows you what the owl has eaten.

Sloughed snake skin Snakes regularly shed the outer layer of their skin as they grow. Even when not growing, the scales become worn and must be replaced by a new, healthy layer. After the old layer is loosened, the snake crawls out of its old skin, typically shedding it in a single piece.

Thrush stone The song thrush can be easily identified because it uses a tool to eat snails when the ground is hard and worms cannot be found. The thrush smashes the snail's shell against a large stone to get at the soft body tissue inside.

Badger track

Deer track

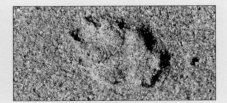

Fox track

Owl pellet

Sloughed snake skin

Thrush stone

GETTING A CLOSE-UP VIEW

Most gardeners will have at one time lifted a stone to reveal many tiny creatures darting here and there to escape the light. Such sightings are a real thrill and, with a bit of patience, you can get a close look at this whole new world. A good way to start is just to sit quietly and watch birds eat on a feeder, or see the butterflies flit from flower to flower. Many species are very shy, though, and you'll need to hide to get a good view.

Above: *By fitting a wall box with a small solar-powered light, you can see night-flying species as they visit, attracted by the glow.*

WHY CREATURES ARE SHY

Many animals are understandably shy of people because their survival depends on their alertness to danger and potential predators. When you observe a creature you're actually like a predator. You stop, turn your eyes directly on the creature and then slowly move towards it – essentially stalking it. Its first reaction is to assume that it's being hunted and to flee. This sort of flight response is instinctive in many creatures as a result of aeons of evolution, and can be difficult to overcome unless you mask your intentions.

THE FLIGHT RESPONSE

There are many ways that creatures detect the presence of a potential predator. Some will pick up scents, so the wind direction will make a difference, while others have very acute hearing.

Movement is an obvious trigger, especially when it's sudden. Even if you have managed to get close without disturbing a creature, it may well be aware of your presence. A sudden movement may be mistaken for the start of an ambush attack and it'll flee. Even if you stay at a respectful distance and keep still, the effect of binoculars or cameras can prove alarming to many creatures. This is simply because they look like large eyes, and seem closer than they actually are.

TEMPORARY CAPTURE

This is a good way of seeing some creatures, provided you are careful not to cause them harm or distress in the process. Remember that their behaviour can be aggressive if they feel threatened. Wild creatures will become as alarmed when encountering you as they do when meeting a predator.

Right: *If you have a very big garden, you could set up a large permanent hide to observe visiting wildlife species without disturbing them.*

The most obvious candidates for capture are pond creatures that can be caught and briefly placed in a jar where they can be studied. Small mammals, such as mice and voles, can be captured in a humane trap, but don't keep them in it for long because this will distress them unnecessarily (the traps are "humane" only in the sense that they do not kill the creatures). Never attempt to trap larger animals – even squirrels or rabbits – because they can become quite aggressive when threatened, and they have sharp teeth that can do a lot of damage. Whatever you do catch, the golden rule is to put it back where you found it as soon as possible, and never handle it.

POND DIPPING

1 *Move a small-gauge net slowly through the water in a gentle, side-to-side swishing motion for about half a minute.*

2 *For identification, carefully empty the contents of the net into a shallow white bowl containing a little pond water.*

3 *The white background makes a good contrast with the creatures so they can be easily identified using a simple "spotter" guide.*

4 *Don't keep the animals in the tray for too long. Always return them to the water as quickly as possible to minimize stress.*

LURES

To get a close look without capturing a creature, use a lure. Moth traps are an obvious example where a light is placed under a white sheet to attract them. Some bird feeders can be secured to a window by suction cups so that you can observe the birds close up. Indeed, feeding is an excellent way of luring even larger animals close to the house, but never overestimate this trust, and avoid trying to interact with them because they can still be aggressive. And never try to make them tame in case they trust all humans, some of whom might be out to kill them.

SPYING

A hide is really just a tent, albeit one made specially for the purpose, with a small opening for you to watch through. If they cannot see you and you remain quiet, animals will often come amazingly close.

Binoculars or a telescope are an excellent aid, and a night scope can yield amazing results. Smaller aquatic creatures in a drop of pond water can be looked at under a microscope. You will be amazed what else is lurking there.

It's now even possible to look into the homes of some creatures. It's relatively easy to put a small surveillance camera in a nesting box, and these micro cameras send a video link direct to a television monitor. If you get one with infrared lighting it is even possible to see what is happening at night.

The simple rules for watching wildlife are to be quiet, avoid sudden, quick movements, give yourself plenty of time and, most of all, be patient. Binoculars, telescopes and a telephoto lens on your camera will enable you to get a close-up view, and see undisturbed wildlife. Never rush or pursue wildlife, be considerate, and always avoid causing unnecessary stress.

Above: *A nest box can become a wonderful opportunity to observe nature by using "spy-camera" technology inside the structure.*

Limit time spent observing wildlife because encounters with people can alter their normal behaviour. Stay clear of mothers with young, nests or rookeries, and never herd, chase or separate a mother from its young or try to handle the young, even if they appear to be orphans – the mother may well be watching from a safe distance.

MAKING A TEMPORARY HIDE

1 *Making a hide doesn't need specialized equipment – just a large cardboard box, paints, stakes and a little creativity.*

2 *Open out the cardboard box and paint it. The pattern or colour is not important; your body shape will be hidden behind it.*

3 *Preparing the hide can be great fun and is something that the whole family or friends and neighbours can join in with.*

4 *To support the cardboard, drive a few thin stakes into the ground until they are firm enough to support the weight of the hide.*

5 *Hides are traditionally made of dull-coloured material, some with military-style camouflage. In the case of a garden hide, the colour is* rarely important. Gardens are often full of extreme contrast, and so why not make a colourful hide that children will love to make?

RECORDING WILDLIFE IN YOUR GARDEN

Once you have designed and established your wildlife garden, you'll probably want to know how successful it has been. Making a record of which animals choose to either visit or take up residence is an important way to judge the success of your garden and can be tremendous fun too. The essential thing to remember is that you should be discreet in your activities. Try not to disturb the animals too much.

Above: *Sketching wildlife can be a relaxing hobby and has the added advantage of teaching you to look closely at the creatures.*

TAKING PHOTOGRAPHS

Photographing wildlife can be a frustrating affair because the creatures in question are so elusive and easily frightened. If they aren't startled by your presence, the camera lens often looks like a big eye and timing that perfect shot can be almost impossible. Even easily seen creatures, such as a familiar garden bird, may fail to pose at the right moment. It is simply a matter of patience.

IDENTIFYING SPECIES

Always try to identify the species of wildlife accurately, and in the case of many creatures that's easily done using illustrated books. Some creatures, though, tend to have a large number of species, many of which look quite similar, birds being a good example. If you get a rare visitor it is often difficult to identify it straight away. Always look closely because most creatures have distinctive characteristics, making later identification possible in books or on the Internet. Assume that it is something common until you have any evidence to the contrary.

Above: *Photographs are an ideal way to accurately record the wildlife in your garden, but getting a really good shot can take a lot of practice and patience.*

MAKING NOTES

The easiest and most obvious way to collate any notes is to keep a diary of what you have seen through the year. This has the advantage of helping you to build a picture of what is happening, and you can compare years to see if your garden is gradually attracting more species and to predict what species will turn up at a particular time.

In addition, you could draw up a plan of the garden and mark where you see most species, perhaps extending those areas that are most successful. You could also record which flowers the bees and butterflies prefer, and when particular flowers start to bloom. Adding notes on the weather will flesh out the picture.

DRAWINGS

Even non-artists can gain a lot from trying to draw a creature. The most important technique is to look carefully and take in the detail. You can use simple sketches for basic shapes, and record something of a creature's movement by using sequences of line drawings, as well as studying typical poses, such as a squirrel sitting upright. Details and notes of the eyes, wings, legs and coloration should all be made.

CALLS AND SOUNDS

If a creature is very difficult to see, there might be a good chance that it gives its presence away by a call or sound. Many creatures – birds being a prime example –

Left: *Make notes about the animals you see, paying special attention to the plants they are visiting and the time of day.*

Right: *A large textbook can be cumbersome; a short field guide showing common species is often much more valuable when you are out and about.*

SETTING UP A GARDEN TRANSECT

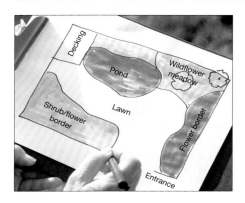

1 *Draw a rough sketch of the area that you intend to keep records on. This needn't be particularly detailed but should show the positions of major habitats in your garden.*

2 *The transect should have several locations where you make observations. Stand still for a few minutes at each and avoid any sudden movements, as this may alarm animals.*

3 *You can always take a portable chair along with you and sit for a set duration of time to record the resident wildlife. Try not to hurry as you might miss some of the shyer creatures.*

communicate using an extensive vocabulary of sounds. These often allow you to identify them without even getting a sighting.

Things are not always as they seem though, and often different sexes have different calls. For example, most people think that the tawny owl goes "twit-twoo". In fact the "twit" (or more accurately "ke-wick") is the female's contact call, and the "twoo" (or more accurately "hoo-hoo-oooo") is the male's territorial call. People assume the "twit-twoo" is one bird when it's actually a conversation between two owls. Learning to recognize the sounds that animals make can take time, but it is a fascinating way to appreciate what is out there without needing to stalk and cause unnecessary stress.

KEEPING RECORDS

Scientists call regular recording sessions that are carried out on a weekly basis using books, binoculars, camera and notebook a "transect". If you want to do the same in your garden, you could simply pick a few different areas around the garden, such as flower borders, shrubs or a woodland edge, and spend five minutes at each place, taking notes about the species seen.

Try to collect similar information each time, including notes on the weather, species seen and which plants they were on, if relevant. Don't forget to add notes about any unusual behaviour or other interesting snippets, sticking in drawings, photographs, feathers, fur, fallen leaves or empty seed cases. All can be kept with information about where and when you found them.

RECORDING A GARDEN TRANSECT

Use a sheet like this to record wildlife in the garden. It is better to choose one species at a time to record. Split the garden into sections and record the different types that visit each section. Record the information on a weekly basis usually from spring through to autumn (and winter if the animals chosen are active in this period). If the records are kept year-on-year you can soon establish if your wildlife numbers are increasing or decreasing, and this will determine if any changes need to be undertaken in your garden to improve the habitat.

Butterfly recording Temperature: 27°C Wind speed: Slight		Date: 18th July Sun/cloud cover: Sunny, no clouds			
Garden sections					
Type of butterfly	Flower border	Wildflower meadow	Pond	Shrub/ wildflower border	Total number
Small tortoiseshell	III			ⅢⅢ	8
Painted lady	I	II			3
Peacock	II			III	5
Comma		I	I		2
Red admiral	III			II	5
Meadow brown		ⅢⅢ IIII	ⅢⅢ ⅢⅢ I		20
Orange tip		I			1
Small white					0
Large white	II	III	I	II	8
Small copper		ⅢⅢ II	ⅢⅢ	I	13
Number of butterflies visiting each section	11	23	18	13	**Total for week** 65

BOOSTING YOUR HABITATS

While natural habitats can be very rich in wildlife and natural diversity, gardens often lack the space that some of the larger species require. Fortunately, though, our gardens can provide their own set of rich pickings, often in the leaner seasons of winter and early spring, when natural food sources are scarce. By planning your garden carefully, you can provide hibernation and nesting sites and a year-round supply of food. You'll give many species a real boost and, in turn, your garden will also flourish, with natural predators promptly getting rid of any pests.

Left: *A habitat stack is the ultimate in purpose-built accommodation for a range of garden creatures, and is great fun to make.*

Above: *While most butterflies are happy to visit garden flowers for food, a butterfly feeder is a great way to see them close up.*

Above: *Birds naturally suffer food shortages in the winter months. They can be boosted by providing food supplements at this time.*

Above: *Standing deadwood is an extremely important home for many species, while for others it provides shelter or hunting grounds.*

HELPING NATURE

By giving nature a helping hand, your garden can become a vital refuge for many species that have been edged out of their natural habitats. You don't need to have a big garden to make a difference, but understanding the needs of these creatures, and why they are in decline elsewhere, is the first step towards helping them. Often only a few minor changes to the way that you look after your garden will be needed, although in time you might find you want to help as many species as you can.

Above: *Many birds naturally nest in holes in dead trees, but our preoccupation with removing these leaves them in short supply.*

INDIVIDUAL RESPONSIBILITY

All places on Earth support life, from the driest deserts to the coldest mountain peaks. What marks out these extremes is that they are hostile to all but a few species, where the balance of nature has been pushed in their favour. In other habitats, such as woodland, wetland or grassland, the climate is more hospitable and so, in time, more species find a home there. The richer a habitat becomes, the more complex the relationships and interrelationships between species are, and, while they are constantly changing, there is a balance that favours a multitude of life forms.

When we interfere with nature to suit our own needs, whether through farming or industrial and urban development, we often make a habitat less hospitable than it was for many species, and they are left either hungry, homeless or, frequently, both. Of course this is the result of a collective, social action and can seem beyond our individual control. A garden, however, is the one aspect of nature over which you can have some control, and by making it more attractive to the needs of wildlife you can help reverse this general decline in natural habitats.

HABITAT DECLINE

Almost all of our natural habitats have experienced some form of decline in the last few centuries. Quite simply, there are more human beings now than ever before, and this burgeoning population has taken an immense toll on the planet's natural resources. That's why even parks, railways and green roadsides stretching into the centres of towns and cities are so important.

These isolated patches of habitat – or *refugia* as they are more properly called – are precious and, in many cases, highly threatened. Many rural creatures, such as foxes and badgers, frequently visit or even live in towns, and some former woodland birds, such as blackbirds, are among the easiest ones to see. This is because there are elements within the urban landscape that can provide what they need to live, feed and breed. Recognizing what these elements are, and recreating them in the garden is, of course, a key to reversing the decline of some of these creatures.

INTENSIVE FARMING

People living in rural areas have often seen great changes to the landscape, as the need to feed ever more of us has led to an intensification of agriculture. This often involves the use of pesticides to kill crop pests, but pests, however inconvenient to farmers, are a part of the food chain. There will thus be many other creatures that are affected by their absence, and pesticides also usually kill other creatures that aren't damaging the crops. In addition, the need to increase efficiency in harvesting crops has meant that a widespread use of herbicides has removed many common wildflower species, which are now often threatened with extinction or marginalized to roadsides and hedge bottoms. Their decline has wrought its toll on creatures that used them as a food supply, many of whom are now also threatened.

Many creatures that have moved into towns have done so because these changes wrought in the countryside have forced them to seek richer pickings elsewhere. Gardens are essentially a little bit of countryside within a city or town, and the rich and varied landscape they provide can be an excellent source of food and shelter

Left: *Derelict buildings are often the ideal place for birds, such as barn owls, to make nests. Renovation of these buildings leaves them without ideal nesting sites.*

Above: *Poppies were once a familiar sight among grain crops in Europe before herbicides were widely used. They benefited from the yearly disturbance of the soil and in turn benefited the insect species that visited them.*

Right: *Intensification of agriculture has led to extensive tracts of land where few wildflowers now grow. These habitats are consequently poorer in species and are described as being "denuded".*

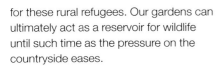

for these rural refugees. Our gardens can ultimately act as a reservoir for wildlife until such time as the pressure on the countryside eases.

INDUSTRIALIZATION AND URBANIZATION

It is a strange irony that, in some cases, a new housing development can actually improve the lot of wildlife by replacing sterile fields with a mosaic of garden diversity. These spaces often have fewer pesticide residues and, in many cases, the occupants actively encourage wild species by providing food. The buildings can provide shelter and nesting places, and the total number of species, as well as their abundance, rises.

Of course the story is not always one of success and, for larger species, or species needing large amounts of open space, cities may be as inhospitable as a desert. The added pollution that urban and industrial development causes will also play its role in the decline of some species. There are also more predators, such as cats, and an increased chance of disease spreading as increasing numbers of a species come into contact with each other. It is a mixed picture, and one for which there is no wonder cure. All we can do as gardeners is to improve our own small patch.

GARDEN AID

Your garden provides the three most crucial elements required by wildlife – food, water and shelter – and planning your garden around these ingredients is absolutely essential. Domestic gardens can actually provide richer wildlife habitats and greater biodiversity than many more rural areas, and recent research has shown that while species are disappearing from the countryside at an alarming rate, there has been a corresponding rise in wildlife diversity in gardens. By creating a valuable habitat, you can attract wildlife to even the smallest area.

Many species find urban gardens to their liking but cannot find suitable nesting sites. Those that nest in holes in trees can be given bird boxes, as can some of the burrowing creatures. Piles of logs and stones mean that some visitors will stay and, by planting the right types of plants, you can provide for their long-term needs. Remember that natural habitats are diverse, so if your garden has room for only one tree, make sure it is different to those in surrounding gardens, thereby making the wider habitat

Right: *The skylark was once common in agricultural lands. Its numbers have plummeted in recent years as its habitat is changed by modern agricultural practice.*

more varied. Try to recreate an analogue (a non-exact but similar copy) of what was there before, using a species found across that region on uncultivated sites, and always decide which wildlife species you intend to target, paying particular attention to its life cycle. Lastly, remember that if every garden were managed with wildlife in mind, the benefits for wildlife would be huge. Your garden is just a small part of a wider habitat and, while it can't provide for every conceivable type of wild creature, it can help those that do live in your area, and as such is a vital resource.

PLANTS AS FOOD

Food is the single most important element that a wildlife garden must provide. Even the smallest window box on an upstairs balcony can act as a feeding station for passing visitors. If creatures find food, one of their most vital necessities is satisfied and they rarely stray too far from it. The real trick is to ensure there is a supply all year round, and the natural seasonality of plants throws up some interesting challenges and ultimately solutions where feeding wildlife is concerned.

Above: *The bright yellow flowers of this* Tagetes *attract many insects, especially bees, which find pollen and nectar there.*

SEASONALITY

When feeding garden wildlife, you need to make sure that you provide food over as long a period as possible, which is why you should try to have some flowering and fruiting plants every month of the year, if possible. Remember, too, that flowers attracting insects will in turn attract predators, such as birds, which may also need to feed.

Winter flowers are useful because they help those few hardy, winter-emerging insects. Late winter is especially important because some species, woken by a mild spell, will not be able to survive until spring without food. You can also stretch the season with annuals – sown in several batches over a few weeks – to add continuity of flower.

FLOWER SHAPE

In general, creatures are attracted to a flower by some reward. Nectar provides an instant source of sugary energy, and pollen is rich in protein. Visiting creatures may eat one or both of them, and the flower is often shaped according to the way in which these visitors feed. As a general rule, flowers that are large and showy, fragrant and nectar-rich, have usually adapted to attract animal pollinators.

These plants, of course, exclude those that have been bred by humans to be large and showy. Double-flowered cultivars often have little in the way of nectar or pollen, and some large-flowered kinds, such as the garden pansy (*Viola* x *wittrockiana*) and its cultivars, have flowers that are so large and slippery that bees cannot easily land on them. In the case of wild pansies, however, they can grip the smaller, more rigid flower and these less showy species are the greatest asset to wildlife.

While there are a number of plant species that attract a whole plethora of creatures, many pollinators have specific preferences as to the types of flower they like to visit. Bees, for example, tend to visit flowers whose petals form a wide surface providing a landing site, whereas butterflies and hummingbirds tend to visit flowers whose petals form a protective cup or tube. Flowers that open at night often target night-flying insects, particularly moths, although certain water lilies (*Nymphaea*)

attract night-flying beetles. Some orchids even attract male moths by mimicking the sexual parts of a female moth, while also producing a pheromone-like scent. It follows that you should choose as wide a variety of flower shapes as you can, and always choose those that most resemble the wild form.

FLOWER SCENT

Bees are usually attracted to flowers that are sweetly fragrant and produce nectar. Moths are also attracted to flowers that have a strong, sweet scent, whereas butterflies generally seem to be guided by the colour of the bloom although they, too, are often attracted to sweet scents, especially that of fallen fruit. Flies are a large and complex group with some, such as hoverflies, preferring open, flat composite blooms or umbels. Some specialized flowers, such as those in the arum family, attract carrion-feeding flies or beetles using a foul odour, although the majority of pollinating beetles are attracted to flowers with a spicy smell.

FLOWER COLOUR

While there is no single best colour for a wildlife plant, certain colours do tend to attract better than others. Remember, though, that the colours that you see may not be the same as those seen by a pollinator. Many pollinators see in ultraviolet, as well as the visible spectrum accessible to us, and the best colours for them may be invisible to us. Bees, for example, often favour flowers that are yellow or blue, but most of them have ultraviolet markings that act like landing lines, guiding the bee in to the nectar.

Hummingbirds almost always favour yellow, orange or red blooms with long necks that bear large amounts of nectar. Butterfly-pollinated flowers are also usually

Left: *Fruit is an ideal food for a whole range of garden wildlife, including insects, some mammals and especially birds that rely on this seasonal bounty to supplement their diets. This often brings conflicts because fruit, such as this raspberry, is as enticing to them as it is to us. Always ensure that there is enough fruit for birds, and protect "your own".*

brightly coloured, with many species being especially fond of purple or red flowers, whereas those used by moths tend to be yellow or white because colour is not important for night visitors. Beetles also seem less enticed by colour, often favouring white, yellow or dull blooms.

FRUIT AND SEED

Once a plant has flowered, gardeners often remove the dead heads before the seed is set. This prolongs flowering and helps them build up food reserves for next season. It also has the unfortunate consequence of removing a valuable food source for wildlife, particularly during the winter. You can help by not deadheading flowers, and if you choose plants that don't eject or drop the seed as soon as it ripens, when it may germinate or rot in the soil, you can ensure a longer-lasting supply of food. Sunflowers (*Helianthus annuus*), many grasses, cardoons (*Cynara cardunculus*) and globe artichokes are good examples of seed heads which persist into winter.

Since berries are a well-known source of nourishment for garden wildlife, berrying trees and shrubs should be grown wherever possible to help birds and mammals. Try to choose a range of species that have berries over a long period. Spring is the time when there are often fewest available; one shrub that does have berries ripening then is the spotted laurel (*Aucuba japonica*).

SACRIFICIAL OFFERINGS

Any serious wildlife gardener will want to make compromises, either by growing plants that are intended to be eaten by visiting creatures, or by encouraging those we normally regard as weeds. Nettles are a prime example of a plant that can support a wide range of wildlife. The stinging nettle (*Urtica dioica*) has a reputation for providing for many species: 100 species have been recorded on it, though it more usually supports up to 40 species. The best results need a patch around 3m² (32sq ft), but if you have a smaller garden you may want to consider growing the related hop (*Humulus lupulus*). Although it supports fewer species, it's an excellent food plant for many butterflies and moths, takes up much less space and doesn't sting. Ultimately, the real message is not to be too upset if a few of your plants are eaten. It is all part of garden ecology, and you should take comfort in the sight of the vast numbers growing healthily.

TOP ORNAMENTAL PLANTS FOR WILDLIFE

The wealth of wildlife found in a garden is determined by the type of plants selected for it. This panel lists some of the best plants to entice wildlife into an area.

	PLANT NAME	WILDLIFE ATTRACTED
TREES AND SHRUBS		
	Butterfly bush (*Buddleja davidii*)	An excellent plant for butterflies and other nectar-feeders, including bees and moths. Can self-seed and become invasive.
	Crab apple (*Malus*, especially *M. sylvestris*)	All apples are excellent for wildlife, especially older specimens with deeply creviced bark. Bees visit the flowers in spring; many species feed on the fruit in autumn.
	Lavender (*Lavandula angustifolia*)	The scented blooms attract many different species of bee and bumblebee, as well as several species of butterflies.
	Rosemary (*Rosmarinus officinalis*)	Almost unrivalled in its ability to attract honeybees, butterflies and hoverflies, all attracted by the copious nectar.
	Rowan (*Sorbus aucuparia*)	The flowers are great for feeding bees and other insects in spring; the berries are consumed by many bird species.
CLIMBERS		
	Golden hop (*Humulus lupulus* 'Aurea')	Caterpillars of several butterflies and moths feed on the foliage, which also attracts other leaf-feeding insects and their predators.
	Honeysuckle (*Lonicera periclymenum*)	Bumblebees, and especially moths, are attracted to the flowers in the evening. Fruit-eating birds take the berries.
HERBACEOUS PLANTS AND ANNUALS		
	Borage (*Borago officinalis*)	Attracts bees when in full bloom due to the abundant nectar. Readily self-seeds and is at home on dry or stony soil, in full sun.
	California poppy (*Eschscholzia californica*)	Attracts hoverflies, bees and bumblebees. Once sown, will self-seed freely around the garden.
	Fern-leaved yarrow (*Achillea filipendula*)	An abundance of hoverflies can be found "nectaring" on the flowers in summer. Also attracts bees and bumblebees.
	Honeywort (*Cerinthe major* 'Purpurascens')	Bees love the blue flowers and congregate in vast numbers. Readily self-seeds, eventually creating large colonies. Loves hot, sunny borders.
	Ice plant (*Sedum spectabile*)	Sedums are loved by butterflies, bees and hoverflies because they're a valuable, late summer source of nectar.
	Michaelmas daisy (*Aster novi-belgii*)	In late summer and autumn, butterflies and bees visit the flowers. Birds also eat the seed after ripening.
	Miss Willmott's ghost (*Eryngium giganteum*)	Extremely attractive to many species of bee and bumblebee during its long flowering period from early to late summer.
	Red valerian (*Centranthus ruber*)	One of the best flowers for butterflies. Rapidly spreads via seed, and can become invasive if not kept in check.
	Summer phlox (*Phlox paniculata*)	Attracts large numbers of various nectar-feeding adult butterflies and moths from late summer to early autumn.
	Sunflower (*Helianthus annuus*)	Birds, such as greenfinches and bullfinches, eat the seeds. Also visited by honeybees and bumblebees when in flower.
	Tall verbena (*Verbena bonariensis*)	Attracts a whole host of butterflies, moths and hummingbirds. It self-seeds easily, with seedlings flowering the same year.
BOG GARDEN AND WATER PLANTS		
	Hemp agrimony (*Eupatorium cannabinum*)	Attracts butterflies and bees. As well as looking fantastic, this plant is one of the best at providing adult butterflies with nectar.
	Water lily (*Nymphaea alba*; one of many superb nymphaeas)	Adult frogs and dragonflies like to bask on the floating oval leaves, which also provide cover for tadpoles that swarm below the surface of the water.

PROVIDING EXTRA FOOD

Cold winters and hot summers can be harsh times for garden creatures for a variety of reasons, and the extremes of temperature often cause intense physical strain to all the creatures within the habitat. Food shortages can occur at such times because insects, fruit or flowers might become scarce during extreme weather. You can help wildlife by providing some extra food, enabling them to endure these lean times.

Above: *A live-food feeder can help a variety of birds that rely on live prey to feed their young. Use them in spring and early summer.*

LIMITED NATURAL FOOD SOURCES

During harsh times of the year, many garden creatures either hibernate or migrate to a better climate and, in so doing, avoid seasonal food shortages. This particularly helps creatures that have specific dietary needs. Hibernating species often emerge in times of relative plenty, but for those species that remain active for the whole year, there are times of extreme hunger, as well as times of surplus. As one group of migratory species leaves the garden to seek food elsewhere, others often migrate into the garden and take their place, so there is no reason why your garden should not be full of life all year round.

The hardest time for most year-round garden residents is during the autumn and winter. Natural foods are still available in the form of berries, seed heads and a few late surviving insects but, as winter really begins to bite, food demands become more

Below: *Natural food, such as these rowan berries (*Sorbus aucuparia*), is always the best option, but seasonal shortages may necessitate additional feeding.*

Above: *Millet bunches hung in the branches of trees and shrubs can help overwintering birds, which will be attracted to the seeds.*

pressing as non-hibernating creatures compete for the dwindling natural resources. Their plight is not helped by the fact that many creatures enlarge their foraging areas, and conflicts may arise when new individuals enter the garden in search of food.

For all the creatures in a garden, additional food can be a lifeline. Not only are you helping the ones that have been present all summer but a wider community, including migratory birds, which may have travelled thousands of miles to be there.

THE BEST FOOD

When deciding which animals to feed, remember that by habituating any wild animal to food in your garden, you are making that place an important part of its territory. Also that all the animals in your garden (save domestic pets) are still wild and, as such, may behave aggressively if

they feel threatened. Even small creatures, such as squirrels, have been known to be highly aggressive once the fear of humans is lost, and you must weigh up the chances of any conflicts before you commence feeding.

As a rule, most mammals are perfectly capable of finding the food they need although some, especially those living in urban areas, will benefit greatly from any additional nourishment that you can provide. If you do decide to supplement their diet, the amount should be limited and targeted for times when their natural food sources are scarce.

Badgers, for example, benefit from additional feeding in the drier months or when the ground is frozen. They are naturally omnivorous and will often eat worms and insects as well as plant material and fruit. They do not hibernate, and the winter can be harsh as food is often scarce. They can be fed small amounts of canned, cereal-based dog food with lightly cooked meat, cheese, peanuts and fruit. Such supplements can help badger cubs survive harsh summer conditions, and it is a good way to entice them to an area where you can watch them. But remember that encouraging badgers into your garden can be a mixed blessing because their natural digging and foraging can be very destructive. And if they extend their territory into your garden, they may come into conflict with domestic pets, and, being large, strong and potentially ferocious, can cause serious injuries.

Some gardeners love to feed squirrels, whereas others resent their habit of stealing bird food and their occasional habit of damaging trees. They do not hibernate, and although they will hide snugly in their drey in really cold spells, they remain active for the whole year. In fact, giving them their own food may actually reduce the incidences of damaging behaviour – since this is usually associated with food shortage – and dissuade them from bothering the bird feeders.

Place food away from windowsills or doorways so as to discourage them from coming into the house, or becoming too familiar with people. No matter how tempting it may be, you should not feed them from the hand or they'll start to associate people with food. And despite their innocent and cuddly look, they can become quite aggressive and inflict a very painful bite. Place their feeding stations away from those for the birds, and consider using a purpose-made squirrel feeder that will not attract birds.

Hedgehogs are one garden visitor that few of us have any qualms about feeding, being non-aggressive, beneficial and the perfect guest. They have a varied diet, and you can encourage them to visit by providing them with dog food mixed with biscuits, or even by providing a specialist dried hedgehog food (any food should always be accompanied by fresh drinking water). While they do hibernate in winter, they are active when the conditions are mild enough to favour their prey – insects, slugs and other invertebrates – and you should only stop feeding them when it is really cold.

WHEN TO FEED WILDLIFE

Winter is the best time to feed because that's when food is scarce. Many mammals that live in gardens all year round are omnivores, and extra food is a good way of ensuring that they are healthy for the following spring. Remember that many birds and some smaller mammals principally visit gardens in the winter to exploit the diversity of food available in this varied habitat.

Above: *A simple butterfly feeder made from a wooden frame contains a sponge soaked with sugar water to tempt insects to feed.*

MAKING A BUTTERFLY FEEDER

1 *Butterflies normally find enough food in flowers, but they will readily feast on ripe fruit and fruit juices.*

2 *Suspend a shallow dish on thin chains and place a range of chopped fruit pieces in the dish.*

3 *To prevent drying out in warm weather, soak the fruit in some fruit juice to keep it moist and release the sugars.*

Gardens are often quieter in the colder months, also making them an ideal retreat. Take stock of what is visiting and feed accordingly.

Spring is a time of seeming plenty but, for many creatures, it can be a hungry gap. While everything is stirring into life, many creatures start their annual cycle of breeding and raising young, adding to the demands of collecting food. Remember that if you have been feeding creatures through winter, more of them survive and demands on natural sources may be temporarily excessive. Keep feeding through spring, judging the demand and reducing the amounts as conditions improve.

Summer is the time when you should provide very little food, except to try to attract more interesting species. Butterflies are best provided with flower nectar, but can be encouraged to visit a purpose-made feeder.

Autumn sees the whole cycle recommence. Gradually reintroduce feeding for your active winter residents, but don't forget about the hibernating species as they need to build up their strength for the coming winter too.

PROVIDING EXTRA FOOD

Whilst wild animals are instinctively very adept at finding food from natural sources, they might well appreciate a bit of help, especially in the winter months.

Pet food Providing a small amount of pet food mixed with water is often an ideal supplement for hedgehogs, foxes and badgers, etc. Only leave a small amount, removing and replacing it daily so that it doesn't go off.

Live food Some species only ever take live food and, while this is difficult to provide in the case of larger animals, small garden visitors, such as songbirds, relish this valuable supplement. Mealworms are ideal and are easily purchased.

Leftovers Kitchen leftovers, such as cake, cooked rice or other natural food items, are generally fine for most wildlife species. Fat drawn from roasted or grilled (broiled) meat is excellent. Avoid any spicy, salty foods, or items that have gone off.

Bought items These include peanuts, raisins and purpose-made foodstuffs formulated for particular species. The latter are usually excellent but can be quite costly. However, they are designed for specific dietary needs and do save a lot of time.

Hedgehog food

Mealworms

Cooked rice

Peanuts and raisins

BIRD FEEDERS

Even a well-stocked garden can be a harsh and unforgiving place for wildlife as the winter draws in. Late autumn marks the time when many birds will visit your garden, seeking extra supplies of food. These birds are welcome visitors, since they add much-needed life and colour as the days grow darker. But feeding can be beneficial throughout the year, especially in spring when the young are born and adults must find even more food to feed their growing families.

Above: *Small perching birds are able to take advantage of hanging bird feeders, safe from competition from larger birds.*

WHY BIRDS NEED EXTRA FOOD

By supplementing bird diets with extra food, you are arguably maintaining a falsely high population of birds in your garden but this, in turn, helps some species to survive when their natural habitats have disappeared. It is therefore important that you keep feeding once you have started because the birds will soon come to depend on it. By choosing the right foods, and offering them in different bird feeders around the garden, you can attract a wide range of species.

POSITIONING BIRD FEEDERS

Different species of birds have different feeding habits. Hanging food is ideal for members of the tit family, placed high enough up so that cats can't get at it. If the food is too exposed, however, the birds may be in danger from sparrowhawks, unless there is nearby cover, such as trees and hedges. Avoid placing feeders near bird boxes because the numbers of attracted birds can put off nesting parents.

The bird tables sold in many garden centres are frequently more ornamental than functional, but have the benefit of being off the ground, thereby reducing the chances of other foraging animals, such as mice and rats, getting at the food. A bird table with a roof can help to keep rain off, but is not essential. The simplest design is usually the best, and often proves to be the easiest to clean and maintain.

Some birds readily forage on the ground, and a few actually prefer this. Putting food on the lawn – away from shrubs that can be hiding places for predators – will favour these species. Don't put too much out at once because this encourages rats and mice, and avoid using the same patch repeatedly so as to reduce the risk of disease.

DRINKING SUPPLY

Maintain a reasonably clean water supply at all times, ideally in shallow containers for the birds to use for bathing as well as drinking. Never add salt or any chemicals to the water, even if there is a tendency for it to turn green. If it does, change the water regularly, cleaning the container and placing it out of direct sunlight wherever possible. A garden pond with shallow areas can also be useful, but a bird bath has the advantage that you can change the water regularly to ensure that the risk of disease is minimized. Water is especially welcome on a cold, frosty morning when natural supplies may be frozen. If a bird bath is on the ground, other animals, such as hedgehogs, can also drink from it.

GIVE BIRDS VARIETY

Birds, like many wild creatures, enjoy a range of food, much of which is easy to obtain. In certain cases this can be leftovers, although this can be a variable commodity so don't solely rely on it. Seed, such as black sunflower seed, peanuts or the wild seed mixes sold for the purpose, is useful and can easily be supplemented with such items as pinhead oatmeal or porridge oats, sultanas, shredded suet and toasted breadcrumbs. Other popular items for the bird table include canned sweetcorn and fresh fruit, broken (not cut) into pieces.

The more different food types can be left in different positions and types of feeder, the better. Whole peanuts are best avoided

---

DIFFERENT FEEDERS

By using a wide range of bird feeders, you can provide a greater variety of food items. In doing this, you will increase the chances of more species visiting your garden.

Bird feeder table – spring Bird tables are excellent for a range of larger birds that perch or stand in order to eat their food.

Buzzard table Not really an option for most gardens, although congregating birds often attract predatory birds that may feed on them.

Glass/plastic feeder – spring Glass or plastic feeders are usually filled with mixed seed, made accessible through a series of small hoppers in the side.

Half a coconut – spring (or any time) A coconut sliced in two is an excellent way of providing food for small, clinging birds. Can be filled with suet or seeds.

Squirrel-proof feeder To discourage squirrels, make bird food inaccessible. This feeder has a cage to protect the seed.

Wire feeder – spring Wire feeders are mostly for peanuts, and are useful because they prevent birds from choking on whole nuts.

Buzzard table

Glass feeder

Half a coconut

Squirrel-proof feeder

MAKING A BIRD FEEDING STATION

1 *Start by choosing a range of glass/plastic, wire, cage and open feeders that will support a wide variety of bird species.*

2 *Either use an existing dead tree or insert a couple of large branches firmly into the ground to act as supports for your feeders.*

3 *Securely attach the feeders to the branches using thin, pliable wire, twisted around the branches or old branch stumps.*

4 *Once you have hung the feeders, check to see which get used. If some remain unused, replace them with more popular types.*

during the nesting season because they can choke young nestlings. They should be chopped, if left on a table, or placed in a mesh peanut feeder from which adult birds can take only small fragments. Always avoid using any form of dried food, such as uncooked rice or dried bread, because this will swell in a bird's stomach and can even be fatal.

Some birds, robins in particular, can benefit from supplements of live food, such as mealworms, particularly during the late winter period when food is scarce and their breeding cycle commences. The worms can easily be purchased from pet shops or by mail order, and can be placed on tables or in specialist feeders. Whatever you decide to place out for the birds, make

sure that you stick to natural foods, rather than chemically altered or processed items, such as margarine.

KEEP IT FRESH AND CLEAN
Only leave out as much food as can be consumed in a day or two, and never allow food or feeding debris to accumulate because it can rapidly spread disease.

DIFFERENT TYPES OF FOOD/SEED
The variety of seed and other food supplements available for birds has increased vastly in the last few years and all of these have their own merits and will be preferred by different species, according to their dietary and feeding preferences.

Black sunflower seed More commonly known as the "oil sunflower", this seed – as its name suggests – is rich in oil and ideal for winter-feeding a range of garden birds.

Coconut fat Half coconuts are ideal for filling with a mixture of suet – rendered animal fat – seed and other dried foodstuffs that suit clinging feeders such as tits.

Dried mealworms These freeze-dried grubs are an excellent source of protein for carnivorous birds.

Fat ball A ball of suet into which other dried foodstuffs have been incorporated. It is usually hung in nets or special feeders.

Fruit suet treats Mainly for bird tables or hanging feeders, this suet-based cake is best made with moist, dried fruit and peanut granules, and is popular with larger birds.

Grain Consists of any commercially grown crops in the grass family, including wheat, millet, maize and oats.

Mixed seed Consists of various seed types for a wide range of birds, and is often of variable quality.

Niger Sometimes called thistle seed, this tiny black birdseed, cultivated in Asia and Africa, is high in calories and oil content, and is quickly devoured, especially by finches.

Scraps A variable commodity, and best included only as extra titbits. Avoid dried foodstuffs that can swell in the stomach; also spicy or over-processed items.

Striped sunflower seed Has a lower oil content than the black variety, and is useful in the spring when natural foods become more abundant.

Suet cake This block type of suet food is used on a table, and contains a seed mix that provides a balanced diet for many species. It is ideal for feeding birds when you are away, although the fat content can sometimes attract scavenging mammals, such as rats, to a table.

Black sunflower seed

Fat ball

Fruit suet treats

Mixed seed

Niger

Suet cake

FEEDING BENEFICIAL CREATURES

In any garden, pests will proliferate if we don't maintain the balance of nature. But for every pest, a natural predator exists. By encouraging these predators, unwanted species can be controlled, but be prepared to give the predators a helping hand to get them started. If pest numbers get too high, the predators might not easily control them. By giving predators an early boost, you can improve their chances of reducing the pests.

Above: *Flowers such as this aubretia are useful for attracting early aphids that in turn allow predator numbers to increase.*

WHY FEED BENEFICIAL CREATURES?

The balance of nature is a cycle whereby different populations rise and fall in direct relationship to the abundance of food. Creatures that hunt widely for dispersed food will need a large territory to satisfy their needs, and creatures that feed on more abundant species will, of course, become more abundant themselves. In the garden, we want to ensure that certain creatures are present to control predators, and if we can feed them, they are more likely to flourish and stay where we want them.

Many beneficial species can be given a boost by providing some form of supplementary feeding to increase their numbers early in the year, or quite simply to attract them to the garden. Once there, they are able to begin eating pests, and feeding

Below: *Hedgehogs are excellent pest-controlling animals, and can benefit from a supplement of dried mixed seed and wax-worms in the spring.*

them means that seasonal fluctuations in their numbers can be avoided. In a small, enclosed garden, for example, it would be quite easy for a hedgehog to be trapped and run out of food. By feeding it, you help it through hungry periods and maintain its useful presence. Equally, some insects, such as ladybirds, can be helped with an artificial food supplement hung in the garden in a special feeder. It attracts and nourishes these useful beetles, and enables them to maintain a high population early in the season. By feeding them, you are maintaining an artificially high number of these useful creatures, and consequently will reduce numbers of their prey.

Many beneficial insects have different needs depending upon their life stage, and a surprising number eat pests when they are larvae but are partly or wholly vegetarian as adults. Plants can be chosen to feed the adults and even to attract their (or their offspring's) prey. To maintain a variety of beneficial insects, then, you will need to make provisions for all these stages. The simplest approach is to maintain a diverse

habitat. The more varied your garden is, the more species you will maintain and ultimately, the more beneficial creatures there will be.

Finally, note that the term "beneficial creature" is really only of particular relevance to gardeners. All garden creatures have some benefit, and it is up to us to recognize what these are, and to seek a balance, according to the needs of our own garden.

FOOD SOURCES

Each species of beneficial insect has its own particular diet, and that may change according to availability or which life stage it is passing through. Some, such as lacewings or hedgehogs, are generalists, feeding on several different species, while others, like hoverfly maggots, exclusively eat aphids and therefore have a specialized diet.

In the case of more general feeders, the garden often contains several alternative kinds of prey. This, of course, increases the chance that the hunters will stay in the garden and perhaps breed there. Specialists, on the other hand, such as ladybirds, will fly away if there are not enough small, soft-bodied insects – such as aphids and scale insects – to support them and, especially, their voracious larvae.

It is a simple fact of life. If you want to encourage predators to take up residence then you first have to encourage their prey – the very pests you want to get rid of.

TOLERATING SOME DAMAGE

While pests sometimes eat more of our garden plants than we would like, a healthy garden has a balanced ecosystem, with severe outbreaks of problem creatures being mercifully rare. As a wildlife gardener, you must learn to accept some level of damage to many of your plants. A few holes in some of the leaves or flowers won't make

MAKING A LADYBIRD FEEDER

1 Ladybird feeders are relatively simple constructions, consisting of a length of bamboo cut at angles so there is a "long side", some ordinary garden twine and a feeding compound.

2 Slightly moisten the food block (bought from a specialist supplier) and break it up so that it forms a spreadable paste, by lightly working it between your fingers until soft.

3 Smear the mixture on to the inside of the feeder, putting it on the shorter side that will hang lowermost on the feeder. Spread it evenly on the bottom and sides of the inside surface.

4 Hang the feeder on a piece of twine with the long side uppermost to keep out the rain and preserve the food paste. Hang it in light shade in an out-of-the-way corner.

them less attractive or useful. Don't be blinded by advertisements and their promise of blemish-free plants. Nature isn't like that.

PLANTING TO ATTRACT "BENEFICIALS"

Many flowering plants will attract the vegetarian adults of beneficial insects whose larvae are predators of pests. The adults need to feed upon the nectar or pollen, and attracting them is a vital first step in encouraging them to mate and lay eggs so that the larvae can start eating the pests. The poached egg plant (Limnanthes douglasii) attracts large numbers of hoverflies, and various parasitoid wasps will be attracted if you plant white alyssum (Lobularia maritima). Both hoverflies and wasps are dependent on proteins from pollen and carbohydrates from nectar because of their active lifestyle, and to form their eggs.

Korean licorice mint (Agastache), feverfew (Tanacetum parthenium), pot marigold (Calendula officinalis) and yarrow (Achillea millefolium) are also excellent at attracting a wide range of creatures, including the "beneficials". The best results are gained when you plant them on the edges of a border or bed in a sunny spot.

Ladybirds and some other beneficial insects will even lay their eggs on some plant species in the absence of aphids. The best plants for such egg-laying are stinging nettles (Urtica dioica), ivy (Hedera), gorse (Ulex) and hawthorn (Crataegus), as well as umbelliferous herbs such as angelica, chervil (Anthriscus cerefolium), parsley (Petroselinum) or coriander (Coriandrum).

Other plants are valuable because they harbour pests, and act as a larder for predators. Nasturtium (Tropaeolum majus) is one such example that is practically guaranteed to attract aphids before the surrounding plants. Aubretia (Aubrieta) and nettles are especially useful because they attract some of the earliest aphids, and enable the army of "beneficials" to get an early season feed. Remember also that many bird species eat aphids or larger pests, such as caterpillars, and by planting seed-bearing annuals, native trees and hedges you can enjoy the benefit of their efforts in spring and summer.

Finally, don't be in too much of a rush to tidy the garden in early winter. Excessive trimming of hedges and cutting back of herbaceous plants means that there will be nowhere for the beneficial insects to shelter. Even when you do clear up, don't burn any garden waste unless it is diseased because it may carry the eggs and pupae of overwintering beneficial insects.

Below: The white alyssum, Lobularia maritima, is a superb plant for attracting highly beneficial parasitic wasp species that flock to feed on the flowers.

PROVIDING NATURAL SHELTER

Shelter is essential if wildlife is to hide from the elements and predators, and many creatures also need cover for nesting. There are many different types of natural shelter, and some can easily be recreated in the garden. The best kinds are those made of natural materials, especially if they are the by-products of other garden tasks, since they will blend in with the surroundings and will not cost you anything.

Above: *A pile of logs is a great hiding or sheltering place for many creatures, especially if it is situated near a food source.*

THE BEST KINDS OF SHELTER

Top of the list come natural forms of shelter. Every part of most natural habitats supports a range of creatures, many of which have specific adaptations enabling them to live there. Fortunately, many of the natural shelters found in the wild can be recreated in the garden.

The first thing to remember is that decay is an essential natural process by which nutrients are cycled and recycled thanks to a whole host of species. If your garden contains a lot of plants, then you will be familiar with the amounts of green waste produced over the year, with one of the most useful habitat-forming materials being deadwood. It provides food and shelter for hundreds of species, including many that eat it or live within its confines. In addition, thicker branches may be used to create specific habitats such as log piles or log pyramids. Building a log pile is quick and easy, and you can make a real five-star habitat by carefully constructing your pile.

LOG PILES

If you have a limited amount of space, just pile up a few old logs or stumps, and partially cover them with leaves and smaller brushwood in an out-of-the-way corner. If you have enough space, though, you could consider making a log-pile hotel. Start by making the base out of six or eight large, untreated logs, ideally with the bark still on, 1.8–3m (6–10ft) long and 10–15cm (4–6in) in diameter. Stack them so that they are stable, with a variety of runways and spaces between to allow access for larger creatures. Once you have finished the base, add large branches criss-crossed to cover the logs. Continue adding more branches of a gradually smaller diameter so that you end up with a domed structure about 1.2–1.5m (4–5ft) high. If you want a smaller pile, just reduce the dimensions accordingly, but try to keep the thickness of the base logs the same. Ideally you should place your log pile between two habitats, and make sure that at least half of it receives direct sunlight.

You can enhance the pile by adding piles of flat stones along the edges to serve as basking sites and tight crevices, and planting some native plants around it to soften its appearance. Remember not to destroy fruiting bodies of toadstools that spring up around the pile as they often harbour dozens of rare insects.

OTHER HABITATS

Standing deadwood is another important habitat that, if it cannot be left on the tree, can be recreated. You can recreate some of its benefits by making a log pyramid. Stand a series of logs of varying thickness in a hole, dug some 30–45cm (12–18in) deep. Leave from one-third to one-half their lengths out of the ground. Fill in around them with the excavated soil, and pile this higher on one side. Plant some native plants around it to soften its appearance, and give additional shelter for other wildlife. Try drilling holes in some of the logs to provide homes for solitary bees.

Left: *Tree bark naturally becomes fissured and gnarled, creating many tiny nooks and crannies for small creatures to hide in.*

Above: *Vegetation is always an excellent source of shelter. A dense planting of grasses and flowers will protect many creatures.*

TIPS ON PROVIDING SHELTER

Providing shelter is an essential part of any wildlife garden and can be done quite simply using a range of naturally occurring materials that are readily available.

Plant a variety of shrubs, trees and herbaceous plants Some bird species may find them attractive as nesting sites, but even if they nest elsewhere, these plants will attract birds, albeit for only a few minutes.

Large evergreen shrubs They provide winter shelter for many species. Low-growing evergreen plants are ideal for small animals, such as shrews, which stay active all year round.

Grass cuttings Left in heaps in a sunny spot, these attract reptiles, such as grass snakes, which use them for egg-laying or as a warm hideout on cool nights.

Mounds Use unwanted rubble to build a stone and earth mound – great for hibernating newts and lizards. Smear yogurt on the rocks to encourage lichens.

Old logs Drill holes in these for solitary bees or place by a pond for an egg-laying site for some dragonflies. Many creatures will hide inside the decaying wood.

Rocks and wood These provide shelter for ground-dwelling species, including toads and voles, which enjoy hiding in small crevices or under decaying logs or stumps. A length of drain or tubular material provides protection from predators and the weather.

Cotoneaster

Old logs

Rocks

Wood

Herbaceous plants are ideal for close planting and provide plenty of cover. This type of planting is helpful to a variety of species, including many insects as well as the creatures that prey upon them, such as shrews and hedgehogs. If the ground is thickly covered with plants, the insect numbers increase, and the plant debris makes useful hibernation sites.

Lawns can also be an excellent habitat, particularly when left to grow long. Many animals, including insects, spiders, toads, frogs, slow worms and small mammals, find cover in areas of long grass throughout the summer months. The grass gives them places to feed, hide from predators and nest. Wait until midwinter before you cut the grass, raking off cuttings and composting them. To add interest, you can try planting late flowering grassland plants in these areas.

Water and poolside planting provides good habitats for aquatic creatures, and also cover for any creatures that are approaching and leaving the pool. If you don't have space for a pond, provide a birdbath or shallow pool, and keep it filled all year round, letting birds drink there and restore their plumage.

Mulch and litter layers covering soil serve as a protected habitat for ground-dwelling creatures, including larger insects, amphibians and some reptiles, which can sometimes be seen basking on mulched surfaces. These are unable to thrive if the soil is regularly cultivated. While cultivating the soil has obvious advantages in terms of growing certain plants, leaving some areas undisturbed has tremendous benefits for these creatures, many of which are useful predators. Not cultivating all your ground at once, and leaving undisturbed areas as wildlife refuges is the best solution, although a hedge bottom or well-mulched shrub border is very useful.

All trees and shrubs are also very beneficial, and support a rich population of invertebrates and larger animals. Evergreen plants are especially good for providing cover all year, and provide all-round structure in the garden. Climbers are a favourite nesting site because the supporting wall on one side and camouflage of leaves on the other provides safe protection. Remember to include some thorny shrubs, such as barberry, pyracantha, mahonia and roses, which offer hide-aways and nesting sites.

MAKING A LOG PILE

1 Begin by digging out a shallow pit to a depth of around 30cm (1ft) in a shady spot where creatures will not be disturbed, preferably in a shrub bed or under a tree.

2 It is best to use a range of logs that are different ages. Arrange some of them in the pit, putting the thickest ones at the base and building up with smaller ones.

3 Fill the spaces between the logs with the excavated soil and pile some up around the edges. Wood chips could also be used.

4 Cover the finished pile in leaves, twigs and old litter. You could plant ferns or ivies to soften the appearance of the log pile.

CONSTRUCTING EXTRA SHELTERS

We cannot pick and choose which creatures enter our gardens – they choose us – but we can definitely maximize the possibilities and opportunities for them. The best policy is to provide shelter for those creatures that you know are nearby. Find out what is in your area by talking to neighbours or asking local wildlife groups; provide the appropriate accommodation and wait to see if those creatures take up residence.

Above: *A bat box in a sheltered, shady spot in the garden can act as a temporary resting place for these night-flying predators.*

NESTING AND BIRD BOXES

It is never the wrong time to create nesting places, and even if it's not immediately used by the intended creature, it will almost certainly be used by some form of wildlife. Remember that nest boxes may be used by one species at a certain time of year, and by another in a different season. Many summer roosting or nest boxes, for example, are used as winter hibernacula (hibernating sites), being vacated in early spring before the summer residents return.

As many gardens lack natural types of shelter for wildlife, the best way to help creatures is to provide them with an artificial substitute. There are many types to choose from that can either be bought ready made or created at home. Over time, and as your

Below: *A butterfly roosting house provides safe, dry shelter for these beautiful insects. Put verbena or buddleja inside to attract them.*

garden habitat improves and diversifies, you may need to increase their numbers according to the needs of the wildlife.

The majority of shelters are essentially boxes mimicking natural crevices in trees that have often disappeared due to human management of forests and woodlands. The relative importance of cavities and crevices varies according to which country you are in. The total number of Australian animals that use tree hollows, for example, is around three times greater than in North America, and twice as great as in South Africa. In situations where hollows are important but in short supply, expect many species to try and take up residence in the boxes provided. The greater the range of sizes and shapes of these artificial crevices, the greater the number of species that might reside in your garden.

CUSTOM-MADE SHELTERS

Until recently, if someone talked about providing boxes in the garden, they'd almost certainly have been thinking of birds. The last few years, however, has seen a surge in

Above: *A toad house placed near water can be an ideal sheltering spot for these useful garden amphibians in daylight hours. Hide it among vegetation to keep it cool.*

interest in the provision of homes for other creatures, and gardeners are now providing breeding and shelter sites for a wide range of animals, including insects, amphibians and mammals. Examples include nest boxes for mason bees, bumblebees, bats and hedgehogs, as well as shelters for ladybirds, lacewings and other insects. Some gardeners prefer the designed look of commercially produced shelters and nest boxes but, if your budget is tight, or you prefer the more rustic look, you can easily make your own.

DIY

While an ever-expanding array of nest boxes is now available, most are very easy to make and require only the simplest tools and equipment. All the facilities found in the more expensive shelters and nest boxes can be provided in other ways. For example, a good hibernating or breeding shelter for hedgehogs can be made by piling up dry leaves in a quiet corner, and leaning a sheet of plywood over it to keep off the worst of the rain.

Shelter for insects and other invertebrates can be made in dozens of simple ways, for example by drilling holes of different sizes into a piece of hardwood and leaving it undisturbed in a sunny corner of the garden, or try a bundle of hollow stems or canes, placed in a pipe, and left in a quiet hot spot. Minimum disturbance is essential.

LACEWING HOTELS

One of the easiest shelters to make is a lacewing "hotel", helping these creatures – whose larvae are voracious predators of aphids – hibernate in large numbers, ensuring that there are always plenty of them. From late summer on they are looking for shelter for the coming cooler months.

Simply cut the base off a large plastic drinks bottle using a pair of scissors, and keep the lid on. Roll up a length of about 1m (3½ft) of corrugated cardboard so it fits loosely inside the bottle, and trim so that it doesn't poke out. Then push a piece of wire through the bottle sides and across the bottom to stop the cardboard falling out, and bend the ends round to keep it in place. Now hang it up using a piece of strong string tied around the neck of the bottle, and place it in a tree, shrub, hedge, or against a fence covered by climbing plants. A particularly good site is near an outside light or lit window. To help attract visitors, spray the cardboard with a widely available pheromone liquid. You can put

Above: *This lacewing hotel is a hibernation site for these useful garden predators. It can be taken down and stored in a shed over winter and put out again in spring.*

the "hotel" in a shed from mid-autumn to late winter in frosty areas, otherwise leave it alone.

BEE BOXES

Solitary bee boxes are also easy to make and can be very simply made, involving nothing more than a few canes or hollow stems. If you are using bamboo canes, you will need six or seven approximately 6–10mm (¼–⅜in) wide; cut them into pieces about 15cm (6in) long, avoiding any knots in the cane. Then gather them into a circular bundle, and tie them firmly together in two places with wire, garden

Above: *Bat boxes fixed to trees should be placed in threes on all but the sunniest side, because bats change their roosting preferences through the year.*

string or twine, twisting it tight. Alternatively, put them inside an old can. Hang the bundle at about eye-level at a slight angle so that the entrance holes are slightly lower than the opposite end, in a sheltered, sunny spot, for example under the eaves of a garden shed.

Lastly, remember that this construct may well become home for other unexpected residents. Nature is no respecter of your intentions. If another creature wants to live there, it will. Some bumblebees, for example, will nest in bird boxes and, although they are very docile, may sting if threatened, so never evict any residents.

MAKING A SOLITARY BEE NESTING BOX

1 *Using an old can (making sure there are no sharp edges) or similar food container, paint the outside to help prevent rusting in wet weather as it ages.*

2 *Cut some old bamboo canes to the approximate length of the can using a fine-toothed saw or a pair of very sharp secateurs. Discard any split ones.*

3 *Place the cut canes into the can and pack them in. Use a hammer to bang the last few in tightly, thereby avoiding glue, which would produce fumes.*

4 *Place the finished can in a sheltered, sunny spot, at around eye level and at a slight angle, so that the open end is just lower than the closed end.*

BIRD BOXES

In recent years, bird boxes have become a familiar sight in many gardens, chiefly because people like to see birds raising their young. Boxes have been extremely valuable for many birds because they provide alternative, artificial nesting sites for many species, but before you erect one, decide what kind of bird you are trying to help. Different birds have different needs. Choosing the wrong type of box or putting it up in an inappropriate place may mean that it is not used.

Above: *The sight of a bird feeding a brood of chicks, such as these common redstarts, is a wonderfully rewarding sight in a garden.*

WHICH BOXES TO CHOOSE

If bird boxes are to be used immediately, they need to be in place by the start of the breeding season, and that usually means late winter. However, there is never a wrong time of year to put one up, and they often provide winter shelter. A box so used is more likely to be used again next season.

Recent years have seen an explosion in the range of commercially produced bird boxes, and numerous designs are now available to suit a range of garden birds from martins and swifts, tawny owls and wrens, to starlings, sparrows and tits. Small-scale specialist producers of bird boxes can be found on the Internet.

Only trust solid, simple designs and beware fussy, ornate ones because they're often useless. If you are buying a box it needs to be waterproof, but it must have a drainage hole in the bottom to allow any water that blows or seeps in to escape. If there's any standing water, it will make the box cold, might lead to disease, and will

DIFFERENT TYPES OF BIRD BOXES

There is no standard, accurate design for a bird box. What birds really need is a secure and weatherproof home, safe from predators.

Do remember, though, that different bird species have different preferences regarding the type and location of a box.

With a front hole The size and shape of the hole varies with the species you intend attracting. Small birds such as tits need round holes around 2.8cm (1⅛) wide whereas larger birds like woodpeckers need rectangular holes that are 6cm (2¼in) or more.

With an open face Many birds, including European robins, wrens, wagtails and thrushes, prefer this design, and the opening width varies accordingly, from 4cm (1½in) for wrens to 12cm (4¾in) for flycatchers and thrushes.

Duck box Usually large and square for attaching to poles sunk in water, keeping predators away. The rectangular entrance is reached via a ramp-like ladder.

Communal box Birds such as house sparrows form communal nests, commonly in the eaves of houses. Modern energy efficiency means that many former nest sites have been sealed off, however, and the house sparrows often have difficulty in breeding. A communal nest box can help these species and is best attached as high as possible on the shady side of a building.

Martin box Swallows and house martins can have difficulty finding nest sites, and the smooth walls of modern buildings often cause nests to fall, sometimes with the young inside. Near roads, vibration caused by heavy vehicles may also shake nests loose. Artificial nests, made of a wood and cement mix, are attached to an artificial overhang and ready for immediate use.

Owl box These vary considerably in their design and are often more of a tube than a box. Smaller owl boxes are used by other large birds as they are often at least three times the size of a standard bird box. While there are many designs, all need a well-drained floor and easy access for cleaning at the end of the season, and are best placed in a large tree in the lower to mid canopy.

Tree creeper box Tree creepers build nests that have contact with the trunks of thick-barked trees such as oak (*Quercus*), alder (*Alnus*), poplar (*Populus*) or pine (*Pinus*), and so the boxes must be open at the back. They are fixed to the tree with wire attached to each side or with wooden blocks and the entrance holes face downward and are located at the side of the box.

Open face box

Duck box

Communal box

Martin box

Owl box

Tree creeper box

MAKING A BIRD BOX

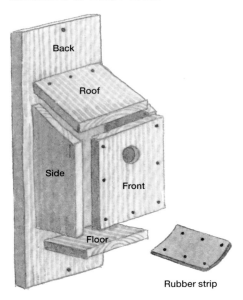

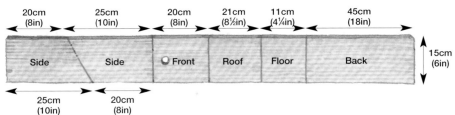

20cm (8in)	25cm (10in)	20cm (8in)	21cm (8½in)	11cm (4¼in)	45cm (18in)
Side	Side	Front	Roof	Floor	Back

25cm (10in) 20cm (8in)

15cm (6in)

Rubber strip

1 *Measure the dimensions and mark them clearly with a soft pencil and a "T" square. Mark the names of each section.*

2 *Cut the pieces using a sharp carpentry saw and put them to one side. Sand off any splintered edges to the wood.*

3 *Carefully screw the sections together. Don't use nails as these can cause the wood to split, allowing water into the box.*

4 *On the front face of the box, make a hole with a large drill bit. Attach the roof, using the rubber strip as a hinge.*

5 *Fix the bird box in the garden, choosing a suitable spot out of direct sun and high enough to be out of reach of predators.*

increase the chances of rotting the box. For the same reason, make sure that the base of the box is inside the sides and not fixed to the bottom or water will seep straight into the bottom. The lid must fit tightly, preferably with a hooked catch to prevent predators, such as squirrels or cats, from getting in and eating the chicks. If a box has a perch under the entrance hole don't buy it because birds will not use it, and it is perfect for hungry (predatory) squirrels to stand on. Lastly, avoid using any boxes that have been heavily treated with preservative. They could prove poisonous to the adults or chicks and, what is more, the fumes will be off-putting to birds.

When you buy bird boxes, make sure that they are accompanied with instructions and other useful information regarding their positioning to maximize the chances of birds taking up residence. The best brands

may also offer advice on how you can improve your garden to suit particular species. Buying a bird box from a reputable supplier is probably the simplest (if most expensive) way to achieve success.

FIXING A BIRD BOX

It is not difficult to fix a bird box, but choosing the right position is important, and it must be fixed securely so that it doesn't fall when occupied. Although boxes can be fixed at 1.8m (6ft) above ground, they can be placed higher than this, and a height of 3.7m (12ft) or more will defeat many predators, as well as preventing overly curious children from investigating.

When positioning a bird box, make sure that it is protected from prevailing cold winds and hot sun, preferably giving it a shady aspect or wall that faces away from the strong midday or afternoon sun. Try to

ensure that the birds have a fairly clear flight path to and from the nest, and try to angle the box slightly downward to help exclude rain. Remember that birds are often territorial and, in most cases, don't like being crowded together. Leave some space between the boxes unless providing for communal species such as sparrows.

MAINTENANCE

Inspect the box in late summer or early autumn, and remove any nesting material or other debris. This helps to remove parasites that otherwise build up and, if you want to make the box attractive for small birds over winter, add some loosely packed clean straw. In late winter, clear the box out again ready for the nesting season. Finally, give the next batch of nesting birds building materials such as string, cloth, wool, dried grass and excess hair from your cat or dog.

HIBERNATION SITES

During winter, many creatures go into a state of suspended animation known as hibernation, usually for several months. They do this to avoid harsh conditions and shortages of food. Many overwintering species (those that do not migrate to avoid the winter) adopt this strategy. Overwintering species choose a wide range of hibernating sites. Many have very specific requirements, and if you provide what's required, you may well see them again next year.

Above: *A rock garden situated next to a pond provides lots of crevices for hibernating animals, including amphibians such as frogs.*

WHAT IS HIBERNATION?

The state of inactivity experienced by many overwintering species is triggered by short day lengths, cold temperatures and scarcity of food. Some larger garden animals hibernate, and most insects do so in response to the shorter days which tell of the approaching winter. Most insects hibernate as eggs or larvae, although a few overwinter as adults. The hibernating animals are quite defenceless at this time and need a secure place to protect them. It is essential, then, that we help these smaller garden occupants, as well as the larger more charismatic creatures.

HOW ANIMALS HIBERNATE

Most insects hibernate as eggs or larvae, emerging as adults in spring or summer. Some species overwinter as adults, and a few, including honeybees and the occasional butterfly, can still be seen flying in mild spells during winter as they forage on winter-flowering plants.

Reptiles, amphibians and insects are all cold-blooded, and must anticipate the onset of cold conditions so as not to be caught out when the temperature drops. They need to find a sheltered, frost-free place to hide and become completely torpid, where they remain until temperatures rise again in spring.

Mammals are different because they generate their own heat to keep themselves warm, getting the energy to do so, and the energy to grow and move about, from their food. They tend to hibernate because food becomes scarce in winter, and they may use up more energy looking for food than is gained from eating what they find. Different mammals have different ways of overcoming the problem, however, and while some react by hibernating, others are active all year round.

MAKING A HABITAT STACK

1 *Place a layer of bricks on to bare ground. Arrange them to provide crevices for animals that like cool, dark places – especially newts.*

2 *Put old pallets on top and stuff them with straw. This offers burrow opportunities for mammals and hibernation sites for invertebrates.*

3 *Place layers of logs and bricks to provide a range of dark, dry recesses for creatures, such as spiders and woodlice, to hide in.*

4 *In the next layer of pallets, roll up sheets of corrugated cardboard, cutting them to the right length. These will encourage lacewings.*

5 *Drill the ends of some of the cut logs to create nest holes for solitary bees and hiding places for other small insects and invertebrates.*

6 *Keep making successive layers, packing old roof tiles with stones to create a drystone wall-type habitat for insects and reptiles.*

7 *There are no real rules about what you can include in your stack. As with all artificial habitats, you should cater primarily for creatures in your own neighbourhood. You can use any materials that you have available to hand, and the finished habitat stack will become a unique and beautiful feature in its own right.*

HELPING HIBERNATING ANIMALS

There are several ways in which you can help hibernating animals. Firstly, don't tidy up any sites too soon, and avoid the urge to dispose of all the organic matter that lies around throughout the year. Many insects hibernate in grass tussocks and hollow, dead plant stems; a late autumn clearance will often devastate their populations. Leave piles of autumn leaves in corners to create hibernation sites for a variety of insects, and avoid raking leaves from borders any later than mid-autumn, so that you avoid disturbing any hibernating creatures.

Nest boxes can be cleared and part-filled with straw in early autumn to help overwintering animals. Nooks and crannies, such as those found in walls, rock piles and elsewhere in the garden, are ideal places for hibernation – don't tidy them.

Artificial homes can also be bought for many species. These will help creatures to survive in greater numbers through the winter. A lacewing box, for example, can increase survival rates for these useful insects – that devour aphids the following spring – from around 5 per cent to as high as 95 per cent.

An alternative to buying artificial lodgings is to make them yourself, using odds and ends from around the house and garden. The ultimate example is a habitat stack, which is a bit like a hibernation city for your garden wildlife, and can incorporate a whole range of hibernation sites in one "multi-storey complex". Many creatures can benefit from such a diverse place, and the whole construction can become a decorative – if eccentric – and interesting feature in your wildlife garden.

Above: *A drystone wall is a wonderful habitat for creatures that make their homes in narrow crevices or use them for shelter. It is also a very attractive ornamental feature.*

DIFFERENT TYPES OF HIBERNATION SITE

The garden can be a great place for wildlife to overwinter in, safely tucked up in their hibernation sites. It is important to know what and where these hibernating creatures are if you want to avoid disturbing them, and vital if you want to provide extra sites for them.

Burrows Some creatures, such as bumblebees, simply burrow down into the soil to avoid the winter weather. Leave some patches of ground uncultivated until spring.

Compost heaps An attractive hiding place for some amphibians and rodents, attracted to the cool, moist conditions. Wait until late winter before moving a heap and disturbing the inhabitants.

Drystone walls Contain a multitude of nooks and crevices, offering safe, secluded shelter for an amazingly diverse array of creatures, including amphibians, reptiles, insects and spiders.

Herbaceous plant stems Leave old plant stems until the following spring to provide many insects with a safe hiding place. Start to clear them away as the weather warms up, but leave on the ground for a few days to let the inhabitants escape.

Insect boxes There is an increasing array available on the market, designed to help garden insects nest and overwinter. You can make your own using common household items such as cans and bamboo stakes.

Leaf piles The perfect place for many species to shelter in. Often rich in overwintering insects and may also contain amphibians, rodents and hedgehogs. Ideally, leave undisturbed through the winter.

Log piles Replicating piles of fallen branches and offering overwintering sites for many amphibians and insects as well as wood-boring beetles, these are excellent and easy features to include in a wildlife garden. Hide them among shrubs for extra cover.

Mulch Often rich in species, such as ground beetles and centipedes, that devour garden pests. They too often hibernate there and, by cultivating the ground in the winter, you can expose and kill them.

Ponds Water is an ideal place to spend winter because the temperature is relatively stable. Most aquatic life does not really hibernate but merely slows down, although male frogs often hibernate in muddy pond bottoms.

Sheds and outbuildings An ideal place for some species, such as butterflies, to spend winter. Any creatures found there are best left until spring.

Standing deadwood Attracts many creatures, especially wood-boring beetles, and will be colonized by numerous fungus species. In searching for grubs, woodpeckers often make holes that may later be occupied by other creatures.

Tree cavities Contain a number of overwintering creatures, such as insects, mammals and even amphibians seeking wind-free shelter. There are few times of the year when such cavities would be empty.

Burrow

Mason bee box

Leaf pile

Log pile

Pond

Standing deadwood

DIRECTORY OF GARDEN WILDLIFE

This part of the book focuses on the more common types of wildlife found in a variety of garden habitats. Each group is described and its benefits to the garden are clearly outlined. Advice on how you can provide for the creatures' needs, as well as essential facts regarding their conservation status, habits and lifestyle, are all included. For species that may cause alarm or become a nuisance, tips are added on the best way to deal with them. This directory is only a sample of common species; for more information about the wildlife in your area, consult a local guide.

Left: *There are many species of beautiful butterfly, such as this painted lady, that visit gardens to feed on the nectar from flowers.*

Above: *Amphibians frequently venture into gardens, and knowing which is which can help you to cater for their needs.*

Above: *Bumblebees are just one of the types of wild bees that will travel to your garden and perhaps take up residence there.*

Above: *Pheasants are a semi-wild species, often introduced as game-birds, and are sometimes seen foraging in gardens.*

INSECT-EATING BIRDS

Insectivorous birds are a familiar sight in the summer garden, and their activities help to control pests. Many of the species seen, though, are seasonal summer migrants that visit to feast upon the abundance of insect life that appears at this time. In addition to this, certain species develop insect-eating tendencies during periods of summer abundance because this offers the richest source of protein and fats for their young, allowing them to raise a family quickly and successfully.

Above: *Wrens are among the smallest of garden birds, but are voracious predators of insects in the summer months.*

ROLE IN GARDENS

In garden settings, birds take insects and small invertebrates, many of which are regarded as pests. They constitute an important food source, especially in regions where insects are most plentiful. Swallows, martins and swifts pursue their insect meals while flying, often swooping down in pursuit, and woodpeckers can sometimes be seen – and more often heard – making holes in wood to find grubs. Even the flocks of starlings that walk across your lawn are systematically searching for insects.

HABITAT PREFERENCES

Whilst some birds are entirely insectivorous, others, including many common songbird species, eat insects only when raising young. Some of these feed the offspring entirely an insect diet, but only a small percentage of their own food is insects. This habit has the obvious advantage that they do not have to change their preferred habitat and can remain in a garden all year.

Some larger birds also eat insects as part of their diet when these are plentiful but revert to other animals at other times of the year. Swallows, on the other hand, are a well-known example of a species that feeds only on insects and so must make radical shifts in its habitat preferences within a single season by migrating vast distances to follow seasonal "gluts" of their prey in different countries.

FEEDING STRATEGIES

Although there are many different species of insect-eating birds, they often adopt similar strategies for catching their prey. Most have fine, narrow beaks, although even this can vary greatly according to species. Ecologists therefore tend to divide insectivorous birds according to their hunting habits, or guilds.

These guilds consist of groups of species that, although not necessarily closely related, behave in similar ways.

Below: *Barn swallows migrate vast distances to follow seasonal abundances of insects.*

Leaf gleaners, such as warblers, pick insects off leaves, whereas bark gleaners, such as nuthatches, pick them off tree trunks. Woodpeckers are wood and bark probers because of their ability to dig out their prey from within the branch.

The air salliers, including flycatchers, sit on a perch waiting for their prey to pass, whereupon they fly out and catch insects

PROFILE

Garden benefits The insect-eating habit of birds should be a delight to most gardeners because their prey includes many potential pests. Incoming migrants also help tackle the rocketing summer population.

Migratory species For insectivorous birds, with their high mobility, migration is the rule rather than the exception. For some, such as swallows and swifts, the journey covers thousands of miles.

Natural diet Insectivorous birds do not only eat insects but will often take a range of invertebrates. Because they gain most of their moisture from these, they drink less frequently than seed-eaters.

Resident species Very few insectivores remain as residents in higher latitudes. Mostly small birds such as the wren, they are very susceptible to cold and limited to mild regions as a consequence.

Supplementary diet Mealworms are an excellent supplement and can be offered in a simple dish or a specialist feeder. In addition, many food suppliers now provide dried food for insectivores.

Left: *There are numerous species of woodpecker that may visit gardens, all of which prefer to feed on wood-boring grubs.*

Right: *Lavender is an excellent plant for attracting insects such as bees and butterflies, which flock to the flowers in search of nectar. In turn, these creatures often become food for many bird species.*

on the wing. The final guild includes the swallows, martins and swifts – gleaners of aerial plankton. In other words, they eat a large number of small insects while on the wing. In reality, however, most birds opt for more than one strategy, particularly if food becomes scarce.

Most insectivorous birds consume several different kinds of insect, often switching their preferences through the season according to the abundance of species available.

MIGRATORY SPECIES

Birds that feed exclusively on insects often face seasonal food shortages if they remain in one place, and that's why they travel in search of food. Swallows and flycatchers in north-western Europe fly south in autumn to spend winter in Africa. It is easy to see why they do so because the cold, dark months offer little reward in terms of insects. What is less easy to understand is why they should return. The simple answer is that countries in high or low latitudes have a large seasonal glut of insects in summer. The birds move from place to place, so that it's always summer, and there's always plenty of food.

Migrating insect-eating birds also prosper because there are often not many resident insectivorous birds in their summer feeding grounds. This means that the migrants have an abundant food supply without facing competition from too many residents. Furthermore, feeding and raising their young in high or low latitudes means that they can use the longer hours of

daylight to gather plenty of food, so they can potentially raise more young. A final, if less obvious, advantage for migratory birds is that they avoid specialist predators trying to feed on them, because few of their predators make the same migratory journey. They and their chicks do, though, suffer from parasites, like any other bird species, and often these parasites have adapted to hibernate in nests where they wait for the host to return.

PLANTS TO ATTRACT INSECT-EATING BIRDS

Evening primrose (*Oenothera biennis*)
Fern-leaved yarrow (*Achillea filipendula*)
Flowering rush (*Butomus umbellatus*)
Golden rod (*Solidago virgaurea*)
Honesty (*Lunaria annua*)
Lavender (*Lavandula angustifolia*)
Lemon balm (*Melissa officinalis*)
Tansy (*Tanacetum vulgare*)

Evening primrose

Golden rod

Honesty

Tansy

THREATS

Pesticides The increased use of pesticides in both urban and rural settings means that insects are now relatively scarce. In addition, many surviving species carry small traces of these poisons, and they can accumulate in the bodies of insect-eating birds.

Predation Small birds are vulnerable to predation from larger species, both birds and mammals. Domestic cats are a big danger in urban gardens, and both squirrels and large birds, such as magpies, will take eggs and the young in the breeding season.

Territory If food becomes scarce, small birds are generally less able to compete with larger birds and become seasonal insectivores. Many need larger territories as a result, and the effort of defending this may use up a large amount of daily energy.

Urbanization Insect-eating birds often find it difficult to find the required amounts of food in very built-up areas. The lack of suitable vegetation and the human tendency to kill insects means that insect prey is often relatively scarce. Vehicular pollution can also limit the insect population because toxins can eventually build up in the urban habitat and ultimately in the insects' bodies.

OMNIVOROUS BIRDS

The changing seasons bring times of alternate plenty and shortage for birds that have highly specialized diets, and unless they are able to migrate, they can face starvation when food is scarce. For the majority of resident garden birds, their need to survive has driven them to adopt an omnivorous diet, thereby allowing them to exploit various foods as they become available. It is a highly successful strategy, and the chief reason behind the success of many species in colonizing our towns and gardens.

Above: *A familiar sight in many European gardens, blue tits exploit numerous food sources, especially during the winter.*

ROLE IN GARDENS

Birds that eat anything digestible/edible are known as omnivores. This is not to say that an omnivorous bird will eat any item of food that is put in front of it, and in most cases omnivores have specific feeding needs that may vary seasonally or perhaps because of local variations in their habitat. In fact the vast majority of birds tend to be somewhat omnivorous, although the tendency is usually most pronounced when their normal food source is in short supply. Being an omnivore is usually the most successful survival strategy in rapidly changing environments, or in places subject to extreme seasonal variation. Also note that many larger birds are omnivores because their body size makes specialization difficult unless a habitat – and therefore food supply – is very consistent all year round.

In time, successful omnivorous species can become very numerous. Members of the crow family, such as magpies and jays, will eat smaller birds and immature chicks. This results in an unusually high number of these large birds while the smaller species are often rarer than might be expected.

HABITAT PREFERENCES

Because omnivores will eat both plant and animal matter, they survive well in many environments and often prove highly adaptable. Some, like the seagull, have no problem adapting to living near humans and have recently started scavenging landfill sites and city streets. This shouldn't be so surprising because modern cities are similar in many ways to tall, rocky cliffs, and as the seagulls often nest or roost on top of tall buildings, safe from predators, it is only natural that they should feed nearby.

As habitats change, those creatures that best adapt to them tend to prosper. Urban bird populations have changed over time, and pigeons now seem to have reached epidemic proportions. Surprisingly, garden birds are often quite urban in their distribution, with higher densities in towns and cities than in the surrounding countryside. The most common species of these urbanized populations are often omnivores, and the garden is an ideal habitat.

FEEDING STRATEGIES

Being omnivorous has obvious advantages, but different foods often require adaptations to the digestive system. Some omnivorous bird species lengthen the digestive tract in winter to get more out of the relatively poor quality food. This allows them to be mostly vegetarian in winter, switching to an insectivorous diet in summer.

The beaks of omnivorous birds are usually relatively long and unspecialized, although this can vary considerably according to their evolutionary history. Feral ring-necked parakeets in the UK, for example, are much more omnivorous than

Left: *Originally from Europe, chaffinches have also been introduced elsewhere. Their varied diet has contributed to their success.*

PROFILE

Garden benefits Omnivores can be a mixed blessing in the garden, particularly if you have a vegetable patch. On the other hand, their varied diet includes many garden pests, and resident omnivores will often begin feeding on them much earlier than migratory insectivores.

Migratory species The vast majority of omnivores are able to avoid the necessity of migrating vast distances, and many – including members of the thrush family – just travel short distances to escape harsh winter weather, and often take up temporary residence in gardens.

Natural diet Many omnivores have set patterns regarding exactly what and when they will eat. Birds are often insect eaters in the summer months, for example, before their digestive tracts adapt for their winter diet of berries and seed.

Resident species Resident species of omnivorous birds often face a bleak prospect during winter. Food shortage, exacerbated by other resident competitors and incoming winter migrants, means that there is a naturally high mortality rate as a consequence.

Supplementary diet Omnivores should be provided with a varied diet. Numerous mixes exist, and the best idea is to provide a full range of food types, including grain, small seeds, suet, fruit and even some live food.

Near right: *The American robin, much larger than its European namesake, eats a mix of insects, worms and many fruits.*

Far right: *The Australian pied currawong has a wide and variable diet, adapting well to both towns and gardens.*

the original wild populations in Africa and Asia that eat fruit, berries, nuts and seed. This is likely to be a result of their foraging in domestic gardens where meat and bacon rinds are often left out on bird tables.

It is this ability to adapt, learn new tricks and exploit unfamiliar food sources that differentiates omnivores from other birds with more restrictive diets.

MIGRATORY SPECIES

Omnivores, like most birds, will migrate if food becomes scarce. They rarely undertake the huge journeys so characteristic of insectivores, however, with starlings or European robins simply travelling a few hundred miles and, even when they do migrate, it will not always be the whole population that does so. In fact the most likely migrants in a normally resident bird population are invariably the females and young. Many common species move from one country to another, while others simply move into the towns from the countryside. Some species regarded as non-migratory will sometimes move large

Below: *The sweet, edible fruits of juneberry* (Amelanchier) *mature in midsummer and are eaten by a wide variety of birds.*

distances when faced with harsh winter conditions, and because these newcomers look just like the residents, their arrival often goes largely unnoticed.

Robins, thrushes, skylarks and blackbirds all tend to undertake short flights to warmer areas, and blackbirds that live in Scandinavian countries fly south-west to spend the winter in countries with a less severe winter. In fact blackbirds often change their habits and distribution over the year, raising families and feeding in gardens

PLANTS TO ATTRACT OMNIVOROUS BIRDS
Blackthorn (*Prunus spinosa*)
Bramble (*Rubus fruticosus*)
Evening primrose (*Oenothera biennis*)
Gooseberry (*Ribes uva-crispa*)
Hawthorn (*Crataegus monogyna*)
Ivy (*Hedera helix*)
Juneberry (*Amelanchier lamarkii*)

Blackthorn **Bramble**

Gooseberry **Hawthorn**

during the spring and summer where they can raise up to three broods. After the breeding season, they must "feed up" for the coming winter, and move out into the surrounding countryside to do so.

THREATS
Competition Omnivores are adaptable and able to exploit new situations, but this brings them into contact with new competitors. Some urban birds are highly aggressive, and often chase away or even kill newcomers.

Disease Any increase in population raises the chances of disease spread. Omnivorous birds often congregate where there is a food source, and disease becomes more prevalent than for birds following a more solitary life.

Habitat changes As changing habitats favour certain incoming species, others are less favoured and some omnivorous birds that were formerly common in cities – such as the raven in London – are now scarce or absent, having been unable to adapt to modern city life.

Predation All birds face predators in either the garden or their natural habitats, and they are usually numerous enough to cope with any losses. In gardens, cats are usually the main threat, although other birds (including birds of prey) also take their toll.

SEED-EATING BIRDS

Once very common, changes in agricultural practices caused a decline in many seed-eating bird species. Fortunately, the increasing popularity of garden feeders has thrown these birds an essential lifeline, and many species now prosper in a domestic setting. These include some of the most engaging of garden birds, many of which are migratory species that flock into towns to escape harsher conditions elsewhere. For many of these species, gardens form an essential part of their continued survival.

Above: *Goldfinches eat mostly seeds but will sometimes peck at and eat buds, sap and occasionally insects through a season.*

ROLE IN GARDENS

The majority of birds using garden feeders will be seed-eaters for at least part of the year, although there are comparatively few that are exclusively seed-eating (most seed-eating species hunt nutritious insects when they are feeding and raising their young). The main problem with being a seed-eater, though, is that the majority of seeds ripen in summer and autumn. By the following spring, seed is in short supply and the birds must switch to a substitute or face a shortage. Feeding seed-eating species therefore helps them through this period, and ensures that they will be in peak condition, ready for the breeding season in spring.

HABITAT PREFERENCES

Recent years have seen a serious decline in many formerly common seed-eating birds. Intensification of agriculture has borne most of the blame, although realistically the shortage of food is the root of the disaster. The seed-eaters' numbers were previously probably artificially high as they prospered under traditional agricultural practices.

If that sounds puzzling, note that large flocks of seed-eaters were often seen feeding on winter stubble before moving on

to land that was ploughed in late winter to find weed seed that had been thrown on to the surface. Before the widespread use of herbicides, crops had many weeds that left seed in the soil. It was these weeds that the seed-eating birds depended on, and modern agricultural efficiency has largely removed them. A second problem is that seed-eaters can no longer feed on spilt grain in the stubble because fields are now ploughed soon after the autumn harvest.

Another traditional agricultural habitat that has declined is the hay meadow. Many were rich in species, but it is actually how they are managed that is important. In fact they do not have to have a great variety of plants to be important for birds, and those that contain dandelion and sorrel are especially useful for seed-eating birds, such as linnets, in summer.

Ironically, housing developments that spread over what was once farmland may yet help save some of these birds. The increasingly popular habit of feeding seed-eating birds has thrown them a lifeline, and many now prosper as a result. It is not the same for all species, though, and the house sparrow, found in many towns and cities, was first attracted to our streets when the only form of transport was horse-drawn. The sparrows fed on the spilt grain in the streets and lived around the stables, common all over the city. The arrival of the car saw the decline in their numbers across much of their original range, although ironically they remain a pest in other countries where they were introduced by European settlers.

Always try to provide as much natural food as possible to ensure that you preserve their natural behaviour patterns. Plants such

as sunflowers (*Helianthus*), and a patch of wildflowers that includes thistles, knapweed (*Centaurea*) and teasel (*Dipsacus*) will help to attract seed-eating birds.

PROFILE

Garden benefits Seed-eating birds are potentially beneficial when they switch to hunting insects in order to feed their young. Their habit of foraging seed from the soil in winter also helps to reduce weed growth the next season.

Migratory species The corn and snow bunting, brambling, siskin and many other finches, for example, tend to migrate in short hops in search of food. They do not always choose a regular destination, and often only a proportion of the birds in an area migrate.

Natural diet Seed-eating birds will eat a whole range of seed, including grain, wildflower and nuts. They prefer oil-rich seed, and will switch their preferences as a season progresses according to the availability of food.

Resident species Resident breeding populations of seed-eating birds are extremely dependent on the availability of food, and almost all non-migratory species move between breeding and wintering areas in order to forage.

Supplementary diet Many seed-eating birds are choosy about what they eat, and prefer oil-rich, high-energy food. The best includes black sunflower hearts (seed with the husks removed), white proso, millet, niger (thistle) and good quality peanuts.

Left: *Although they have a variable diet, great tits are mostly dependent on seeds throughout the year, especially in winter.*

Above: *Siskins have smaller bills than other finches, this being ideal for extracting seeds from birch, alder, spruce and pine cones.*

Traditionally, feeding birds was limited to the winter, although recent evidence suggests that serious shortages are experienced in summer by many species when they are rearing their families. Summer feeding with sunflower hearts and other seed can help the birds to lay more eggs and rear a healthier brood. Always make sure you buy from a reputable supplier because commercial bird food brands can be quite variable, and may not be formulated or intended to meet all the nutritional needs of the seed-eaters.

FEEDING STRATEGIES

The seed-feeders generally have short, thick, strong beaks that are good for crushing or cracking open seed, and they can take some time to learn which foods are safe or good for them to eat. They often have an instinctive wariness about any change in their habitat, and you will need to be patient when you try to feed them. They will always prefer their natural food sources, and when they come to the garden for the first time they may not actually recognize supplementary foods.

Try offering black sunflower, white proso, millet, niger (thistle) and peanuts, but remember that most of these foods are supplements and can't always meet all of the bird's nutritional needs. Gradually add variety once they become accustomed to feeding at the site. They will soon overcome their caution and start to experiment.

PLANTS TO ATTRACT SEED-EATING BIRDS

Amaranth (*Amaranthus caudatus*)
Dandelion (*Taraxacum officinale*)
Fat hen (*Chenopodium album*)
Field forget-me-not (*Myosotis arvensis*)
Millet (*Panicum miliaceum*)
Red clover (*Trifolium pratense*)
Sunflower (*Helianthus annuus*)
Teasel (*Dipsacus fullonum*)

Amaranth

Red clover

Sunflower

Teasel

The seed-eaters are naturally more gregarious in winter, probably because of their tendency to form large flocks at this time (though in summer they'll defend their territory). This often helps them locate food and feed more efficiently than when alone, also making them less vulnerable to predators.

MIGRATORY SPECIES

Seed-eaters tend to be resident species, but some of the buntings and finches do migrate in search of food, moving to areas

Below: *Dunnocks have a variable diet through the seasons but depend heavily upon small seeds during the winter months.*

THREATS

Competition The winter is a time when birds naturally flock, and this can cause aggression and tension. Birds at a winter feeder are forced together, and aggression is likely. Try to spread food around, and for aggressive species such as robins, you should put food out separately to avoid conflict.

Habitat loss Intensification of farming has meant that many species of once common birds are in serious decline due to loss of habitat and food sources. Oil-rich wildflower seed is vital for these species, and many now remain abundant only in gardens.

Herbicides Weedkillers have been used with increasing regularity in many countries, both to control crop weeds and to improve the look of the garden. But letting some weeds flourish is vital for foraging seed-eaters.

Predation The seed-eaters' habit of feeding on the ground makes them vulnerable to attack by cats, especially where the latter can hide and wait under garden bushes.

where the climate is milder and food more accessible. These winter migrants return to their breeding grounds in spring, although in some bird populations (e.g. goldfinches) only part of the population migrates. Other species simply move to lower ground.

Below: *Dandelions are generally regarded as weeds by gardeners but their seed is an ideal food for smaller seed-eating birds.*

FRUIT-EATING BIRDS

Fruit is an abundant and nutritious source of natural food, and one that many bird species have learned to exploit. In cooler climes, fruit tends to be a seasonal bounty, and so in these regions there are very few birds that exclusively eat fruit. Those that do tend to be limited to the tropics where this food source is available all year round. Most fruit-eaters alternate their diet, eating insects or other protein-rich foods in summer, and switching to fruit in the cooler months.

Above: *Redwings eat insects in summer, but migrate to gardens in autumn, when their dietary preference changes to fruits.*

ROLE IN GARDENS

Berries grow on a wide variety of plants including trees, bushes, climbing plants and even some herbaceous and ground-cover plants. When they are ripe, birds often descend on them and can clear a bush in a matter of hours, with some species (such as thrushes) switching almost totally to a fruit diet in late summer and autumn.

Birds and berries are a remarkable example of how plants and animals have evolved together, with one exploiting the other. The fleshy pulp of a berry is surprisingly nutrient-rich, and contains a good deal of starchy carbohydrate or sugars that conceal and protect the seed within. Most berries are also full of vitamins. The trade-off is simple. The birds benefit from the nutrients contained in the soft flesh, and spread the seed in their droppings.

The major limitation for most birds with a fruit diet, however, is that it is not available for enough of the year. Late winter to midsummer is a time when there is precious little fruit around, and the birds must find an alternative. Even when fruit is plentiful, many fruit specialists still supplement their diet with insects or other animal protein to ensure that they have a balanced diet.

PROFILE

Garden benefits It is rather difficult to say exactly what benefit fruit-eating birds actually have in the garden. They have an important role ecologically in dispersing seed, but are most useful in the summer when they switch to insect eating.

Migratory species While there are fewer migrant fruit eaters, many bird species that move short distances in winter will eat fruit in winter. Waxwings, on the other hand, are unpredictable in their movements but travel long distances in search of food.

Natural diet Fruit is rarely the sole part of any bird's diet for the whole year, but it does form an important part of some species' diet from midsummer into the colder months. Even fruit specialists occasionally take alternative food types.

Resident species Birds will often widen their territories to forage, and may even defend them to protect their fruit. Many species flock together in winter and adopt a methodical feeding approach that is different to their summer behaviour.

Supplementary diet Fruit-eating birds will quite happily take substitutes for fruit, provided they are able to recognize what it is. Pieces of broken apple and dried raisins may prove popular, and specialist suppliers now sell dried fruit especially for these birds.

HABITAT PREFERENCES

Fruit availability varies according to the season and, in most temperate climates, is available from midsummer until late winter. The fruit of the guelder rose (*Viburnum opulus*) or currants (*Ribes*) are quite short-lived and, if not consumed immediately, will fall from the plant and rot. However, fruit of the cotoneaster and holly (*Ilex*) remains on the plant for many months, being a vital food reserve for much of the winter.

Always choose a range of plants that produce fruit over a long period. Remember that most species of fruit-eating birds have their favourites that they will take first, and that some fruit will remain on the plant for a long time before it is taken. Early fruiting bushes, such as currants and wild strawberries, are just as important as the late berries, and even a small garden can accommodate some of these plants.

FEEDING STRATEGIES

Fruit is extremely important for many songbirds that switch from a summer invertebrate diet to a winter one based on berries. This is especially important when cold weather arrives and frozen ground prevents resident species foraging for worms, grubs or fallen seed. It is at these times of year, when food is short, that nourishing fruit is most vital.

Some birds tend to descend en masse to take berries when ripe, with starlings, for example, being highly systematic in their approach, methodically stripping bushes and trees from the top down. They also drop far fewer berries than other birds, and leave bushes picked clean. The thrushes, on the other hand, are well known for their tendency to defend their territory, and will often defend a berrying tree or shrub against all-comers. This acts as a larder that will see them through the winter, and if hard

Left: *Yellow warblers are a migratory species in North America that fatten up on fruit before heading south for winter.*

Above: *Elderberry is an excellent source of berries in midsummer. The berries are especially liked by blackbirds and thrushes.*

times do not materialize the birds gain a great advantage in having food to the end of winter, enabling them to nest early.

MIGRATORY SPECIES

As with most bird species, harsh winter weather is often a trigger for them to move south. While most only move short distances, there are a few that cover much greater distances and the movements of berry-feeding birds are always inextricably linked to the availability of the fruit itself.

Possibly the most famous migratory berry-eaters are the waxwings. In both Europe and North America these beautiful birds leave their forest homes and move to warmer climes, often descending on

PLANTS TO ATTRACT FRUIT-EATING BIRDS

Blackcurrant (*Ribes nigrum*)
Elderberry (*Sambucus niger*)
Herringbone cotoneaster (*Cotoneaster horizontalis*)
Holly (*Ilex aquifolium*)
Guelder rose (*Viburnum opulus*)
Mezereon (*Daphne mezereum*)
Rowan (*Sorbus aucuparia*)
Wild strawberry (*Fragaria vesca*)

Cotoneaster   **Holly**

Mezereon   **Rowan**

gardens to feast on berries. They are communal feeders with individuals eating up to 500 berries each day, and in Holland they are called *pestvogel*, meaning invasion bird, due to their habit of appearing suddenly and clearing away all the fruit.

The cedar waxwing of North America is also migratory and equally fond of berries. Flocks of these birds show a high degree of cooperation when they feed, and when the end of a twig holds a supply of berries that

THREATS

Competition Even if there is plenty of food at the start of winter, harsh weather may force the birds to eat more of it and shorten the supply. In addition, migrants moving into the area compete for resources and visiting flocks may even strip an area clean.

Habitat loss Changes to the countryside caused by agriculture have meant that many native berrying shrubs have been destroyed, particularly when hedgerows are removed from field margins, and bird numbers often fall as a consequence.

Poor fruit years In some years the amount of fruit that sets on a tree or shrub will be considerably less than usual, mainly because the weather damaged blossom or deterred pollinators. The following winter shortages may therefore occur.

Predation The tendency to seasonal fruit-eating among many bird species often attracts them to settled areas where domestic cats are common predators. Ironically, the very shrubs they are feeding on often give cover to these ambush specialists.

only one bird can reach at a time, members of a flock will even line up along the twig and pass berries from beak to beak down the line so that each bird gets to eat.

Left: *The American cedar waxwing eats berries and sugary fruit all year, but takes insects during the breeding season.*

Above: *Although naturally migratory, the availability of supplements in gardens means that some blackcaps overwinter.*

CARNIVORES AND INSECTIVORES

Carnivorous mammals are rare and exciting garden visitors and, although smaller insectivores are more numerous, these too are rarely seen, being shy and often nocturnal. Mammals that capture and eat other animals or insects in order to feed themselves are important elements of many habitats, and if you keep your garden wildlife-friendly you should be rewarded with a glimpse of one of these exciting, if reclusive, animals.

Above: *Polecats are mainly carnivorous, feeding largely on frogs and voles, but they will also catch rats and other small prey.*

ROLE IN GARDENS

Mammals, like any other group of animals, have developed into those that eat plants and those that eat other animals. The latter are carnivores, and they play a vital role in controlling the number of plant-eaters in a habitat. A surprisingly high proportion of mammals eat other animals, and it is widely believed that the earliest mammals may all have been carnivores. Fossils of ancient mammals are those of small, insect-eating creatures known as insectivores, and indeed a great many mammals still pursue this strategy.

When we refer to carnivorous mammals, it usually means those species that capture and eat other vertebrates, including other mammals. Some carnivores are large and dangerous mammals like bears, but there are a number of smaller carnivores, such as stoats and small cats. They are no less fierce than their larger counterparts, and some of the smaller mustelids such as stoats, weasels and minks often attack, kill and eat prey that is even larger than they are. Ultimately, though, it is their small size alone that means we can live in close proximity to them.

Above: *Stoats, common throughout Europe, Canada and the United States, often catch prey that is larger than they are.*

The most common mammals found in gardens eat insects, and also worms, woodlice and other small invertebrates. The garden therefore often represents an ideal hunting ground, and the abundance of insects can limit the mammals' need for a very large territory. Shrews are commonly found in gardens and, though rarely noticed, consume vast amounts of invertebrates, often 125 per cent of their body weight each day. Others, such as the hedgehog of Europe and Asia, are more obvious.

HABITAT PREFERENCES

Most predatory mammals do not have very specific preferences, and all that is required is dense cover for them to shelter in or possibly to mount ambushes from. Long grass and thickets are essential if you want

to encourage insectivores, such as hedgehogs or shrews, and of course the greatest asset in encouraging a predatory mammal into the garden must be an abundance of its preferred prey.

You can always give some species a helping hand, though, and bats in particular need roosting sites in which to stay during daylight hours. They naturally occupy a crevice in rocks or trees, but may be helped by positioning bat boxes in the garden that keep them safe and allow them to sleep soundly, well out of the way and hidden from larger day-hunting predators.

Left: *Hedgehogs are common visitors to European gardens, feeding on a range of invertebrates, including some pest species.*

PROFILE

Garden benefits The most obvious advantage of carnivores and insectivores in the garden is their ability to control pests. Many mammal predators are at, or near, the top of the food chain and, as such, help maintain a balance of nature.

Nuisance behaviour Many smaller carnivores can become a problem because they forage for food. Moles are a prime example, their excavated earth mounds ruining a smart lawn.

Risk to people or pets Remember that any wild animal can, and often will, bite if threatened. Carnivores are specially adapted to bite and tear flesh. Some species may also attack pets if given the chance.

Supplementary diet Carnivorous and insectivorous animals are best left to their own devices. Feeding them can result in their becoming too habituated and possibly aggressive.

WHAT IS A MAMMAL?

Essentially warm-blooded, the skin of a mammal is virtually covered in hair. With the exception of one small group of Australian egg-laying mammals, all give birth to more or less fully developed young that are then fed milk by their mothers. Also, mammals live in most places, and although most are ground-dwellers, many habitually climb up rocks or trees, and most are capable of swimming. One group, the bats, has even evolved the ability to fly in pursuit of their prey.

Mammals are extremely variable in size, with the pigmy shrew being so small it weighs just 2–4g (½-⅙oz), while the blue whale reaches almost 200 tons. Among them are numerous carnivores (e.g. cats and stoats), omnivores (raccoons and hedgehogs), and herbivores (rabbits and squirrels). While most gardens will harbour relatively few (if any) mammals, a number of species are likely to visit, with a few usually smaller species of herbivores even becoming residents.

Above: *Overgrown areas with plenty of decaying vegetation and logs provide both shelter and hunting ground for carnivores.*

THREATS

Competition Many mammal species face increased competition, partly due to shrinking habitats, but more often because they face a threat from an introduced species. Feral domestic cats in the United States and Australia and mink in Europe are examples of such invasive competitors.

Habitat loss Many hunting animals need to maintain a territory in order to have access to sufficient numbers of their prey. Larger mammals need larger territories and, as humans encroach upon them, the predatory species often suffer as a result.

Pesticides The use of insecticides in gardens and the wider countryside has meant that many species have become rare. This is partly because prey species are in short supply, but also because animals higher in the food chain accumulate these toxins from prey species to lethal levels.

Persecution Many predator species have been persecuted by humans. Often this is because they are seen as vermin or a threat to domesticated animals. They have also been relentlessly pursued both for their fur and as trophies, leading to some species becoming rare or endangered as humans encroach upon their natural habitats.

FEEDING STRATEGIES

Many carnivores are stealth hunters and tend to capture their prey by ambush. Insectivores, on the other hand, are rarely ambush predators, usually preferring to locate their prey by a combination of smell, sound and sensitive whiskers. Their hunting might appear erratic to us, but their progress through their territory is usually systematic and effective. They consume prey as soon as they find it, and are often either nocturnal or tend to live and hunt in dense vegetation and, as a consequence, are less reliant on sight than some of the other larger carnivores.

Moles are also insectivores but have evolved a highly specialized lifestyle, spending almost all their life underground, digging long, deep tunnels and, as a result, they are almost blind. Their tunnels act as a trap for many invertebrates, especially worms that fall into them and are quickly located and eaten by the patrolling mole.

Not all the insect-eating mammals are ground-dwelling, and the night brings forth the bats, a group of mammals that are widely misunderstood and much maligned. There can be few garden creatures that polarize our views as much as these small but useful creatures. Bats have been around for over 50 million years, and have developed the ability to "see" at night. While the expression "blind as a bat" is inaccurate – they have eyes and can see – they do not use them at night. Instead, they use a complex system of high-pitched sounds called echolocation to navigate in flight, as well as to locate and capture their prey.

Below: *Bats like this pipistrelle are often seen in gardens, pursuing insects feeding on plants such as honeysuckle at dusk.*

PLANTS TO ATTRACT BATS

Common honeysuckle (*Lonicera periclymenum*)
Common jasmine (*Jasminum officinale*)
Evening primrose (*Oenothera biennis*)
Heliotrope (*Heliotropium arborescens*)
Night scented stock (*Matthiola bicornis*)
Tobacco plant (*Nicotiana affinis*)

Honeysuckle

Jasmine

Heliotrope

Tobacco plant

HERBIVORES

In direct contrast to the shy and secretive carnivores and insectivores, the plant-eating (herbivorous) mammals are often more easily seen, although many of the smaller ones remain hidden in dense vegetation and are often nocturnal. Herbivores are extremely important in many habitats because many carnivorous animals depend upon them as a food source, and while the idea of them consuming your valuable garden plants may seem alarming, the majority are relatively non-destructive.

Above: *Water voles mainly eat grass and plants near flowing water, but occasionally eat fruits, bulbs, twigs, buds and roots.*

ROLE IN GARDENS

It is widely believed that herbivorous mammals evolved from omnivorous ancestors. They are an extremely successful group and occupy almost every habitat on the planet. They are often more numerous in gardens than other mammal types, although the only evidence you might see is the damage they have done to your plants. Of the herbivorous mammals, rodents are the most likely garden visitors, being by far the most numerous of all mammals, comprising around 41 per cent (or 1,750 species) of all mammalian species. Unfortunately, many are regarded as pests, both in the garden and in the home. They are characterized by highly specialized, chisel-like, gnawing incisors and have extremely strong jaw muscles, allowing them to chew through even the toughest plant material. These incisors grow continuously throughout their life.

There are many more herbivores on the planet than there are carnivores, and the vast majority are small and inconspicuous.

Below *Deer are large herbivores that only visit gardens near countryside. They can cause considerable damage in a short time.*

Above: *Brown hares, and their relatives the jackrabbits, feed mainly on herbs during summer, and grasses in the winter.*

Their success and large numbers have made them important species when it comes to shaping and maintaining habitats.

It is hard to see the value of herbivorous mammals in the garden because their habit of eating prize plants can instantly turn them into pests. They are, however, an important link in the food chain with predatory mammals, birds and reptiles, such as snakes, depending on them for their survival.

The majority of smaller herbivorous mammals are relatively non-destructive in the garden, and prefer to forage only for the richest foods. The result is that they are mostly seed- or fruit-eaters and do little harm, particularly if a wild area is left for them. They also help to cycle nutrients (via their droppings), and may even help control certain kinds of weed.

HABITAT PREFERENCES

The sorts of herbivorous mammals you find will vary with the type and design of your garden, as well as the range of nearby habitats. Gardens bordering woodland, for example, will doubtless get mammals such

PROFILE

Garden benefits All herbivores are termed primary consumers, and their feeding helps shape habitats and cycle nutrients. They can help control certain weed species, although their true value may be in supporting populations of predatory mammals.

Potential for nuisance behaviour Certain plants may be repeatedly targeted, and it is probably easiest to avoid growing them rather than persecute the responsible animals.

Risk to people or pets Any large animal can be potentially dangerous, but smaller mammals are relatively benign. They are all wild, though, and will react if threatened or cornered. Squirrels are often quite aggressive if frightened, and will bite.

Supplementary diet Herbivorous mammals don't generally need a supplementary feed, and often ignore most items left out for them, preferring wild food. Squirrels are a notable exception, and some suppliers produce food mixes for them.

as squirrels and wood mice, although many former woodland species now have a permanent home in city gardens and parks. Remember, though, that they will only stick around – and indeed continue to visit – if there is food and shelter.

Rabbits and hares are examples of slightly larger herbivores that sometimes visit rural gardens. They will not only eat plants – preferring young and freshly planted ones – but will dig holes, destroying

HERBIVORES AND FOOD CHAINS

Herbivores are a vital part of all terrestrial habitats, and many mammals have adopted this feeding strategy. As primary consumers they turn plant nutrients into animal matter, and their droppings are quickly recycled and may even be exploited as a niche by certain invertebrates and microbes.

The vast majority of the world's mammals are herbivores. Most are small mammals, with rodents (rats, mice and squirrels) accounting for over two-fifths of all mammal species. Many of these small herbivorous mammals are liable to be eaten by birds or other predators because their sheer numbers make them a valuable food source. They are often most vulnerable to attack when feeding. Consequently they are extremely fast runners and often have keen senses, employ camouflage, and live in dense cover or are nocturnal.

Above: *Where herbivores are likely to be problematic, newly planted areas like this hedge will need adequate protection.*

other plants in the process. In small numbers, and with the proper protection for young or treasured plants, they can be tolerated although many gardeners would prefer not to see them at all.

Larger herbivorous mammals are much rarer and hardly ever visit gardens because they mostly range over extensive areas, and are shy of humans. Deer, on the other hand, are an example of a large mammal type that is becoming increasingly common, and are now often found on the fringes of urban and suburban areas. They often enter inhabited areas at dusk to feast on garden plants and drink from a pond before retreating early the next morning. Despite their grace and beauty they can be destructive, and although repellents can dissuade them, their numbers are increasing and the damage can be extreme. Fencing is often the only solution.

FEEDING STRATEGIES

Just about everything except leaf litter and mature tree bark is eaten by herbivorous mammals and, in common with most mammals, they tend to be opportunistic. They will often exploit different food sources at different times of year due to changing availability. This allows them to survive fluctuations in the numbers of different plants, and often allows many species that are common in gardens to adapt to changes in their habitat. There are exceptions to this, of course, with Australian koalas having restricted feeding habits, consuming only the leaves of a few eucalyptus species. Such specialized diets are rarely catered for in gardens due to the diversity of plants.

Herbivores must consume a large amount of plant material each day because it mostly consists of cellulose with water and some carbohydrates, but very few fats

PLANTS TO ATTRACT SQUIRRELS

English oak (*Quercus robur*)
Hazel (*Corylus avellana*)
Scots pine (*Pinus sylvestris*)
Sweet chestnut (*Castanea sativa*)

English oak

Hazel

Scots pine

Sweet chestnut

THREATS

Disease Animals moving into urban areas can catch diseases from domestic or introduced species and, in some cases, lack any immunity, resulting in plagues that can wipe out populations.

Habitat loss Certain mammals are extremely specialized in their habitat requirements for food, shelter and nesting sites. The loss of any one of these factors, as a consequence of development, can mean that they are unable to live in an area.

Introduced predators Herbivores have evolved behavioural traits in the presence of particular predators. When faced with introduced predators – such as domestic cats in the United States – they often lack the ability to escape, and their numbers decline as a result.

Pesticides Plants often accumulate a variety of environmental toxins, including pesticides, in their tissues. Herbivorous mammals must consume large amounts of vegetation to satisfy their food requirements, and these poisons can accumulate in their bodies to lethal levels.

and proteins. This renders it considerably lower than meat in energy content, which is why most herbivorous mammals spend more time eating than carnivores. To overcome these problems, smaller herbivores often feed on seeds or fruits as both of these provide a far more nutritious diet than leaves.

Below: *Red squirrels naturally eat tree seeds in forest regions and may visit gardens to forage where tree seeds occur.*

OMNIVORES

Mammals that eat both animal and plant matter are called omnivores. They are generalist feeders, and some will hunt and kill prey when it is available. However, all have the common ability to adapt to new surroundings, including our gardens. This has led to many omnivorous species becoming highly successful town-dwellers, and many are now more numerous in areas of human habitation than they were formerly in their original "natural" habitats.

Above: *Raccoons are adaptable American omnivores, renowned for being clever and mischievous, and are often seen in gardens.*

ROLE IN GARDENS

Omnivores are capable of consuming both animal and vegetable matter as part of their diet. Their teeth are often less specialized than those of herbivores and carnivores, and are a mixture of sharp cutters and flat grinders, allowing them to deal with a wide range of foods. Being an omnivorous species, however, does not necessarily mean that their diet is in any way indiscriminate, and neither does it mean that the animals eat equal amounts of meat and plants. It does mean, though, that mammals with this trait can live on different types of food according to what's available throughout the year, and this is especially useful where seasonal variation means that food sources are variable.

Omnivores have typically descended from carnivorous ancestors, and their varied diet may well reflect changes that occurred in their habitats over time. Raccoons, skunks and badgers are all examples of mammals called mustelids that were originally predators. Their ability to consume many different types of food has meant that they can exploit a range of different habitats, and these creatures have adapted well to changes in the landscape wrought by humans. They are frequent visitors to

PROFILE

Garden benefits Omnivores can be a mixed blessing in the garden, particularly in the case of larger animals, such as foxes and raccoons. However, they hunt and kill certain pests, and play a vital role in the absence of other predators.

Potential for nuisance behaviour Most of the nuisance behaviour you are likely to encounter will be destructive activity that is associated with foraging for food or nesting, although this is not always particularly serious.

Risk to people or pets This depends largely upon the mammal. Raccoons and badgers are extremely strong and will take on domestic dogs or even people if cornered.

Supplementary diet Deciding whether to feed an omnivore is tricky, though most species don't need it. Occasionally feed titbits, such as grated vegetable, raisins and pet food mixed with water, if conditions are very harsh.

gardens, and are often far more common than similar-sized carnivorous mammals both in and around gardens.

Not all omnivores are descended from carnivores, however, and some, such as the rat, obviously have a herbivorous ancestry. In fact many carnivores and herbivores take other types of food where the opportunity arises, and this type of "opportunistic omnivorousness" is common in mammals, although those species that can truly be classed as omnivores are in the minority.

It is too tempting to see omnivores as "nature's dustbins", although for some species – such as the rat – the term does seem appropriate. In the majority of cases, however, omnivores are opportunists that can switch their feeding habits according to the availability of food. In gardens they will do the same, and often their presence is the result of your providing a habitat or food source to their liking.

Omnivores are often a mixed blessing in the garden because their foraging activities can be both useful and highly destructive, and even exciting creatures, such as badgers, are sometimes reviled due to their habit of digging in lawns, stealing root crops, and – if they learn the habit – overturning dustbins. Other omnivores, such as raccoons

Left: *The red fox is the most widespread member of the dog family, owing its success to its adaptability and wide-ranging diet.*

Right: *Rats are very common omnivores which have spread widely in association with human habitation and agriculture.*

Above: *Gardens with plenty of tall plants and some open space provide an excellent foraging ground for most omnivores.*

and skunks, often cause similar problems, and larger types (e.g. pigs and some bear species) could become downright dangerous if they take a liking to your garden. Having said that, they are a part of a natural ecosystem, and they can hardly be blamed for following their own instincts.

HABITAT PREFERENCES

As generalists, many omnivores are not particularly fussy about their surroundings. This is borne out when we see creatures such as foxes taking up residence even in heavily built-up inner-city areas, and other creatures, such as raccoons, living in and around domestic dwellings.

As a rule, most gardens are too small to act as the total territorial area for either individuals or groups of omnivores, although some of the smaller rodent omnivores may be perfectly content in your garden for their whole life. But, in general, most mammalian omnivores are small to medium-sized creatures that will visit, rather than reside in, a garden. Having said that, they will need to live somewhere. If they decide to live in your garden and you are concerned, seek advice from your local wildlife society.

FEEDING STRATEGIES

The extent of an omnivorous mammal's territory may depend a lot on the environment. Most omnivores naturally forage over quite a large area, in keeping with their adaptive tendency, but may disappear shortly after appearing if food is sparse. In addition, solitary omnivore species have often evolved to live in changing and variable habitats, moving on when the pickings become slim.

Animals that have moved from a herbivorous to an omnivorous existence often eat more vegetable matter. They are often quite eclectic in their tastes, and are not natural hunters. Omnivores that are descended from carnivores, however, are quite able to capture, kill and eat prey, and many omnivores, such as foxes, badgers and raccoons, will readily do so. These animals have a wide gape to their jaw structure and well-developed musculature and teeth that enable them to kill and consume prey, even though the majority of their diet is comprised of plant foods and killing is a rare part of their behaviour.

Below: *Badgers are shy, nocturnal creatures that eat earthworms, insects, small animals, berries, nuts, roots, and other plant matter.*

REPTILES

A very misunderstood group of animals, reptiles are often met with fear or trepidation when encountered in the garden, or indeed elsewhere. They are an important and ancient group of creatures, though, that fulfil a significant role as "pest controllers" in many habitats. Whilst most common in warmer climates, a number of species make their homes in places that have a marked variation in the seasons, where they tend to hibernate in winter and are thus only seen in the warmer months.

Above: *Common lizards hunt insects, spiders, snails and worms, which they stun by shaking before swallowing them whole.*

ROLE IN GARDENS

Reptiles are mostly very beneficial in gardens, provided that they are of a non-venomous type. Lizards often eat insects and help control the number of pests in a garden, and many snakes are specialists in hunting small mammals. They are often especially sensitive to their habitats, and their presence is a clear indication that your garden habitat is both balanced and healthy.

Many reptile species face an uncertain future, chiefly because their habitats have been lost, fragmented, neglected or unsympathetically managed. They are mostly creatures of the wild, although certain species regularly visit or even take up residence in gardens. There is little to fear, and you should consider yourself fortunate to have spotted what will usually be a shy and retiring creature.

Reptiles are fascinating animals, and play an important part in the ecology of some habitats. Their somewhat secretive

Below: *Sand lizards mainly feed on slugs, spiders and insects, but will also feed on other foods, such as fruit and flower heads.*

behaviour in gardens means that they often go largely unnoticed or, at best, are only glimpsed fleetingly before they disappear into the nearest cover. They are a somewhat misunderstood group of animals, and this often leads to a needlessly fearful response when they are noticed.

There are three types of reptiles that you may encounter in a garden – the lizards; the legless, snake-like slow worms or glass lizards; and true snakes. In addition, you may more occasionally encounter a turtle or tortoise, although they are much rarer and more specialized in their habitat preferences and, because they rarely venture into gardens, they are not dealt with here.

LIZARDS, SLOW WORMS AND GLASS LIZARDS

The largest group of reptiles, with more than 4,300 species worldwide, these resemble salamanders but have dry, scaly skin, external ear openings and usually clawed feet. Most lizards are small, with four legs and a long tail.

The legs of some lizards are greatly shortened, or vestigial, making creatures such as the slow worm or glass lizard rather snake-like, although they are easily distinguished from true snakes by their movable eyelids (snakes have no eyelids and cannot close their eyes).

SNAKES

An exciting and important part of many habitats, snakes are the only group likely to harm people. Despite their fearsome reputation, though, most snakes are harmless and will quickly slither away, although all are best treated with caution

Right: *Slow worms are not snakes but legless lizards. They hunt slow-moving prey, such as slugs and earthworms, at dusk.*

PROFILE

Diet A few reptiles, such as iguanas and tortoises, are herbivorous but the vast majority are carnivores or insectivores that capture, kill and eat live prey. Lizards mostly eat insects whilst snakes take larger prey such as small mammals, birds or other reptiles.

Garden benefits Most lizards are harmless to the plant life in your garden and prove beneficial by controlling insect populations. In turn, some of the commoner types are a source of food for larger mammals and birds, and are therefore a part of the garden food web.

Potential for nuisance behaviour Reptiles are generally no trouble in the garden but can prove alarming. The best answer is usually to avoid contact with them, and they'll invariably keep out of your way.

Risk to people or pets There are comparatively few reptiles that pose a significant threat to people or pets, but poisonous snakes can occasionally be dangerous, particularly if cornered or threatened.

WHAT IS A REPTILE?

Reptiles have lived on the Earth for over 300 million years. All have dry, scaly skins and rely on external heat sources to maintain their body temperature (hence the term "cold-blooded"). Unless they are warm, they tend to be very sluggish and make a surprisingly easy meal for cats, foxes, badgers and birds of prey.

All reptiles regulate their temperature by basking, particularly in the morning, first finding a warm site to heat up their bodies before moving away into the shade. This behaviour prevents them from overheating and, during hot periods, particularly in summer, many species then seek a cooler, shadier site.

Most reptiles continue to grow throughout their lives and periodically shed their outer skin. Also, all have eggs with a waterproof shell, although a few species – such as vipers – retain them internally until they hatch. The four surviving groups of reptiles are turtles and tortoises, snakes and lizards, the crocodile family, and the tuatara from New Zealand.

Above: *A pile of dry wood provides a good sheltering place for many reptiles, particularly in hot summer weather.*

and respect. Indeed, many snakes are actually very vulnerable and have particular environmental needs, and a number of species have legal protection for this reason. There are also some venomous types and, while few will harm you, they should not be provoked.

HABITAT PREFERENCES

The needs of reptiles vary, but in general all need a place to shelter, nesting and hibernation sites (in cooler locations), and a ready source of food. The ideal habitats provide a good mixture of cover and open, sunny areas for basking, such as rough grassland or patches of shrubby vegetation.

Rock and log piles provide excellent shelter and basking sites, and also serve as an excellent habitat for many of the reptiles' preferred prey. On cloudy or wet days, reptiles may well shelter in these retreats and avoid coming out in the open because cool weather slows them down and makes them vulnerable to predators. Reptiles are often easiest to see in the mornings, warming up by basking on rocks or on top of vegetation. As the day becomes hotter, they often return to their shelters or other shady places.

FEEDING STRATEGIES

The diet of lizards varies depending on species, although most of the species you will encounter in gardens are insectivorous. They ambush their prey and eat them quickly there and then, and rarely attack prey that is so large that it cannot easily be overpowered. For snakes, on the other hand, catching and eating prey would seem to be potentially more problematic. They have no claws with which to grab, tear or hold their food, and are unable to chew because their teeth and hinged jaws aren't designed for that purpose. Instead, they either poison or crush their prey.

Venomous snakes strike suddenly and inject venom into the victim, which first paralyzes it, and later assists the digestive processes. Most snakes have no venom, though, and use strength alone to immobilize their victims, having first grabbed their prey with their mouth. Constrictors wrap their body in tight coils around the victim to suffocate it, whereas others start swallowing immediately so that the animal is eaten alive. Snakes habitually catch and kill quite large animals because they are able to dislocate their upper and lower jaws, and spread their mouth and throat open to swallow them.

PLANTS TO ATTRACT REPTILES

Bilberry (*Vaccinium myrtillus*)
Cranberry (*Vaccinium oxycoccos*)

Cross-leaved heath (*Erica tetralix*)
Ling (*Calluna vulgaris*)

Bilberry   Cranberry   Cross-leaved heath   Ling

THREATS

Collection for pet trade The pet trade has had a severe effect upon the numbers of wild reptiles, and some species are now legally protected to prevent their capture in the wild. Tortoises suffered badly in this respect, and consequently many species are now rare.

Disturbance Reptiles are easily startled and retreat at the first sign of danger. In a garden, human activities may severely disrupt their normal behaviour, such as feeding and basking, and most species do not tolerate constant human incursions into their habitat.

Habitat loss Reptiles are particularly sensitive in their habitat requirements, and only a few species ever take up residence in gardens or developed areas. Loss of habitat often adversely affects the availability of a food source, and many formerly common species are now rare.

Persecution Reptiles are often the object of needless fear, and snakes have been persecuted for hundreds, and perhaps thousands, of years despite the fact that most species are harmless and even useful.

AMPHIBIANS

Amphibians are very widespread and are often quite common across much of their range, being frequent garden visitors and even residents. There are three types of amphibian that you are likely to encounter in the garden: frogs; toads; and salamanders and newts. As their name suggests, amphibians are almost equally at home on land or in water and, although the adults of many species are almost entirely land-based, all must return to water to lay their eggs.

Above: *Adult frogs often stay quite near to water, where they hunt insects or small animals that they catch with a sticky tongue.*

ROLE IN GARDENS

Amphibians perform a vital role because they are predators of invertebrates, including many that might eat your prize plants. All amphibians are particularly sensitive to environmental stresses, and their presence is a sure sign of a healthy, natural garden. By encouraging them, you are also paving the way for other forms of wildlife. Ultimately, a plentiful population of amphibians could be just what your garden needs.

HABITAT PREFERENCES

While you don't actually need a pond to have amphibians living in your garden, they do need a pool in which to breed. Although the pond does not need to be large, always make the largest one possible so that plenty of species can use it. More important than size, though, is its maximum depth, and that's ideally 60–90cm (2–3ft). It should have at least one side that shelves out gradually, allowing good access, preferably into surrounding rough vegetation for feeding and hibernation. Use a good mix of native pond plants, but avoid too many overhanging trees; many amphibians prefer to breed in ponds that receive full sun and warm up more quickly in the spring, thereby speeding up the development of the young.

Left: *Newts live both in and out of water, eating anything small enough to swallow, such as slugs, worms and beetles.*

FEEDING STRATEGIES

Most amphibians eat anything that is small enough to fit into their mouth, although distasteful objects may be spat out again. They are extremely efficient hunters and

PROFILE

Climate change Warming temperatures across the planet are affecting many amphibians. It is widely believed that climate change reduces the effectiveness of immune response to disease in many species, and it may also affect their habitat in other ways.

Diet All amphibian adults are carnivores or insectivores, and capture and eat a wide variety of prey. The tadpoles, on the other hand, begin life as herbivores and gradually switch to meat as they change into adults.

Garden benefits Frogs, toads, salamanders and newts enhance the environmental and aesthetic value of the garden. They also perform a vital role in hunting and eating many common garden pests.

Potential for nuisance behaviour Amphibians tend to be fairly problem-free. Their vocalizations may become quite loud in the evening, particularly around the breeding season.

Risk to people or pets There are very few dangers associated with garden amphibians and, in most cases, they are the vulnerable ones. Some toads and salamanders do exude a toxic poison, however, and it is best to avoid handling any amphibian if possible.

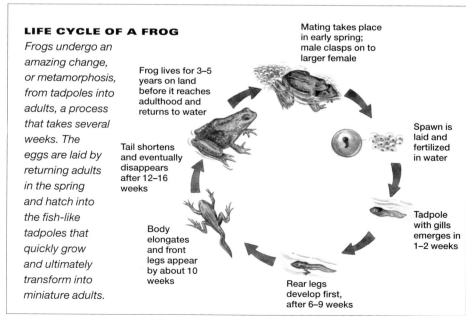

LIFE CYCLE OF A FROG

Frogs undergo an amazing change, or metamorphosis, from tadpoles into adults, a process that takes several weeks. The eggs are laid by returning adults in the spring and hatch into the fish-like tadpoles that quickly grow and ultimately transform into miniature adults.

Frog lives for 3–5 years on land before it reaches adulthood and returns to water

Mating takes place in early spring; male clasps on to larger female

Spawn is laid and fertilized in water

Tadpole with gills emerges in 1–2 weeks

Rear legs develop first, after 6–9 weeks

Body elongates and front legs appear by about 10 weeks

Tail shortens and eventually disappears after 12–16 weeks

WHAT IS AN AMPHIBIAN?

Amphibians are cold-blooded animals that differ from reptiles because they lack scales, do not produce eggs with a waterproof shell, and generally return to the water to breed. The three types of amphibians are the frogs and toads, salamanders and newts, and the strange and rarely seen caecilians – mostly tropical, worm-like amphibians that live underground.

Generally eggs are laid in a big mass in the water and fertilized externally. Without water, their eggs (which are not protected by a shell) would quickly dry out and the young would die before they hatched. The small, fish-like young (tadpoles) are completely unlike the adults and metamorphose over a period of a few weeks into a tiny replica of the adult. Once the metamorphosis is complete, the young adults leave the water and disperse into the surrounding vegetation, where they remain until it is time to breed.

Above: *Amphibians are vulnerable when they leave the water so they prefer to inhabit ponds with plenty of bank-side vegetation for cover.*

are extremely fast when capturing prey, often doing so in a fraction of a second using a long, sticky tongue.

When in water, salamanders and newts are voracious feeders and will snap at any small passing creature with lunging body movements. Frogs and toads, on the other hand, feed almost entirely on land, catching prey with their tongue.

FROGS, TOADS, SALAMANDERS AND NEWTS

Probably the best-known of all amphibians, frogs are popular with gardeners for their ability to capture and eat insects, and many people derive immense pleasure, if not pride, from watching "their" frogs return to breed year after year. As wild habitats become increasingly scarce, our gardens (especially those with a suitable pond) provide a vital refuge for these fascinating creatures.

Though similar to frogs, toads differ in having a warty skin – frogs have a smooth, shiny skin – and they generally walk rather than leap. Having said that, toads do resemble frogs in their appearance and life cycle, and often eat the same prey.

Salamanders and newts are considerably different and much more reminiscent of the first amphibians that were the original vertebrate life forms to colonize the land, some 375 million years ago. When encountered for the first time, salamanders and newts can cause quite a stir because people often mistake them for lizards. Despite their looks, however, these common little amphibians are quite harmless to us, and are useful because they eat garden insects and invertebrates.

A LIFE CYCLE IN TWO HALVES

All the amphibians you are likely to encounter in the garden must return to water in order to breed and, although the exact time and way in which this takes place may vary according to the species and geographical location, the life cycle is basically the same for all of them. The adults return to breed in ponds, usually in late winter or early spring and, once they arrive, a frenetic spate of breeding usually ensues. Breeding is often synchronized so that the spawn (egg masses) in a pond is laid over a short period. This ensures that there is too much for predators to eat, so that some eggs will hatch.

PLANTS TO ATTRACT FROGS

Flag iris (*Iris pseudacorus*)
Duck weed (*Spirodela polyrhiza*)
Marsh marigold (*Caltha palustris*)
Water mint (*Mentha aquatica*)
White water lily (*Nymphaea alba*)

Flag iris **Marsh marigold**

Water mint **White water lily**

Once they do hatch, the young amphibians are considerably different from their parents. These tadpoles are born and live entirely in water, and have tails that allow them to swim like a fish. They also have gills so that they can breathe under water. As the tadpoles grow into adults, they lose their gills and, in the case of frogs and toads, their tails. All develop legs for moving on land and, like their parents, spend much of their time on land, although they'll also swim in water.

THREATS

Disease Amphibians all over the world have been falling prey to a disease called *Amphibian chytridiomycosis* that is an infection of their skin cells by a microscopic fungus. The reasons for its spread are still unclear but many species are affected.

Habitat loss The loss of wetlands for both agricultural and urban development has taken a very heavy toll on amphibian breeding grounds. In addition the habitats occupied by adult amphibians are also under threat in some cases and many species are rare as a result.

Pesticides Many amphibians have very sensitive skin that is not entirely watertight, and is protected by a layer of mucus. This enables them to absorb oxygen when submerged, but also means that they tend to absorb poisons easily.

AQUATIC LIFE

Ponds are an important part of any wildlife garden, although few of us ever see or appreciate the true richness of the habitat that lies just below the water surface. Aquatic habitats are some of the most interesting and diverse habitats that it is possible to create in a garden. Their murky depths hide a constant and ongoing struggle between species to survive and breed, with many of these being highly specialized – often with a colourful, sometimes strange, and occasionally unique appearance.

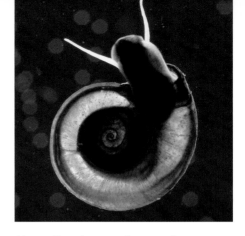

Above: *Ramshorn snails generally eat the most delicate plants, preferring algae, although they may also eat decaying matter.*

ROLE IN GARDENS

Many of the creatures that live in a garden pond are from familiar groups of animals, and the aquatic realm has creatures from almost all the major groups of land animals. Consequently, a great many of them must rise to the surface to breathe, and some have adult forms that live as dry-land dwellers.

Freshwater habitats are very fertile and, as with many land habitats, are extremely rich in microscopic life. This is of vital importance in sustaining those larger creatures that exist further up the food chain. Often the rich soup of micro-organisms in ponds serves to make these habitats somewhat cloudy, so that all that can usually be seen are the more sizeable creatures, and even they are small and flea-like. The larger creatures are much more visible, though, and can sometimes be seen as they move around in the murky shallows.

Creatures that live in fresh water are essentially divided into two types: those that live in still water (e.g. a pond) and those that must have flowing water (and live in streams or rivers). There are relatively few creatures that fall into the latter category, and many of the creatures that will commonly inhabit a garden pond may also be found in streams and slow-flowing rivers.

PROFILE

Algal bloom This condition particularly affects ponds with raised nutrient levels or an imbalance in the ecosystem. Pond environments must be balanced, and a small pond should have plenty of floating-leaved plants and not contain fish that eat small algal feeders.

Garden benefits A pond is always a positive benefit because it provides a source of drinking water for many land animals, and because many of the species that dwell in the water emerge when adult, enriching the wider habitat.

Potential for nuisance Summer mosquitoes are a major nuisance, as breeding females suck animal blood before laying eggs in shallow pools. Encourage bats, which will eat the adults, and wear mosquito repellent.

Risk to people or pets The main source of danger is the water itself, with its inherent risk of drowning, especially to young children.

HABITAT PREFERENCES

Aquatic life is, in many ways, a completely separate habitat from the rest of the garden. Its most obvious benefit may be that larger terrestrial garden visitors can get a quick drink, and a few, such as herons, can feed here.

Many of the species in the water are only aquatic for part of their life, with some insects, for example, having entirely aquatic larvae that become entirely land- (or air-) dwelling adults. Mosquitoes hatch on the water surface and then take to the air, being the preferred prey of many smaller night-flying bats, such as the little brown bats of North America or the pipistrelle of Europe and Asia. Pregnant females of these species actually come close to eating their own body weight in mosquitoes in a single night.

Other species form part of a seasonal glut when they emerge from the water. Young amphibians, for example, emerge in their thousands although most of them fall prey to larger land animals in their first couple of years. Insects, such as the mayfly, emerge in synchronized "hatchings", usually over just a few days, in which time they fill the air and cause a feeding frenzy among birds and larger flying insects. The pond is also a breeding

Left: *Sticklebacks are extremely widespread fish that feed at night upon worms, insect larvae, small snails and water fleas.*

Above: *Backswimmers swim upside down near the surface of the water, eating tadpoles, small fish and aquatic insects.*

THREATS

Climate change This threatens many species worldwide, including a vast number of aquatic organisms. Gradual changes in temperature and rainfall patterns over time may well result in the loss of certain key species that may, in turn, affect the populations of other pond-dwellers.

Habitat loss As natural wetlands and ponds disappear, so the numbers of animals that depend on them diminish. While some are able to relocate, others are unable to migrate as a land-living relative might, and have often become rare.

Invasive species Some species, whether deliberately or accidentally introduced, are termed "invasive" because they tend to grow rapidly, spread easily, and frequently out-compete native species. If they escape into wild habitats they may wreak havoc.

Pesticides These often accumulate in a pond if the water that drains from the surrounding land into them becomes contaminated. Over time, pesticides can reach toxic levels, and it is often the smallest animals at the base of the food chain that are the first to suffer the consequences.

ground, and occasional refuge, for many useful species including amphibians and the spectacular dragonflies that are excellent predators of garden insects and pests.

A new garden pond is often quite devoid of life, and it can take a couple of years before the ecology builds up. The complexity will develop over time and, as it does, more creatures will take up residence, so that after just a few short years the pond becomes an important element in both the garden and the wider habitat. The best ponds for wildlife have a variety of habitats, including deep and shallow shelves where the water can warm up during the day. In addition, there will be plenty of vegetation to give cover and oxygenate the water, whilst offering a variety of cover for the animals to hide in, make shelters, lay their eggs and raise the next generation.

BENEFITS OF HAVING FLEAS, LICE AND SNAILS IN THE POND

All three are a sign of a well-balanced, healthy habitat. For a pond to have clear water, free of mats of floating algae (algal bloom), these creatures are a "must".

Many are very small crustaceans, belonging to three important groups - the water fleas, the ostracods, and the copepods, with the water fleas, such as *Daphnia*, being the largest. They are extremely important in the food chain of a pond because they are very numerous, they harvest tiny, floating algae, and clear the water before being eaten by larger animals. Water lice are also crustaceans, being closely related to the familiar land-dwelling woodlice that they resemble, although they have a flatter body. Water snails often breathe air, and can be seen coming up to the surface. They feed on the tiny algal "meadows" that often coat the plants and pond sides, and therefore help keep the water clear, which in turn keeps the plants healthy.

FEEDING STRATEGIES

Pond-dwelling creatures can be grouped into three types of feeders: herbivores; filter feeders that eat detritus (all the semi-decayed fragments of plants or animals); and predators.

Many herbivores, such as pond snails, unlike their land-based relatives, do not actually eat the pond plants, but graze on the algae growing on them and on the pond sides, when the water gets sufficient light. The filter feeders, or detritivores, are often slow-moving creatures at the pond bottom that usually escape our attention, and include a variety of worms, molluscs and crustaceans, such as the water lice and so-called "water fleas" that move around in the water with jerky movements. They are very important in keeping water clear and are, in turn, eaten by larger creatures, thus forming an essential part of the pond's food chain.

The most exciting and often the most visible aquatic creatures are the predatory ones, such as backswimmers. These will pursue and overpower prey that is significantly larger than themselves,

Above: *Pond water will stay clear when daphnia, or water fleas, are present. These will also provide food for larger predators.*

including tadpoles and small fish. Not all predators are as noticeable, however. Dragonfly larvae, though rarely seen, are super predators that catch prey with lightning speed, using their unique mouthparts to ensnare their hapless victims.

PLANTS TO ATTRACT AQUATIC LIFE

Use the following plant types to attract different aquatic species. A range of plants is essential to provide different habitats for as many different species as possible.

Marginal/emergent plants, e.g. water mint
Water lilies and deep water aquatics

Oxygenators, e.g. *Elodea*
Free-floating plants, e.g. water soldier

Water mint

White water lily

Elodea

Water soldier

SPIDERS AND SCORPIONS

Probably some of the most feared creatures in the garden, spiders and scorpions can invoke severe bouts of arachnophobia. Despite this, both are important in nature, with spiders being particularly beneficial because they feed on insect pests. The hunting prowess of both spiders and their distant relatives, the scorpions, means that they help to control the numbers of other species and so play a vital role in the garden habitat.

Above: *Golden silk spiders, common in the southern USA, spin large webs to catch flies, bees, wasps, moths and butterflies.*

ROLE IN GARDENS

Spiders and scorpions are distantly related, and are among the oldest of all land animals, belonging to a group of creatures called the *Arachnids*. Both have four pairs of walking legs and fangs (called *chelicerae*) that are adapted for liquid feeding.

Spiders are extremely diverse and have the distinction of being the largest group of predatory animals. Some of the most familiar types are the big-eyed jumping spiders, small sheet-web spiders, orb-weaving spiders, cobweb spiders, non-web-weaving wolf spiders and crab spiders. Scorpions are the largest arachnids, with some tropical species reaching over 20cm (8in) long. The long body ends in a narrow, tail-like structure with a curved stinger held up over the back that delivers venom and paralyzes larger prey. They are mostly nocturnal, and all tend to have the peculiar property of fluorescing at night under an ultraviolet lantern.

While both spiders and scorpions are important predators, spiders are the most abundant and most ecologically important group, being found in almost every habitat.

One Eurasian spider family (*Argyronetidae*) even lives underwater in ponds and lakes where it makes silken "diving bells" that it fills with air brought from the surface.

Because of their abundance, spiders rank among the most important predators in many ecosystems, and their numbers can often exceed 100 per m² (sq yd). In short, their combined weight in a habitat often exceeds that of larger predators, albeit fewer in number, such as birds.

As all spiders are predators, mainly eating insects, they are a great benefit in the garden, controlling many pests and balancing insect populations. Despite this abundance however, spiders cannot reproduce faster than their insect prey, and so if populations are damaged by insecticides, the surviving insect pests often grow to larger population sizes than before the insecticide was applied – a phenomenon known as resurgence. Of course many spiders also become a meal for others, and they can be an important food source for birds, lizards, wasps and other creatures. Spider silk is also an important material for

some birds when building nests, with many songbirds, and nearly all species of hummingbird, heavily dependent on it.

HABITAT PREFERENCES

Spiders occupy just about every habitat in the garden, and if you keep your garden pesticide-free their numbers soon grow, with many newcomers actually parachuting in by ballooning. This involves attaching long strands of silk to a firm anchor point before

Below: *Garden spiders are common on bushes and other vegetation, where they feed on flying insects caught in a sticky web.*

Below: *Harvestmen, only distantly related to spiders, have many omnivorous species that eat insects, fungus and decaying matter.*

PROFILE

Diet Although spiders and scorpions often have particular prey specialities, the variety of forms and species means that they are mostly generalist feeders taking advantage of any available prey. All are predatory.

Garden benefits Both spiders and scorpions are important in controlling the number of insects in a habitat. Spiders are particularly important in this respect, often more so than many larger predators.

Life span This varies according to the species, with most scorpions appearing to live for about 3–4 years, although some exceed this. Spiders are much more variable, and while some live just one year, most live longer with some tarantulas surviving for 30 years.

Risk of bite or sting Most spiders and scorpions have venomous bites or stings, although their potency and willingness to use them varies greatly. Despite a scorpion's reputation, few pose a real threat to humans but, if you are stung, seek medical attention immediately.

Above: *The desert hairy scorpion, native to the southern USA, is a burrowing species, but can also be found under stones or logs.*

rising air currents lift the spiders up and into the breeze, dispersing them to new habitats. These spiders are usually small and immature, and are the familiar "money spiders" seen in the summer and autumn.

Scorpions tend to move more slowly than this, but if they are common in your area and you have a garden that is to their liking, they soon colonize it. They are rarely seen, typically preferring cool, shady areas where they hide in the day. A drystone wall, rock or log pile is often the best site, whence they emerge at dusk to commence a night of hunting.

FEEDING STRATEGIES

All spiders and scorpions are predators, and the majority are generalist predators, eating many different kinds of insects and other small animals. Most rely on their venomous bite or sting to subdue their prey. The greatest variety is seen among the spiders, with some feeding on certain types of prey. Most use a web of carefully constructed sticky silk fibres to ensnare their prey, while others – the wolf and jumping spiders – do not use a web but subdue their prey by pouncing on them.

Crab spiders are experts at ambush and often hide in flowers, from where they deliver fatal bites with pinpoint accuracy to bees, butterflies, and other would-be pollinators.

Scorpions are nocturnal feeders that either lie in wait to ambush prey, or actively hunt. Their diet includes insects, centipedes, millipedes, snails, spiders, other scorpions and even small reptiles and mice. They detect them by air movement over the long, sensory hairs on the body that trigger a dash to capture the prey. The victim is caught by pincers and stung to subdue and kill it, before it is eaten head first. Scorpions do not eat every day and some can survive from 6–12 months without food. On any one night, therefore, only a small percentage may be seen feeding; the population may be much greater than a search might suggest.

PLANTS TO ATTRACT SPIDERS

Blackthorn (*Prunus spinosa*)
Hawthorn (*Crataegus monogyna*)
Ivy (*Hedera helix*)
Lawson cypress (*Chamaecyparis lawsoniana*)

Blackthorn

Hawthorn

Ivy

Lawson cypress

Above: *Many spiders and scorpions need an area of dense undisturbed vegetation in which to hide from larger predators.*

THREATS

Habitat loss Many spider species are restricted to particular habitats, such as wetlands, that are threatened by human development, resource extraction, and agricultural activities, with some species being very rare as a result.

Persecution Spiders have much more to fear from us than we do from them, and indeed the overblown fear of both spiders and scorpions has led to their being remorselessly persecuted in the home and garden.

Pesticides Spiders are extremely sensitive to the effects of pesticides in the environment, and often decline when they are used. The effects of pollution, acid rain, and climate change also pose a major threat.

Predators While scorpions and spiders are well equipped for survival, they are not without their natural enemies. Scorpions not only feed on each other but are prey to other animals, while spiders fall prey in large numbers to wasps and birds.

BUTTERFLIES AND MOTHS

Almost universally loved, butterflies are the epitome of insect activity on a warm summer afternoon. They are beautiful and graceful and, with their night-flying cousins, the moths, form an important group in many habitats. The larvae, or caterpillars as they are known, eat vegetation and, although we may regard them as pests for this, they form an important food item for larger animals in the garden.

Above: *Moths differ from butterflies, with their ability to fold their wings horizontally and their short, feathery antennae.*

ROLE IN GARDENS

Many gardeners claim to love butterflies, although they show considerably less concern for the larval stages. In fact, some gardeners develop an almost unnatural horror at the sight of a caterpillar, making open warfare that has led, in some cases, to an unprecedented decline in the numbers of certain species. With the additional loss of suitable breeding and feeding habitats, the picture for many butterfly and moth species looks bleak.

Both butterflies and moths are important elements of many habitats, as a source of food for many predators and as herbivores because their larvae often eat a considerable amount of plant material. From hatching to pupation a caterpillar increases its body size more than 30,000 times, and all this plant material that is converted into body tissue can be a rich source of protein for other animals. A few

Below: *Butterflies are almost always day-fliers, unlike most moths, and have brightly coloured wings and clubbed antennae.*

moths are infamous pests, such as the cabbage white, tortrix and tomato moth, but others actually eat weeds.

Moths, in particular, are extremely numerous and often form an extremely important part of the diet of many bat species. The bats locate the moths using high-pitched echolocation, although moths have sensitive "ears" and when some species hear the ultrasonic squeak of a bat, they close their wings, and drop like a stone out of harm's way. Other species even send out a jamming sound that effectively blinds the bat to their presence. In fact, it is widely believed that butterflies actually evolved from moths and became active by day to avoid night-flying predators.

Despite their basic similarities, butterflies and moths are quite easy to distinguish. The simplest way – if you can get close enough – is to look at the antennae. Butterfly antennae have a ball (or club) on the end of the antennae. Moths never have a club, and have either plain or feathery antennae. In addition, the majority of butterflies rest with their wings folded up above the body, whereas most moths rest with their wings folded along the body or outspread. Butterflies also have thinner bodies than moths and generally have a slower wing beat, tending to flutter; moths produce a whirring motion.

HABITAT PREFERENCES

Most butterflies prefer a sunny feeding site by day, whereas moths need suitable species of night-scented flowers with nectar. Of equal importance to both, however, is a larval food plant in sufficient numbers to guarantee that enough caterpillars pupate and reach adulthood to maintain the population. Both adults and their young need your help, and plants should be chosen accordingly.

PROFILE

Climate change The habitats of some butterflies have started to change and are now less suitable. Butterflies would normally migrate to combat this, but habitat fragmentation may make this impossible for some species.

Collection The wings of many butterflies and some moths are often sought by collectors, making some species scarce. Despite the legal protection of some species, the problem continues.

Garden benefits Both butterflies and moths are important elements of the food chain, and pollinate many plant species. Their grace and beauty also enhance the summer garden.

Potential for nuisance Despite their reputation, don't kill caterpillars because they may be doing no harm to ornamental plants. Bug screens across open windows will prevent moths from entering rooms on warm nights.

Risk to people or pets Some butterflies and moths variously hiss, mimic stinging insects or even have what look like eyes on their wings to ward off predators. They are harmless to us, but many caterpillars have irritant hairs that can cause rashes if touched.

Supplementary diet Butterfly-feeders contain a sponge chamber filled with honey or sugar water. Moths can be attracted using a solution of dark beer, molasses, brown sugar and a dash of rum, painted on to tree trunks.

FEEDING STRATEGIES

Both butterflies and moths have a long, tube-like mouthpart kept in a tight coil. Once unfurled it's dipped into a flower for sucking out the nectar. Butterflies generally land on the flower or flower head to do this, whereas moths more commonly hover in front of the bloom when feeding, although all show a preference for scented flowers with long, tubular throats. Caterpillars, on the other hand, are simply eating machines

Right: *Some adult moths and butterflies have vivid eye spots on the wings. These are very effective in confusing or dissuading would-be predators.*

that consume vast amounts of plant material to convert it into body tissue, which they do with tremendous efficiency over quite a short period.

A LIFE IN TWO HALVES

Both butterflies and moths have larvae that look nothing like the adults, and undergo a complete metamorphosis during the pupal stage. This cycle starts with the female butterfly laying eggs on or near a food plant. The young caterpillars hatch from the eggs after a few days or weeks, although eggs laid in autumn will not hatch until the following spring.

These young caterpillars are literally eating machines whose main purpose in life is to change plant matter into body tissue. Amazingly, they may eat 10 times their own eventual weight in food. As they grow, they fill their skins, shed them, and emerge with a new skin, four or five times, before turning into a chrysalis (the pupal stage). To do this, the fully grown caterpillar makes a button of silk that it uses to attach itself to a twig before shedding its skin, one last time. The new, exposed skin layer is hard and often golden (the word chrysalis means gold), although it usually darkens in time.

Right: Verbena bonariensis *is an absolutely wonderful butterfly attractor, even rivalling the well known* Buddleja *in this respect.*

Inside the chrysalis, the body turns to a soupy liquid before, gradually, the wings, legs and other parts of the butterfly form. When the butterfly emerges from the chrysalis, its wings are initially wrinkled and gradually open. The butterfly hangs upside down and gently beats its wings, pumping air and liquid from the body into the wings before finally taking flight.

LIFE CYCLE OF A BUTTERFLY

The butterfly undergoes a complete change between the larval and adult stages. The caterpillars look like a different species, and need to eat large amounts of vegetation to grow. The adults live for a short time, mating and reproducing.

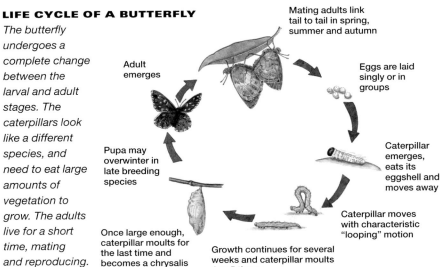

Mating adults link tail to tail in spring, summer and autumn

Adult emerges

Eggs are laid singly or in groups

Caterpillar emerges, eats its eggshell and moves away

Caterpillar moves with characteristic "looping" motion

Growth continues for several weeks and caterpillar moults 4 or 5 times

Once large enough, caterpillar moults for the last time and becomes a chrysalis

Pupa may overwinter in late breeding species

BEETLES AND BUGS

With about a quarter of a million species, beetles are by far the largest group of insects and probably the dominant group on the planet. They include a number of important garden predators among their ranks, as well as many strange and interesting species that fulfil a vast array of roles within almost every conceivable habitat in a garden. Bugs, on the other hand, while less diverse, include many familiar insects, comprising a number of both pests and predators.

Above: *Ladybirds are a widespread and familiar group of beetles, well known to gardeners for their aphid-eating habits.*

ROLE IN GARDENS

Beetles occur almost everywhere on the planet except for Antarctica, and are common in gardens. They can easily be recognized by the front wings that have hardened and modified into protective shells called elytra that usually cover the whole abdomen in most species. There are exceptions, of course, and they are very short in rove beetles and are completely absent from the female glow-worm, or firefly as it's sometimes known.

All species have biting mouthparts, although they can be extremely variable between different species. While most beetles can fly, some have no hind wings at all, and their elytra are fused together and immovable. As for those with the power of flight, most prefer to walk, scuttling away when disturbed, or simply dropping to the ground and "playing possum" (lying still and feigning death), with their legs held tight against the body.

The life cycle of many species is somewhat complex, and involves a metamorphosis with four or more larval stages and a pupa before the adult finally

Below: *Most beetles are easily recognized by their hardened front wings, modified into protective shells that cover the abdomen.*

emerges. The larvae are very diverse, sometimes legless, but nearly always with a well-developed head and biting jaws.

While bugs sometimes resemble beetles, their elytra always overlap. In addition, bugs have a piercing beak (or rostrum) that is never seen in beetles. Bugs also have a life cycle that involves an incomplete metamorphosis where the young (or nymphs) generally resemble small, wingless adults, although their colours and markings may be very different. Many species have young that exist with the adults and feed in the same way, whereas others, such as cicadas, have nymphs that are specialized for burrowing and appear quite different from the adults.

Both beetles and bugs fulfil a whole range of roles in the garden, acting as herbivores, predators and decomposers, at which some are highly specialized. Some beetles, such as the sexton or burying beetles, actually find and bury the carcasses of small rodents, using them as a food store for their young. Scarab beetles remove dung, and a whole host of beetles of all sizes chew their way through deadwood, helping to recycle and break it down. The sheer number of beetles and bugs (that, in turn, are taken by other predators) makes it possible only to generalize about their role in the garden, but they are possibly the most important creatures in any given habitat and, as such, a valuable part of the garden food chain.

HABITAT PREFERENCES

Both bugs and beetles can be found almost anywhere, including aquatic habitats. Beetles are especially common in gardens because their tough elytra give them added protection, and allow them to occupy places that are denied to other winged insects. Many of them, for example, live in

the soil and under stones while others spend their lives groping their way through leaf litter and compost heaps. Water beetles use the spaces between their elytra and their bodies as rechargeable air cylinders that enable them to spend long periods under the water, whereas water bugs often breathe through a tail-like siphon that connects them to the air.

PROFILE

Diet The diet of both bugs and insects is very eclectic because they live in virtually every type of ecosystem, both above and beneath the ground, as well as under water. They eat decomposing plant or animal material, living plants, or are predators.

Life span The life span of most adult beetles and bugs is short, although some wood-boring beetles live for more than 40 years, albeit mostly as larvae. Cicadas (a bug) also live for a long time, spending 3–17 years as nymphs.

Risk of bite or sting If roughly handled, many beetles discharge obnoxious fluids, and may squeak or buzz to alarm you. Large specimens can also inflict a sharp nip with their jaws, and some bugs, such as the aquatic backswimmer, can give very painful bites.

The largest animal order All beetles belong to the order *Coleoptera*, the largest order in the entire animal kingdom (there are more species of beetles than plant species). In total there are an estimated 350,000 named species, and many more still unnamed ones, constituting 30 per cent of all insects.

GARDEN BENEFITS OF BEETLES

Beetles can be very useful in the garden, consuming slugs, snails and caterpillars. In certain circumstances, however, they can compete for resources with other garden creatures, and attack and cause much damage to plants, furniture and buildings.

Beetles and their larvae are also an important source of food for many larger birds and mammals, and they are eaten by badgers, foxes, and toads as well as by many birds, such as thrushes, wrens, woodpeckers, crows and nuthatches. You will also often see crows, magpies and, occasionally, gulls, searching for chafer grubs in fields or, more annoyingly, in lawns, although this usually causes less long-term harm than the grubs might cause. Beetles also help in breaking down larger organic matter, such as carrion, dung and plant material, and some even aerate the soil and act as pollinators.

Above: *Leaf litter is home to many beetles, some of which feed upon it directly, whilst others hunt in its moist, shady shelter.*

PLANTS TO ATTRACT LADYBIRDS

Alpine cinquefoil (*Potentilla crantzii*)
Bugle (*Ajuga reptans*)
Fern-leaved yarrow (*Achillea filipendula*)
French marigold (*Tagetes patula*)
Penstemon (*Penstemon strictus*)
Prairie sunflower (*Helianthus maximiliani*)
Speedwell (*Veronica spicata*)
Tansy (*Tanacetum vulgare*)

Fern-leaved yarrow

French marigold

Speedwell

Tansy

FEEDING STRATEGIES

Beetles eat a very wide range of foods, both animal and vegetable, living and dead. Most beetle larvae are rather stout and slow, but adults vary in size and shape, with some, such as longhorn beetles and impressive stag beetles, being very large indeed. Others, such as some of the pollen beetles, are merely tiny black specks to our eyes.

Of the predatory types, ground beetles and ladybirds are probably the best-known examples, both being excellent controllers of pests. Ground beetles are long-legged and fast, and while some have a beautiful metallic sheen, the majority are dark. They live in litter layers above the soil, and hunt slugs and other ground-living invertebrates. Ladybirds are also voracious predators that hunt on the plants themselves, feeding on aphids (greenfly), coccids (scale insects), mealybugs, whitefly and, occasionally, on other garden insect pests and crop plants, in both their larval and adult stages.

Bugs are similarly diverse, and have adapted to a wide range of habitats and lifestyles. Most bugs are herbivores and use their piercing "beaks" to suck plant sap directly from the cells or veins of leaves and stems. Possibly the best known is the aphid, that often plagues gardens in the summer, although many more plant-sucking bugs, such as leaf hoppers, capsid bugs and shield bugs, are also familiar garden species.

THREATS

Habitat loss While many beetles in gardens are common and widespread, other species are very specific in their requirements. Many wood-boring beetles need deadwood for their larvae to eat and grow in.

Human intervention Beetles and bugs are often feared when encountered, and may be killed by people ignorant of their garden value. Some species are also taken by collectors, particularly if they are brightly coloured.

Pesticides Many beetles are predators, and they are extremely susceptible to even quite small residues of pesticide. This is most serious when prey species develop a resistance, and relatively large amounts of pesticide may accumulate in their body tissue.

Predators Beetles, like any other garden insect, have their enemies, and if they are large predators their protective armour will not be enough to save them. Foxes, badgers and even bats will take beetles if given the opportunity, or if other food is scarce.

LIFE CYCLE OF A LADYBIRD

The ladybird's larva is an even more voracious predator than the adult, and commences feeding as soon as it hatches. It often goes unnoticed because both it and the pupa resemble a bird dropping – an effective camouflage.

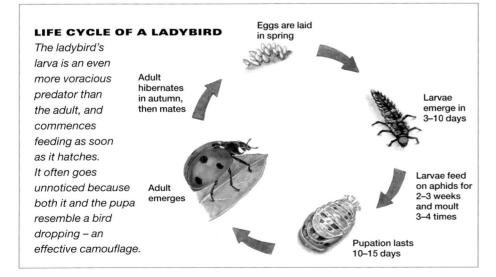

Eggs are laid in spring

Larvae emerge in 3–10 days

Larvae feed on aphids for 2–3 weeks and moult 3–4 times

Pupation lasts 10–15 days

Adult emerges

Adult hibernates in autumn, then mates

BEES AND WASPS

Both bees and wasps play a vital role in maintaining a balanced, healthy ecology in our gardens: bees are very effective pollinators, and wasps are good at controlling insect pests throughout the growing season. The latter especially may be hard to love, but without them, life outdoors would actually be more difficult. Wasps' hunting activities are extremely important in controlling numbers of potentially devastating garden pests, such as caterpillars, thus helping to reduce damage to plants.

Above: *Bees are important natural pollinators of plants. Without them, many trees, such as this apple, would not be able to bear fruit.*

ROLE IN GARDENS

Bees are immensely important in any habitat that contains flowering plants, and are the single most important insect pollinator in gardens. Around 80 per cent of the food we eat comes from crops that have been pollinated by bees and, without their efforts, many species would become rare and eventually die out in the wild. Ironically, bees originally evolved from solitary hunting wasps, becoming vegetarian in the process, and today there are about 19,000 known species of bee; while many remain numerous, some are rare or endangered.

Wasps differ from bees principally in the fact that they feed their young on meat – such as insect larvae and scraps of carrion – rather than nectar and pollen. Although there are some 75,000 different species of wasp, most of the attention is given to the larger, social wasps, so named because they live in colonies that can number thousands. They are also highly beneficial insects (eating their way through tens of thousands of garden pests each season), and are only annoying because some species have adapted to living in close proximity to us. Unlike the honeybee, social wasps have not developed methods of storing food for winter, which means their colonies last for only one season. In the autumn, new queen wasps leave the colony to search for a sheltered spot where they can spend the winter.

HABITAT PREFERENCES

Most bees in the world are solitary with a short lifespan, living as adults for only about 6–8 weeks. A range of species has evolved to exploit particular environmental niches, and they emerge at different times of the year. Many have no sting because they do not store honey (and don't need a defensive weapon), and because their nest is only open for short intervals of time. Mated

Above: *Social wasps, such as these yellow jackets, live in large colonies that they may fiercely defend using their stings if they are threatened.*

Left: *Wasps are excellent hunters, but only the larvae are carnivorous, with the adults depending upon sugary liquids instead.*

female bees live alone in a hole or burrow in well-drained soil, in soft brick mortar, in wood (in the case of carpenter bees), or any other convenient hole that suits their needs.

Bumblebees and honeybees, on the other hand, live together in colonies (a hive) and store both honey and pollen to feed on in periods of food shortage or bad weather. Wasps are mostly solitary and, even in the case of the social wasps, the only individuals that survive a winter are the young fertilized queens.

PROFILE

Diet Bees are exclusively vegetarian, and feed on a diet of sugary nectar and pollen. Wasps, on the other hand, are active hunters although many species have adults that are vegetarian, having a taste for sugar, while others feed on pollen or meat.

Life span In general, the life of an adult bee or wasp is relatively short, ranging from a few weeks to a few months. Few last longer than a season, and the only real exception is the queen honeybee that lives three or more years.

Risk of bite or sting For most people this is a mild, albeit painful annoyance, but a significant minority are allergic to stings and suffer extreme reactions.

And if you are stung ... The proper way to remove a bee sting is to scratch it out. Never pull one out because this forces venom from the sac into the skin, causing more swelling. Wasp stings are not left in the skin. Antihistamine cream will help reduce the swelling or other allergic reaction.

DIFFERENCE BETWEEN POLLEN AND NECTAR

Nectar and pollen are produced by flowers, and both form an important part of the diet of bees. Nectar is a liquid that is extremely rich in sugars, and is produced in glands called nectaries, generally at the base of the flower cup. Pollinators are made to brush the flower's reproductive parts to reach it. Nectar that is produced outside the flower is generally produced to attract predatory insects, which eat both the nectar and plant-eating insects.

Pollen is produced by the male part of a flower, and its role is to fertilize the ovaries of the female part of a flower and promote diversity. As insects, or other pollinators, brush past the male parts of the flower when they gather nectar, they often become coated in it, and involuntarily transport it from flower to flower, thereby playing an important role in many plants' reproductive cycles. Bees actually eat the pollen and collect it by brushing it into pollen sacs, situated on their rear legs.

FEEDING STRATEGIES

Bees are characteristically busy because they must constantly forage across their range to gather enough nectar and pollen for their young to feed on.

Wasps are all carnivorous as larvae, although the adults often feed on high-energy food such as nectar and other sugary liquids. Of the 25,000-odd known species, about 16,000 are parasitic, feeding on the bodies or eggs of other insects or spiders. Other larger hunting wasps catch

and kill insects that they chew into round food balls and carry home to the larvae. The larvae then secrete a sugary liquid that the adult social wasps feed on, and it is this that cements the bond in their hives.

Wasps vary greatly in size with some of the parasitic species being so small that several may develop in a small insect egg, while other species can reach a body length of about 5cm (2in). In gardens, you're most likely to see social wasps, especially in autumn when they're attracted to ripening fruit. As the adults begin to starve, with the number of grubs gradually decreasing from late summer, they desperately seek nutrition elsewhere, being attracted to sugary liquids. The combination of cooler weather and fermenting fruit often makes them highly irritable and more likely to sting.

Left: *Bees need plenty of flowering plants that bloom over a long period to provide them with enough food.*

LIFE CYCLE OF A BUMBLEBEE

Bumblebees are social bees, meaning that they form cooperative colonies of very closely related individuals. Unlike honeybees, bumblebees don't survive the winter: a new colony is formed each spring, when the queen seeks a suitable nest site such as a rodent burrow.

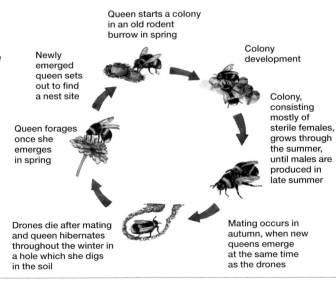

Queen starts a colony in an old rodent burrow in spring

Colony development

Colony, consisting mostly of sterile females, grows through the summer, until males are produced in late summer

Mating occurs in autumn, when new queens emerge at the same time as the drones

Drones die after mating and queen hibernates throughout the winter in a hole which she digs in the soil

Queen forages once she emerges in spring

Newly emerged queen sets out to find a nest site

PLANTS TO ATTRACT BEES

Shrubby plants
Blackberry (*Rubus fruticosus*)
Lavender (*Lavandula stoechas*)
Laurustinus (*Viburnum tinus*)

Lavender   Laurustinus

Herbaceous and annuals
Bee balm (*Monarda didyma*)
Catmint (*Nepeta racemosa*)
Giant yellow hyssop (*Agastache nepetoides*)

Bee balm   Catmint

THREATS

Habitat loss Many bee species entered a decline during the twentieth century, and a number of species have already become extinct as a result. It is estimated that around 25 per cent of wild bees are currently either rare or threatened with extinction.

Parasites Almost all species of wasps and bees have parasites that attack them, particularly when they are larvae.

Pesticides Bees are very sensitive to many pesticides, especially insecticides that are absorbed by the plant. They can end up in the nectar and poison both the bees and their young. Wasps or their larvae often succumb to a build-up of insecticide residues from their prey.

Predators Both wasps and bees may be eaten by other insects or larger predators. Some birds, such as bee eaters and honey buzzards, specialize in eating bees or their young, and badgers often dig into wild bee nests to raid the honey and young grubs.

EARWIGS AND FLIES

There are many species of earwig, easily recognized by their pincer-like appendages (or cerci) on the tail end that are straight-sided in females but curved and larger in males. They are omnivores, rarely causing serious damage to plants, but eating some garden pests. Flies, on the other hand, are extremely diverse, and aside from the familiar, irritating houseflies, count many useful predatory species in their ranks. Ultimately, both earwigs and flies form an important food source for other garden inhabitants.

Above: *Earwigs are a common sight in many gardens, where they feed on decaying plant and animal matter and other insects.*

ROLE IN GARDENS

The word earwig comes from the old English word *earwicga*, meaning ear beetle, following the old European superstition that these insects crawled into people's ears while they were asleep and bored into their brains.

Earwigs are unusual among insects because the females remain and care for both the eggs and young nymphs. In spring, the female, sometimes assisted by the male, builds a nest underground in which to lay her eggs. She then evicts the male and carefully attends to the eggs, turning them regularly and cleaning them until they hatch, after which she continues to tend and feed them until they can forage for themselves.

Flies belong to an immense order of insects known as *Diptera*, or the "true flies", with approximately 122,000 known species. It's an extremely diverse group, having evolved into a multitude of forms. Flies are generally recognized through their minute, pin-shaped hind wings, known as balancers, that act as gyroscopes and help maintain balance during flight.

Above: *Adult hoverflies feed mainly on nectar and pollen, but their larvae are often voracious predators of aphids.*

The fly life cycle is composed of four stages: egg, larva (or maggot), pupa and adult. The eggs are laid in, or near, the preferred habitat or food source of that particular species, which variously includes decaying flesh, animal manure, live prey, plants and pools of stagnant water.

Earwigs, particularly the European earwig, are often regarded as garden pests primarily due to their habit of chewing the flowers and young leaves of dahlias, clematis, chrysanthemums, lettuces and strawberries, etc. They can also be valuable predators of insect pests, such as aphids and mites. While most species are omnivorous, plant material almost always constitutes the bulk of the diet. Fortunately, earwig damage is not usually particularly severe, mostly restricted to a few species, and on the whole, their beneficial attributes of pest control and as a source of food for larger creatures outweigh this.

Left: *The late flowers of ivy (*Hedera) *offer a drink of nectar and some nutritious pollen to flies and other insects late in the season.*

Flies, on the other hand, are a much more mixed group and include some serious pests, such as the carrot and onion fly, as well as some of the most beneficial insects in the garden. The latter include the hoverflies and some midge species that are excellent controllers of aphids. The vast majority of the flies you see, however, act as scavengers and recyclers, feeding mostly

PROFILE

Diet Earwigs are omnivorous, feeding on a wide variety of insects as well as live or decaying vegetation, and occasionally attacking garden plants. Flies have evolved to exploit just about every imaginable food source, and are ecologically very important.

Garden benefits Both earwigs and flies are important creatures in the garden, helping to recycle nutrients and maintain the balance of other animal populations, serving as both predators and prey within the garden ecosystem.

Life span Earwigs can live for as long as two years, although many perish before this as a result of predation. Flies, on the other hand, tend to be shorter lived, often living for just a few weeks, although some temperate species have a total life cycle covering a whole year.

Risk of bite or sting Earwigs cannot bite humans, and even their impressive pincers are capable of delivering only a puny nip. Most flies are also harmless, although some species (e.g. mosquitoes, horse and march flies) can bite humans.

LIFE CYCLE OF A HOVERFLY

The hoverfly is often visible in gardens, where it is sometimes mistaken for a bee or wasp. The larvae or maggots of certain species of hoverfly are predatory, and eat aphids during the summer months. The adults feed mainly on nectar and pollen.

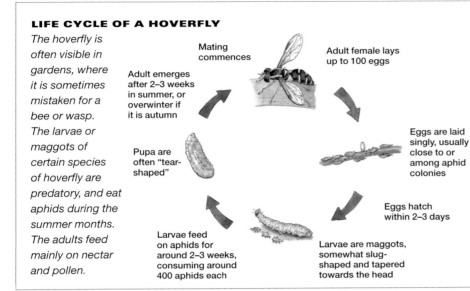

Mating commences

Adult female lays up to 100 eggs

Adult emerges after 2–3 weeks in summer, or overwinter if it is autumn

Eggs are laid singly, usually close to or among aphid colonies

Pupa are often "tear-shaped"

Eggs hatch within 2–3 days

Larvae feed on aphids for around 2–3 weeks, consuming around 400 aphids each

Larvae are maggots, somewhat slug-shaped and tapered towards the head

on decaying waste, such as dung and dead animals, and, ultimately, all become food for other insects and many birds. Flies are also extremely important pollinators, coming a close second to bees and wasps.

HABITAT PREFERENCES

Earwigs live in a variety of habitats but many species spend part of their life below ground. They are mostly active at night, hiding in moist, shady places beneath stones, and among debris during the day. While many species do have wings, they rarely fly and are unable to crawl long distances. Despite this, they are often inadvertently transported long distances by humans, with some species – such as the European earwig – now being widely distributed as a result.

Flies, on the other hand, are masters of the air and disperse readily. Their larvae are less mobile, though, and many species have young with a particular diet; hoverfly maggots, for example, eat aphids. The parents are therefore restricted to areas that can provide such food, although in certain cases, such as the housefly, human activities have resulted in it becoming extremely widespread across the entire planet.

FEEDING STRATEGIES

Earwigs are rapid runners that feed on a variety of foods that they consume with their biting and chewing mouthparts. While they fulfil a minor predatory role, feeding on aphids and other small invertebrates, they are primarily scavengers of dead plant material, although some do feed on live plants.

Adult flies feed almost exclusively on liquids, although a few hoverflies are able to crush pollen grains as part of their diet. Most use a variety of mouthparts to feed, ranging from the pad of the housefly that is used to regurgitate digestive juices on to the food before it and the food are sucked up, to piercing mouthparts that are used to suck the juices from plants or live prey. The larvae, on the other hand, have much simpler mouthparts that are used to swallow food or attack prey.

Tachinid flies, robber flies, bee flies and hoverflies are all carnivorous at some stage, and provide effective pest control in the garden. Other fly species, however, such as mosquitoes, horse and march flies, are bloodsuckers. While no adult flies ruin cultivated plants, the larvae of many species, including the carrot fly, leaf miner and leatherjacket, happily munch their way through garden plants and, if numerous, can become extremely damaging.

THREATS

Habitat loss Certain species of fly have a regular, seasonal life cycle, with their emergence coinciding with the appearance of a particular food source for them or their young. Changes in habitat can mean that this cycle and food availability is interrupted.

Persecution Both earwigs and flies are often unfairly singled out as undesirable elements of the garden insect population, despite the fact that all earwigs and most flies are harmless to humans. Generally, most species cause little damage to garden plants.

Pesticides Pesticides, especially those aimed at a broad spectrum of species, often affect flies, particularly the carnivorous types. However, pesticides in the food chain, and particularly their prey, can lead to a build-up in their own bodies that proves lethal.

Predators The abundance of many fly and earwig species means that they are an essential part of many food chains and, as such, many are caught and eaten by larger predators such as spiders. This is an essential part of their natural population control.

Flies will always be difficult to love in the garden, possibly because of their association with disease, death and decay, but also because they can be downright irritating when they buzz around you on a hot summer's day. Remember their importance as food for other animals, though, and that most species are actually on your side.

PLANTS TO ATTRACT HOVERFLIES

Black-eyed Susan (*Rudbeckia fulgida*)
Carrot (*Daucus carota*)
Coriander (*Coriandrum sativum*)
Dill (*Anethum graveolens*)

Fennel (*Foeniculum vulgare*)
Lobelia (*Lobelia erinus*)
Wood betony (*Stachys officinalis*)
Yarrow (*Achillea millefolium*)

Black-eyed Susan   **Coriander**   **Lobelia**   **Wood betony**

GRASSHOPPERS AND CRICKETS

Forming a large and varied group of insects, grasshoppers and crickets are mostly big, easily recognized creatures that are commonly found in gardens and beyond. They can be an important source of food for many larger garden inhabitants. More often heard than seen, their distinctive noise provides a familiar soundtrack throughout the day and on into the night during the warmer months of the year.

Above: *Grasshoppers are quite common in many areas, but need areas of long grass in which to hide and complete their life cycle.*

ROLE IN GARDENS

Although some species of grasshopper can become garden pests, most are quite happy to live their lives in long grass and rarely venture into the more ornamental parts of the garden. A few, such as the locust, are capable of devastating crops and gardens, which means that in some parts of the world all grasshoppers are tarred with the same brush and are persecuted.

While most grasshoppers are vegetarian, many crickets are omnivores and never attack garden plants. In addition, both are an abundant and nutritious food source that is eaten by a number of predators, including spiders, centipedes, birds, reptiles, amphibians and small mammals.

Grasshoppers and crickets are closely related, and often bear quite a close resemblance at first sight. But closer inspection shows that grasshoppers have short antennae and are predominantly active during the day, whereas most crickets have antennae that reach their abdomens (and normally further), and are often nocturnal. Despite this, it can be difficult to tell them apart, and some of the insects that we call grasshoppers are actually more closely related to crickets than they are to other grasshoppers.

Although you often find both crickets and grasshoppers in a garden, most species are restricted to their favoured habitats. The most noticeable feature of grasshoppers and most crickets is their long, jumping hind legs that enable them to leap well over twenty times their body length. They are also noted for their ability to make a variety of sounds, many of which are intended to protect territory or attract mates. Only male grasshoppers make these noises as a rule, and in some species they use both sound and vision to impress potential partners. A few species may be

Left: *Whilst closely related, grasshoppers differ from crickets by their shorter antennae and by being active during the day.*

PROFILE

Diet Grasshoppers are mostly vegetarian but can become pests of certain crops. Crickets are much more eclectic in their tastes and, while the vast majority are omnivores, some have become almost entirely carnivorous.

Garden benefits Grasshoppers are vegetarian by nature, but are little threat to garden plants, while they are an important food source for various creatures. Many crickets are predatory.

Life span Most grasshoppers and crickets live for less than a year, and often have quite short adult lives. Eggs that are laid in late summer overwinter and hatch in the spring, and just occasionally nymphs or adults overwinter and lay eggs the following season.

Risk of bite or sting While the majority of grasshoppers cannot bite, some of the larger species of cricket are capable of delivering a bite that, in a few cases, can be quite painful. The sting-like ovipositor (or egg-layer) on the tail of some crickets is harmless.

LIFE CYCLE OF A GRASSHOPPER

Most species have a yearly cycle that sees the young larval stage emerging in the spring and growing to maturity in late summer. Adults rarely overwinter and most will die by the late autumn, having mated and laid eggs that will overwinter and hatch next spring.

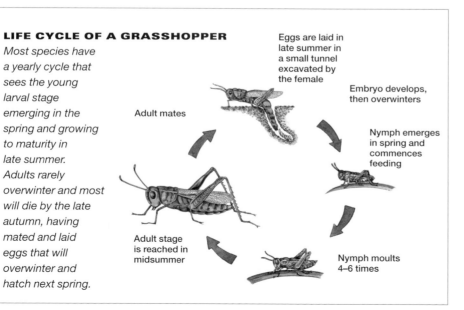

Adult mates

Eggs are laid in late summer in a small tunnel excavated by the female

Embryo develops, then overwinters

Nymph emerges in spring and commences feeding

Nymph moults 4–6 times

Adult stage is reached in midsummer

Above: *Long, flower-rich grassland provides the ideal habitat and food source for many grasshoppers and certain cricket species.*

seen in the summer taking short flights and flashing their brightly coloured wings while snapping them together, to produce a distinct sound. Such short-flight noises are called crepitation and are usually species specific. Males more commonly make a sound by scraping the hind leg against the hard outer wing casing (stridulation) to produce the characteristic rasping sound so commonly heard in summer. Crickets also stridulate, but they produce the noise by scraping one outer wing case over another, and are more generally known for doing this in the evening and at night.

Left: *The oak bush-cricket is a mostly carnivorous species, although it does eat some succulent plant material as well.*

HABITAT PREFERENCES
Grasshoppers tend to inhabit grassland and are predominantly active during the day, especially during sunny weather. They can be quite choosy about which plants to eat, and many species are specialists, feeding on only a few particular grass types.

Crickets tend to be more general in their distribution, with some even living partially or entirely underground, or in caves. They are also more commonly active at night, and their dull colouration makes a very effective camouflage. Most crickets hide during the day and are hard to see, the only evidence of them being the sound they make at night.

FEEDING STRATEGIES
Grasshoppers are mainly vegetarian, and often consume relatively large amounts of vegetation daily that they chew using their well-developed mandibles. They are mostly

specific in terms of their preferred food plants, but if numbers increase and food becomes short, they may switch their attention to other plants. This reaches its greatest extreme in the case of plagues of locusts that are capable of stripping all the vegetation from an area. Crickets, on the other hand, are mostly omnivores.

THREATS
Habitat loss Many species of grasshopper and cricket rely on a particular food source, but changes in habitat can affect its availability. The behaviour of hunting crickets may also depend on particular habitats.

Persecution Being vegetarian, grasshoppers may be considered pests despite their being mostly harmless. Most species cause no real damage to garden plants. Crickets are often mistaken for cockroaches and killed.

Pesticides Pesticides aimed at one particular pest species often affect other species, particularly the carnivorous types of cricket, leading to a lethal build-up in their bodies.

Predators Both crickets and grasshoppers are an essential part of many food chains and, as such, many will be caught and eaten by larger predators, including mammals and even birds of prey.

PLANTS TO ATTRACT GRASSHOPPERS

Cock's foot (*Dactylis glomerata*)
Creeping bentgrass (*Agrostis stolonifera*)
Crested dog's tail (*Cynosurus cristatus*)
Red fescue (*Festuca rubra*)

Cock's foot   Creeping bentgrass   Crested dog's tail   Red fescue

DRAGONFLIES AND DAMSELFLIES

Often considered to be the glittering jewels of the insect world, dragonflies and damselflies are a very successful group, with fossils dating back over 300 million years. Their colour and behaviour never fail to excite, but, far from being just beautiful, they are highly effective hunters, grabbing smaller prey in flight with their bristly legs. These rapacious insects have larvae that are some of the most effective hunters in freshwater ponds.

Above: *Dragonflies are large and powerful hunters, whose body design has not changed in over 350 million years.*

ROLE IN GARDENS

Dragonflies are some of the largest and perhaps most spectacular insects in the garden, often seen hovering and flitting over ponds. They even mate on the wing when a pair can be seen flying together, in tandem. Both dragonflies and damselflies have a high acceleration rate and speed, and they share the ability to hover or fly backwards and forwards. In fact, they are unmatched for speed and agility in the air, and hunt by sight, often ambushing prey with amazing accuracy.

There is often confusion between dragonflies and the smaller damselflies, but distinguishing between the two orders is easy when you see them resting. Dragonflies always sit with their wings open and flat, while the more diminutive damselflies close their wings and fold them tightly along the length of their body, often making them harder to spot when resting.

HABITAT PREFERENCES

Some dragonflies insert their eggs into plant stems growing in the pond shallows, whereas others simply release them on to the water surface to sink or be trapped amongst the plants. Once hatched, the nymphs remain as nymphs from one to two years (sometimes three) and, during this time, they increase their size by periodically moulting their hard outer casing, swelling their body and bursting through this outer layer.

Eventually the nymphs climb out of the water, up the stem of a marginal plant, mostly under cover of night. After a short period, often as the first light of day returns, they moult one last time, splitting open the outer casing along the back. From this shell, the new adult emerges, and remains there while it pumps blood through the veins in its wings to fill them out to their full size. Once the wings have dried in the early morning sun, the adult may take to the air where it will spend much of its adult life.

All dragonfly species need a stable pond environment, and suitable surroundings with good feeding and roosting sites. Warmth is essential, and the best breeding ponds are those that are sunny and sheltered from the wind. Plenty of vegetation, both in and around the water, is another key ingredient.

FEEDING STRATEGIES

While both the nymph and adult dragonfly are carnivores, they catch their prey in very different ways. The nymphs are entirely aquatic and hunt by stealth, catching their prey using an unusual mouthpart called a

PROFILE

Diet Adults prey on other flying insects, particularly midges and mosquitoes, but they will take any prey that is small enough to catch. The larvae live in water and eat almost anything including small fish, tadpoles, bloodworms or other insect larvae.

Garden benefits Dragonflies are extremely effective hunters and eat large numbers of flying pests, given the right habitat. They also provide food for larger garden creatures, and their aerial antics are reason enough to want them.

Life span A dragonfly's minimum life cycle from egg to adult death is about six months, although it can be six to seven years with some of the larger dragonflies. Most of this time is spent in a pond in the larval form, with the adult stage only lasting a few months at best.

Risk of bite or sting While larger dragonflies may try to bite if held, their jaws are not powerful enough to break the skin. Despite stories to the contrary, no dragonfly can sting; they overcome their prey by strength.

Above: *Dragonflies are mostly larger than damselflies, and rest with their wings held out flat and away from the body.*

Above: *Damselflies are mostly smaller than dragonflies, and rest holding their wings upright above their body, like butterflies.*

PLANTS TO ATTRACT DRAGONFLIES

Oxygenating plants These are a must to provide cover and oxygen for the larvae.
Curled pondweed (*Potamogeton crispus*)
Eurasian water milfoil (*Myriophyllum spicatum*)
Hornwort (*Ceratophyllum demersum*)
Water starwort (*Callitriche stagnalis*)

Curled pondweed

Hornwort

Water lilies, deep-water aquatics and free-floating plants Plants with floating leaves are useful for hiding larvae and providing basking sites for adults.
Floating pondweed (*Potamogeton natans*)
Frogbit (*Hydrocharis morsus-ranae*)
Water crowfoot (*Ranunculus aquatilis*)
Water lilies (*Nymphaea*)
Water smartweed (*Polygonum amphibium*)

Frogbit

Water lily

Marginal plants These are essential for the larvae as they climb out of the water, also providing perching, roosting and egg-laying sites for the adults.
Bogbean (*Menyanthes trifoliata*)
Flowering rush (*Butomus umbellatus*)
Water horsetail (*Equisetum fluviatile*)
Watermint (*Mentha aquatica*)
Yellow flag (*Iris pseudacorus*)
Brooklime (*Veronica beccabunga*)
Bulrush (*Typha minima*)
Burr reed (*Sparganium erectum*)
Pickerel weed (*Pontederia cordata*)
Water forget-me-not (*Myosotis scorpioides*)

Watermint

Yellow flag

mask. This appendage shoots out incredibly quickly to capture its victim in the sharp terminal pincers, and the prodigious speed of the mask makes it one of the fastest animal movements in nature. They detect prey mostly by sight, touch and vibrations, and devour everything from water fleas and other insects to larger prey, such as newts, small fish and even each other.

The adults, on the other hand, always catch their prey on the wing and this usually involves one of two strategies. Broadly speaking, dragonflies are either "darters" or "hawkers" because of the way they hunt. Darters perch on reeds or other vegetation, waiting for the prey to come past, and then dart out and catch it. Hawkers patrol up and down a territory, looking for prey to swoop on, grabbing smaller flying insects with their bristly legs before landing and consuming them. Whether a darter or hawker, all

Above: *An ideal dragonfly pond should have a mixture of plants to provide cover for the larvae and stems for them to climb out.*

THREATS

Collection Dragonflies have long been admired, not only for their speed and agility in flight but also for the patterns and dazzling colours on their eyes, bodies and wings. Over-collection of some species has made them rare.

Habitat loss Many species of dragonfly and damselfly rely on water for their breeding cycle, and the loss of wetland is a serious threat. In addition, changes in the surrounding habitat might mean an absence of prey.

Pesticides Dragonflies are predatory in their larval stages and also when they are adults. If pesticides end up in tiny amounts in their prey, dragonflies can be poisoned through this.

Predators Despite their incredible aerial abilities, many adult dragonflies are caught by spiders, larger insects, mammals and even birds of prey.

dragonflies and damselflies share brilliant flying abilities, being both fast and agile, easily outmanoeuvring their prey.

They can actually make themselves invisible to airborne prey and territorial rivals. They do this by moving in such a way that they appear to be a stationary object blending into the background. This "motion camouflage" allows dragonflies to stalk their victims undetected.

LIFE CYCLE OF A DRAGONFLY

Dragonflies are instantly recognizable when they are seen flying during the summer months. However, this stage is only a short part of their life – they actually spend most of their life as nymphs underwater, feeding on a range of aquatic species. After emerging, the adults hunt on the wing, feeding on insects.

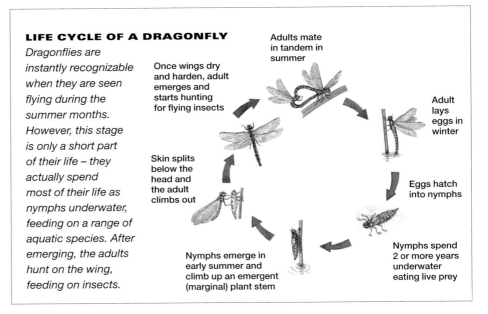

Once wings dry and harden, adult emerges and starts hunting for flying insects

Adults mate in tandem in summer

Adult lays eggs in winter

Eggs hatch into nymphs

Nymphs spend 2 or more years underwater eating live prey

Nymphs emerge in early summer and climb up an emergent (marginal) plant stem

Skin splits below the head and the adult climbs out

WORMS

Familiar creatures to most gardeners, worms are elongated, soft-bodied creatures that lack both legs and backbone, and are usually found in the soil. Many worms are extremely useful in helping to break down dead and decaying plant material and aerating the soil. The best known worm is probably the earthworm, frequently encountered when digging. Worldwide, however, there are many thousands of species in almost every conceivable habitat, including a number of predatory species.

Above: *Earthworms are a familiar sight in many gardens, where their feeding and tunnelling activities enrich and aerate soil.*

WHAT ARE WORMS?

There are thousands of different kinds of worm – the largest measures several metres long, and the smallest cannot be seen without the aid of a microscope. Only a limited number actually live in our gardens, and the vast majority of these live in the soil or in rotting plant litter, while a few inhabit ponds. The majority of the larger species eat decaying plant material, but a few feed on animals, and some of the microscopic types live as parasites in animals and plants causing a number of diseases.

There are three main groups of worms that you would expect to live in a garden. The flatworms are mostly aquatic, and are usually carnivorous or parasitic. Many species are very small but some larger species, such as the New Zealand flatworm, are carnivores that capture and eat earthworms. Roundworms (or nematodes) are tiny, usually microscopic worms and are one of the most common groups of animals with over 20,000 known

Below: *Worms are very common in gardens, and tend to be eaten by a wide range of animals, such as this toad.*

Above: *Brandling worms live in decaying plant material, such as compost heaps, and are very useful in helping decomposition.*

species. They often outnumber other animals in a habitat, both individually and in the number of species. There are many parasitic forms, including some that cause disease to garden plants. However, nematodes can be beneficial because certain predatory ones kill garden pests, such as vine weevils and cutworms.

The segmented worms (or annelids) include the more familiar garden earthworms, but also include bloodsucking leeches. Earthworms are often highly abundant in gardens, and are especially numerous in soil that's rich in organic matter. They tunnel deeply into the ground, and bring soil from the lower layers closer to the surface, helping to mix the topsoil. In addition, the slime that they secrete to ease their passage through tunnels contains nitrogen, and helps bind together clusters of soil particles into aggregates.

Worms don't have true eyes, although they are able to sense light and quickly move away from a bright source. Indeed, if they are unable to escape this they can become paralyzed if the light exposure lasts

an hour or more. They can also be damaged and die if their skin dries out, as this is the prime way in which they breathe. For this reason, they often prefer a damp site, although they can easily drown if the ground becomes waterlogged. The likelihood of drowning makes them rush to the surface if they sense rain, and many birds exploit this by lightly pecking at the ground to simulate raindrops, catching the worms as they emerge.

PROFILE

Diet The vast majority of larger worm species found in gardens eat decaying organic matter, and recycle nutrients. Many smaller worms are parasites or carnivores, and leeches are always carnivorous or blood-sucking.

Garden benefits Worms fulfil a huge variety of roles and functions, particularly in the soil, and are an essential part of this and many other food chains. Earthworms, in particular, are especially useful as decomposers of decaying matter.

Life span Worms vary in their lifespan according to species, but an earthworm may well live for up to eight years, and many other worms show a similarly long lifespan. However, few reach that age, being eaten by other creatures.

Risk of bite or sting Most garden worms are unable to bite (unlike some of their marine relatives), and are completely harmless. Some leeches, on the other hand, are bloodsuckers, even though few attack people.

LEECHES

Chiefly because of their reputation as ruthless bloodsuckers, leeches are a much-maligned group of worms. While all leeches are carnivorous, most feed on a variety of invertebrates, such as worms, snails, insect larvae and crustaceans. Only a very few are parasitic bloodsuckers, and most of those limit this activity to amphibians, reptiles, waterfowl and fish, with only small numbers attacking mammals (including humans).

The best-known bloodsucker is probably the European medicinal leech that was once used to control diseases believed to be the result of an excess of blood. Though this now seems extraordinarily naïve, some surgeons are now using them following operations to reattach severed limbs or digits. Researchers have discovered that leeches are better at controlling and even reducing any swelling in the reattached limb during the healing process than conventional medicine, and additional research is being carried out into the anticoagulant secreted by leeches as they feed. This could also be medicinally useful.

Despite their predatory nature, leeches have many predators, including fish, aquatic insects, crayfish and even other leeches. They are to be found in most freshwater habitats and, although some are terrestrial, they mostly require warm, moist conditions.

Above: *The humid conditions and abundant plant material in a compost heap make it an ideal place for many worm species.*

ROLE IN GARDENS

Worms play a diverse role in garden ecosystems, depending on the species concerned. Earthworms, for example, help maintain the fertility of the soil. Their tunnelling helps increase the amount of air and water that gets into the soil, and their feeding aids the breakdown of organic matter. Ultimately, their continued activity helps turn the soil.

Brandling worms (or redworms) are a special type of earthworm adapted to life among layers of decaying organic material, and are often found in compost and manure heaps. Their ability to speed up the conversion of green waste into compost means that they are used in worm composters. Finally, leeches are useful as they catch small prey.

HABITAT PREFERENCES

While worms of all descriptions are widely distributed and differ in their habitat requirements, most prefer darkness and avoid light, emerging from cover only at night. This means that they are safe from many predators, although many nocturnal creatures actively hunt them, and creatures such as moles actually seek them out in their tunnels.

Earthworms form a burrow by entering the soil head first to a depth of several centimetres, before tunnelling back to the surface at a different point. They make this burrow partly by using the pointed head end to push soil particles aside, but also by taking in soil that passes through the body, being left as castings at the entrance to the burrow. In the winter or periods of drought, earthworms retreat deep into the soil.

FEEDING STRATEGIES

Worms that spend some of their time above ground, such as earthworms, tend to be nocturnal feeders, and spend the daylight hours with the head just below the soil surface of the exit. They often hide this exit with a pebble or piece of leaf drawn over the opening, and at night they come part way out of the ground, leaving the tail end in the burrow to make a hasty retreat if necessary. In this position they feed on decaying plant and other organic matter, before retreating back at the first sign of dawn.

Leeches rarely eat, often surviving for months on a single meal. Some are bloodsucking but the majority eat smaller prey, such as snails and other worms, that they mostly capture under cover of darkness.

Below: *Despite its name, the pond-dwelling horse leech does not suck horse blood, but feeds on worms and decaying flesh.*

THREATS

Habitat change Increased cultivation and reliance on synthetic chemical fertilizers often results in a decrease in soil organic matter (especially at the surface), which is a worm's prime food. This layer also helps keep soil cool and moist in summer, and warm in winter.

Pesticides Carelessly applied pesticides frequently reach the soil, and decaying plant matter often has residues. Even if the worms are not killed by this toxicity, they can accumulate pesticides in their bodies that, in turn, lethally affect the wildlife that feeds on them.

Pollution Synthetic chemical fertilizers can have a disastrous effect on earthworm populations, many tending to create acid conditions that are often fatal to worms. Pollutants can also accumulate in their bodies to levels around twenty times higher than in the soil they inhabit.

Predators Earthworms have many predators, but introduced predators can wreak havoc. In the UK they are threatened by the accidentally introduced New Zealand flatworm that feeds on the earthworm, but lacks any natural predators. Worms are a vital food source for many larger creatures, and their loss may in turn cause food shortages for these animals.

OTHER INVERTEBRATES

There are too many types of invertebrates to mention in this book. Many are commonly encountered in gardens, and it is often tempting to assume that they are pests if they seem unfamiliar. Most, if not all, creatures play a significant (albeit small) role in the garden, and it is only when their numbers are out of balance or when species are introduced to areas where they formerly never occurred that they are likely to become a problem.

Above: *The praying mantis feeds primarily on other insects, although larger species can consume small reptiles, mammals or birds.*

COCKROACHES

These are an ancient group of insects, whose basic body design of a flattened body, bristly legs and long antennae has remained unchanged for hundreds of millions of years. They can eat almost anything, giving them the edge when competing with other species for food. Only a few species ever venture into our homes, with most being the outdoor, nocturnal kind. By day they hide in crevices, or under rocks, logs or in burrows, and are often important elements in the food chain, being eaten by larger predators.

MANTISES

The mantises, or "mantids" as they are sometimes called, are a distinctive group of insects, being related to cockroaches and crickets. They're widely distributed throughout warmer areas of the world. They prefer areas rich in plants and other insects, and are carnivores feeding primarily on other invertebrates, although it is not

Below: *Termites are extremely common in warmer regions. They are tremendously important recyclers of plant matter.*

Above: *Cockroaches often invoke revulsion when encountered, but most are outdoor-living and few species ever enter our homes.*

uncommon for larger mantises to consume small reptiles such as geckos, and even small mammals or birds. Mantises are often extremely well camouflaged, moving slowly and blending in with their surroundings while they wait for their prey to come within striking distance. They use their front legs to snatch their victim quickly, which is immediately devoured. In turn, mantises are devoured by bats, the larger birds, spiders, and even bigger mantises.

TERMITES

Termites are very simple insects in their design, but have an astonishingly complex social behaviour, often involving several different "castes" of adults that undertake specific roles in the colony. They play an essential role in the decomposition and recycling of plant material, being especially abundant in drier or tropical environments. They feed on wood, grass and other plant matter, according to species, and also eat fungus that some species cultivate in dark, humid parts of their nest or find growing on moist wood. Termites are often mistakenly called white ants because of their social

habits, but are actually most similar to cockroaches, with which they are thought to share a common ancestry.

STICK INSECTS AND LEAF INSECTS

These are plant-eating insects (most being closely related to cockroaches, grasshoppers, crickets and mantises) that are mainly restricted to tropical regions, with only a few species in temperate places. As their name suggests, they are usually long and slender, and bear an uncanny resemblance to the structure and colour of twigs and leaves of the woody plants on which they live and eat. They move very slowly – if at all – during daylight hours, and most species tend to restrict their movements and other activities, including feeding, to the hours of darkness.

ANTS

Living in large, highly cooperative colonies, ants often function as if they were one large organism. They are most closely related to

Below: *Ants are extremely common in gardens everywhere, and in many cases they are important predators and recyclers.*

Above: *Millipedes have long cylindrical bodies with many tiny pairs of legs, and if disturbed often form a defensive coil.*

wasps and, in many ways, an ant resembles a wasp without its wings, and indeed the flying forms of ants (the new queens and males) greatly resemble and are often mistaken for wasps.

Ants are extremely important elements of many habitats, and are important predators of some insects that they capture and kill for their young. Like social wasps, the adults have a sweet tooth and their search for sugary substances, as well as their wide-ranging search for food, often brings them into conflict with home owners.

CENTIPEDES AND MILLIPEDES

With their long, segmented, elongated bodies, centipedes have one pair of legs per segment. They range in size from 2cm (¾in) to giant specimens in warmer regions that can reach 15–20cm (6–8in) long. All are fast-moving predators that feed on any small creatures, with smaller species preying mostly on insects. The larger centipedes often sport bright colours to warn that they can inflict a painful bite. All species lack a waxy layer on their outer shell and are prone to desiccation. They consequently shun the sun, being mostly nocturnal, or spend their lives underground.

While they resemble centipedes, millipedes have long, cylindrical bodies with two pairs of legs on each segment. They are found worldwide (except in polar regions), being most abundant in tropical climates, and all species feed on decaying organic material. Like centipedes they are nocturnal and prefer a humid environment, and often spend most of their time underground. If disturbed, millipedes roll into a defensive coil and some species exude foul-tasting chemicals so that they aren't eaten. They don't bite.

Above: *Woodlice are unusual in being land-living crustaceans that breathe with gills, so they prefer living in damp or humid places.*

WOODLICE

Also known as pillbugs, woodlice are easily recognized by their flattened or round-backed profile, seven pairs of legs, and sharply angled antennae. While they look a little like insects, they are in fact crustaceans, being closely related to lobsters, crabs or shrimps, and are the ones from this group to have successfully colonized land. They breathe by means of gills and, for this reason, prefer damp, humid places, such as leafy compost heaps, where they feed on dead vegetation. All species are nocturnal and only venture into the open at night. Some species roll into a ball when disturbed – hence the name "pillbug".

SLUGS AND SNAILS

These are molluscs, and belong to the same group as shellfish (e.g. oysters and clams). They are legless creatures that glide along on a path of mucus and are invariably regarded as pests, with herbivorous species feeding during the night. The shiny mucus trail left behind is the only clue as to where

Below: *Slugs are molluscs that lack a protective shell. Whilst some species are pests, most eat carrion or decaying material.*

Above: *Areas of dense vegetation, particularly if they are near water, often harbour a rich diversity of invertebrates.*

they have been. Their damage to plants can be very significant, generally being worse in damp conditions when they emerge en masse from their hiding places. They are an important part of many habitats, and many species of slug and a few snails eat only decaying matter and cause precious little damage to garden plants, with a few species being carnivorous.

While slugs and snails are a severe irritation to any gardener, they are a vital and rich source of food for many other garden predators, so you should never attempt to poison them with chemicals – such chemicals may end up being ingested by one of the predators. Instead of focusing on killing slugs and snails, try encouraging the predators instead.

Below: *Snails are frequently a problem when they attack garden plants, but are preyed upon by many other garden animals.*

DIRECTORY OF PLANTS

Choosing plants is one of the most exciting aspects of landscape or garden design. For all species in this directory, the particular types of wildlife that they attract are clearly outlined, so that you can select the best plants for the creatures that live in your area. The plants are grouped into standard categories – annuals and biennials, bulbs, perennials, herbs, shrubs, hedges, trees, climbers, pond and bog plants, and fungi and decomposers – with tips on how they are cultivated, wildlife benefits and suggestions for closely related species.

Left: *Insects are a vital part of the food chain. Careful plant selection will ensure that food and shelter are provided for them.*

Above: *Huge quantities of nectar produced by lupin flowers attract several species of bee. The blooms brighten up garden borders.*

Above: *Heleniums are good in herbaceous borders or naturalistic plantings. Their bright daisy flowers attract many insects.*

Above: Verbena bonariensis *is probably the best plant to attract garden butterflies. It flowers for a long period in the summer.*

HOW PLANTS ARE NAMED

All living things are classified according to a system based on principles that were devised by the 18th-century Swedish botanist, Carl Linnaeus. This system states that a particular plant genus (plural: genera) is a group of plants containing similar species. Beyond that there may be plants that are simply a slight variation of a species, or are a hybrid (cross) of different species or variations.

Above: *All plants in the directory are divided into groups. This yellow flag iris can be found in the Pond and Bog Plants section.*

SCIENTIFIC NAMES

Under this system, plants have botanical names – often Latin but also derived from other languages – that consist of the genus name (for example, *Verbena*), followed by the name that denotes the particular species (for example, *hastata*). Some genera contain a huge number of species that may include annuals, perennials, shrubs and trees, while others contain just one species. Although all members of a genus are assumed to be related to each other, this is not always visually obvious.

It is useful to keep in mind that a species is defined scientifically as consisting of individuals that are alike and tend naturally to breed with each other.

Despite this system, botanists and taxonomists (the experts who classify living things) often disagree about the basis on which a plant has been named. This is why it is useful for a plant to retain its synonym (abbreviated to syn. in the text), or alternative name. Incorrect names often gain widespread usage, and in some cases, two plants thought to have separate identities, and with two different names, are found to be the same plant.

A well-known example of naming confusion is the genus *Pelargonium*. Until the 19th century, pelargonium plants were included in the genus *Geranium*, and despite being classified separately for over a century, they are still popularly known as geraniums.

VARIATIONS ON A THEME

Genetically, many plants are able to evolve over time to adapt to a changing environment. In the wild, individuals within a species that are not well adapted will not survive, so all survivors will look the same. The average garden is a more controlled environment, so gardeners can choose to encourage and grow on variations within a species that have small but pleasing differences such as variegated leaves and double flowers. The terms for these variations are subspecies (abbreviated to subsp.), variety (var.), form (f., similar to variety and often used interchangeably) and cultivar (cv.). A cultivar is a variation that would not occur in the wild but has been produced and maintained solely by cultivation. Variations are given names in single quotes, for example *Papaver orientale* 'Allegro'.

HYBRIDS

When plant species breed with each other, the result is a hybrid. Rare in the wild, crossing is very common among plant-breeders, and is done specially in order to produce plants with desirable qualities such as larger or double blooms, variegated foliage and greater frost resistance. A multiplication sign (x) is used to indicate a hybrid, and the name often gives a clear idea of the hybrid's origins.

GROUPS

A Group of plants is a group of very similar variations. Their names do not have quotation marks around them – for example *Tradescantia* Andersoniana Group.

HOW THE DIRECTORY IS ARRANGED

Within the plant directory, plants are arranged alphabetically, by genus. Each main entry features a general introduction to that genus, plus specific information such as tips on propagation and which hardiness zone the genus belongs to. This is followed by a selection of plants from that genus, also arranged alphabetically according to their most widely accepted names. One of these entries might be a species, a hybrid (or group of hybrids), a variety, form or cultivar. Each is given a description that may include height and spread.

Left: *The Japanese rose is classified as a shrub but can also be found in the Single-Species Hedges section because it forms an excellent barrier.*

HOW TO USE THE PLANT DIRECTORY

Within the plant directory, the plants are arranged principally according to their habit of growth and life cycle. The plants are split into sections such as Annuals and Biennials, Bulbs, Perennials etc, which makes it easier to use. Each main entry features the common and botanical names, the plant's family and where it is originally a native. This is followed by a general introduction to that genus, including a description of the plant, including the leaves, flowers and height. There are also brief cultivation notes and propagation tips, as well as information relating to its hardiness zone.

Notes on each plant's uses show how it can be used in the garden, and the section on wildlife benefits describes the range and types of creatures it might normally attract. Lastly, the directory suggests a selection of closely related species that may fulfil a similar role in the garden.

Photograph
Each entry features a full-colour photograph that makes identification easy.

Caption
The full botanical name of the plant in question is given with each photograph.

Genus and species name
This is the internationally accepted botanical name for a group of related plant species. This starts with the current botanical name of the plant in bold, and this can refer to a species, subspecies, hybrid, variant or cultivar. If a synonym (syn.) is given, this provides the synonym, or synonyms (alternative names) for a plant. A common name may be given after the botanical name.

Common name
This popular, non-scientific name applies to the whole of the plant genus.

Family
This shows the larger grouping to which the plant belongs and can reveal which plants are related to each other.

Native
The nativity of a species refers to its original home range although it often occurs outside this range now as a result of cultivation.

Cultivation
This section gives the level of sun or shade that the plant either requires or tolerates, with advice on the best type of soil in which it should be grown. Methods of propagation are listed, as well as any other helpful tips that might be appropriate.

Uses
This section advises on how to get the best from a plant, for example using it in borders or containers or to brighten up dark corners. In some cases, suggestions are also given for plants that complement each other well.

Wildlife benefits
The plant is intended to be useful for wildlife and so the principal species they normally attract are listed here. The list is not always exhaustive and most plants will attract many others as well.

Closely related species
This section provides information about common types that are available and other recommended plants to look out for. Both wild plant species and cultivars are listed. In several cases, plants that are not beneficial to wildlife are also listed. This will help you to decide which plants to avoid when planning a wildlife garden.

Ceanothus thyrsiflorus

Ceanothus thyrsiflorus
CALIFORNIAN LILAC
Family: Rhamnaceae
Native: California and S Oregon
The Californian lilac is one of the best shrubs to attract huge numbers of bees. It is a large, vigorous, evergreen shrub growing to 6m (20ft) high.
Cultivation Grow in full sun in a sheltered location, protected from cold winter winds. The roots favour fertile, well-drained soil. Propagate by semi-ripe cuttings in mid–late summer. ❀ ❀ ❀ Zone 8.
Uses Ideal for planting in a large shrub border, or train against a sunny wall where it provides a valuable source of food for insects. Also, several species of birds are likely to nest in the network of branches.
Wildlife benefits A huge favourite with bees and bumblebees seeking mainly pollen and, occasionally, nectar. The leaves are eaten by caterpillars of several common butterflies and moths. Songbirds feast on the numerous visiting insects that take refuge in the dense foliage.
Closely related species Research has shown that *C.* 'Ray Hartman' is a fantastic plant to attract bees. *C. impressus* is another real favourite, attracting several species of insect. It is an evergreen shrub with dark blue flowers in mid- to late spring.

Genus description
This provides a general introduction to the genus and may state the number of species within that genus. Other information featured here may include general advice on usage, preferred conditions, and plant care, as well as subspecies, hybrids (indicated by an "x" in the name), varieties and cultivars (featuring names in single quotes) that are available.

Size information
The average expected height and spread of a genus or individual plant is frequently given, although growth rates may vary depending on location and conditions. Metric measurements always precede imperial ones. Average heights and spreads are given (as H and S) wherever possible and appropriate, and more consistently for perennials and bulbs, although it must be noted that dimensions can vary a great deal.

Plant hardiness and zone
A plant's hardiness and zone are given at the end of this section. Zones give a general indication of the average annual minimum temperature for a particular geographical area. The smaller number indicates the northernmost zone it can survive in and the higher number the southernmost zone that the plant will tolerate. In most cases, only one zone is given. (See page 256 for details of hardiness symbols, zone entries and a zone map.)

PLANT SELECTION

The plants in this directory can be used internationally in ornamental gardens, and have been chosen for their ability to benefit wildlife. Unfortunately, only a limited number could be included, but additional information can be found in each section on closely related species.

ANNUALS AND BIENNIALS

Agrostemma githago
CORN COCKLE
Family: Caryophyllaceae
Native: S Europe and W Asia
A delightful summer-flowering hardy annual that was formerly a common weed in cereal crops but is becoming rare due to modern farming practices, such as increased use of herbicide and good seed-cleaning techniques. It reaches a height of 60–90cm (2–3ft), has lance-shaped green leaves and is graced with pretty, open, trumpet-shaped pink flowers, 8cm (3in) wide. The seed is poisonous.
Cultivation Grows best in full sun, in well-drained soil with low fertility. Fully hardy, surviving temperatures down to -15°C (5°F). Sow direct in the ground in spring or early autumn; after germination, thin out and transplant when the seedlings are small. Protect overwintering seedlings with pea sticks that will then support the willowy growth. Deadhead to promote new flowers. ❀ ❀ ❀ Zone 4.
Uses A popular garden plant that is widely used in annual or mixed borders, and is often used in cottage gardens. It is also commonly found in annual meadow mixes, along with annual poppies, corn marigolds and annual corn flowers.
Wildlife benefits The flowers are a great source of nectar for bees and the occasional butterfly.
Closely related species The following *A. githago* cultivars are excellent nectar producers: try 'Milas' with plum-pink flowers, 'Milas Cerise' bearing deep red flowers and 'Milas Rosea' with pale lilac-pink flowers.

Alcea rosea

Alcea rosea
HOLLYHOCK
Family: Malvaceae
Native: Unknown – probably Turkey or Asia
A tall, majestic biennial that can often survive three or more years. The erect stems can grow to 3m (6–7ft) or more, and bear spikes of rosette-like flowers 5–10cm (2–4in) across in a range of colours, from white to pink or purple, and sometimes pale yellow. The green leaves are rounded, lobed and have a rough texture.
Cultivation Although fully hardy, it needs a sunny location with well-drained soil. Propagate in late summer for flowering the following year. ❀ ❀ ❀ Zone 5.
Uses Gives height to herbaceous borders, also terrific in mixed borders when planted sporadically throughout the border. Very effective in cottage gardens.
Wildlife benefits The large flowers are popular with bees looking for nectar. Avoid double-flowering cultivars of hollyhock, such as *A. rosea* 'Charters Double Hybrids', as

they have little wildlife benefit.
Closely related species Single-flowering cultivars, such as *A. r.* 'Indian Spring' and *A. r.* 'Nigra', are ideal for visiting bees. *A. rugosa* is a tall, elegant species that bears pale yellow flowers and is also a good nectar producer.

Amaranthus caudatus
LOVE-LIES-BLEEDING
Family: Amaranthaceae
Native: Peru, Africa and India
An exotic, late-summer hardy annual, growing to 1.5m (5ft) tall. Used for its plume-like tassel flower heads that reach 45cm (18in) long, and contain hundreds of tiny, crimson flowers. The pale green leaves turn beautiful bronze in autumn.
Cultivation Although it can tolerate poor ground, it thrives in any fertile, well-drained soil in full sun. Sow direct outside in mid-spring or, for an earlier show, sow indoors in early spring and then plant out, after hardening off in late spring. ❀ Zone 5.
Uses Excellent in a tropical bedding scheme with the likes of *Canna* 'Orange Perfection', *Dahlia* 'Bishop of Llandaff' and *Salvia uliginosa*. A real talking point if grown in pots in prominent places.
Wildlife benefits The seed is a popular choice with many birds, including collared doves, reed buntings, dunnocks, sparrows and finches.
Closely related species *A. tricolor* is also a favourite with birds. Gardeners particularly like the cultivars *A. t.* 'Joseph's Coat' with scarlet, green and yellow oval leaves and *A. t.* 'Molten Fire' with crimson, bronze and purple leaves.

Agrostemma githago

Amaranthus caudatus

Antirrhinum majus

Antirrhinum majus
SNAPDRAGON
Family: Scrophulariaceae
Native: SW Europe and
Mediterranean

Grown in cottage gardens for centuries, it's still a big favourite. Although it is classed as a short-lived perennial, it is best grown as a half-hardy annual. The lance-shaped leaves are borne on stems that can reach 90cm (3ft) high; flowers are normally pink or purple.

Cultivation Grows best in full sun in fertile, well-drained soil. Add organic matter to the soil before planting if necessary. If grown as a half-hardy annual, sow indoors in early spring and plant out after the risk of frost has passed, usually in late spring or early summer. Deadhead to promote new flowers. ❀ Zone 7.

Uses Most commonly used in annual bedding schemes because of the range of colours and sizes. With other tall varieties, like the Rocket Series, it can be used for cut flowers, while dwarf varieties ('Tom Thumb') are ideal for window boxes and tubs.

Wildlife benefits The fragrant flower spikes are full of nectar, and are a great temptation to bumblebees that either snap off the flower heads or eat the corolla tube to obtain the nectar if the entrance to the flower is too small.

Closely related species *A. molle* is a small hardy perennial, shrubby species

which has pale pink, white or yellow flowers, and is ideal for the rock garden or for naturalizing in walls. *A. sempervirens* is another dwarf, shrubby species that suits a free-draining area and has nectar-rich cream-white or yellow flowers.

Borago officinalis
BORAGE
Family: Boraginaceae
Native: Europe

A beautiful annual herb that grows to 60cm (2ft) high, with hairy stems, simple leaves and flowers that are sky blue with tinges of white and pink. The edible flowers can be picked for salads, or frozen in ice cubes and served in summer drinks.

Cultivation Thrives in a sunny location in free-draining, fertile soil. Sow seed outdoors *in situ* about late spring; it will self-seed, coming up year after year. ❀ ❀ ❀ Zone 7.

Uses Can be used in annual borders, mixed borders and dotted around vegetable gardens to encourage pollinators. The leaves taste of a salty cucumber, and can be used in salads.

Wildlife benefits Excellent at attracting many different bee species. It is pollinated by honeybees and bumblebees attracted by the abundance of nectar.

Closely related species *Borago officinalis* 'Alba' has white flowers and 'Variegata' has variegated leaves; both good at encouraging bees. *B. pygmaea* is a short-lived perennial for woodland edges, preferring moister soil.

Borago officinalis

Calendula officinalis

Calendula officinalis
ENGLISH MARIGOLD
Family: Asteraceae
Native: Origin unknown

A brightly coloured hardy annual that is a big hit with many different wildlife species. A spring- or summer-flowering bushy plant, it can often grow to 60cm (2ft) high, with lance-shaped, strongly aromatic, pale green leaves. The stunning disc of flowers ranges from yellow and brown to orange.

Cultivation Thrives in full sun in well-drained soil. Sow *in situ* in autumn for early spring flowering, or in mid-spring for summer flowering. Deadhead at regular intervals to prolong flowering. ❀ ❀ ❀ Zone 6.

Uses The brightly coloured flowers liven up a vegetable patch and encourage beneficial insects, providing natural pest control. Can also be used in hardy annual borders, as fillers for mixed borders, and in window boxes and hanging baskets.

Wildlife benefits A favourite with pest-controlling hoverflies, it also attracts pollinating honeybees and bumblebees and the occasional butterfly. Always plant single-flowering cultivars or the species to encourage wildlife. Avoid the double-flowering *C.* 'Art Shades' and Calendula Fiesta Series.

Closely related species The field marigold (*Calendula arvensis*) is an annual, 30cm (1ft) high. The colour ranges from yellow to brown, and is excellent for bees.

Cerinthe major
HONEYWORT
Family: Boraginaceae
Native: S Europe

An eye-catching hardy annual that produces stunning bright blue bracts and nectar-rich yellow and purple flowers with smooth, hairless, lance-shaped foliage. The stems, which may need supporting with pea sticks, can quickly reach 60cm (2ft) high.

Cultivation An undemanding species that will grow in most free-draining garden soils, in full sun or partial shade. The fleshy roots can rot in prolonged wet weather. Propagate by seed *in situ* in autumn or spring, or start off in the greenhouse and harden off before planting in its final position. ❀ ❀ ❀ Zone 5.

Uses Looks great in a mixed border, especially amongst grasses and with purple-leaved plants, such as *Physocarpus opulifolius* 'Diabolo' or *Sambucus nigra* 'Black Beauty'. Can also be used in annual borders, although it does tend to self-seed freely around the garden.

Wildlife benefits It attracts so many honeybees you can hear them clearly humming on the plant as you walk past. One of the best bee plants for a large or small garden.

Closely related species Without doubt the best cultivar of *Cerinthe major* is 'Purpurascens'; the deep purple colour of the bracts is absolutely amazing, and it's just as attractive to bees. *C. minor* is an annual or short-lived perennial for the shady flower border. It reaches 60cm (2ft) high and has nectar-rich yellow, violet or purple flowers.

Cerinthe major

Daucus carota

Daucus carota
WILD CARROT
Family: Apiaceae
Native: Europe to India

We always think of the carrot as a big, orange, edible root, but its not-so-well-known flowers that appear in the second year of growth are both simple and elegant. This 1m (3ft) high biennial produces dense umbels of white flowers that are often tinged purple in the centre in late summer, and have finely cut foliage.

Cultivation Grows best in free-draining, slightly acidic soil in full sun, although it will grow well in most soils. Sow *in situ* in spring or autumn, and it will flower the following year. ❀ ❀ ❀ Zone 5.

Uses Carrots can be used in all sorts of situations. Try planting in tubs, plant randomly in mixed borders or use as fillers in herbaceous borders. Another good tip is to allow a certain percentage of carrots from the vegetable garden to overwinter and flower next year, attracting many species of beneficial insects into the garden, helping to control pests. Wild carrot is commonly used in wildflower meadow mixes, but tends to die out as the meadow matures.

Wildlife benefits The leaves are a food plant for the caterpillars of the swallowtail butterfly, and the flowers are an excellent source of nectar and pollen for bees and various species of hoverfly.

Closely related species *D. carota* subsp. *sativus* is the garden carrot with an orange, fleshy taproot; it's equally beneficial to wildlife.

Dianthus barbatus
SWEET WILLIAM
Family: Caryophyllaceae
Native: S Europe

A gorgeous, short-lived perennial that is normally grown as a biennial, growing to 60cm (2ft) high. Sweet William produces beautifully fragrant flowers in large, dense heads that are white, pink or red in late spring and early summer, with lance-shaped leaves.

Cultivation Grows well in an open, sunny situation in free-draining, fertile soil. Sow seed in late spring to plant out in early autumn, and it'll flower the following spring. Deadhead to promote new flower heads. ❀ ❀ ❀ Zone 4.

Uses A cottage garden favourite that can be used in spring bedding displays with wallflowers (*Erysimum cheiri*) and pansies (*Viola* x *wittrockiana*), and a selection of spring-flowering bulbs. Dwarf cultivars, such as *Dianthus barbatus* Roundabout Series, are ideal for tubs and window boxes.

Wildlife benefits Nectar-hunting butterflies and bumblebees are attracted to the fragrant flowers. Avoid the many double-flowered cultivars because they are unproductive for visiting insects; only single-flowering species should be selected.

Closely related species Another good wildlife-attracting species is *D.* 'Brympton Red', which is an old-fashioned pink with bright crimson single flowers with deeper shading. *D. deltoides,* a maiden pink, is another single-flowering species that is ideal for the rockery or stone wall.

Dianthus barbatus

Digitalis purpurea

Digitalis purpurea
FOXGLOVE
Family: Scrophulariaceae
Native: Europe

A fantastic plant with tall spikes of tubular white, pink or purple flowers, with spotted markings inside, that blooms from late spring to early summer. Its nectar-rich flower spikes can reach heights of 90cm–1.5m (3–5ft), and the rough-textured, deep green leaves are found in a basal rosette. It is usually grown as a biennial, but is often a short-lived perennial; every part of the plant is poisonous.

Cultivation Grow in moist but well-drained soil that is rich in humus. Foxgloves are a natural woodland plant that can grow in full sun but thrive in semi-shade. Sow seed *in situ* from late summer to autumn for flowering the following year. ✿ ✿ ✿ Zone 4.

Uses An excellent plant to brighten up a shady border, especially if using the naturally occurring white form, *D. alba*. It is also a winner if planted randomly throughout a mixed or herbaceous border, and can be an inexpensive way of providing colour in large drifts under trees.

Wildlife benefits Excellent for bumblebees seeking nectar. Fallen seed will be eaten by birds foraging in the border. Don't cut back the old flower stems because many insects spend winter inside them in the tubular flowers.

Closely related species All *Digitalis* species are particularly good nectar-producing species, although some flowers are smaller than others, hampering bee visitation. Bees will then drill into the side of

the flower to obtain the nectar. *D. ferruginea* has rust red flowers. *D. grandiflora*, the large yellow foxglove, has pale yellow flowers netted with brown veins.

Dipsacus fullonum
COMMON TEASEL
Family: Dipsacaceae
Native: Europe, Asia and N Africa

A majestic architectural biennial that produces nectar-rich, egg-like flower heads on erect stems that can reach 2m (6½ft) high. The pale lilac flowers are borne from midsummer on, and open a few at a time, prolonging the flowering period. Water collects at the base of the stem leaves, providing drinking pockets for small insects.

Cultivation Prefers full sun or dappled shade in good, fertile soil, including heavy clay. Sow seed *in situ* in autumn or spring. ✿ ✿ ✿ Zone 3.

Uses Best used in a wild garden where the plant can seed freely, or use in a wildflower meadow mix. Teasel can be used in cultivated mixed borders but self-seeding can be a big problem.

Wildlife benefits The flowers are visited by bees and butterflies seeking nectar. The seed is loved by birds, such as goldfinches and crossbills, because they have bills long and narrow enough to reach them. The larvae of the marsh fritillary butterfly feed on the leaves.

Closely related species Fuller's teasel (*Dipsacus sativus*) is similar in height but has extremely stiff seed heads and, like common teasel, has fleshy seed with an oily coating.

Dipsacus fullonum

Erysimum cheiri

Erysimum cheiri
WALLFLOWER
Family: Brassicaceae
Native: S Europe

A sweet-scented, short-lived perennial that is cultivated as a biennial predominantly for spring bedding displays. It is variable in height, ranging from 25–80cm (10–32in); the stems are sturdy, bearing lance-like leaves, and the flower heads range from purple-green to bright yellow, orange and striped red-purple.

Cultivation Prefers full sun but will grow in dappled shade in any well-drained soil, especially in alkaline conditions. ✿ ✿ ✿ Zone 7.

Uses One of the main ingredients in spring bedding displays. This is mainly because it flowers reliably, but also due to the great range of height and colours that many of the cultivars provide. It is one of the better species for planting into old walls, and can then be allowed to naturalize.

Wildlife benefits The sweetly scented flowers attract bees to the pollen and nectar, and butterflies can be seen sitting on the flattened flower parts drinking nectar in spring.

Closely related species The cultivar *E.* 'Bowles Mauve' is a bushy, short-lived perennial that has nectar-rich, purple-mauve flowers from late winter to early spring, providing a welcome early source of nectar. The short-lived perennial species are also good for wildlife. *E.* x *allionii* is a pretty, bright orange flowering cross that grows to 60cm (2ft). *E.* x *kewensis* flowers from winter through to summer and sports orange-yellow flowers that will turn purple.

Eschscholzia californica

Eschscholzia californica
CALIFORNIA POPPY
Family: Papaveraceae
Native: NW America

A really pretty hardy annual that provides an inexpensive splash of colour during the spring and summer months. Variable in height and colour, often reaching 60cm (2ft), with flowers ranging from pale yellow to bright orange. The divided foliage has a blue tinge that nicely complements the flower colours.

Cultivation Like many annuals, it requires full sun for optimum germination and will grow well in any light, well-drained soil. Sow *in situ* in spring or autumn. ❁ ❁ ❁ Zone 6.

Uses California poppies can be used to fill gaps in mixed borders. They are also ideal to use in traditional hardy annual borders, and can even be sown as a filler in a rocky dry garden. They will look good planted next to the purple-flowering *Salvia nemerosa* and the silver-leaved small shrub, *Artemisia* 'Powis Castle'. A very versatile plant that is both heat- and drought-tolerant. Once it has been sown, it will self-seed and come back year after year.

Wildlife benefits The bright orange flowers are great at tempting beneficial insects, such as hoverflies, into the garden for nectar. The flowers are also a favourite of bees and bumblebees searching for food.

Closely related species The tufted *Eschscholzia caespitose* is smaller than *E. californica*, and is ideal in a rock garden. It has bright yellow flowers and reaches 25cm (10in) high.

Helianthus annuus
SUNFLOWER
Family: Asteraceae
Native: N and S America

Sunflowers are a great favourite with children, and it's easy to see why when they bear huge, yellow, daisy-like flowers from summer to autumn on stems that can grow up to 5m (17ft) high. The leaves are pale green. Modern cultivars offer a range of tall, medium and dwarf sizes, and a range of colours to suit all tastes.

Cultivation To obtain the best growth from a sunflower, grow it in well-drained, fertile soil in full sun. Stake the taller varieties as they grow. Can be sown direct outside in mid-spring, or start off indoors in early spring, hardening off before planting out in late spring. ❁ ❁ ❁ Zone 4.

Uses Excellent in a children's garden, and also looks great if planted in large groups in annual borders or dotted around mixed or herbaceous borders. Dwarf varieties, such as *H.* 'Teddy Bear', can be used in tubs and window boxes, intermediate varieties (*H.* 'Taiyo') are ideal for bedding, and the tall *H.* 'Russian Giant' gives height in herbaceous or mixed borders.

Wildlife benefits Honeybees and bumblebees love its nectar and pollen, and the flowers are visited by the occasional butterfly. When the flowers fade, the oily seed attracts many birds, including collared doves, greenfinches, nuthatches, long-tailed tits, crossbills and bramblings, as well as other seed-eaters.

Closely related species *Helianthus x laetiflorus*, reaching 2m (6½ft) high, and *H. salicifolius*, 3m (10ft), are both perennials that can be used effectively in a wild garden or at the back of herbaceous borders.

Helianthus annuus

Heliotropium arborescens

Heliotropium arborescens
HELIOTROPE
Family: Boraginaceae
Native: Peru

Heliotrope is a half-hardy shrub that is treated as a half-hardy annual because it doesn't withstand the frost. It bears heads of small, tubular, white, or purple to pink flowers with oblong, rough-textured leaves. It can grow up to 45–60cm (1½–2ft) when grown as an annual. The smell is like sweetly scented marshmallows, which will attract many night-flying insects.

Cultivation Prefers full sun but will also grow in dappled shade, in fertile, well-drained soil. Sow seeds in spring, or alternatively take semi-ripe cuttings in autumn before frost damage occurs. ❁ Zone 10.

Uses Heliotrope has been used for many years in traditional summer bedding schemes, but it can also be used to fill gaps in mixed borders. When positioning heliotrope, try to plant it around doors and paths to gain maximum benefit from the strongly scented flowers. It's also a big success when used in containers.

Wildlife benefits Bees and bumblebees seek out the nectar-rich flowers. The tubular flowers make the nectar accessible to many species of butterfly, such as the comma, painted lady and the colourful peacock. Day-flying moths, for example the hummingbird hawk moth, find the nectar irresistible.

Closely related species One of the most popular cultivars is *H. a.* 'Marine', with compact, bushy growth, purple flowers and a height of 45cm (18in).

Hesperis matronalis
SWEET ROCKET
Family: Brassicaceae
Native: S Europe to Siberia

A gorgeous, scented, summer-flowering biennial or short-lived perennial. The flowers are strongly scented in the evening and are violet to white; their stems grow to 75cm (2½ft) high, and the leaves are smooth and narrowly oval.

Cultivation Sweet rocket requires free-draining, neutral to alkaline soil, in a sunny position. Sow seed *in situ* in autumn or spring. ❀ ❀ ❀ Zone 3.

Uses Great for planting in mixed borders or as a gap-filler in herbaceous borders. Violet-flowering strains look striking when planted next to the dark foliage of the smoke bush (*Cotinus coggygria* 'Royal Purple') and *Iris* 'Matinata'. Also useful in a wild garden.

Wildlife benefits The leaves are a food source for the caterpillars of the orange tip butterfly, and a nectar source for many species of butterfly.

Closely related species *Hesperis bicuspidata* is a small, violet-flowered perennial growing to 30cm (1ft) high, and is suitable for growing in rock gardens. *H. tristis* is ideal in the wild garden and for planting in old walls. It is a biennial or short-lived perennial that produces white or cream flowers with the occasional purple.

Iberis amara
CANDYTUFT
Family: Brassicaceae
Native: W Europe

A lovely, summer-flowering hardy annual with masses of fragrant, white- and pink-domed flower heads with fine, lance-

Iberis amara

shaped leaves. Fast growing, it quickly reaches 30cm (1ft) high.

Cultivation Likes well-drained, chalky soil in a sunny situation. Candytuft will even tolerate poor, dry soils, and also ones with low levels of acidity. Sow *in situ* in spring. ❀ ❀ ❀ Zone 7.

Uses A great addition to an annual border, or sow in bare spots to fill up herbaceous beds, a mixed border or a special butterfly border.

Wildlife benefits The fragrant, nectar-rich flowers attract bees seeking pollen and nectar. Also a great butterfly plant for nectar-hungry adults, such as the small gatekeeper.

Closely related species *Iberis umbellata* Fairy Series is a popular choice. Its heads of small, four-petalled flowers in shades of purple, pink, red or white appear from summer to early autumn and are really

popular with butterflies. *I. saxatilis* is a dwarf evergreen sub-shrub which produces numerous small white flowers in late spring and early summer. Excellent in the rock garden, or as an edging plant in a mixed border.

Limnanthes douglasii
POACHED EGG PLANT
Family: Limnanthaceae
Native: California and S Oregon

A stunning, fast-growing hardy annual reaching just 15cm (6in) high. The prolific white flowers with yellow centres are cup-shaped, and appear from early to late summer; the feathery leaves are light green.

Cultivation Easily grown in moderately fertile soil with added organic matter to aid moisture retention. Position in full sun for the best growth. Sow direct into the soil in autumn or spring. ❀ ❀ ❀ Zone 8.

Uses Ideal for a hardy annual border, or as edging for mixed or herbaceous borders. To create an informal look to a pavement or patio, sow the seed between the cracks; the young growth will soften the look of the hard landscape and add colour. If you have a hedge that's bare at the bottom and facing a sunny location, benefit the wildlife by sowing seed here. It'll create a fantastic display of flowers in summer, that's also a haven for several species of insects.

Wildlife benefits The brightly coloured, lightly scented flowers are an excellent nectar source for bees. They also attract an abundance of hoverflies that are great predators of garden pests, such as aphids.

Closely related species *Limnanthes douglasii* var. *sulphurea* has stunning yellow flowers that are just as attractive to visiting insects.

Hesperis matronalis

Limnanthes douglasii

Lobelia erinus
EDGING LOBELIA
Family: Campanulaceae
Native: S Africa

This small perennial is normally grown as a short annual, 7.5–15cm (3–6in) high, in summer bedding schemes. The slender stems support small, ovate leaves, and the flowers are white to blue and violet.

Cultivation Sow seed indoors in early spring. Harden off before planting outside in late spring in rich, moist soil. Grow in full sun or light shade for best results. ❀ Zone 9.

Uses Choose between the upright edging and trailing kind. Upright cultivars, such as *L.* 'Cambridge Blue', are ideal plants for edging summer bedding schemes and lining pathways. Trailing cultivars, such as *L.* 'Colour Cascade', are one of the best pendulous plants for window boxes, hanging baskets and tubs.

Wildlife benefits The flowers are a favourite with bees, daytime moths and butterflies seeking nectar. At night, as the light fades, take a torch outside and you will marvel at the number of night-flying moths visiting the flowers for their sugary drink. One plant can often be covered in many different species of moth.

Closely related species *Lobelia cardinalis* is a short-lived perennial that flowers profusely in late summer, growing to 90cm (3ft) high. The spikes of stunning, scarlet, tubular flowers attract day-flying moths and butterflies. Best planted in drifts in a bog garden or by a stream edge.

Lobelia erinus

Lunaria annua

Lunaria annua
HONESTY
Family: Brassicaceae
Native: C and S Europe

A biennial, growing 90cm (3ft) high, with lanceolate to cordate leaves that are coarsely toothed. Honesty produces beautiful, purple-red flowers in late spring and summer. The seed heads are flat and rounded and, as they mature, turn attractive silvery grey, making them more frequently used in floral arrangements than the flowers.

Cultivation Grow in well-drained soil in full sun or dappled shade. To attract the greatest number of insects, place in full sun. Sow seed *in situ* in late summer to have flowering plants the following year. ❀ ❀ ❀ Zone 8.

Uses If you have a shady corner of the garden, honesty is the ideal candidate to brighten up the area. Can also be used to provide a rich nectar source around a woodland edge, and is excellent when naturalized in a wild garden.

Wildlife benefits The scented flowers attract butterflies and moths, and bees and birds are often observed feeding on insects on the plant. The leaves of honesty are the larvae food plant of the orange tip butterfly. When the plant sets seed, it's quickly eaten by bullfinches.

Closely related species Perennial honesty (*Lunaria redivia*) is similar to *L. annua*, except the leaves are finely toothed and the plant lives for three years or more. The flowers are also scented and attract visiting insects.

Myosotis arvensis

Myosotis arvensis
FIELD FORGET-ME-NOT
Family: Boraginaceae
Native: Europe, NE Africa and Asia

A pretty annual (or sometimes biennial) that will grow to 50cm (20in) high. It has lance-shaped leaves, and the spring to autumn flowers are bright blue to dark purple, being followed by a healthy production of seed.

Cultivation Will grow in sun or semi-shade, and likes fertile, well-drained soil. Propagate by seed in autumn. ❀ ❀ ❀ Zone 6.

Uses Good for naturalizing in the wild garden. The closely related *Myosotis sylvatica* and its hybrids are used in spring bedding to provide a splash of colour after the dull winter months. Plant with wallflowers (*Erysimum cheiri*), tulips and pansies (*Viola* x *wittrockiana*) for a stunning spring display.

Wildlife benefits Bees and bumblebees seek out the flowers in spring for pollen and nectar. Occasionally butterflies drink the nectar. In autumn, birds such as chaffinches, linnets and a number of finches feast on the seeds.

Closely related species The water forget-me-not (*M. scorpioides*) is an excellent perennial that's a spring-flowering marginal plant. Unlike *M. arvensis*, which prefers well-drained soil, the roots of this species flourish at the edge of a pond in moist soil or shallow water. Colourful cultivars of *M. sylvatica* include 'Blue Ball' (a small, compact plant with rich indigo flowers), 'Blue Bird' (tall with deep blue flowers), and 'Rosea' (tall with pink flowers).

Nicotiana sylvestris
TOBACCO PLANT
Family: Solanaceae
Native: Argentina

A perennial (grown as a half-hardy annual) that's best described as graceful, elegant and simple. The large, elliptic leaves are a terrific feature, as are the 1.5m (5ft) stems with long, white, tubular flowers that are sweetly fragrant on summer evenings. All *Nicotiana* species are poisonous.

Cultivation Thrives in well-drained garden soil in sun or shade. Can be grown as a biennial if late spring flowering is required, in which case sow in late summer under glass, and plant out in early to mid-autumn after hardening off. ❀ Zone 8.

Uses Good for height in summer bedding schemes. It also looks extremely lush if used in tropical bedding schemes, especially if planted with sunflowers (*Helianthus annuus*), cannas and busy lizzies (*Impatiens*). One of the great assets of the tobacco plant is that it grows extremely well in sun or shade, making it one of the most versatile annuals.

Wildlife benefits The fragrant evening flowers are a big attraction to moths and, as the food chain progresses, bats. Day-flying moths are also drawn to the long, white, tubular flowers for a satisfying drink of nectar.

Closely related species All nicotianas are great for attracting moths. *N. alata*, often called jasmine tobacco, is a perennial (grown as an annual) that is often used in summer bedding schemes and pots. The

Nicotiana sylvestris

Oenothera biennis

cultivars are uniform in growth reaching 75cm (30in) high. *Nicotiana* 'Domino Series' are cultivars that are relatively slow-growing bushy annuals in a range of colours from white to pink and red; ideal for window boxes.

Oenothera biennis
EVENING PRIMROSE
Family: Onagraceae
Native: E North America

A true biennial with tall spikes of yellow scented flowers reaching up to 90cm (3ft) tall in summer. The leaves have a bluish tinge, with the basal rosette leaves being 10–30cm (4–12in) long and the stem leaves 8–15cm (3–6in) long.

Cultivation Needs full sun on sandy, well-drained soil. Sow seed in late spring and early summer for next year's flowers. ❀ ❀ ❀ Zone 4.

Uses Can be used in a mixed border or to fill gaps in herbaceous borders. Excellent for naturalizing in wild areas where birds can forage about in the undergrowth for its seed.

Wildlife benefits The evening-scented flowers attract late flying bees to collect pollen and night-flying insects, such as moths, for a nightcap of nectar. Other insects drawn to the plant are hunted by hungry warblers. Evening primrose is a prolific seeder, and attracts birds such as finches, crossbills, chaffinches and siskins seeking an easy meal.

Closely related species *Oenothera speciosa*, the white evening primrose, is a short-lived summer-flowering perennial that grows to 45cm (18in) high. *O. caespitosa* is

Papaver rhoeas

only 12cm (5in) high and ideal for the rock garden. Its white, fragrant flowers open at sunset in summer. Both are excellent nectar and pollen producers.

Papaver rhoeas
CORN POPPY
Family: Papaveraceae
Native: Temperate Old World

This tall annual, up to 90cm (3ft) high, bears big, bright red flowers from late spring to summer. They are commonly seen on waste ground and in gardens. After flowering, the plant has heads full of nutritious seed.

Cultivation Grow in full sun in any well-drained soil. Sow seed direct in the soil in early spring. ❀ ❀ ❀ Zone 5.

Uses A welcome addition to an annual border, providing a big splash of colour. Also commonly included in an annual cornfield wildflower mix.

Wildlife benefits A popular insect plant, with the flowers attracting bees and bumblebees, hoverflies and the occasional butterfly. The seed is eaten by sparrows, siskins, linnets, dunnocks and a number of finches.

Closely related species The Oriental poppy (*Papaver orientale*) and opium poppy (*P. somniferum*) are excellent in gardens. The former is a bold plant, loved by bees, and can be used in herbaceous or mixed borders. It comes in many colours, from white, red and purple to pink. The latter can be used similarly to *P. rhoeas,* and the flower colour ranges from white to purple.

Petunia x *hybrida*

Petunia x *hybrida*
PETUNIA
Family: Solanaceae
Native: Garden origin

An excellent, versatile half-hardy annual that can be used in many situations. Grow as an upright bedding plant or as a trailing plant for hanging baskets and tubs. It produces large trumpet flowers, that vary in colour from white, pink and purple to reds and yellows, throughout summer until the first frosts. The leaves are green and lance-shaped.

Cultivation Petunias thrive in hot, dry summers but languish in wet, cool weather when root rot can occur. Requires a sunny situation that is sheltered from the wind. Remove deadheads to encourage new flowering. Can be prone to cucumber mosaic virus and tomato spotted wilt. ❈ Zone 7.

Uses The trailing cultivars are ideal for hanging baskets. Cultivars found in the Cascade Series are excellent for wildlife because they have single flowers, making the nectar more accessible. The Recoverer Series includes a number of upright cultivars that are ideal for incorporating in summer bedding displays. Do not grow double cultivars such as the Bonanza Series.

Wildlife benefits Bees are keen daytime visitors to the trumpet flowers, whereas moths are drawn to the sweet-smelling flowers in early evening.

Closely related species *Petunia axillaris* offers simplicity and has large white flowers, while the relatively prostrate *P. integrefolia* bears violet to rose red flowers. Petunia cultivars 'Resisto' and 'Plum Crazy' perform better in wet and windy conditions.

Silybum marianum
MILK THISTLE
Family: Asteraceae
Native: Mediterranean,
SW Europe to Afghanistan

A fantastic biennial that looks just as spectacular in the wild as it does in the garden. It grows to 1.5m (5ft) high, and produces tall, purple-pink thistle flowers in summer that are slightly scented. The leaves have unusual white veins and sharp spines around the edges.

Cultivation Grow in full sun in well-drained soil. Sow in autumn for flowers the following summer. The young growth is prone to snail damage. ❈ ❈ ❈ Zone 7.

Uses A brilliant plant, ideally suited to the wild garden, or cultivate and control in a mixed border. Remove any unwanted plants or it'll take over.

Wildlife benefits Bees and bumblebees are frequent visitors. When the seed matures it is a real favourite with goldfinches.

Closely related species *Silybum eburneum* is very similar to *S. marianum* except the stems are white to pale green, and the leaves have yellow-brown spines and are at least twice as big.

Tagetes patula
FRENCH MARIGOLD
Family: Asteraceae
Native: Mexico and Guatemala

The subtle orange flowers are a real winner for many insects. This is a half-hardy annual which grows to 20–50cm (8–20in) high and flowers all summer until the first

Silybum marianum

Tagetes patula

frosts. The deeply divided leaves are attractive and add a tropical look to a border.

Cultivation Prefers full sun in fertile, well-drained garden soil. Sow indoors in early spring and plant out in late spring after hardening off. Deadhead to prolong the flowering period. ❈ Zone 9.

Uses An excellent edging plant for a summer bedding scheme. A mix of just African marigolds (*Tagetes erecta*) and French marigolds with a simple dot plant in the middle to provide height is absolutely stunning. Both can also be used as companion plants in vegetable gardens to attract beneficial insects to prey on pests, or act as pest deterrents.

Wildlife benefits Select species or single-flowered cultivars, as they are popular with many species of hoverfly and several butterflies. The hoverflies (and their larvae) will feed on 40–50 aphids daily. Avoid the many double-flowered cultivars, such as 'Honeycomb', because they are of little use to wildlife due to the many petals produced.

Closely related species All single-flowering *Tagetes* are excellent for wildlife, and many are also used in companion planting. *T. minuta* has been effective in helping to prevent the spread of garden weeds, such as celandine (*Ranunculus ficaria*) and ground elder (*Aegopodium podagraria*). *T. minuta* can also be used for planting between potato rows to provide a deterrent against the destructive keeled slugs. However, *T. patula* doesn't reliably protect brassicas against the cabbage butterfly.

Tropaeolum majus
NASTURTIUM
Family: Tropaeolaceae
Native: Columbia to Bolivia

This strong-growing annual climber is a great asset to any wildlife garden. It produces trumpet-shaped flowers in reds, oranges and yellows from early summer to the first frosts. The trailing stems grow to around 60cm (2ft) long, and are clothed with bluish-green leaves.

Cultivation Nasturtiums thrive in poor, well-drained soil in a sunny site or partial shade. If grown in fertile soil, too much leafy growth will be made at the expense of flowers. Sow *in situ* in late spring. ❀ Zone 8.

Uses Adds colour in herb containers, vegetable hanging baskets and window boxes. Often grown in the vegetable garden to lure aphids away from other more valuable crops. The cabbage white butterflies tend to lay their eggs on the nasturtiums' leaves instead of on brassicas, such as cabbages.

Wildlife benefits The nectar-rich flowers are visited by butterflies and bees. Ladybirds, parasitic wasps and hoverflies, all voracious aphid-eating insects, are also drawn to the plant.

Closely related species Cultivars come as trailing plants and dwarf, bushy types. Choose cultivars with single flowers, such as Tom Thumb Series, with flowers in a range of colours and about 25cm (10in) high. The herbaceous climber, Canary creeper (*Tropaeolum peregrinum*), grown as an annual, hits 2m (6½ft) high with bright yellow flowers set off by grey-green leaves.

Tropaeolum majus

Verbena bonariensis

Verbena bonariensis
TALL VERBENA
Family: Verbenaceae
Native: S America

The abundance of butterflies, bees and moths that visit the clusters of nectar-rich flowers of this annual (or short-lived perennial) is astounding. It grows to 1.8m (6ft) high and bears blue, violet and purple flowers. The leaves are toothed and lance-shaped.

Cultivation Grows best in a sunny site in any well-drained soil. Because it seeds freely around the garden, it will need to be thinned to stop it becoming invasive. Best to sow indoors and plant out where required. ❀ ❀ Zone 8.

Uses Ideal for an annual bedding scheme, especially if height is needed. It also looks great if used to add colour in mixed borders. A good wildlife idea is to plant it as the sole plant along the sunny side of a path for about 6m (20ft). When in flower there should be dozens of butterflies nectaring on the flowers, clearly visible from the path.

Wildlife benefits It attracts more butterflies than the butterfly bush (*Buddleja davidii*) because it flowers for longer. It also flowers when many other nectar plants have finished, and it therefore gives butterflies an essential energy boost, especially if they are to survive the winter months. The hummingbird hawk moth, a day-time flying species, loves the flowers, as do many night-flying species that visit the flowers at dusk.

Closely related species *Verbena* x *hybrida* and *V. rigida* are half-hardy annuals which are used frequently in hanging baskets and window boxes. They are both popular with wildlife, especially moths.

Zinnia elegans
ZINNIA
Family: Asteraceae
Native: Mexico

A half-hardy annual with pretty, daisy-like florets from summer to the first frosts. The tiny petals range in colour from red, white, yellow and orange to pink, scarlet, lilac and purple. The stems can reach from 60–90cm (2–3ft) in height, and are graced with simple, lance-shaped green leaves.

Cultivation Zinnias grow extremely well in full sun, in free-draining soil. Warm, dry summers are best; they'll perform poorly in cold, wet seasons. Deadhead regularly to promote new flowers. ❀ Zone 9.

Uses A colourful addition to any summer bedding scheme, window box or container. Also use in tropical bedding schemes or summer bedding displays. The cultivars' flowers can be any colour except blue, making them ideal for any colour scheme.

Wildlife benefits The flowers are visited frequently by bees seeking nectar and pollen. They also attract the occasional butterfly.

Closely related species Cultivars of *Zinnia elegans* are available in many different flower shapes. The dahlia-flower kind, such as the pom-pom types (as in the Marvel Series, or cultivars resembling the cactus-flowered dahlia, for example *Z.* 'Burpees Zenith') are very pretty, but by far the best for wildlife are the simple daisy blooms of the old-fashioned *Z. haageana* 'Old Mexico'. The annual *Z. angustifolia* is ideal for the rock garden. It grows 40cm (16in) high and bears orange, yellow-brown flowers with black or deep purple centres.

Zinnia elegans

BULBS

Allium giganteum
ORNAMENTAL ONION
Family: Alliaceae
Native: C Asia

This spring-flowering ornamental onion has large, round flower heads that can reach 10cm (4in) across, on stems 90cm–1.8m (3–6ft) tall. The scores of tiny individual flowers are star-shaped and purple or, occasionally, white. The grey-green foliage contrasts well with the flower colour.
A wonderful genus, excellent at providing nectar for bees and many other insects.
Cultivation Alliums like well-drained soil in a sunny location. Plant bulbs 15cm (6in) deep, and leave the flower heads on the plant after flowering to provide a habitat for insects and because they look very attractive, especially adorned with frost. ❈ ❈ ❈ Zone 8.
Uses For maximum visual impact, plant bulbs throughout herbaceous or mixed borders, from the middle ranks to the back (with the tallest plants). *Allium giganteum* is thrilling next to plants with silver, blue or purple foliage or flowers, for example sea holly (*Eryngium giganteum*), the smoke bush (*Cotinus coggygria* 'Royal Purple') and honeywort (*Cerinthe major* 'Purpurascens').
Wildlife benefits Good at attracting bees, white butterflies and many other insects seeking a rich source of nectar. Choose carefully to have several allium species in flower over a long period, ensuring a steady supply of nectar.
Closely related species All alliums are an excellent source of nectar for wildlife. *A. christophii*, the star of Persia, reaches

Allium giganteum

Chionodoxa luciliae

20–50cm (8–20 in) in height, and supports purple-violet flower heads. *A. cernum*, the wild onion, has flowers ranging from white through pale and deep pink, to maroon.

Chionodoxa luciliae
GLORY OF THE SNOW
Family: Hyacinthaceae
Native: W Turkey

A pretty bulb with soft violet-blue flowers and a small white centre; the leaves can be 20cm (8in) long, and the flowers open on stalks 30cm (12in) high. It's closely related to *Scilla* and the two species, both spring flowering, are sometimes difficult to distinguish.
Cultivation Glory of the snow is easy to grow, thriving in any good, well-drained soil in full sun or light shade. Plant the extremely small bulbs in autumn. ❈ ❈ ❈ Zone 4.
Uses Ideal in the wild garden, or for planting beneath shrubs and taller plants in the mixed border. It can also be planted in large drifts in grassed areas that are cut down in summer. This looks really eye-catching, and provides a nectar-rich restaurant for spring-flying insects.
Wildlife benefits Many species of insect, especially bees, visit the nectar- and pollen-rich flowers. Cultivars of *Chionodoxa luciliae* include 'Alba' with white flowers and 'Rosea' with pink flowers, both good insect attractors.
Closely related species *C. forbesii* bears deep blue flowers and a white centre, is as beneficial as *C. luciliae*, and grows up to 30cm (12in) high. *C.* 'Tmoli' is a dwarf cultivar with bright blue flowers reaching 10cm (4in).

Crocus chrysanthus

Crocus chrysanthus
CROCUS
Family: Iridaceae
Native: Balkans and Turkey

A spring-flowering bulb that is an important early source of pollen and nectar for bees. The colour ranges from creamy yellow to golden, with the petals arranged in a tube that can be up to 10cm (4in) long. The narrow leaves are dull green and contrast well with the flowers.
Cultivation Provide well-drained, moderately fertile soil in sun or partial shade, sheltered from the wind. Plant in autumn, possibly encasing the bulbs in wire mesh when there's a danger that burrowing mice, rabbits and other pests may eat them. ❈ ❈ ❈ Zone 4.
Uses It is ideal for naturalizing in grassland or creating colourful pockets in shrub or mixed borders. The cultivars range from blue, violet, purple and white to many different shades of yellow, making it easy to select one for a particular colour theme.
Wildlife benefits Bees visit the tubular flowers for nectar and pollen. Cultivars can also be used in the wildlife garden, including 'Blue Peter' with rich, deep purple petals on the outside and soft blue inside. 'Zenith' is a lovely violet-blue on the outside and silver-blue inside.
Closely related species Many species of crocus will not tolerate large amounts of summer rain, and care is therefore needed when selecting those for the garden. *Crocus tommasinianus* and *C. vernus* are more robust than most species, and suit a range of conditions.

Eranthis hyemalis
WINTER ACONITE
Family: Ranunculaceae
Native: S Europe

One of the first flowers of the year to emerge, starting in late winter and ending in early spring. It provides a display of bright yellow, buttercup-like flowers, and reaches 10cm (4in) high. Many tubers need to be planted to make an effective carpet of flowers.

Cultivation Winter aconites naturally occur in damp woodland and shady places, and in gardens thrive in deep, humus-rich, preferably heavy soil in full sun or partial shade. Like the snowdrop (*Galanthus*), it is difficult to establish from dry tubers. Divide clusters and replant when still in leaf ("in the green"). ❀ ❀ ❀ Zone 5.

Uses It tolerates partial shade and is therefore ideal for planting under deciduous trees, brightening up parts of the garden that would otherwise be devoid of foliage and colour in late winter. Also plant the tubers under winter-flowering shrubs, such as honeysuckle (*Lonicera fragrantissima*) or Persian ironwood (*Parrotia persica*). Plant in large groups for the best effect.

Wildlife benefits An early source of pollen for bees and the first of the emerging insects. The cultivar 'Aurantiaca' sports orange flowers and is equally good for wildlife. Birds may peck at the open flowers.

Closely related species *Eranthis cilicica* and *E.* x *tubergenii* are ideal for growing in pots and displaying in a cold conservatory or alpine house. *E. cilicica* flowers later than *E. hyemalis* and has leaves that are tinged bronze when first opening. It is a good pollen producer whereas *E.* x *tubergenii* is a sterile hybrid with abortive anthers; no pollen is produced, and it has little value to wildlife.

Eremurus stenophyllus

Eremurus stenophyllus
FOXTAIL LILY
Family: Asphodelaceae
Native: C Asia to W Pakistan

An excellent, eye-catching architectural plant for any garden. This species and its cultivars have flower colours ranging from beautiful rich golden colours and coppery yellows to orange, red and pink. The tall flower stems can reach up to 1.5m (5ft) and are complemented well by the linear, sometimes hairy, dark green leaves.

Cultivation As the foxtail lily naturally occurs in rocky, semi-desert areas, it requires fertile, well-drained soil and full sun. Winter is a crucial time – if the ground is too wet the rhizome may rot and die, but without a cold spell it won't flower well. Taller cultivars and species require staking, especially in a windy site. Mulch with bracken in winter to prevent frost damage. ❀ ❀ ❀ Zone 5.

Uses Very effective when planted in large numbers. The most economical way to create new plants is by dividing clumps after flowering. Looks magnificent when used among old-fashioned roses, poking up through the bushes, and in mixed borders. Place amongst hot colours, such as *Sambucus racemosa* 'Plumosa Aurea' whose leaves turn from bronze to flashy yellow.

Wildlife benefits The striking hot colours of the flower spikes are great attractants for nectar-hunting bees and bumblebees.

Closely related species All *Eremurus* species are good at attracting summer bees to the garden. A white species,

E. himalaicus, produces gorgeous flowers 2–2.5m (6–8ft) tall, and *E. robustus* sports pink blooms at much the same height. A small species, *E. spectabilis*, reaches 1.2m (4ft) high and bears pale yellow flowers with red anthers in early summer.

Fritillaria imperialis
CROWN IMPERIAL
Family: Liliaceae
Native: S Turkey to Kashmir

An exotic bulb with a tall stem reaching up to 1.5m (5ft) high, adorned with bright green, glossy leaves. The stem culminates in an impressive flower head of bright orange flowers in spring. The individual flowers are bell-shaped and nodding.

Cultivation The crown imperial prefers well-drained, fertile soil in semi-shade or full sun. The bulbs need to be planted at a depth of 20cm (8in) in autumn. ❀ ❀ ❀ Zone 4.

Uses Plant in the peripheral areas of a woodland garden, to brighten up a border or mixed scheme. The flower heads are best displayed against a solid green background, for example an evergreen shrub such as laurel (*Prunus lusitanica* or *P. laurocerasus*), or a yew (*Taxus baccata*) hedge.

Wildlife benefits A fantastic source of nectar for several species of birds, including blue tits and black caps. Bees and bumblebees frequently visit the large orange flowers.

Closely related species Nectar-rich cultivars are available in red and yellow forms. *Fritillaria imperialis* 'Rubra Maxima' is very sturdy, bearing red flowers, whereas *F. i.* 'Lutea' has lovely yellow flowers. The species, *F. persica*, flowers in spring after reaching 1.5m (5ft) tall. The flowers are brown, with 10–20 on any one head.

Eranthis hyemalis

Fritillaria imperialis

Fritillaria meleagris

Hyacinthoides non-scripta

Fritillaria meleagris
SNAKE'S HEAD FRITILLARY
Family: Liliaceae
Native: Europe

The beautiful, solitary flowers appear in spring. They are found in different shades of purple and white, in a checkerboard pattern, reaching to 30cm (12in) high on slender stems. The narrow leaves are grey-green.

Cultivation The snake's head fritillary's natural habitat is a damp water meadow, meaning it needs damp garden soil when the bulb is in full leaf. Site in full sun or semi-shade. Propagate by seed when ripe. ❀ ❀ ❀ Zone 4.

Uses Best planted in areas of grass that can be left long, not being mown until the bulb's leaves have died down in summer. Plant numerous bulbs together for maximum impact. They can also be used in mixed borders, but avoid soil that might dry out.

Wildlife benefits The chequered flowers produce an important, early source of nectar for many insects, especially bees and butterflies. The white 'Alba' is also favoured by bees.

Closely related species *F. pyrenaica* is a spring-flowering species with lance-shaped, grey-green leaves and nodding, solitary, deep brown or blackish flowers. It grows 15–30cm (6–12in) tall and is ideal for the herbaceous border. *F. verticillata*, to 90cm (3ft) high, is another good spring-flowering species.

Hyacinthoides non-scripta
ENGLISH BLUEBELL
Family: Hyacinthaceae
Native: W Europe

It has drooping heads packed with blue-violet (or occasionally pink or white) tubular flowers. The leaves are narrow and curved, and both leaves and flowers can reach 40cm (16in) high.

Cultivation Its natural habitat is oak or beech woodlands. It therefore flourishes in gardens where the soil is rich in humus, and there's partial shade. If planted in a sunny area, the intense light will bleach the flowers. Propagate by division of established colonies. ❀ ❀ ❀ Zone 5.

Uses Plant in large groups under deciduous trees, in woodland gardens or in flower beds. Excellent if used in a shady area where it is allowed to naturalize. Do not plant beside the Spanish bluebell (*H. hispanica*) because the two species will hybridize, and *H. hispanica* will eventually take over.

Wildlife benefits Bluebells are loved by bees seeking pollen and nectar in spring, and by the occasional butterfly. The white *H. h.* 'Alba' and pink 'Rose' also attract insects.

Closely related species *Hyacinthus orientalis* can be grown outside, reaches 25cm (10in) high, and is packed with scores of tiny flowers. The different cultivars provide a wide range of colours, and attract bees seeking pollen and nectar.

Muscari armeniacum
GRAPE HYACINTH
Family: Hyacinthaceae
Native: SE Europe to Caucasus

A colourful spring-flowering bulb reaching 20cm (8in) tall. The bright blue, fragrant flowers are bell-shaped and produce good quantities of rich nectar. The green leaves are long and narrow, often being paler on the upper surface. The grape hyacinth is a real favourite with wildlife gardeners.

Cultivation The bulb prefers full sun to dappled shade. Plant in autumn to a depth of 7.5cm (3in), in large groups to give a strong, bold effect. Divide occasionally to improve the show. ❀ ❀ ❀ Zone 4.

Uses Excellent for a mixed border, woodland edge or for lining a path. The grape hyacinth is not an ideal species for growing in grass because it can't cope with the competition. It can also be used in hanging baskets in spring for extra colour, alongside cowslips, polyanthus and forget-me-nots, as well as other bulbs, such as dwarf daffodils and tulips.

Wildlife benefits Grape hyacinth is an early source of nectar for insects, particularly for bees and butterflies such as the brimstone and small tortoiseshell. Do not use 'Saphir' because the flowers are sterile and of little value to wildlife.

Closely related species The tassel grape hyacinth (*M. comosum*), a late spring-flowering bulb with brownish-yellow flowers, is good at attracting wildlife. The cultivar, *M. c.* 'Plumosum' is sterile and of limited use to wildlife. *M. azureum* bears bright blue flowers.

Muscari armeniacum

Narcissus pseudonarcissus

Narcissus pseudonarcissus
WILD DAFFODIL
Family: Amaryllidaceae
Native: W Europe to N England

There are scores of different daffodil cultivars, vastly ranging in size and strengths of yellow, orange and white. *N. pseudonarcissus*, sometimes called the lent lily, will grow to 30cm (12in) tall and bears yellow trumpet-shaped flowers in spring and long, linear leaves with a blue tinge.

Cultivation Daffodils grow in any good garden soil, in full sun or semi-shade. Plant in autumn to a depth of 7.5cm (3in). When the bulbs stop flowering in abundance, lift, divide and replant. This will allow them to flower profusely again. ❀ ❀ ❀ Zone 4.

Uses A versatile plant that can be used in numerous situations. Daffodils can be naturalized in grass in large numbers for the best effect. Use under deciduous trees or in groups in mixed borders. Dwarf cultivars can be used in rock gardens, hanging baskets, window boxes and tubs. The taller cultivars can also be used in spring bedding schemes.

Wildlife benefits The trumpet-shaped flowers provide a welcome early nectar source for bees and bumblebees. Do not use double flowering varieties, such as 'Texas', because they have no wildlife value.

Closely related species Several small species are excellent for wildlife. The hoop-petticoat daffodil (*N. bulbocodium* subsp. *bulbocodium*) is a vigorous species reaching 8–15cm (3–6in) tall, which successfully naturalizes in grass. *N. cyclamineus*, which grows to 15cm (6in) high and flowers from late winter to early spring, produces delicate, nodding flowers with reflexed petals. *N.* 'February Gold', an early spring flowering cultivar, is 30cm (12in) tall.

Sternbergia lutea
AUTUMN DAFFODIL
Family: Amaryllidaceae
Native: Spain to Afghanistan

An autumn-flowering bulb with sweetly scented, crocus-like flowers. The flowers are deep yellow and grow to 2.5–20cm (1–8in) tall. The bright green leaves are slender and narrow, appearing with or just after the flowers.

Cultivation It prefers a hot, sunny site with free-draining soil that dries out in summer. The bulbs are naked at this time of year, and it is essential that they are dry or they will rot. Although the plant is frost hardy, it needs the protection of a sunny wall in colder areas. Propagate by division of offsets when dormant. ❀ ❀ Zone 7.

Uses Plant out in a sunny herbaceous or mixed border; rock gardens are also ideal. The autumn-flowering daffodil can also be used in borders against a conservatory or greenhouse, which will offer extra warmth and protection during the winter months, when frost damage can kill the plants.

Wildlife benefits This nectar-rich plant is a real autumn bonus for insects, especially bees and bumblebees, because many of their abundant nectar suppliers have finished flowering.

Closely related species One of the most robust species for the garden is *S. sicula*, which has funnel-shaped yellow flowers that grow from 2.5–7cm (1–2¾in) in autumn. Another reliable species is *S. clusiana*, which produces yellow or greenish-yellow autumn flowers which are 4–8cm (1½–3in) with grey-green leaves.

Sternbergia lutea

Tulipa biflora

Tulipa biflora
TULIP
Family: Liliaceae
Native: S Yugoslavia and SE Russia

A real winner with wildlife, *T. biflora* sports yellow-centred white flowers in early spring with a lovely, sweet smell. It is a small species, just 5–10cm (2–4in) high with narrow, oval, green-grey petals and thin leaves with a bluish edge and red tip.

Cultivation Tulips thrive in full sun. Plant the bulbs 15cm (6 in) deep in well-drained, fertile soil. Avoid using fertilizer that's high in nitrogen or fresh manure because they encourage soft growth that is susceptible to disease. Propagate by seed in autumn. ❀ ❀ ❀ Zone 7.

Uses Ideal for planting permanently at the front section of a mixed border, or in a rock garden. Alternatively, grow the bulbs in pots and stand them around the garden to provide spring colour. When the bulbs have finished flowering, replace the pots in late spring with summer bedding plants. This is an excellent way to keep changing the look of your garden.

Wildlife benefits Recent observations at a tulip trail with many different species and cultivars showed that *T. biflora* was the most frequently visited plant. It was a magnet mainly for bees, though bumblebees also sought out the nectar and pollen.

Closely related species
T. kaufmanniana, an early flowering species that has red and cream striped flowers, reaching 20cm (8in) high, is a great attraction for bees and bumblebees seeking pollen and nectar. *T. sprengeri*, with bright red flowers, and *T. sylvestris,* bearing golden blooms that are sometimes tinged pink, are the best species for naturalizing in grass.

PERENNIALS

Achillea filipendula
FERN-LEAVED YARROW
Family: Asteraceae
Native: Caucasus, Iran, Afghanistan and C Asia

A graceful, upright plant, culminating in large, flat, yellow flower heads during summer. The flat heads provide an ideal landing platform for many visiting insects seeking nectar. The stems grow up to 1.2m (4ft) high, and bear fern-like foliage that is extremely attractive.

Cultivation Prefers a site in full sun in any good, well-drained soil. Propagate by division in autumn or early spring. ❀ ❀ ❀ Zone 3.

Uses An excellent structural plant for the herbaceous border, the flat flower heads providing an unusual shape. Plant next to species with red or orange flowers, such as crocosmia and rudbeckia, to create a focal point.

Wildlife benefits Hoverflies swarm to the nectar, while bees, bumblebees and numerous other species of insects are also frequent visitors. Favoured by insect- and seed-eating birds, especially house sparrows, tits and chaffinches.

Closely related species All achilleas are great insect attractors. *A. millefolium* is one of the best, being a firm favourite with hoverflies, wasps and bees. Birds feed on the insects and mature seeds.

Achillea filipendula

Agastache foeniculum

Agastache foeniculum
ANISE HYSSOP
Family: Lamiaceae
Native: N America

A great perennial for attracting wildlife, it grows to 60cm (2ft) high and bears small leaves, shiny green above and bluish below. The flowers are lilac but occasionally white. Although *A. foeniculum* is one of the hardier species, it will not survive severe frosts.

Cultivation Anise hyssop thrives in a sheltered location in full sun. Plant in any free-draining soil. Propagate by seed or division in early spring. ❀ ❀ Zone 8.

Uses An excellent plant for the front of the herbaceous or mixed border. It is also an ideal plant for rock gardens, or can be grown as an annual, especially in colder regions.

Wildlife benefits The upright flower heads are a real magnet for bees and bumblebees. Garden butterflies, for example red admiral and painted lady, are also frequent visitors. Seed-eating birds, such as goldfinches, eat the mature seeds during winter.

Closely related species *A. rugosa* and *A. urticifolia* are both as hardy as *A. foeniculum*. *A. rugosa* grows to 1.2m (4ft) high and bears rose or violet flowers, whereas *A. urticifolia* reaches 1.8m (6ft) high and produces violet to rose flowers.

Ajuga reptans

Ajuga reptans
BUGLE
Family: Lamiaceae
Native: Europe, Iran and Caucasus

A versatile plant that can be used in many situations. Bugle is a ground-cover plant that reaches only 20cm (8in) high. Popping up from the matt of green foliage are spikes of nectar-rich, blue-purple flowers during summer. Over 20 different cultivars are available, many from North America.

Cultivation Bugle prefers partial shade, in humus-rich, moist soil with some added leaf mould. Propagate by division in autumn or early spring. ❀ ❀ ❀ Zone 6.

Uses One of the best ground-hugging plants, it's ideal in a woodland garden or under shrubs to create ground cover. It is also very effective in hanging baskets or tubs where it will trail over the sides.

Wildlife benefits The flowers are frequently visited by bees and bumblebees seeking nectar. Butterflies, ladybirds and hoverflies also visit large patches of flowering bugle, especially if conditions are calm and sunny.

Closely related species The pyramid bugle (*A. pyramidalis*) is an evergreen perennial with blue, nectar-rich flowers. *A. genevensis* is taller, bearing blue flowers and reaching 40cm (16in). The latter prefers full sun.

Anthemis tinctoria

Anthemis tinctoria
YELLOW CHAMOMILE
Family: Asteraceae
Native: Europe, Caucasus and Iran

An extremely good-value garden plant, producing masses of yellow to pale cream daisy flowers from spring through until autumn. It is a clump-forming perennial that bears evergreen, fern-like, crinkled, mid-green leaves which are slightly hairy. The stems easily reach 60–90cm (2–3ft) high in one season.

Cultivation Yellow chamomile thrives in an open site in full sun and needs well-drained soil. Propagate by basal cuttings in spring or semi-ripe cuttings in late summer. ❀ ❀ ❀ Zone 6.

Uses A great plant for herbaceous and mixed borders, providing a burst of bright colour. It is also ideal for adding height to summer-bedding containers. For good colour combinations, plant with blue-purple trailing lobelia, petunias and fuchsias.

Wildlife benefits Numerous beneficial insects feed on the pollen and nectar, particularly hoverflies, lacewings, parasitic wasps, ladybirds and tachinid flies. Leave the old foliage until spring before cutting back to provide good hibernating sites for insects.

Closely related species 'E. C. Buxton' is often said to be the prettiest cultivar of *A. tinctoria*, sporting beautiful lemon-coloured flowers. *A. punctata* subsp. *cupaniana* bears aromatic silver foliage, adorned by sharp white flowers in summer.

Aquilegia vulgaris
COLUMBINE
Family: Ranunculaceae
Native: W, C and S Europe

A typical cottage-garden plant that produces unusual, pretty flowers which have nectar-rich spurs. The flowers are borne in late spring and early summer, their colour ranging from blue to purple, red or white. Columbines can grow up to 60–90cm (2–3ft) high, and bear deeply divided leaves that are dark green with a flush of blue.

Cultivation Plant in organic-rich soil to retain moisture over summer in full sun or semi-shade. Propagate by seed in late summer. ❀ ❀ ❀ Zone 4.

Uses Fantastic for a woodland garden because it can withstand shade and provide a real splash of colour in the under-storey. Plant in drifts along pathways for the best impact. Allow the columbines to self-seed in a wild or naturalistic garden.

Wildlife benefits The nectar-rich spurs found at the back of the flower head attract mainly insects able to reach far into the flower, particularly long-tongued bumblebees, butterflies and moths. Leave seed heads uncut for foraging birds in autumn.

Closely related species All species aquilegias are good nectar producers and an asset to wildlife, especially *A. canadensis*, a native of NE North America with yellow to red flowers in spring and summer. *A. skinneri* has green-orange and bright red flowers in summer.

Asclepias tuberosa
BUTTERFLY WEED
Family: Asclepiadaceae
Native: E and S North America

A brightly coloured border plant that's a winner in drought-tolerant gardens. It can easily grow up to 90cm (3ft) high and produces red, yellow or orange flowers in summer that are fantastic nectar producers. The stems bear mid-green leaves that are long and lance-shaped.

Cultivation It prefers dry, free-draining soil and should be located in full sun. Propagate by tip cuttings or seed throughout spring. ❀ ❀ ❀ Zone 3.

Uses An extremely good herbaceous border plant that will provide a real focal point, especially if planted beside red or yellow flowering plants. *A. tuberosa* is often selected when short-listing plants for a specialist butterfly border.

Wildlife benefits The nectar-rich flowers attract the monarch butterflies, and its caterpillars feed on the leaves of the plant. A chemical substance within the leaves makes the grubs unpalatable to birds. Bees and other butterflies also frequent the flowers in large numbers.

Closely related species *A. syriaca*, with pink to mauve flowers, is best suited to the wild garden and naturalistic plantings, and is particularly good at providing nectar for bees. Swamp milkweed (*A. incarnata*) prefers damp habitats and grows to 2m (6½ft) tall, bearing white to pink flowers.

Aquilegia vulgaris

Asclepias tuberosa

Aster novi-belgii

Aster novi-belgii
MICHAELMAS DAISY
Family: Asteraceae
Native: N America

A classic autumn perennial that provides a welcome boost of nectar in gardens as winter approaches. The flower heads can reach 90cm–1.2m (3–4ft) and contain many violet-blue flowers with yellow centres. The leaves are lance-shaped and prone to powdery mildew in dry summers.

Cultivation Michaelmas daisies thrive in full sun and prefer the soil to be slightly moist. Propagate by division in spring or autumn. ✤ ✤ ✤ Zone 2.

Uses A brilliant plant for herbaceous or mixed borders. Many different cultivars are available, enabling small or very tall cultivars of *A. novi-belgii* to be selected for the front or back of the border, and with most colour schemes.

Wildlife benefits The flowers are a real favourite with butterflies, especially species preparing to overwinter. The rich nectar helps to build up their body weight to help them through hibernation. Seeds provide food for various birds, such as crossbills and finches.

Closely related species *A. novae-angliae* grows to 1.5m (5ft) high and bears purple flowers with a yellow centre. *A. lateriflorus* produces white flowers with a dark centre, and *A.* 'Coombe Fishacre' is one of the best single-flowering cultivars with pink-tinged flowers.

Aubrieta deltoidea
AUBRETIA
Family: Brassicaceae
Native: Aegean

During the spring months when aubretia is in flower, the leaves are hardly noticeable because the lilac-red flowers are so numerous. Though only 10cm (4in) high, it is a prolific spreader, either on a slope or down a wall. It is also fairly drought-tolerant, which is an excellent quality if used in dry gardens, walls and containers.

Cultivation Grows well in full sun in any good, free-draining garden soil. Propagate by softwood cuttings in summer. Cut back hard after flowering to maintain a good shape. ✤ ✤ ✤ Zone 7.

Uses Aubretia looks delightful when planted in dry banks and cracks in walls, where it hangs down, softens the hard surface and offers a vibrant splash of colour when in flower. It is also useful for planting in a rock garden or in spring-flowering hanging baskets and containers, where it is used as a trailing plant.

Wildlife benefits It attracts early flying butterflies, bees and bumblebees in spring. Birds are then drawn to the area to feed on the visiting insects. The flowers are often taken by garden birds for use in nesting.

Closely related species Take care to avoid double-flowering cultivars, for example *A. d.* 'Doctor Mules'. A better bet for insects is the single-flowered *A. d.* 'Gurgedyke' with purple flowers in spring.

Aubrieta deltoidea

Aurinia saxatilis

Aurinia saxatilis
YELLOW ALYSSUM
Family: Brassicaeae
Native: C and SE Europe

This traditional rock-garden plant, formerly known as *A. saxatile*, originates from rocky and mountainous habitats. It grows 20cm (8in) high and produces numerous rich chrome-yellow flowers from late spring to early summer. The stems bear leaves that are linear, grey and slightly hairy.

Cultivation Yellow alyssum grows in any garden soil, but will perform well even in poor ground. Site in full sun. Propagate by soft cuttings in early summer. ✤ ✤ ✤ Zone 3.

Uses Although ideal for rock and gravel gardens, the plant, especially the flowering heads, can become unruly and invasive, therefore care needs to be taken when positioning it. Yellow alyssum can also be used when planting in containers, particularly for spring bedding ones.

Wildlife benefits Produces an early source of pollen for bees to take back to their hives and feed the larvae. Emerging butterflies drink from the nectaries to build up their strength before breeding begins.

Closely related species *A. s.* 'Citrinum' is good for wildlife, bearing bright lemon flowers. *A. petraea,* with yellow flowers, is very similar to *A. saxatilis*, but is more compact and less hardy. *A. rupestris* is a low-growing species bearing white flowers with attractive silver-grey leaves, and again is less hardy.

Baptisia australis
FALSE INDIGO
Family: Papilionoideae
Native: E North America

A graceful, upright perennial reaching up to 75cm (2½ft) tall. The delicate, pea-like violet flowers are borne on flower spikes throughout the summer months. The stem bears attractive bright green leaves that are divided into ovate leaflets. Ornate, dark grey seedpods form after flowering, and often persist on the plant over winter.

Cultivation False indigo thrives in full sun, in free-draining soil that is neutral or acid. Propagate by division in early spring or by seed in autumn. ❀ ❀ ❀ Zone 5.

Uses Owing to its upright habit, false indigo is ideal in herbaceous or mixed borders. It is also often grown with old-fashioned roses and other beauties, especially polemoniums, aquilegias and lupins.

Wildlife benefits False indigo is a real winner with bumblebees and the occasional butterfly. Avoid cutting back in autumn because seed-eating birds are readily drawn to the mature seedpods from autumn to winter.

Closely related species Both *B. alba*, which grows to 1.8m (6ft) tall with creamy white flowers, and *B. bracteata* var. *leucophaea*, bearing white to yellow-orange flowers and stems up to 60cm (2ft) high, are particularly suited to dry, sunny banks. Most *Baptisia* species naturalize in wild areas if sown or planted.

Baptisia australis

Campanula latifolia

Campanula latifolia
BELLFLOWER
Family: Campanulaceae
Native: Europe to Kashmir

This is one of the showiest herbaceous perennials for the back of a border. The tall stems, 1.2m (4ft) high, bear pale blue or light lavender bell-shaped flowers in summer. The foliage is long and ovate at the base, becoming distinctly rounder and more ovate near the top of the plant.

Cultivation Although the greater bellflower can be grown in full sun, it prefers light shade. It will grow in most soils but thrives in damp, fertile ground. Propagate by division in spring. ❀ ❀ ❀ Zone 3.

Uses An extremely useful plant for placing at the back of the herbaceous border, providing height and a showy display. For a bigger impact, plant with other perennial species such as *Phlox*, *Delphinium* and *Monarda*.

Wildlife benefits Bees are attracted to the flowers' pollen and nectar, and insect-eating birds are often found feeding on aphids around the flower head. Do not cut back the old stems until spring because the dense foliage offers protection through winter to hibernating insects.

Closely related species Harebell (*C. rotundifolia*) grows in grasslands. It has fine leaves and nodding blue flowers, and can be grown in meadows or rock gardens. *C. punctata* has large pale blue to white flowers in summer and grows to 1.5m (5ft) tall.

Cardamine pratensis
CUCKOO FLOWER
Family: Brassicaceae
Native: Europe

A delicate perennial, often associated with meadows and natural areas, the cuckoo flower sports beautiful white flowers flushed with lilac, and distinctive yellow stamens. It grows up to 30cm (1ft) high, with the stems producing deeply cut, glossy dark green foliage.

Cultivation The cuckoo flower is great for growing in full sun or light shade. Grow in damp soil with low fertility. Propagate by seed or division in autumn. ❀ ❀ ❀ Zone 4.

Uses An ideal plant for incorporating into a meadow mix for sites where the soil remains damp for prolonged periods. The cuckoo flower is also well suited to wild gardens, where it can easily naturalize and self-seed around an area.

Wildlife benefits The leaves of the cuckoo flower are the caterpillar food plant for the orange-tipped, green-veined, various brown and white butterflies. Bees are often observed visiting the flowers seeking nectar.

Closely related species *C. trifolia* is a creeping perennial suitable for rock gardens, bearing pure white flowers in late spring. *C. bulbifera* is useful for wild or naturalistic plantings. Do not select double-flowering cultivars of *C. pratensis*, such as 'Edith' and 'Flore Pleno', for example, as they are of little benefit to wildlife.

Cardamine pratensis

Centaurea montana
PERENNIAL CORNFLOWER
Family: Asteraceae
Native: Mountains of Europe

A wonderful, spreading perennial that produces an abundance of lance-shaped leaves with flower heads popping through, reaching 50cm (20in) high. The early summer thistle-like flowers are surrounded by a ray of slender petals which are purple, pink, blue or white.

Cultivation Prefers full sun in any well-drained soil, even if it is infertile, dry or chalky. Propagate by division in spring or autumn. Alternatively, take root cuttings in spring and place in an open propagating case in a sandy compost. ❊ ❊ ❊ Zone 3.

Uses A great plant for the front of the herbaceous border or for a large rock garden. The pale blue foliage of *Cerinthe major* 'Purpurascens' and the dark blue-purple flowers of *Centaurea montana* complement each other well.

Wildlife benefits The gorgeous blue flowers are irresistible to bees and bumblebees seeking nectar in summer. The seeds mature in autumn and are often eaten by greenfinches, goldfinches, crossbills, linnets and blue tits.

Closely related species Cornflower (*Centaurea cyanus*) is an annual reaching up to 90cm (3ft) high with violet to blue flowers. It is ideal for using in wildflower mixes or wild areas. *C. dealbata*, to 90cm (3ft) high, bears deeply cut silver foliage with lilac-purple flowers.

Centaurea montana

Centranthus ruber

Centranthus ruber
RED VALERIAN
Family: Valerianaceae
Native: Europe, N Africa and Asia Minor

The beautiful flowers, which range from crimson to pale red, are commonly seen in gardens in summer and autumn. The stems reach up to 60cm (2ft) high, and bear succulent, pale green foliage that allows the plant a degree of drought tolerance.

Cultivation Grow in full sun to obtain maximum flowering. They enjoy poor, dry soil, making them ideal candidates for growing in walls and rockeries. Propagate by seed in spring or autumn. ❊ ❊ ❊ Zone 3.

Uses A fantastic plant for rock gardens, and for growing in planting pockets in walls. The surface will be softened by the flower heads that cascade down the brickwork. Also very effective in herbaceous and mixed borders.

Wildlife benefits A renowned nectar provider for bees and several species of butterfly, including red admirals and small tortoiseshells. Moths, particularly hawk moths, are attracted by the fragrant flowers and seek nectar in the evening.

Closely related species Common valerian (*Valeriana officinalis*) is one of the best perennials for attracting many species of insects, especially beneficial ones. It is closely related to *C. ruber*, and bears spikes of white to deep pink flowers throughout summer.

Cichorium intybus
CHICORY
Family: Asteraceae
Native: Europe, W Asia and N Africa

The electric blue flowers are stunningly beautiful and eye-catching, especially on a sunny day. The flowering period is long, and ranges from late spring to early autumn. Growing out of a basal rosette of leaves are stems that can reach up to 1.2m (4ft) high.

Cultivation Site in full sun in any moderately fertile, well-drained soil. Take care when using chicory because it can freely seed in the garden. Propagate by seed in spring or autumn. ❊ ❊ ❊ Zone 3.

Uses Chicory will look amazing if used in meadows, especially when planted with colourful perennials such as milky bellflower (*Campanula lactiflora*), *Knautia macedonica* and campion (*Lychnis calcedonica*). Also use in the wild garden and allow it to self-seed freely around an area.

Wildlife benefits The flowers are visited by bees and bumblebees seeking nectar and pollen. The nectar production will peak in the morning because each individual flower will only last for one day. Leave the stems uncut over winter to aid overwintering insects.

Closely related species *C. spinosum* is a dwarf perennial that grows to 20cm (8in) high and produces blue, occasionally white or pink flowers in summer. Endive (*C. endivia*) is very like *C. intybus*, but is normally an annual or biennial.

Cichorium intybus

Cirsium rivulare

Coreopsis verticillata

Cirsium rivulare
PLUME THISTLE
Family: Asteraceae
Native: SW Europe

Often thistles are thought of as weeds, but this species is particularly ornamental though still invasive if left to self-seed. The tall, erect stems reach up to 1.2m (4ft) high and produce round, button-like, purple flower heads with 2–5 in a cluster. Leaves are narrow, oval and deeply cut.

Cultivation Plume thistle prefers sun or semi-shade in any type of soil except one that is constantly wet. Best propagated by seed in autumn. ❀ ❀ ❀ Zone 5.

Uses C. rivulare is ideal for growing in the wild garden where it's free to self-seed and spread. It is better here than in the herbaceous border where it tends to die out on a frequent basis and constantly needs replacing.

Wildlife benefits The pincushion blooms attract many species of insect, particularly bees and bumblebees seeking nectar. Do not cut down the seed heads after flowering because they attract dunnocks, linnets, finches and crossbills.

Closely related species The closely related musk thistle (Carduus nutan) has the same cultivation requirements as C. rivulare. It's a big attraction for bees and butterflies seeking nectar from the semi-nodding, crimson flowers.

Coreopsis verticillata
TICKSEED
Family: Asteraceae
Native: Maryland and W Virginia to S Carolina

A brightly coloured perennial, native to the east coast of North America. The stems grow to 60cm (2ft) high and produce deeply divided, dark green leaves, and culminate in branched stems bearing numerous golden-yellow daisy-like flowers in summer.

Cultivation Tickseed thrives in full sun in fertile, well-drained soil. C. verticillata is fairly tolerant of dry soils. Propagate by seed or by division in spring. ❀ ❀ ❀ Zone 6.

Uses Excellent in the herbaceous or mixed border. The brightly coloured flowers look stunning if planted next to other perennials, such as Salvia nemorosa 'May Night' with almost purple-black flowers, and the purple Cirsium rivulare 'Atropurpureum'.

Wildlife benefits Honeybees seek out the bright yellow flowers that are rich in pollen and nectar. It is also excellent for encouraging butterflies, hoverflies and ladybirds. Do not cut back after flowering because birds, especially finches, devour the mature seeds in autumn.

Closely related species
C. pubescens, to 1.2m (4ft) high, can be naturalized in wild gardens, and it flowers in several flushes from spring to late autumn. C. tripteris, to 3m (10ft) high, is a back-of-the-border plant but can also be planted in the wild garden and in partial shade.

Dahlia Collerette Group
DAHLIA
Family: Asteraceae
Native: Garden origin

The Collerette Group of dahlias was raised in France at the beginning of the twentieth century. The blooms have an open centre, and are surrounded by an inner circle of short florets (the collar). There are one, sometimes two, rows of normally flat outer ray florets. The cultivars grow to 1.2m (4ft) high, and are found in a range of colours.

Cultivation Dahlias grow well in a sheltered, sunny site, with high light levels and rich, well-drained soil. Propagate by division of the tubers or cuttings in spring. ❀ Zone 9.

Uses Dahlias can be used for seasonal interest in summer-bedding schemes, tropical borders, tubs and containers. They are also very effective at filling gaps in herbaceous borders, especially if used in large groups making plenty of impact.

Wildlife benefits The open flowers of species dahlias or Collerettes are excellent for providing nectar to butterflies and bees. Dahlias in other Groups, for example the Pompon and Cactus, have too many petals covering the sexual parts to be of any benefit.

Closely related species The Collerettes include several excellent cultivars, including D. 'Clair de Lune' with yellow ray petals and an inner circle of paler yellow petals. D. 'La Cierva' has purple-tipped white outer petals with a white collar.

Dahlia Collerette Group

Deschampsia flexuosa

Echinacea purpurea

Deschampsia flexuosa
WAVY HAIR GRASS
Family: Poaceae
Native: Europe, Asia, NE North America and S America

It produces one of the most attractive flower heads with panicles of golden flowers, tinged purple in late summer. The leaves are thread-like and will reach up to 20cm (8in) high, but the flower heads grow to 90cm (3ft) tall.

Cultivation Although wavy hair grass will grow in most soils, it will thrive in acid ground in full sun or semi-shade. Propagate by division in spring. ❈ ❈ ❈ Zone 5.

Uses A wonderful plant to use in naturalistic plantings with perennials including rudbeckias, eryngiums and fennel. Wavy hair grass can also be used to create movement in winter borders, and can be sited on the edge of woodland gardens because it tolerates partial shade.

Wildlife benefits Many different insects shelter and hibernate amongst the thick foliage over winter. It is also the food plant for the caterpillars of the ringlet butterfly.

Closely related species All grasses should be left uncut over winter to offer a home to many species. Tufted hair grass (*D. cespitosa*) is an evergreen perennial grass reaching up to 1m (3ft) high. It produces panicles of minute, pale brown spikelets in summer.

Echinacea purpurea
CONEFLOWER
Family: Asteraceae
Native: E North America

Produces a beautiful, erect daisy-like flower that is both eye-catching and a fantastic plant for attracting numerous species of wildlife. The deep crimson-pink flower heads, with conical brown-pink centres, are borne singly in late summer, and the lance-shaped leaves are dark green with a rough texture.

Cultivation The coneflower prefers full sun but will tolerate partial shade. Plant in humus-rich soil that is well drained. Propagate by division in spring. ❈ ❈ ❈ Zone 3.

Uses A versatile plant that can be used in many different situations. It looks superb in naturalistic plantings when planted in large drifts with rudbeckias, verbenas, grasses and campanulas. Also very effective in herbaceous or mixed borders.

Wildlife benefits The coneflower is very popular with bees and bumblebees taking nectar from the conical brown centres that produce petal-less flowers. Butterflies and hoverflies are occasional visitors seeking nectar.

Closely related species *E. pallida*, to 90cm (3ft) high, is very similar to *E. purpurea* and produces purple flower heads in late summer. *E. angustifolia*, which grows to 1.5m (5ft) high, has decidedly smaller light purple to rose-pink flowers.

Echinops ritro
GLOBE THISTLE
Family: Asteraceae
Native: C and E Europe

A striking architectural plant grown for its globe-like, spiky flower heads that appear in summer. The purple-blue flower heads can reach up to 1.2m (4ft) high. The attractive, large foliage is striking, silver-grey and deeply divided.

Cultivation Plant out in full sun in well-drained soil. It will grow adequately in poor ground, though the tall stems may need staking. Propagate by division or seed in autumn. ❈ ❈ ❈ Zone 3.

Uses Very popular for the back of the herbaceous or mixed border, giving height and structure. Globe thistles are stunning when sited next to plants with purple foliage, for example the smoke bush (*Cotinus coggygria* 'Royal Purple').

Wildlife benefits Extremely attractive to bees and bumblebees. Butterflies are also frequent visitors to the round blue flower heads. The autumn seed is eaten by the likes of goldfinches.

Closely related species Other excellent insect attractors are the 1.2–1.5m (4–5ft) high *E. bannaticus* with pale to mid-blue flower heads. *E. sphaerocephalus* is an extremely large perennial growing to 2m (6½ft) high with greyish-white flower heads.

Echinops ritro

Eryngium alpinum

Eryngium alpinum
SEA HOLLY
Family: Apiaceae
Native: Europe

A superb eye-catcher and structural plant for any border. Sea holly produces basal rosettes of heart-shaped, deeply toothed, glossy foliage. The stems bear purple-blue flower heads surrounded by metallic blue bracts with large, soft spines throughout the summer months. This unusual plant will reach 75cm–1m (2½–3ft) high.

Cultivation Sea holly thrives in full sun in moderately fertile, free-draining soil, although it will tolerate a range of soil conditions. Propagate by seed in autumn. ❀ ❀ ❀ Zone 5.

Uses A versatile plant at home in a dry or seaside garden, sea holly can also be used in a herbaceous or mixed border. The beautiful purple-blue colours contrast well with silvers, pinks and purples, making it ideal in an old-fashioned rose garden.

Wildlife benefits It attracts bees and bumblebees that congregate in large numbers, seeking the nectar-rich, thistle-type flowers. The occasional butterfly and a rare beetle visiting the flower head have also been recorded.

Closely related species All the eryngiums are excellent nectar producers and benefit many insects. *E. giganteum* is another attractive species that is equally beneficial to wildlife. It is a biennial or short-lived perennial bearing blue flowers with silver bracts. *E.* x *oliverianum* has lavender-blue flowers and grows to 1m (3ft).

Festuca glauca
BLUE FESCUE
Family: Poaceae
Native: Europe

A wonderful plant that is frequently used in modern planting schemes. It is an evergreen tuft-forming grass growing up to 10cm (4in) high and produces narrow, blue-silvery white foliage. The foliage is definitely the most attractive part of the plant because the flower spikes are small and insignificant.

Cultivation Fescues are easily grown in poor, dry conditions, in full sun. Constantly remove the dead leaves to promote good leaf colour. Divide every 3–4 years in spring. ❀ ❀ ❀ Zone 5.

Uses The colour of the fine leaves is one of the loveliest shades of blue in the garden. The grass is also ideal in containers and winter hanging baskets because it gives a good colour boost in the dull, dormant months. Blue fescue can also be used effectively in a dry garden, or in herbaceous or mixed borders.

Wildlife benefits The thick tufts offer shelter to overwintering insects and small mammals. Larvae of several different species of butterfly will use the fine leaves as their food plant. Small insects will use the dense foliage to shelter in during summer and winter.

Closely related species Sheep's fescue (*F. ovina*) is excellent for wildlife. Similar to *F. glauca*, it is an important caterpillar food plant for garden butterflies, and is ideal in wildflower meadow mixes.

Festuca glauca

Foeniculum vulgare
FENNEL
Family: Apiaceae
Native: Mediterranean

A wonderful plant that provides good structure in borders. The soft, fern-like foliage adorns the rigid zigzag pattern of the green stems. The foliage is aromatic, especially if crushed or brushed past. The large, flat flower heads are full of small yellow flowers borne from summer to autumn.

Cultivation Fennel thrives in full sun in any well-drained garden soil. It will set seed freely and can become a problem in a small garden, so frequent weeding is needed to remove the seedlings before they take over the border. Propagate by seed or division in spring. ❀ ❀ ❀ Zone 5.

Uses Excellent in the herbaceous border or wild garden where it's allowed to self-seed and naturalize freely. Grow amongst echinaceas and verbenas.

Wildlife benefits The nectar-rich flowers attract many species of insects including lacewings, ladybirds, parasitic wasps, wasps and bees. The caterpillar of the swallowtail butterfly will eat the leaves of fennel. Many species hibernate in the uncut, hollow stems.

Closely related species Giant fennel (*Ferula communis*), a close relative, also attracts insects, and reaches 1–3.7m (3–12ft) high. A summer-flowering perennial, it's grown for its bold architectural form and yellow flower heads.

Foeniculum vulgare

Geranium maculatum
GERANIUM
Family: Geraniaceae
Native: NE North America

Geraniums create excellent ground cover and provide lovely drifts of colour if planted in large groups. The saucer-shaped, upward-facing flowers are light to deep pink and appear from spring to summer. They are borne above deeply cut, mid-green leaves.

Cultivation Plant in full sun or partial shade in any well-drained soil. Cut back after flowering to promote a second flush. Propagate by division in autumn or spring. ✿ ✿ ✿ Zone 4.

Uses All geraniums are excellent as ground cover. They can be planted under shrubs and trees, can be used at the front of herbaceous borders or naturalized in meadows.

Wildlife benefits The dense leaf cover provides protection for a host of species that will hide and forage in the foliage. Being long-flowering, it is an essential plant for the wildlife garden, especially for bees seeking nectar.

Closely related species Most geraniums provide good ground cover and are attractive to bees. *G. sylvaticum* and *G. pratense* can be naturalized in meadows and wild areas. *G. psilostemon*, a taller geranium, has flashy magenta flowers with a deep purple centre.

Helenium autumnale
SNEEZEWEED
Family: Asteraceae
Native: N America

It is grown for its daisy-like flowers that appear in late summer and autumn. Each flower head has a round central disc and a nectar-rich, bright yellow ray floret. Thin, lance-shaped leaves adorn the stems that grow to 1.5m (5ft) high.

Cultivation Sneezeweed will grow in any fertile soil, except when it's very dry, in full sun. Propagate by division in spring or autumn, or by seed in spring. ✿ ✿ ✿ Zone 3.

Uses An ideal plant for using in herbaceous or mixed borders to add height and colour. Plant beside tall grasses, such as cultivars of *Miscanthus sinensis*, *Panicum virgatum* and other late-flowering species for a graceful autumnal effect.

Wildlife benefits The yellow flowers of sneezeweed are a beacon for bees and bumblebees; the colour sends out a message that nectar is available. Butterflies, especially sulphurs, are also drawn to the flower heads when seeking late-season nectar.

Closely related species *Hymenoxys hoopesii*, to 90cm (3ft) high, occurs naturally around woodland edges and is a welcome addition to any dappled, shady area. *H. bigelovii* grows to 90cm (3ft) high and is a moist, meadowland plant that is suitable for naturalizing in meadows and wild gardens.

Holcus lanatus
YORKSHIRE FOG
Family: Poaceae
Native: Europe

Holcus lanatus is a perennial grass that can grow up to 90cm (3ft) high. It bears ornamental seed heads in a dense panicle up to 15cm (6in) long, and they appear above the slender, grey-green leaves, which are slightly hairy. It produces strong, rhizomatous creeping roots that can become invasive when planted next to less vigorous species.

Cultivation Grow in full sun in well-drained soil that is also moisture retentive.

Holcus lanatus

Propagate by division in autumn or spring, or by seed when ripe. ✿ ✿ ✿ Zone 5.

Uses Ideal for growing in meadows or the wild garden. One drawback is that this species can overwhelm finer grasses that have essential benefits to wildlife, making creeping soft grass (*H. mollis*) a better all-round choice for a wildflower mix.

Wildlife benefits The leaves of Yorkshire fog are eaten by the caterpillars of the speckled wood and small skipper butterflies. The dense foliage is ideal for small mammals and invertebrates that hide and forage around in it.

Closely related species *H. mollis* is best suited to acid soil in slightly shady areas or hedge banks. It is slightly smaller than *H. lanatus*, growing up to 60cm (2ft) high, and produces wider foliage that is soft and velvety.

Geranium maculatum

Helenium autumnale

Knautia macedonia

Knautia macedonia
KNAUTIA
Family: Dipsacaeae
Native: C Europe

A beautiful, graceful perennial that is ideal in the ornamental garden and wildflower meadow. The slender stems reach up to 90cm (3ft) high and, in summer, bear deep purple to crimson flowers in round, pincushion flower heads. The stems bear many narrow, deeply divided, oval-shaped leaves.

Cultivation Site in full sun and in any free-draining soil. Propagate by seed in autumn or by basal cuttings in spring. ❀ ❀ ❀ Zone 6.

Uses A lovely plant to use in naturalistic plantings. It works extremely well with *Miscanthus,* rudbeckias and verbenas. *Knautia* is a firm favourite in herbaceous and mixed borders, providing a good splash of colour over several weeks.

Wildlife benefits The flowers are visited by bees and butterflies, particularly the red admiral and painted lady. They are drawn to the nectaries by nectar guides that are invisible to the naked eye, but not to insects. Birds will eat the seed in autumn if the old flower heads are left uncut.

Closely related species Field scabious (*K. arvensis*) can be grown in lightly shaded areas or full sun, preferably on calcareous soil. It grows up to 1.5m (5ft) high, and bears pale purple-blue flower heads. Use in a wildflower meadow mix or in a wild garden.

Lamium album
WHITE DEAD NETTLE
Family: Lamiaceae
Native: Europe to W Asia

Lamiums are well known for their nectar, and draw large numbers of bee species to the white, tubular summer flowers. The erect, square stems reach up to 90cm (3ft) tall, and bear green, kidney-shaped leaves with toothed margins.

Cultivation *L. album* is at home in sun or semi-shade, and grows best in humus-rich soil. Propagate by potting up rooted running stems, or by seed in autumn. ❀ ❀ ❀ Zone 4.

Uses White dead nettle is a natural woodland plant and is therefore best suited to light shade. Grow under trees, in woodland edges and in drifts in a woodland garden, although it can be invasive. Excellent as ground cover in a wild garden.

Wildlife benefits Adored by bees and bumblebees that visit the flower to drink from the generous nectaries. White dead nettle also produces an abundance of foliage, which provides valuable cover for many species at ground level, including insects and spiders. The nutlets are eaten by birds such as finches.

Closely related species Other excellent nectar-producing species include the herbaceous perennial *L. orvala* that grows to 60cm (2ft) high, and bears red to purple, tubular flowers. *L. maculatum,* to 60cm (2ft) high, is a fantastic plant for ground cover, producing red to purple flowers.

Lamium album

Liatris spicata

Liatris spicata
GAYFEATHER
Family: Asteraceae
Native: E North America

Valued for its late summer, rose-purple flowers borne in spikes to 60cm (2ft) high. The flower heads are unusual because they start to flower from the top downwards, and are set off beautifully by the grass-like, mid-green leaves. The rootstocks are thickened, corm-like structures.

Cultivation *L. spicata* prefers fertile, free-draining soil, which also retains moisture, and flourishes if planted in full sun. Propagate by division in spring, or seed sown in autumn. ❀ ❀ ❀ Zone 3.

Uses Excellent when used in large clumps and planted in drifts to create a real impact. Gayfeather is also ideal in herbaceous and mixed borders. It is often used in partial shade, but in dry conditions can be prone to powdery mildew, which will affect its growth and flowering.

Wildlife benefit The nectar-rich flowers are a real magnet for bees, moths and butterflies. Dry, blackened seed heads are visited in late autumn and winter by birds, particularly finches seeking a protein-rich meal.

Closely related species Cultivars worth growing of *L. spicata* include 'Alba' with white flowers, and 'Floristan Violett' with deep violet flowers. Another species native to North America is *L. squarrosa* that grows to 60cm (2ft) high. It produces red-purple flowers in late summer–autumn.

Linaria vulgaris

Lupinus nootkatensis

Linaria vulgaris
TOADFLAX
Family: Scrophulariaceae
Native: Europe

Toadflax is often seen flowering in roadside verges and on dry banks, being especially noticeable in drier years when more flowers are produced. The flowers are pale to bright yellow with a coppery spur, and appear from spring to autumn. The stems grow to 30–90cm (1–3ft) high and bear delicate, linear, mid-green leaves.

Cultivation Easily grown in dry, sandy soil in full sun. Propagate by division in spring or by seed in spring or autumn. ❉ ❉ ❉ Zone 4.

Uses It is best grown in a hedge bank, wildflower meadow or wild garden because of its fantastic ability to self-seed. Ideal for using on free-draining soil that dries out easily.

Wildlife benefits Bees and bumblebees almost fight at the flower base to land and collect pollen and nectar. Beneficial insects, including hoverflies and parasitic wasps, are also attracted to the nectar.

Closely related species Purple toadflax (*Linaria purpurea*) carries beautiful spikes of purple-blue flowers, and is ideal for the herbaceous border. *L. alpina* is a tuft-forming, short-lived perennial with yellow-centred purple flowers, and is suitable for a rock garden.

Lupinus nootkatensis
LUPIN
Family: Papilionaceae
Native: NW North America

A highly attractive plant grown for its beautiful foliage and large violet, pink, white or multi-coloured flower spikes. The individual flowers are pea-like in appearance, and the deeply divided mid-green leaves are borne on stems reaching up to 60cm (2ft) high.

Cultivation Prefers moist soils with good drainage, in full sun. Raise from fresh seed in autumn, or by cuttings from basal shoots in spring. ❉ ❉ ❉ Zone 4.

Uses Although short-lived, lupins are one of the very best plants for the herbaceous border because their magnificent flower heads provide a great splash of colour. Also widely used in wildflower meadows and the wild garden.

Wildlife benefits The brightly coloured flowers and sweet-smelling secretions are a great draw for bees and bumblebees seeking pollen. The plant is prone to attack from aphids that, in turn, attract birds, ladybirds and lacewings.

Closely related species
L. polyphyllus and *L. arboreus* were the main breeding species used to create the ornamental lupin cultivars grown today. *L. polyphyllus* grows to 1.5m (5ft) high with blue, purple, pink or white flowers. Excellent in a wildflower meadow.

Monarda didyma
BERGAMOT
Family: Lamiaceae
Native: Canada

Also called bee balm, it attracts various species of bee seeking the flowers' nectar. The flower heads are rounded discs with sterile, bright crimson, tubular flowers sited around the peripheral area of the head.

Cultivation Plant in full sun in fertile, free-draining soil that stays moist. Propagate by division of clumps or by seed, both in spring. ❉ ❉ ❉ Zone 4.

Uses A classic herbaceous perennial that is as popular today as it was 30 years ago. Great for the middle to the back of the herbaceous bed, or in a mixed border to create drifts of colour. Grow beside *Achillea* 'Goldplate' for a good colour combination.

Wildlife benefits The flowers produce high yields of nectar that are a magnet for bees, bumblebees and parasitic wasps. Leave the stems on over winter, and all the small crevices and hollows will provide a site for small insects, including ladybirds.

Closely related species
M. russeliana bears pink flowers with purple spots and *M. bartlettii* produces magenta flowers. *M. citriodora* is an annual with white or pink flowers that is another good bee attractor.

Monarda didyma

Nepeta x *faasenii*
CATMINT
Family: Lamiaceae
Native: Garden origin

This lovely, ornamental, herbaceous perennial has lilac-blue flowers from early summer to late autumn, and is adored by cats, which rub themselves against the grey-green foliage, releasing the scent. It is a rampant spreader and reaches 45cm (18in).

Cultivation It thrives in sunny locations in free-draining soil (avoid any other kind or the growth might be severely affected). Propagate by division in spring or autumn. ❀ ❀ ❀ Zone 3.

Uses It looks delightful when used as an edging plant amongst old-fashioned roses. Also use at the front of herbaceous borders or mixed borders where it is best placed next to plants with silver, purple or pink foliage or flowers.

Wildlife benefits Bees and bumblebees visit the small purple flowers seeking nectar. There are also occasional visit from butterflies and parasitic wasps. The dense foliage provides excellent cover for insects and small mammals that hide and forage here.

Closely related species *N. grandiflora* is a taller species with attractive, rich blue flowers. Catnip (*N. cataria*) is believed to repel rats, but the essential oils that are released when it is crushed are irresistible to cats. Both attract masses of bees.

Papaver orientale
ORIENTAL POPPY
Family: Papaveraceae
Native: SW Asia

Ornamental poppies are big, blowsy and great fun. The solitary flowers are red, orange or pale pink with a purple blotch at the base. The stems reach up to 90cm

Papaver orientale

(3ft) high and bear deeply divided, large, hairy leaves that are light green-blue. Many cultivars are now available.

Cultivation Poppies thrive in a sunny location in free-draining, fertile soil. Propagate by division in early autumn or spring, or by seed in spring. ❀ ❀ ❀ Zone 3.

Uses The huge flowers and beautiful seed heads are a must for any mixed or herbaceous border. Do not plant at the front of a border because they die back early in the season, and leave a big, obvious gap. Grow beside *Limonium* or *Gypsophila* to help fill the gaps.

Wildlife benefits The flowers have easily accessible nectaries, making it a popular site for bees and hoverflies. The seed head is like a "pepper pot" filled with small seeds that get shaken out unless eaten by birds such as dunnocks, sparrows, linnets and finches.

Closely related species Other poppies useful to wildlife are the corn poppy (*P. rhoeas*), a tall annual herb that bears large scarlet flowers. The Icelandic poppy (*P. nudicaule*) is best grown as a biennial and bears pretty yellow, orange, peach, white or pale red flowers in summer.

Penstemon barbatus
PENSTEMON
Family: Scrophulariaceae
Native: New Mexico to Utah, Arizona and N Mexico

Penstemons are one of the best value garden plants because they flower for weeks and are really easy to grow. *P. barbatus* grows to 90cm (3ft) high or more, and produces beautiful tubular

flowers that are red with a tinge of pink to carmine throughout summer. The thin, mid-green leaves are lance-shaped.

Cultivation Penstemons are best grown in well-drained soil in full sun, although they tolerate light, partial shade. Propagate by semi-ripe cuttings in late summer. ❀ ❀ ❀ Zone 3.

Uses Without a doubt penstemons offer huge bursts of radiant colour in herbaceous or mixed borders. Plant in large groups to create the best colour effect, and site at the front of a border.

Wildlife benefits The flowers are very popular with bees and bumblebees. If the flower parts are too small to enter, the bees will puncture a hole at the base of the petals with their mouthparts to access the nectaries. Hoverflies and ladybirds are occasional visitors.

Closely related species Bees also favour rock penstemon (*P. rupicola*), which has deep rose-coloured flowers and is just 10cm (4in) tall. It is ideal for a rock garden.

Nepeta x *faasenii*

Penstemon barbatus

Phlox paniculata
SUMMER PHLOX
Family: Polemoniaceae
Native: N America

A majestic herbaceous perennial, it is great for providing late summer colour in the garden. The tall flower heads reach up to 1.2m (4ft) high, and produce tubular, scented, white, purple or pink flowers that are ideal for attracting butterflies and moths. Long, mid-green leaves are carried right up the stem; they are lance-shaped with toothed margins.

Cultivation Summer phlox will grow in almost any soil but prefers rich, moist but free-draining ground in full sun or semi-shade. Propagate by division in early spring. ❀ ❀ ❀ Zone 4.

Uses Often used in herbaceous beds, mixed borders or in a specialist butterfly border. Plant beside other butterfly-attracting species, such as *Scabiosa*, *Sedum* and *Verbena*, to create a nectar-rich haven for butterflies and other insects.

Wildlife benefits Butterflies, in particular swallowtails, fritillaries and skippers, are daytime visitors lured by the sweetly scented flowers for nectar. Hawkmoths may hover around the flowers from late afternoon until dusk, and several species of night-flying moths are also attracted.

Closely related species Other species popular with butterflies and moths include annual phlox (*P. drummondii*) that grows up to 30cm (1ft) high and produces purple-pink flowers. Prairie phlox (*P. pilosa*) grows to 60cm (2ft) high with lilac-purple flowers.

Phlox paniculata

Polygonum bistorta

Polygonum bistorta
COMMON BISTORT
Family: Polygonaceae
Native: Russia and Turkey

P. bistorta is an extremely showy plant when in flower, and can grow up to 60cm (2ft) high. It grows in meadows and at the bottom of hedgerows. The stems produce triangular leaves and culminate in dense, cylindrical spikes of pink, occasionally white, flowers that appear in summer.

Cultivation Plant common bistort in full sun or semi-shade in moisture-retentive soil that is not too fertile. Propagate by division in autumn or spring. ❀ ❀ ❀ Zone 4.

Uses Fantastic in herbaceous borders or for providing colour in a woodland garden. Plant in large drifts at the edge of a woodland garden to provide colour in the under-storey, and use with species such as *Astilbe* and *Doronicum*.

Wildlife benefits During summer the pink flowers attract bees and bumblebees in large numbers. After flowering the plant produces red-brown fruits that, when ripe, attract many bird species, particularly dunnocks, finches and sparrows.

Closely related species *P. affine* is an evergreen, ground-hugging perennial producing dense spikes of rose-red flowers in autumn. *P. amplexicaule* is a taller perennial which grows up to 1.2m (4ft) high and produces delicate, rich red flowers from summer to autumn.

Primula veris

Primula veris
COWSLIP
Family: Primulaceae
Native: Europe and W Asia

When this beautiful grassland plant flowers, it's a sign that spring has arrived. The yellow flowers, with an orange mark, are slightly nodding and sweetly scented. Due to the ground-hugging habit of the green, crinkled leaves it is able to withstand periodic mowing or grazing.

Cultivation Plant in the garden in full sun or semi-shade in any good garden soil. Propagate by seed when fresh. The seed will need a cold spell before germination occurs. ❀ ❀ ❀ Zone 5.

Uses It is extremely well suited to meadows, and will also thrive if planted in borders. As it withstands semi-shade, it is ideal for planting around the base of deciduous shrubs and trees to provide an early source of nectar.

Wildlife benefits The cowslip is an excellent nectar source for overwintering butterflies and bees. It is also eaten by the caterpillars of the Duke of Burgundy butterfly. The seeds are eaten by chaffinches, and sparrows occasionally attack the flowers.

Closely related species With similar benefits to wildlife, the primrose (*P. vulgaris*) is also an early flowering species and is found in hedgerows and woodlands. The seeds of the plant are eaten by chaffinches.

Pulmonaria officinalis
LUNGWORT
Family: Boraginaceae
Native: Europe

A very effective ground-cover plant, no more than 30cm (1ft) tall, for shady borders. It has green hairy leaves that bear white to silver blotches, and spring flowers that are pink when shut, but are violet-blue when open.

Cultivation Prefers moist soil rich in humus, and full or semi-shade. Divide in autumn after flowering. ❀ ❀ ❀ Zone 6.

Uses Produces excellent ground cover in borders or woodland gardens. As lungwort will thrive in full shade, it can be planted in a woodland or dark, shady border. *Dicentra* and *Primula denticulata* are ideal woodland garden companions.

Wildlife benefits The flowers are a firm favourite with early flying bees seeking nectar. Solitary bees, such as the spring (hairy footed) flower bee, have been seen with their long tongues still out between taking nectar from one flower and the next. Plant in large groups to provide a valuable source of early nectar.

Closely related species Although there are many cultivars of *P. officinalis*, the species is the best provider of nectar for visiting wildlife. *P. angustifolia* has narrow, lance-like leaves, produces heads of pink-tinged, deep blue flowers, and may be naturalized in a meadow.

Rudbeckia fulgida
CONEFLOWER
Family: Asteraceae
Native: SE North America

The coneflower adds vibrant colour from late summer to autumn. The plant produces flower heads with long, bright yellow petals with dark, almost black centres. The stems are 60–90cm (2–3ft) tall, and the lance-shaped leaves are rough and hairy.

Cultivation Although it will grow in almost any soil, it does require full sun or part-day shade. Propagate by division in spring. ❀ ❀ ❀ Zone 4.

Uses Great for using in drifts in naturalistic planting and in herbaceous and mixed borders. Also ideal next to other late summer-flowering plants, such as crocosmias, dahlias and various grass species.

Wildlife benefits The flowers are visited by bees and bumblebees for nectar. Late flying butterflies, such as painted ladies and small tortoiseshells, have been noted in large numbers taking nectar in early autumn.

Closely related species Popular cultivars of *R. fulgida* are var. *sullivanii* 'Goldsturm', which has narrow golden petals and is a real gardener's favourite, and var. *deamii*, which is extremely drought-tolerant. Many other species, including *R. hirta*, *R. nitida* and *R. californica*, are also excellent insect attractors.

Salvia nemerosa

Salvia nemerosa
WOOD SAGE
Family: Lamiaceae
Native: Europe to C Asia

Definitely one of the best plants to attract different bee species into the garden. In summer, wood sage produces nectar-rich flowers that are violet to purple but occasionally white or pink. The stems reach up to 90cm (3ft) high, and bear narrow, oval, mid-green leaves with a rough texture.

Cultivation An easy-to-grow perennial that will grow in almost any soil in full sun. Propagate by softwood cuttings at any time of the growing season. ❀ ❀ ❀ Zone 5.

Uses An attractive species that belongs to the front of the herbaceous or mixed border, but note it can self-seed and spread prolifically. The better option might be to use it in a meadow mix or the wild garden.

Wildlife benefits One of the best plants for attracting bees and bumblebees into the garden. At times the flower spikes will bend due to the sheer number of insects taking nectar. Plant in large groups to attract butterflies because they are less likely to visit single specimens.

Closely related species

S. x *sylvestris* bears dark violet flower spikes, *S.* x *superba* produces bright violet to purple flowers, and meadow clary (*S. pratensis*) has violet flower heads. All are herbaceous perennials, superb for herbaceous borders or wild areas.

Pulmonaria officinalis

Rudbeckia fulgida

Scabiosa caucasica

Scabiosa caucasica
SCABIOUS
Family: Dipsacaceae
Native: Caucasus

A wonderful showy plant that produces large, lilac-blue flower heads with pincushion-like centres from summer to late autumn. It has light green lance-shaped basal leaves and deeply cut, grey-green stem leaves, and will easily reach 60cm (2ft) high.

Cultivation Site in full sun in neutral to alkaline free-draining soil. Propagate by seed or basal cuttings in spring. ❀ ❀ ❀ Zone 4.

Uses Ideally place to the front of the herbaceous or mixed border, with *Knautia macedonica* and *Polygonum bistorta* to provide a strong focal point. Can also be used in specialist butterfly borders. Plant in large drifts to create the best visual effect.

Wildlife benefits *S. caucasica* is popular with several different species of butterflies, and is also a winner with bees. This is due to the large amount of nectar produced and because of its long flowering period, offering insects food for many weeks.

Closely related species *S. lucida* has rose-lilac flowers and *S. columbaria* red-purple or lilac-blue flowers. Both are suited to a sunny area in a wild garden, and are an invaluable source of pollen and nectar to many insects, particularly bees and butterflies.

Syn. *Sedum spectabile*
(*Hylotelephium spectabile*)
ICE PLANT
Family: Crassulaceae
Native: China and Korea

A lovely structural plant for the garden. The succulent foliage and stems are light green and bear large, flat heads of small, pink-red flowers from late summer to the first frosts. It remains rigid in the dormant season and, if left uncut, will add structure to the border.

Cultivation It is essential that the ice plant is given full sun and free-draining soil. Propagate by division in autumn or spring. ❀ ❀ ❀ Zone 6.

Uses One of the best plants for a naturalistic planting alongside coneflowers (*Rudbeckia*), grasses (e.g. *Deschampsia*) and fennel (*Foeniculum*). It is also an ideal plant for the front of the herbaceous or mixed border.

Wildlife benefits Overwintering butterflies, particularly small tortoiseshells, peacocks and red admirals, drink large amounts of nectar to survive hibernation. The flowers are also a popular choice with bees and other insects.

Closely related species *Hylotelephium telephium* is equally loved by insects and is ideal for a flower border, growing to 60cm (2ft) high. It bears purple flowers with purple-tinged foliage.

Syn. *Sedum spectabile*

Silene dioica

Silene dioica
RED CAMPION
Family: Caryophyllaceae
Native: Europe

A pretty wild flower of woodland edges and hedgerows. It produces attractive rose-pink flowers from spring to early summer on leafy stems reaching up to 45cm (18in) high. The leaves, found all the way up the stem, are ovate and decrease in number as they reach the flower head.

Cultivation Red campion prefers light, well-drained soil in full sun, and will also thrive in semi-shady conditions. Propagate by seed when fresh. ❀ ❀ ❀ Zone 6.

Uses Best suited for growing in meadows, but it will also grow extremely well in herbaceous borders and woodland edges. Light blue bluebells make good planting companions, mixing well with the light pink.

Wildlife benefits The flowers are a good early source of nectar for butterflies and moths. The leaves are eaten by the caterpillars of several moths. Leave the old stems uncut to allow the seed to drop freely for birds and small mammals, and to create hibernation sites.

Closely related species *S. latifolia*, which grows to 90cm (3ft), bears white, scented flowers in summer. Bladder campion (*S. vulgaris*) is best suited to grasslands in a sunny location. All species attract butterflies and moths to their nectar.

Solidago virgaurea
GOLDEN ROD
Family: Asteraceae
Native: Arctic and W Europe

A fantastic insect attractor that produces tall spikes of golden flowers with lance-shaped green leaves, and reaches up to 90cm (3ft) high. The flowering period is long, from summer to autumn, when golden rod produces large amounts of nectar, making it invaluable to any wildlife garden.

Cultivation It prefers full sun with its roots in any type of well-drained soil. Propagate by division in autumn or spring. ❀ ❀ ❀ Zone 5.

Uses *S. virgaurea* is best suited to the wild garden where it can run rampant. Garden cultivars are a better choice for more managed gardens where they can be grown in herbaceous or mixed borders.

Wildlife benefits The nectar-rich flowers are very attractive to bees, butterflies and moths. Ladybirds and parasitic wasps are also frequent visitors, with soldier beetles hiding in the dense foliage. Seeds are eaten by birds, particularly finches and linnets.

Closely related species *S. virgaurea* and *S. canadensis* have been crossed to produce garden-worthy hybrids such as *S.* 'Cloth of Gold' and *S.* 'Golden Mosa'.

Stachys officinalis
BETONY
Family: Lamiaceae
Native: Europe and Asia

A wonderful woodland plant that produces large, showy flower heads that contain numerous lilac-purple, very occasionally pink or white, flowers. They are borne throughout summer on stems that grow to 90cm (3ft) high, and bear oblong leaves with a heart-shaped base.

Cultivation Plant around the garden in full sun or partial shade. It will grow in any soil, ideally one enriched with humus. Propagate by seed or division. ❀ ❀ ❀ Zone 5.

Uses The attractive flowers are a welcome sight when used in large drifts along a woodland edge. Plant with other shade-tolerant plants, in particular heucheras and dicentras. Can also be used in herbaceous and mixed borders, or in a wild garden.

Wildlife benefits If planted in large numbers it provides welcome colour and a rich nectar store for insects. The flowers are attractive to both bees and butterflies.

Closely related species Annual hedgenettle (*S. annua*) and *S. alpina* are ideal for hedge banks and wildflower areas because they are excellent nectar producers, and attract many species of bee and butterfly. Downy woundwort (*S. germanica*) is ideal for a wild garden.

Symphytum grandiflora
COMFREY
Family: Boraginaceae
Native: Europe

A low-growing perennial reaching up to 30cm (1ft) high, producing a thick mat of leaves making excellent ground cover. The rich green leaves are hairy and rough. The creamy, drooping, tubular flowers appear in spring and are borne on one-sided racemes.

Cultivation Comfrey will grow in most soils but thrives in moist, free-draining

Symphytum grandiflora

ground in sun or, better still, dappled shade. Propagate by division in autumn or spring. ❀ ❀ ❀ Zone 5.

Uses A welcome addition to the front of the herbaceous border or group of old-fashioned roses. Annual maintenance may be required if a clump is becoming too invasive, or grow it in the wild garden.

Wildlife benefits The nectar-rich flowers are a magnet for bees and bumblebees. Group several plants together to create good ground cover that will encourage shy birds into the garden looking for seeds, insects and shelter.

Closely related species The flowers of *S. officinalis* are also good at attracting bees. It is commonly grown in vegetable gardens to make liquid tea, or is cut and added to the compost heap to provide a source of potassium.

Solidago virgaurea

Stachys officinalis

Taraxacum officinale
DANDELION
Family: Asteraceae
Native: Northern Hemisphere

Although thought of as a weed, dandelions have beautiful, round, nectar-rich flowers with sterile, golden-yellow petals around the edge. The heads can reach up to 5cm (2in) wide, and appear from spring to autumn. The mid-green leaves are oblong with toothed edges.

Cultivation Dandelions enjoy a sunny spot in any type of soil. The plant will naturally self-seed if the yellow flowers are left on. ❀ ❀ ❀ Zone 5.

Uses Leave even a small area of grass to grow long and dandelions will naturally appear, giving the area a boost of colour. They will also pop up in meadows and along hedgerow bottoms that aren't too shady, and will look completely at home in the wild garden.

Wildlife benefits Dandelions are a fantastic nectar and pollen plant for honeybees and bumblebees. They also provide nectar for butterflies and other insects. The leaves are eaten by caterpillars of the white ermine moth, and the seeds are eaten by birds, particularly goldfinches and greenfinches.

Closely related species Russian dandelion (*T. glaucanthum*) grows to 30cm (1ft) high and bears pale to bright yellow flowers striped grey underneath. *T. alpicola* grows up to 30cm (1ft) high and has orange to yellow flowers all summer.

Taraxacum officinale

Trifolium pratense
RED CLOVER
Family: Papilionaceae
Native: Europe

Red clover is a profuse flowering perennial, growing up to 30cm (1ft) high. The round flower heads are red to purple or pink, and occasionally cream, appearing in late spring and summer. The leaves are divided into three leaflets.

Cultivation Thrives in any well-drained garden soil, in a variety of types. Place in full sun for best flowering results. Propagate by seed in spring or autumn. ❀ ❀ ❀ Zone 6.

Uses They are used in wildflower areas for their attractive flowers and nectar. *T. pratense* can be used as a green manure in vegetable gardens, or in areas that will lie dormant for several weeks, because the roots fix nitrogen in the soil.

Wildlife benefits An excellent plant for providing nectar for bumblebees, and feeding several species of butterfly caterpillar. Birds also peck at the flowers, hunting pollinating insects as a quick meal. The seeds are eaten by birds, especially finches.

Closely related species White clover (*T. repens*) is less attractive, but is still worth including in a wildflower meadow mix. Its leaves provide food for caterpillars of the common blue and clouded yellow butterfly. It can also be used in an ornamental lawn seed mix. The sowing rate is 50 per cent clover and 50 per cent grass mix.

Trifolium pratense

Urtica dioica

Urtica dioica
STINGING NETTLE
Family: Urticaceae
Native: Northern Hemisphere

One of the best herbaceous plants for attracting a large number of species into the garden. It is not every gardener's favourite, though, because of its invasive roots and stinging leaves. It will, however, attract beautiful species of butterfly into the area. It grows 1.2m (4ft) tall, and produces insignificant green flowers.

Cultivation The nettle is a good indicator of rich soil because it thrives in fertile areas. To attract butterflies to lay their eggs on the plant, the nettle has to be positioned in full sun. If planted in shade it's of limited use to the surrounding wildlife. Excellent spreader. ❀ ❀ ❀ Zone 5.

Uses Grow in wild gardens or areas of long grass. As it has insignificant flowers, plant alongside red campion and cow parsley to bring colour to a grassland area. Cut down a small patch halfway through the season and allow to regenerate because late egg-laying butterflies prefer to lay on young foliage.

Wildlife benefits Caterpillars of many species of garden butterfly, including peacock, red admiral and the small tortoiseshell, feed on the leaves of the plant and, in turn, attract many bird species, including the sparrow, chasing an easy meal. The seeds are eaten by bullfinches and siskins.

Closely related species The annual nettle (*U. urens*) has blue-green leaves that sting if touched. It flowers from summer to autumn.

Verbascum olympicum
MULLEIN
Family: Scrophulariaceae
Native: Turkey

This tall, majestic plant can be classed as a biennial or perennial. Its stems are white and hairy and produce large, woolly textured, lance-shaped basal leaves. The flower heads contain hundreds of individual flowers that are bright golden-yellow.

Cultivation Mullein enjoys full sun, and thrives in well-drained soil. Although it will grow in almost any type of soil, it prefers chalky ground. Propagate by seed in spring. ❁ ❁ ❁ Zone 6.

Uses A brilliant border plant, giving structure and height. Use in herbaceous or mixed borders. It can be used effectively when randomly spaced around a dry garden, between grasses, globe thistles and knautias.

Wildlife benefits Bees are frequent visitors to the flowers collecting pollen for their larvae. Butterflies will occasionally take nectar from the flowers.

Closely related species All verbascums (except doubles) are good for visiting wildlife. Good single-flowering species include dark mullein (*V. nigrum*), which is 1.2m (4ft) high with purple-centred yellow flowers, and nettle-leaved mullein (*V. chaixii*), with yellow flowers and purple hairy anthers. The stems can reach up to 90cm (3ft).

Veronica spicata
SPIKED SPEEDWELL
Family: Scrophulariaceae
Native: Europe

A lovely herbaceous perennial that is extremely popular. It produces strong growth, reaching 60cm (2ft) tall and is a welcome addition to any border. The lance-shaped foliage knits together closely giving rise to spikes of purple-blue flowers in early summer.

Cultivation Veronicas prefer full sun with their roots in any type of free-draining soil. Propagate by division in spring or autumn. ❁ ❁ ❁ Zone 3.

Uses Plant in large clumps in herbaceous or mixed borders to create the best effect. *V. spicata* looks good planted next to silver-leaved plants, such as *Stachys byzantina*, and red-pink flowering plants, for example *Persicaria affinis*.

Wildlife benefits A real winner with bees seeking pollen and nectar. Leave the stems uncut during winter because the tight-knit foliage offers refuge for hibernating beneficial insects. Cut back the stems in early spring.

Closely related species There are many other species in the genus that benefit bees, and are ideal for ornamental borders. They include *V. gentianoides*, 60cm (2ft) high, *V. peduncularis* at 20–25cm (8–10in), and *V. austriaca* at 30cm (1ft).

Viola odorata

Viola odorata
SWEET VIOLET
Family: Violaceae
Native: Europe

A pretty little woodland ground-cover plant that is named after its scented purple, lilac, white or occasionally yellow flowers that appear in early spring. The delicate flowers rise just above the deep green, heart-shaped leaves. It reaches no more than 15cm (6in) high.

Cultivation Grows best in semi- or full shade in soil that contains large quantities of humus, especially leaf mould. This will help the soil to retain moisture during the summer months. Propagate by division in late spring or early autumn. ❁ ❁ ❁ Zone 8.

Uses An ideal little plant for using as ground cover in the woodland garden or a shady border. Plant at the front of a border, or under trees and shrubs in large numbers to create a carpet of flowers. Inter-plant with dwarf daffodils, such as *N.* 'February Gold', for a dramatic effect.

Wildlife benefits The leaves of *V. odorata* are eaten by caterpillars of several fritillary butterfly species. The flowers are visited by bumblebees in spring, and the seeds are eaten by several species of birds, including bullfinches and coal tits.

Closely related species Common dog violet (*V. riviniana*) is a woodland plant that is similar in size but with smaller lilac flowers and purple leaves. It is another very important early nectar source for insects, and a caterpillar food plant for fritillary butterflies. The pansy (*V.* x *wittrockiana*) is usually grown as an annual, and is used in bedding schemes and containers.

Verbascum olympicum

Veronica spicata

HERBS

Allium schoenoprasum
CHIVES
Family: Alliaceae
Native: Europe

Chives are hardy perennials that bear gorgeous pale purple or pink flowers in early summer. This frost-tender culinary herb produces 30cm (12in) tall, thin, cylindrical leaves that, with the flowers, are used in salads.

Cultivation Provide an open, sunny situation and free-draining soil. Grows well if left undisturbed for several years to form large clumps. Easily propagated by seed in autumn, or by dividing the clumps in spring. ❀ ❀ ❀ Zone 5.

Uses Often used with foxgloves (*Digitalis*) and wallflowers (*Erysimum*) as a companion plant for apples. Chives also make excellent ornamental plants, ideal for tubs, hanging baskets (especially when grown with colourful nasturtiums and fuchsias), borders (herbaceous and mixed), and herb gardens.

Wildlife benefits Chives are a big draw for bees and bumblebees seeking abundant quantities of nectar. Chives are also occasionally visited by butterflies.

Closely related species Alliums are ideal for the wildlife garden, producing plenty of nectar, and come in a wide range of heights. At one extreme is *Allium insubricum* that flowers in summer, bearing nodding, pinkish-purple, bell-shaped flowers, and reaches 15–30cm (6–12in) high. A real gardener's favourite is *Allium cernuum*, 30–70cm (12–28in) high with pink to white cup-shaped, nodding summer flowers.

Allium schoenoprasum

Anethum graveolens

Anethum graveolens
DILL
Family: Apiaceae
Native: SW Asia

An attractive annual with a strong anise scent, and bluish-green leaves that are finely divided and look very similar to its close relation, fennel (*Foeniculum*). Dill will grow to 60cm (2ft) tall if left unpicked, and will then bear tiny yellow flowers in terminal clusters. The foliage and seed are commonly used in fish dishes, and in pickling spice mixtures.

Cultivation Plant in rich, well-drained soil and site in full sun. Keep watered in dry periods because it has a tendency to bolt in poor, dry soil. Propagate from seed in spring. Sow direct in the open ground as they don't transplant well. ❀ ❀ ❀ Zone 8.

Uses Dill is ideal in the herb or vegetable garden. It's also an attractive plant that works well in tubs and mixed borders. Looks particularly good when planted next to *Geranium phaeum* or sage (*Salvia nemorosa*).

Wildlife benefits The plants attract many species of hoverfly that enjoy feeding on the nectar-rich flowers. By increasing the number of hoverflies in the garden, it will decrease the number of aphids. Dill also attracts several types of bee, lacewings and ladybirds. By leaving the hollow stems intact over winter, small insects can hibernate inside; they re-emerge in spring to provide food for hungry birds.

Closely related species Cow parsley (*Anthriscus sylvestris*) is loved by various insects, including flies.

Angelica archangelica
ANGELICA
Family: Apiaceae
Native: N and E Europe, C Asia and Greenland

A statuesque biennial that often lives for three years. It grows 1.2–2.4m (4–8ft) high, and has hollow stems with large, deeply divided, light green leaves. The globular flower heads are magnificent, producing clusters of green flowers in early summer.

Cultivation Angelica thrives in rich, damp soil, but will tolerate most conditions except extreme dryness. Site in sun or partial shade. ❀ ❀ ❀ Zone 4.

Uses Great architectural plant for the mixed or herbaceous border. Place it at the back of the border, where staking may be necessary. Stunning if planted beside black elder (*Sambucus* 'Black Beauty') or other purple-leaved plants.

Wildlife benefits The large flower heads are rich in nectar and are frequently engulfed by buzzing, beneficial insects, such as lacewings, ladybirds and parasitic wasps. In turn they attract insect-eating birds, e.g. swifts and wagtails. Blue tits and greenfinches enjoy the autumn seed.

Closely related species All angelicas are great insect attractors. *Angelica atropurpurea*, the American angelica, has dark purple stems and white flowers, *A. sylvestris* is the wild European kind and bears white or pink flowers, and the attractive *A. gigas*, the Korean version, has purple stems and pink flowers but dies after flowering.

Angelica archangelica

Carum carvi

Carum carvi
CARAWAY
Family: Apiaceae
Native: Asia and C Europe

A pretty biennial, 30–60cm (1–2ft) tall, with clusters of white flowers in the second year of growth. The bright green feathery leaves contrast well with the flower heads. The seed is often used in culinary dishes or as an organic breath-freshener.

Cultivation Prefers deep, well-drained soil (although it will tolerate heavy ground) in a sunny position. Sow in its final position in spring because the seedlings dislike being moved. ❀ ❀ ❀ Zone 3.

Uses As with many herbs, especially those in the Apiaceae family, caraway is brilliant at attracting beneficial insects to the garden. Grow small groups every few metres throughout a mixed or herbaceous border, vegetable or fruit garden.

Wildlife benefits The attracted beneficial insects, such as hoverflies, ladybirds and lacewings, are major predators of aphids. The more caraway you grow, the more effective the pest control.

Closely related species Caraway is a near relative of the carrot, another excellent insect attractor. Its roots can be prepared and eaten in a similar way to carrot and parsnip. Note, if you want caraway to flower (which occurs in the second year), you won't get the roots because by then they'll be tasteless.

Coriandrum sativum
CORIANDER
Family: Apiaceae
Native: N Africa and Mediterranean

An aromatic annual that can reach 30cm (1ft) high, with small white to mauve flowers in spring. The pungent, finely divided leaves are narrow and feathery. It has been in cultivation for thousands of years (seed was found in Tutankhamen's tomb).

Cultivation Succeeds in well-drained, fertile soil that is moisture retentive, in a sunny site. Young plants start producing seed if ample water is not given in periods of dry weather. ❀ ❀ ❀ Zone 3.

Uses If coriander is left to flower, it is one of the best plants for attracting beneficial insects. Grow clusters of coriander in mixed and herbaceous borders to provide natural pest control. Also very effective in the fruit and vegetable garden to attract pollinators.

Wildlife benefits Coriander is loved by ladybirds, lacewings and particularly hoverflies, which visit the small, whitish flowers laden with nectar. All (both adults and larvae) are voracious eaters of aphids. Parasitic wasps are also visitors to the flowers, seeking nectar.

Closely related species Many of the plants in the Apiaceae family (formerly known as the Umbelliferae family) are good at attracting insects, especially dill (*Anethum graveolens*), *Ferula assa-foetida* and cumin (*Cuminum cyminum*).

Coriandrum sativum

Hyssopus officinalis

Hyssopus officinalis
HYSSOP
Family: Lamiaceae
Native: S and E Europe

A lovely herbaceous perennial, growing to 60cm (2ft) high. It bears violet, blue or, occasionally, white flowers from late summer to autumn. The small, dark green leaves are pungent and, when chopped, emit a strong, peppery aroma.

Cultivation Needs well-drained (preferably alkaline) soil in a sunny location. Hyssop does not divide particularly well, and propagation by seed or cuttings is best. ❀ ❀ ❀ Zone 3.

Uses Great in pots, or borders (herbaceous or mixed), or grow as a low hedge. Beekeepers often plant such hedges near their hives because of the good-quality nectar. Also plant in the fruit and vegetable garden to attract pollinators, and for its attractive appearance.

Wildlife benefits Butterflies occasionally visit the plant for nectar. Spiders are also attracted, making webs between the stems and sunbathing on the sunny side of the plant. Because many insects hibernate in the foliage, delay cutting back until spring.

Closely related species Plants in the Lamiaceae family are renowned for their nectar. To attract bees, also grow white deadnettle (*Lamium album*), sage (*Salvia nemorosa*), and spearmint (*Mentha spicata*).

Lavandula angustifolia
LAVENDER
Family: Lamiaceae
Native: Mediterranean

An aromatic shrub with grey-green leaves, it grows 60–90cm (2–3ft) high and produces small, purple flowers rich in nectar from midsummer to autumn. Lavender is as important to wildlife as it is for its aesthetic qualities.

Cultivation Provide well-drained soil in plenty of sun. Best propagated by cuttings. ❀ ❀ ❀ Zone 5.

Uses Lavender hedges look great and smell amazing. Plants can also be used in mixed and shrub borders, in tubs and containers. Site next to silver-leaved plants, such as wormwood (*Artemisia ludoviciana* subsp. *mexicana* var. *albula*) or *Santolina chamaecyparissus*, for a cool, calming effect, or with *Perovskia atricifolia* and *Phlomis italica* for a Mediterranean look.

Wildlife benefits Great clouds of white butterflies are often seen in large patches of lavender in late summer, looking for nectar. They have to share it with several species of bee competing for the sugary drink. Goldfinches and other seed-eaters devour the seed from autumn on.

Closely related species Lavender (*Lavandula angustifolia* 'Hidcote') has neat, erect growth making it ideal for hedges or lining paths, especially of old, characterful properties. *L. a.* 'Munstead' is more compact at 30–45cm (12–18in) high, and is very effective in tubs.

Lavandula angustifolia

Levisticum officinale

Levisticum officinale
LOVAGE
Family: Apiaceae
Native: E Mediterranean

A tall, hardy, vigorous perennial reaching 1.8m (6ft) high, bearing insignificant, dull yellow flowers in summer. The leaves are deeply divided, with a pungent smell, and taste of celery. The roots are long and fleshy.

Cultivation It tolerates most conditions, except heavy clay, and grows best in rich, deep soil in sun or partial shade. Propagate from seed in spring, or by division in spring or autumn. ❀ ❀ ❀ Zone 4.

Uses Great in a herb garden or to the back of a scented border, next to red and orange flowers because the glossy green foliage brings out the vibrant colours. Due to its vigorous growth, be careful where it's planted or it'll quickly swamp less vigorous neighbours. Excellent in a wildflower meadow or wild garden.

Wildlife benefits Attracts hoverflies and bees to the nectar-rich flowers, and beneficial wasps seeking nectar in late summer. The lush foliage shelters ground beetles that prey on young slugs.

Closely related species Nectar-rich relatives include the carrot (*Daucus carota*), parsley (*Petroselinum crispum*) and one of the best wildlife plants, fennel (*Foeniculum vulgare*).

Melissa officinalis

Melissa officinalis
LEMON BALM
Family: Lamiaceae
Native: S and C Europe

Lemon balm is a vigorous herbaceous perennial. It has small, white flowers borne in summer on stems up to 75cm (2½ft) high. The leaves are deeply veined and smell of lemon.

Cultivation It grows in almost any soil in full sun or semi-shade, with shelter from strong winds. It is easily propagated by division in spring or autumn, or by seed in spring. ❀ ❀ ❀ Zone 4.

Uses If using in a small herb garden, grow it in a pot to restrict the root spread. The plants need to be left to flower and therefore produce nectar to be of any benefit to wildlife. Due to its vigorous growth, take care that neighbouring plants aren't swamped. The ideal solution is to let it naturalize in a wild garden.

Wildlife benefits Bees are attracted by the smell of the leaves and the nectar. The foliage can be used to ease the pain of insect stings or bites.

Closely related species Balm (*Melissa officinalis* 'Aurea') has variegated foliage and is better for a smaller garden because it is less vigorous. *M.* 'All Gold' has bright yellow leaves, and should be planted in partial shade because it can scorch in full sun.

Mentha spicata

Mentha spicata
SPEARMINT
Family: Lamiaceae
Native: S and C Europe

When gardeners think of planting mint, they immediately worry about root invasion, and spearmint is certainly a vigorous species, spreading everywhere and growing up to 60cm (2ft) tall. The leaves are dark green with prominent patterning, and purple flowers in summer.

Cultivation Mint enjoys full sun or semi-shade, and thrives in almost any fertile soil that doesn't dry out. Best to propagate by cuttings in summer, or by division in spring. ❀ ❀ ❀ Zone 3.

Uses Most gardeners prefer to grow mint in pots to limit its spread. Either stand it on a patio or sink a large container in the ground.

Wildlife benefits Predatory wasps, flies, bees and butterflies are attracted to the nectar-rich flowers all summer, and spiders find shelter beneath the leaves. The mature seed is eaten by birds.

Closely related species All mints are good producers of nectar, usually over summer. Pennyroyal (*Mentha pulegium*) is a smaller plant that prefers moister soil in sun or partial shade, and produces a profusion of mauve flowers in whorls, whereas the variable peppermint (*M.* x *piperita*) grows 30–90cm (1–3ft) tall and has pink flowers.

Myrrhis odorata
SWEET CICELY
Family: Apiaceae
Native: Europe

A vigorous, pleasantly scented herbaceous perennial, it has a strong taproot and grows to 90cm (3ft) tall. It bears fern-like leaves and produces clusters of fluffy white flowers in late spring. Often used to sweeten stewed fruits and rhubarb.

Cultivation Grows in full sun or thrives in semi-shade, being a natural hedgerow plant. Prefers moist, humus-rich soil. Propagate by seed or by root division in spring. ❀ ❀ ❀ Zone 5.

Uses Sweet cicely is a lovely plant, ideal in a cottage garden. It is invasive and self-seeds everywhere, so is only suitable in an unkept or wild cottage garden, or as part of a natural-looking woodland garden. It is extremely hard to eradicate once established, so think carefully before planting.

Wildlife benefits The nectar-rich flowers are a real winner for attracting bees in late spring. Beneficial wasps and flies are also tempted by the flat, white flower heads. Flies are often seen visiting Apiaceae flowers and, although you would not want too many in the garden, they are a vital part of the food chain and support a great number of birds and other creatures.

Closely related species Cow parsley (*Anthriscus sylvestris*) is closely related to sweet cicely. This herbaceous perennial is also ideal for naturalizing in long grass, attracting many insects, particularly flies.

Myrrhis odorata

Ocimum basilicum

Ocimum basilicum
BASIL
Family: Lamiaceae
Native: India and Middle East

A multi-stemmed, tender annual that grows to 40cm (16in) high. It produces bright green leaves that vary in pungency and flavour, depending on the growing conditions, with constant watering diluting the flavour. To be of value to wildlife, don't pick the foliage and leave the small, white summer flowers, a real magnet for bees.

Cultivation Sow seed in early spring under glass. Plant out in late spring and early summer after hardening off. Plants thrive in well-drained soil in full sun, ideally against a sheltering wall. ❀ Zone 10.

Uses Plant in garden containers, pots and hanging baskets, mixing it with ornamental plants, such as fuchsias, trailing lobelia and thyme (*Thymus*). Pick only some of the leaves for the kitchen, and then allow the plant to produce nectar-rich flowers.

Wildlife benefits Carry out several sowings over summer, and plant out when large enough. This will ensure an everlasting supply of nectar for the hungry bees.

Closely related species *Ocimum basilicum* 'Citriodorum' has lemon-scented leaves and *O.* 'Crispum' has leaves that are curled along the edges. *O.* 'Minimum' is ideal for growing in pots because it's just 15–30cm (6–12in) high.

Origanum majorana

Rosmarinus officinalis

Origanum majorana
SWEET MARJORAM
Family: Lamiaceae
Native: Europe

A half-hardy perennial, often grown as an annual, that can reach 60cm (2ft) high in a season. It has pale green leaves and bears small, white to pink flowers in distinctive clusters from mid- to late summer.

Cultivation It thrives in well-drained, fertile soil in full sun. Sow seed in early spring under glass, and plant out in late spring or early summer after the last frost. ❉ ❉ ❉ Zone 7.

Uses Great in herb gardens and borders (herbaceous and mixed). Place to the front of a border and also use as ground cover. Alternatively, grow in pots with other herbs or in hanging baskets with a mix of ornamentals and vegetables.

Wildlife benefits The nectar-rich flowers are excellent for attracting bees and butterflies all summer long. Plant in a sheltered, sunny position to attract large numbers of insects. Seed-eating birds start to forage on the plant from autumn on, while the many crevices of the stems and leaves provide a good site for hibernating insects.

Closely related species All *Origanum* species produce plenty of nectar. Pot marjoram (*O. onites*) is a sturdier grower than sweet marjoram, and produces hairy green leaves and pinkish-purple flowers. Oregano (*O. vulgare*) is very pungent and has a thyme-like scent.

Rosmarinus officinalis
ROSEMARY
Family: Lamiaceae
Native: Mediterranean

A long-flowering evergreen shrub, rosemary has pale blue flowers all along the stems from spring to summer, and will even flower sporadically in autumn and winter. Stems reach 2m (6½ft) high if left unpruned, and produce needle-like aromatic leaves that are green on top and silvery beneath.

Cultivation Enjoys a sheltered, sunny location, and thrives in well-drained soil requiring little moisture. Propagate by semi-ripe cuttings taken in summer. ❉ ❉ Zone 6.

Uses A great plant for a splash of colour in a shrub or mixed border. Also ideal for a dry garden where little or no irrigation is used. Grow beside other drought-tolerant plants, such as the globe thistle (*Echinops ritro*), sea holly (*Eryngium alpinum*) and red hot poker (*Kniphofia caulescens*).

Wildlife benefits The flowers attract bees, hoverflies and the occasional butterfly. Also, the flowers often open when there are few other flowers present rich in nectar, giving a welcome meal for hungry insects. Birds forage around in the foliage looking for a quick meal, usually aphids.

Closely related species The dwarf *Rosmarinus officinalis* 'Blue Boy' is ideal for growing in pots, whereas 'Miss Jessop's Upright' is tall and erect, making it ideal for a shrub border. *R. eriocalyx* is a prostrate shrub rarely reaching 90cm (3ft) high, and can only be grown in frost-free conditions.

Salvia officinalis
COMMON SAGE
Family: Lamiaceae
Native: S Europe

People either love or hate the smell of the leaves that are grey-green with a rough texture. Spikes of tubular, violet-blue flowers are borne from early to late summer, reaching to 60cm (2ft) high.

Cultivation Best grown in light, well-drained soil in a sunny location. Propagate from seed in spring or by cuttings in summer. ❉ ❉ ❉ Zone 5.

Uses Sage is a good all-rounder and can be used in many different garden locations. It is a real winner at the front of a shrub border, in a herb garden, and looks superb in a pot. The foliage of box (*Buxus sempervirens*) nicely complements the pastels of sage. The latter also marries well with pink- and purple-flowering plants, such as the coneflower (*Echinacea purpurea*) and *Cirsium rivulare*.

Wildlife benefits Visited by bees seeking nectar and the occasional butterfly. In late summer the flowers are well known for providing a source of pollen when many other plants have finished flowering. If left uncut over winter, the intricate mass of stems creates many crevices and homes for insects.

Closely related species Two ornamental cultivars of sage, equally good at attracting wildlife, are *Salvia officinalis* 'Icterina', with yellow and green variegated leaves, and 'Purpurascens', with purple foliage, but both are less hardy than the species. *S.* x *sylvestris* and *Salvia nemorosa* are two of the best bee plants for an ornamental garden.

Salvia officinalis

Satureja montana

Satureja montana
WINTER SAVORY
Family: Lamiaceae
Native: Mediterranean

Winter savory was celebrated by Virgil (70–19BC) who said it was one of the most fragrant plants for growing near beehives. This semi-evergreen sub-shrub grows to 38cm (15in) tall and has dark green, aromatic leaves. The stems also bear small white flowers in summer.

Cultivation Thrives in well-drained soil in a sunny location. Propagate by seed or by division in spring. ❀ ❀ ❀ Zone 6.

Uses Plant in a nectar-rich herbaceous border, herb garden or mixed border. Can also be grown in pots with other herbs, although its growth can be a little untidy. Can be used in companion planting to ward off aphids.

Wildlife benefits Winter savory is still one of the best plants for attracting bees into the wildlife garden. The flowers provide an important source of nectar throughout summer. It can be brought on to flower in winter, hence its name.

Closely related species Summer savory (*Satureja hortensis*) is equal to winter savory in its ability to provide nectar for bees. It is a small, busy, hardy annual, slightly shorter than the winter kind. It bears small white or lilac flowers in summer.

Tanacetum vulgare
TANSY
Family: Asteraceae
Native: Europe and temperate Asia

A vigorous, popular herb, tansy grows up to 1.2m (4ft) tall. The stems bear aromatic, finely cut foliage and culminate in flower heads with button-like clusters of yellow flowers that attract many insects.

Cultivation Grows well in dry, free-draining soil in full sun or semi-shade. Propagate by seed, division or by cuttings in spring. ❀ ❀ ❀ Zone 4.

Uses Looks at home in any herbaceous border, adding bright colour from summer to early autumn. In fact tansy is one of the showiest flowers in the herb garden, and is best in a mixed border next to the dark green leaves of bay (*Laurus nobilis*) and yew (*Taxus baccata*).

Wildlife benefits The flowers attract many insects, including lacewings, ladybirds, parasitic wasps and hoverflies. The blooms are especially attractive to bees, bumblebees and butterflies seeking nectar. Leave the stems uncut in the winter to provide a home for hibernating insects.

Closely related species Feverfew (*Tanacetum parthenium*) also attracts many insects. It is a bushy, hardy perennial that grows up to 1m (3ft) high. It produces masses of white flowers with yellow centres in early to midsummer.

Tanacetum vulgare

Thymus vulgaris

Thymus vulgaris
THYME
Family: Lamiaceae
Native: W Mediterranean

Thyme is an excellent plant for attracting wildlife. This species creates a neat dome up to 30cm (1ft) high. The stems bear small, aromatic leaves and a profusion of tiny, mauve flowers.

Cultivation It grows well in poor, stony soil, neutral to alkaline, in a sunny position. ❀ ❀ ❀ Zone 7.

Uses All thymes are ideal for planting between cracks in a patio or path, and in rock gardens or dry borders. They can also be grown in a herb or vegetable plot or in a hanging basket.

Wildlife benefits Hoverflies and butterflies are frequent visitors to the numerous flowers seeking nectar. Bees and bumblebees are attracted to the nectar and collect pollen for their young. Plant in a sunny position for increased nectar production.

Closely related species *Thymus polytrichus* subsp. *britannicus* needs excellent drainage, making it ideal for growing in the cracks between paving stones. *T. serphyllum* bears small, purple-red flowers from early to midsummer and reaches 25cm (10in) tall. It is often used in tubs and hanging baskets.

SHRUBS

Amelanchier lamarckii
JUNEBERRY
Family: Rosaceae
Native: E Canada

This beautiful plant can be classed as either a large shrub or a small tree, and can grow up to 10m (33ft) high. The white flowers are a joy to see in spring and are followed by round, juicy, dark fruit in autumn. The newly emerged leaves have white hairs that quickly fall off. They are oblong and dark green, turning orange and red in late summer.

Cultivation The juneberry prefers well-drained, acid soil that's fertile and moist. Site in full sun or partial shade. Sow seed when ripe or take semi-ripe cuttings in summer. ❈ ❈ ❈ Zone 4.

Uses It flowers all over, not just at the crown, and is best grown as a specimen in a wildflower meadow. It can also be sited in a shrub or mixed border, and is ideal for giving height in a small garden without being invasive.

Wildlife benefits Many pollinating insects, especially solitary bees and butterflies, are drawn to the spring flowers. The fruits are eaten by birds, particularly starlings, garden warblers, thrushes, chaffinches and greenfinches, and mammals, such as squirrels and foxes.

Closely related species The allegheny serviceberry (*A. laevis*), a native North American, has a spreading, shrubby habit with white flowers and good autumn colour before leaf drop. The shadbush (*A. canadensis*) is a suckering species with similar attributes.

Amelanchier lamarckii

Berberis darwinii
BARBERRY
Family: Berberidaceae
Native: Chile and Argentina

The barberries have the best shrub species for wildlife. This particular shrub is a vigorous evergreen with spine-toothed, glossy, dark green leaves. Pendulous, dark orange flowers appear in spring and occasionally in autumn. They are followed by blue to black round fruits.

Cultivation The shrubs grow in most well-drained soils. Nectar production, fruiting and autumn colour are best if the plants are sited in full sun. Take semi-ripe cuttings in summer. ❈ ❈ ❈ Zone 7.

Uses All the species are excellent when used as an informal single-species hedge. *B. darwinii* is also an excellent choice in shrub beds and mixed borders because of its many attributes, which include attractive flowers, late-summer fruits and evergreen foliage.

Wildlife benefits The nectar-rich flowers are loved by bees and bumblebees. The fruits are eaten by birds, particularly blackbirds, thrushes, nuthatches, tits, garden warblers and finches. And small birds often nest amongst the thorny branches because they offer protection from predators.

Closely related species *B. julianae* is one of the species' best nectar producers and, like *B. darwinii*, makes a fantastic hedge. It is an evergreen and bears yellow flowers with a red tinge. *B. thunbergii* is deciduous and can be used in informal or formal hedging.

Berberis darwinii

Buddleja davidii

Buddleja davidii
BUTTERFLY BUSH
Family: Buddlejaceae
Native: China and Japan

If you want to attract clouds of adult butterflies, plant *B. davidii* in the garden. It is a large, fast-growing shrub which can easily reach 3m (10ft) high, with tall, arching shoots bearing lance-shaped green to grey leaves. The lilac to purple honey-scented flowers are borne in 30cm (12in) long panicles from summer to autumn.

Cultivation The butterfly bush likes fertile, well-drained soil in full sun. Propagate by semi-ripe cuttings in summer, or hardwood cuttings in autumn. ❈ ❈ ❈ Zone 5.

Uses *B. davidii* is great in mixed and shrub borders. It has many cultivars in a range of colours, making it easy to select for a colour-themed border. In North America research indicates that butterflies prefer to visit pink- and lilac-coloured flowers more frequently than the dark purple- and white-flowering cultivars.

Wildlife benefits The large panicles of nectar-rich flowers are a magnet for many butterfly species, particularly peacocks, red admirals, commas and small tortoiseshells, and are also visited by several species of bees. The seeds are eaten in winter by birds and small mammals.

Closely related species *B. alternifolia* and *B. crispa* also attract butterflies and other insects.

Calluna vulgaris

Calluna vulgaris
LING
Family: Ericaceae
Native: N and W Europe to
Russia, Turkey and Morocco

A wonderful evergreen shrub that is extremely popular with gardeners, and provides excellent ground cover if planted in large groups. Ling produces flower spikes of bell-shaped flowers in many different colours including red, purple, pink and white. The leaves lie flat along the stem and are short, linear and dark green.

Cultivation Ling prefers an open site in full sun. These ericaceous plants enjoy humus-rich, well-drained acid soil. Propagate by semi-ripe cuttings in midsummer. ❁ ❁ ❁ Zone 4.

Uses *C. vulgaris* has over 500 different cultivars with a wide colour range. They are best planted close together in large groups to create drifts of colour. Once knitted together, they provide excellent ground cover for small mammals and insects.

Wildlife benefits The bell-shaped flowers are very popular with bees and bumblebees seeking nectar. Butterfly larvae of the silver-studded blue butterfly and the emperor moth eat the foliage, and the seeds are eaten by siskins, crossbills and other finches.

Closely related species Do not select double-flowering varieties, such as 'Elsie Purnell', because the double pale pink flowers are inaccessible to bees. Recommended cultivars include 'Allegro' with ruby red flowers, and 'Beoley Gold' with yellow foliage and white flowers.

Caryopteris x *clandonensis*
BLUEBEARD
Family: Verbenaceae
Native: Garden origin

A delicate shrub grown for its grey-green, silver-haired foliage and soft blue, nectar-rich flowers carried in terminal heads from late summer to autumn. The shrub reaches up to 90cm (3ft) high, and is ideal in the small garden but needs careful siting because it is extremely prone to frost damage.

Cultivation Likes moderately fertile, free-draining soil. Site in full sun; it thrives in colder areas against a sunny, warm wall. Propagate by softwood cuttings in late spring. ❁ ❁ ❁ Zone 7.

Uses Ideal for a mixed or shrub border, planted beside silver or purple foliage plants, particularly *Cotinus coggygria* 'Royal Purple' and *Elaeagnus angustifolia* 'Quicksilver'. Other good planting combinations include *Perovskia atriplicifolia* and lavender cultivars.

Wildlife benefits The blue flowers are an excellent late-season source of nectar, and are very popular with a number of insects, especially honeybees and butterflies. Leave the seed heads untouched during the winter months because they provide a snack for small birds.

Closely related species One of the best cultivars is the erect 'Heavenly Blue' with dark blue flowers and 'Worcester Gold' with yellow leaves. The species *C. incana* is slightly larger with bright violet-blue flowers, and makes a dense mound-forming shrub.

Caryopteris x *clandonensis*

Ceanothus thyrsiflorus

Ceanothus thyrsiflorus
CALIFORNIAN LILAC
Family: Rhamnaceae
Native: California and S Oregon

The Californian lilac is one of the best shrubs (occasionally classed as a tree) to attract huge numbers of bees. It is a large, vigorous, evergreen shrub growing to 6m (20ft) high in a relatively short space of time. The arching branches sport ovate, glossy, mid-green leaves and, in spring, it bears pale to dark blue flowers in large panicles.

Cultivation Grow in full sun in a sheltered location, protected from cold winter winds. The roots favour fertile, well-drained soil. Propagate by semi-ripe cuttings in mid–late summer. ❁ ❁ ❁ Zone 8.

Uses Ideal for planting in a large shrub border, or train against a sunny wall where it provides a valuable source of food for insects. Also, several species of birds are likely to nest in the network of branches. Clematis can be trained up through the stems.

Wildlife benefits A huge favourite with bees and bumblebees seeking mainly pollen and, occasionally, nectar. The leaves are eaten by caterpillars of several common butterflies and moths. Songbirds feast on the numerous visiting insects that take refuge in the dense foliage.

Closely related species Research has shown that *C.* 'Ray Hartman' is a fantastic plant to attract bees. *C. impressus* is another favourite, attracting several species of insect. It is an evergreen shrub with dark blue flowers in mid- to late spring. *C. dentatus* bears dark blue flowers in spring.

Chaenomeles japonica
JAPANESE QUINCE
Family: Rosaceae
Native: Japan

The early flowers borne by Japanese quince are a joy to see after the dull winter months. This deciduous thorny shrub can reach up to 90cm (3ft) high, and produces clusters of orange-red, scarlet or crimson flowers in spring before leaf burst. The small leaves are oval with serrated edges. The flowers are followed by yellow-flushed, apple-shaped fruit.

Cultivation Japanese quince enjoys fertile, well-drained soil. Position in sun for optimum flowers and fruits, though the shrub will also grow well in partial shade. Propagate by semi-ripe cuttings in summer. ❀ ❀ ❀ Zone 5.

Uses Excellent in a shrub border or as an informal hedge. A good companion plant is common ivy (*Hedera helix*), which can be used for the under-planting; it makes good ground cover and helps show off the brightly coloured flowers.

Wildlife benefits In spring, the flowers are pollinated by early bees and butterflies that welcome the nectar. Birds, especially bullfinches, are known to eat the sugar-rich flowers, and the fruits are eaten by blackbirds and starlings.

Closely related species Insects and birds also use *C. speciosa*, a more vigorous shrub that easily reaches 2.5m (8ft). Very effective in large shrubberies or for training against walls. A valued garden plant is *C. x superba* 'Crimson and Gold' with deep red flowers and showy yellow stamens.

Chaenomeles japonica

Cornus sanguinea

Cornus sanguinea
DOGWOOD
Family: Cornaceae
Native: Europe

A large, deciduous shrub generally grown for its attractive, reddish-green winter stems, but it needs coppicing annually to promote the attractive new growth. Alternatively it can be left to grow into a large shrub. The latter is the most beneficial to wildlife, and if allowed to grow for two years or more it bears white flowers in summer, followed by dull blue-black fruits in autumn.

Cultivation To achieve the best winter stem colour, grow *C. sanguinea* in free-draining soil in full sun. Propagate by hardwood cuttings in autumn. ❀ ❀ ❀ Zone 5.

Uses To allow dogwood to flower and fruit freely, it needs to be planted in a shrub or mixed border where it grows without annual pruning. Dogwood is also ideal in a wild garden, and is commonly used in a mixed hedge.

Wildlife benefits The flowers are popular with bees and other pollinating insects. Caterpillars of the green hairstreak butterfly eat the leaves, and the blue-black berries are eaten by birds, especially thrushes, tits, woodpeckers and finches, and small mammals.

Closely related species Cornelian cherry (*C. mas*) is a vigorous, deciduous shrub, or small tree, that bears nectar and pollen-rich yellow flowers on bare branches in late winter. On acid soils, *C. canadensis* provides excellent ground cover for birds and small mammals.

Cytisus scoparius
COMMON BROOM
Family: Papilionaceae
Native: W Europe

A terrific garden plant providing plenty of colour when in flower. It is a relatively short-lived shrub, usually reaching its peak in 8–10 years. Upright and deciduous, it can reach 1.5m (5ft) in a short period of time. The stems bear bright yellow, pea-like flowers in late spring, and leaves that are small and palmate.

Cultivation Brooms like basking in full sun and will thrive in well-drained, poor, acid soil, although most are lime tolerant. Plant when small because they do not transplant well. Take semi-ripe cuttings in summer. ❀ ❀ ❀ Zone 5.

Uses Excellent in a shrub border or dry garden. Brooms look at their best if planted next to other Mediterranean species, such as rock roses (*Cistus*), lavender (*Lavandula*) and *Phlomis*. Mulch with various grades of pebbles to create a dry-garden look.

Wildlife benefits Flowers are pollinated by bees and the occasional butterfly seeking nectar. They are also eaten by waxwings, and the black seed pods are devoured by rooks, greenfinches and hawfinches. The leaves are eaten by the larvae of the green hairstreak butterfly.

Closely related species Pineapple broom (*C. battandieri*), with scented yellow flowers and silvery leaves, is a tall, vigorous species that is ideal at the back of a very large shrub border, or it can be trained against a wall. *C. decumbens* is a prostrate deciduous shrub with yellow flowers.

Cytisus scoparius

Corylus avellana

Corylus avellana
HAZEL
Family: Betulaceae
Native: Europe and Turkey

A natural woodland plant that bears beautiful, pendent, yellow male catkins 4–6cm (1½–2¼in) long in late winter and early spring. The female flowers are small and insignificant, but produce edible nuts. Though a deciduous shrub, it can be sometimes classed as a multi-stemmed tree and produces heart-shaped leaves with rounded ends.

Cultivation Hazels thrive in fertile, well-drained soil in full sun or partial shade. They grow in most soils, but favour chalky ones. Propagate by seeds when ripe, or layer in autumn. ❀ ❀ ❀ Zone 4.

Uses An excellent shrub for structure planting in a woodland garden or shrub border. The corkscrew hazel ('Contorta') has twisting shoots that look fantastic in winter. The plant can also be grown in a mixed-species hedge.

Wildlife benefits An important plant for wildlife, it supports up to 70 different species. Bees feed on the early source of pollen, while the nuts are eaten by small mammals and birds including nuthatches, tits, great spotted woodpeckers, hawfinches and crossbills.

Closely related species The filbert (*C. maxima*) is similar to *C. avellana* except it is slightly taller, growing up to 6m (20ft). An excellent purple cultivar is *C. maxima* 'Purpurea' with dark purple foliage, and purple-tinged catkins and fruit husks.

Cotoneaster lacteus
COTONEASTER
Family: Rosaceae
Native: China

An extremely ornamental evergreen shrub, it can reach up to 4m (13ft) high and produces arching branches bearing thick ovate, dark green, deeply veined leaves. The milky white flowers with pink anthers are abundant, with up to 100 per branch. They are followed in the autumn by red berries that can stay on the plant if uneaten over the winter.

Cultivation Cotoneasters enjoy fertile, well-drained soil, and tolerate dry soil in sun or partial shade. Propagate by semi-ripe cuttings in late summer. ❀ ❀ ❀ Zone 6.

Uses Excellent in a shrub border, giving height, while the berries and evergreen foliage provide winter colour. It can also be used to form a single-species hedge, or be trained against a wall to help soften the hard structure.

Wildlife benefits Honeybees and bumblebees seek out the nectar-rich flowers. The overhanging foliage and branches favour birds – especially shy ones such as wrens and dunnocks – that like to use the branch system to roost and hide in. The berries are eaten by many species of birds, particularly thrushes, starlings, tree sparrows and finches.

Closely related species All cotoneasters are good for wildlife, one of the best being *C. horizontalis*, a spreading, deciduous shrub with pink-tinged flowers produced in late spring, followed by red fruit in late summer.

Cotoneaster lacteus

Daphne mezereum

Daphne mezereum
MEZEREON
Family: Thymelaeaceae
Native: Europe, Caucasus and Turkey

Fragrant, sweet-smelling flowers adorn this deciduous shrub in late winter and early spring. The flowers range from pink to light purple, and are borne on bare stems before the pale green, lance-shaped leaves appear. The flowers are followed by round, red, fleshy fruits in summer. The shrub will ultimately reach 1.2m (4ft) high, making it ideal for the small garden.

Cultivation Daphnes thrive in humus-rich soil, which should be well drained without drying out for long periods. Site in sun or partial shade. Propagate by semi-ripe cuttings in late summer. ❀ ❀ ❀ Zone 4.

Uses Use *D. mezereum* to provide late winter colour in a shrub border, or use in a special winter border. Under-plant with snowdrops and dwarf daffodils to add interest when in flower. Also plant next to an evergreen to act as background for the flowers.

Wildlife benefits The flowers are a great source of early pollen and nectar for insects, especially bees. Blackcaps have also been known to drink the nectar from the flowers. The red fruits are eaten by finches, thrushes, starlings, tits and warblers.

Closely related species *D. blagayana*, a prostrate evergreen (sometimes semi-evergreen), bears sweet-smelling, cream-white flowers in spring. Spurge laurel (*D. laureola*) is a bushy evergreen, flowering in late winter.

Fuchsia magellanica

Fuchsia magellanica
LADIES EAR DROPS
Family: Onagraceae
Native: Chile and Argentina

A wonderful, floriferous shrub that produces small, tubular flowers with red petals that are occasionally pink or white, with large sepals and long, purple corollas. Oblong red-purple fruits follow the flowering. The branches can reach up to 3m (10ft) high, and bear ovate leaves.

Cultivation Fuchsias enjoy fertile, well-drained soil that retains some moisture. For this reason, when planting smaller cultivars in pots use a loam-based compost instead of peat. Site in sun or partial shade. Propagate by softwood cuttings. ❀ ❀ Zone 6.

Uses *F. magellanica* will make a fantastic single-species hedge in areas that do not encounter severe frosts. The hedge doubles as a barrier, and flowers throughout summer. Also ideal in a shrub or mixed border.

Wildlife benefits The pollen and nectar-rich flowers of fuchsias are extremely popular with bees and bumblebees, so do not select fancy double-flowering varieties. Butterflies also seek the nectar, and the leaves are eaten by the caterpillars of elephant hawk moths.

Closely related species 'Riccartonii' is an extremely hardy, upright shrub with single flowers, scarlet tubes and sepals, and dark purple corollas. Use as a hedge, as a shrub, or in mixed borders. 'Mrs Popple' is popular in borders and containers.

Hebe salicifolia
HEBE
Family: Scrophulariaceae
Native: New Zealand

An important genus with many ornamental species. *H. salicifolia* is a tall species, which grows up to 2.5m (8ft) high and bears narrow, pointed, lance-shaped leaves. The flowers are white or pale blue-lilac, and are borne in drooping racemes up to 20cm (8in) long all summer.

Cultivation Grow in any well-drained soil that is neutral to alkaline. Grows best in a sunny, sheltered position but will also tolerate partial shade. Propagate by semi-ripe cuttings in late summer. ❀ ❀ ❀ Zone 7.

Uses Hebes are an excellent choice for use at the back of a shrub or mixed border. This species can be used as a tall hedging plant in coastal locations, although it can become bare at the bottom through age. It can be incorporated in a specialist butterfly border to provide evergreen colour and height.

Wildlife benefits A popular plant with bees and bumblebees seeking nectar. Several species of butterfly, particularly small tortoiseshells and red admirals, will visit the flowers looking for nectar.

Closely related species
H. brachysiphon and *H.* 'Great Orme' are great plants for an informal hedge.

Hebe salicifolia

Helianthemum nummularium
ROCK ROSE
Family: Cistaceae
Native: Europe and Asia Minor

A pretty, evergreen, bushy shrub that grows to 10–50cm (4–20in) high and flowers from late spring to late summer. The flowers are saucer-shaped and light yellow, golden yellow, pink or orange. The attractive, grey-green leaves are lance-shaped and slightly hairy underneath, and cover the whole of the stem.

Cultivation The rock rose prefers an open, sunny site in well-drained soil. Cut back plants after flowering to promote a second flush of flowers in late summer. Propagate by softwood cuttings in late summer, and after the cuttings have rooted, pinch them back to produce bushy plants. ❀ ❀ ❀ Zone 5.

Uses *H. nummularium* is excellent for use in dry gardens because it has naturally adapted to grow in areas of low rainfall with free-draining soil. It is also well suited to rock gardens because of its low-growing, mound-forming habit.

Wildlife benefits The flowers attract bees and other insects, including butterflies. The small shrub produces a dense mat of stems and foliage providing an ideal environment for small invertebrates to hunt and forage in.

Closely related species All rock roses are good nectar producers. *H. appeninum* is a sub-shrub reaching 50cm (20in) high, and produces linear, grey leaves and yellow-white flowers. *H. croceum* is a compact shrub reaching 30cm (1ft) high, with white, yellow or apricot flowers.

Helianthemum nummularium

Ilex aquifolium 'J. C. van Tol'

Mahonia aquifolium

Ilex aquifolium
COMMON HOLLY
Family: Aquifoliaceae
Native: S and W Europe, N Africa and W Asia

A tall shrub or tree, it can grow up to 25m (82ft) high and produces prickly, dark green leaves. The nectar-rich flowers are small and white, and are borne in spring. To obtain a show of late summer and autumn red berries, you'll need to plant separate male and female plants.

Cultivation Holly will tolerate most soils, except ones that are waterlogged. Site in any position, including full sun to full or partial shade. Propagate by cuttings in late summer. ❀ ❀ ❀ Zone 6.

Uses A popular plant for a wildlife garden because it has so many uses. It is also excellent in a woodland garden in deep shade or sun, a shrub border, or as a formal hedging or windbreak plant.

Wildlife benefits Honeybees feast on the nectar-rich flowers in spring. After the flowers finish, the plant attracts a great number of bird species. In particular, robins, finches and thrushes feed on the berries, as well as nesting in the branches. The holly blue butterfly is a widespread species throughout the Northern Hemisphere that feeds upon holly for some of the year. The adults that emerge in spring nectar upon the holly flowers and lay eggs on the plant. Once the spring brood have become adults, however, they mate and lay their eggs on ivy for the overwintering brood.

Closely related species *I. aquifolium* 'J. C. van Tol' is a good producer of berries and does not require cross-pollination. It reaches 6m (20ft) high and produces oval, slightly spiny leaves. Use as a hedge or in a container. *I.* x *altaclerensis* is similar, with much broader leaves and smaller spines.

Lavatera olbia
TREE LAVATERA
Family: Malvaceae
Native: W Mediterranean

A highly floriferous shrub producing showy, solitary, red-purple flowers similar to a hollyhock. The flowers are borne throughout summer on stems that can easily reach up to 2m (6½ft) high, and bear 3–5 lobed, semi-evergreen, sage-green leaves that are slightly hairy.

Cultivation Site is full sun, sheltered from cold winds, in poor, free-draining soil. Propagate by softwood cuttings in early summer. ❀ ❀ ❀ Zone 5.

Uses *L. olbia* is a welcome addition to any shrub border because of its long flowering period and abundant clusters of flowers. It can also be used in mixed borders where it mixes well with perennials, such as blue delphiniums and purple aconitums.

Wildlife benefits The bright nectar-producing flowers attract bees, butterflies and a host of other insects. Leave the

Lavatera olbia

foliage uncut over winter before hard pruning in spring because several beneficial insects hibernate amongst the stems.

Closely related species *L. trimestris*, to 1.2m (4ft) high, is an annual that produces an abundance of foliage and white-pink flowers from spring to autumn. *L.* 'Silver Cup' and *L.* 'Mont Blanc' are popular cultivars, and *L. arborea*, a tree-like biennial, is ideal for the wild garden.

Mahonia aquifolium
OREGON GRAPE
Family: Berberidaceae
Native: NW North America

A pretty evergreen shrub producing fragrant, bell-shaped, golden flowers in tight clusters during spring. They are followed by blue-black berries in late summer. The stems, up to 1.2m (4ft) high, have deeply fissured bark and produce bright glossy green leaflets that often turn red-purple in winter.

Cultivation Plant in partial shade in moist, well-drained soil and protect from strong winds. Propagate by semi-ripe cuttings in summer. ❀ ❀ ❀ Zone 5.

Uses It is a valuable, medium-high ground-cover plant because it tends to sucker. Use for its evergreen foliage in a woodland edge or in the dappled shady area of a shrub border. Plant yellow daffodils beside it because the colours complement each other.

Wildlife benefits The flowers are a welcome source of early nectar for bees. Birds, particularly house sparrows and blue tits, attack the flowers seeking nectar and pollen. The blue-black berries are eaten by mistle thrushes and blackbirds.

Closely related species *M. japonica* grows to 1.8m (6ft) high and produces highly fragrant yellow flowers.

Morus nigra
BLACK MULBERRY
Family: Moraceae
Native: SW Asia

A long-lived, round-headed shrub or tree that has been cultivated since at least ancient Egyptian times. It can reach up to 12m (40ft) high and is grown for its attractive, heart-shaped foliage and edible fruits. The tree produces inconspicuous flowers in spring but, by late summer and early autumn, it bears edible, dark purple fruits.

Cultivation Requires full sun and fertile, well-drained soil. Protect from cold winds and frost. Propagate by softwood cuttings in midsummer. ❀ ❀ ❀ Zone 5.

Uses *M. nigra* is best shown off as a specimen tree, for example on a lawn, but avoid a shrub border where it can easily be lost amongst other plants. In colder areas grow against a south-facing wall to provide extra heat and protection.

Wildlife benefits The twisted, gnarled bark provides a home for overwintering insects taking refuge in the cracks. The fruits are eaten by birds, particularly finches, sparrows, tits and waxwings, and the windfalls are taken by small mammals.

Closely related species The white mulberry (*M. alba*) is a deciduous tree growing to 15m (50ft), with oval, pink-red or purple fruits that ripen in summer. The fruits are less palatable than *M. nigra*. Red mulberry (*M. rubra*) is a native of North America and grows to 15m (50ft) high with orange to red fruits.

Morus nigra

Olea europaea

Olea europaea
OLIVE
Family: Oleaceae
Native: Mediterranean

Olives are one of the most important economic plants of hot, dry regions because they provide oil, fruit and timber. *O. europaea*, reaching 7m (23ft) high, is grown for its attractive, narrow, grey-green leaves with silvery undersides and large, oval, green fruits that turn purple. The flowers are tiny, fragrant and white.

Cultivation *O. europaea* thrives in a frost-free environment and will be severely damaged if temperatures hit -10ºC (14ºF). Site in full sun and in deep, fertile soil with good drainage. ❀ ❀ Zone 8.

Uses Old gnarled and twisted plants are fantastic, and are best used as a specimen tree. They are often planted as a central focal point in a herb garden, under-planted with annuals, or grown in terracotta containers on terraces.

Wildlife benefits The flowers are wind pollinated, but the mature fruits are eaten by many species of birds, particularly blackbirds, tits, sparrows, starlings, song thrushes and many finches. Several species use the narrow leaves for nesting material.

Closely related species Black ironwood (*O. capensis*) is a large tree, reaching 20m (66ft). The leaves are lance-shaped and the flowers are small and white, with round, black fruits to follow.

Perovskia atriplicifolia

Perovskia atriplicifolia
RUSSIAN SAGE
Family: Lamiaceae
Native: Afghanistan and Pakistan

Grown for its deeply cut, silver-green, aromatic foliage with serrated edges, and its strong, erect, silvery stems. This upright, deciduous sub-shrub produces grey-white stems that reach 1.5m (5ft) high. The long flower spikes bear numerous violet to soft blue flowers from late summer through to autumn.

Cultivation Russian sage is completely hardy and requires full sun in free-draining soil. Cut back, almost to the base of the plant, each spring. Propagate by softwood cuttings in late spring. ❀ ❀ ❀ Zone 6.

Uses It's a versatile plant that can be used in several areas around the garden, including dry gardens, shrub and mixed borders, herb gardens and fragrant borders. It is extremely floriferous, and is ideal planted next to herbs such as lavender and sage.

Wildlife benefits The open flower spikes are a real favourite with bees and bumblebees collecting nectar. Hoverflies are also frequent visitors to the flowers, as they too are seeking nectar.

Closely related species Another excellent nectar producer is the sub-shrub *P. abrotanoides* that grows to 90cm (3ft) high, and bears panicles of pink-violet flowers in late summer. Its grey-green leaves are deeply divided.

Pyracantha coccinea

Pyracantha coccinea
FIRETHORN
Family: Rosaceae
Native: Italy to Asia Minor

A stunning large shrub that bears autumn fruits after a profusion of small white flowers in spring. Cultivars of this species bear fruits in colours ranging from yellow and orange to bright red. They stand out in winter against the shrub's lance-shaped, dark evergreen foliage.

Cultivation Although firethorn can tolerate poor soil, it grows best in any fertile, well-drained soil. Propagate by semi-ripe heel cuttings in autumn. ❀ ❀ ❀ Zone 6.

Uses It is extremely versatile and can be grown as a freestanding shrub in a border if given plenty of room. It is probably more commonly grown as a wall shrub, being pruned back annually to keep it under control.

Wildlife benefits In spring, bees and bumblebees visit the flowers for pollen and nectar. The autumn fruits are devoured by birds, particularly blackbirds and songbirds. The thorny branches make ideal safe nesting sites for birds.

Closely related species Another evergreen, *P. rogersiana* is slightly less vigorous than *P. coccinea*, and bears fruits in the same colour range. The gardener's favourite must be *P.* 'Flava' with interesting, bright yellow fruits, one of the last berried plants to be eaten by birds because they usually go straight for red and orange berries.

Rhamnus frangula
ALDER BUCKTHORN
Family: Rhamnaceae
Native: Europe, Turkey and N Africa

Alder buckthorn is classed as either a deciduous shrub or tree, and is grown for its beautiful autumn colour and wildlife value. The plant grows 2–5m (6½–17ft) high and bears oblong to lance-like leaves and flowers borne in clusters from late spring to early summer. The ornamental fruits are red, maturing to black.

Cultivation Grows best in sun or semi-shade, in moist, relatively fertile soil. Propagate by seed in spring or by softwood cuttings in early summer. ❀ ❀ ❀ Zone 3.

Uses Alder buckthorn is not a classic ornamental plant, and is therefore not usually included for use in a shrub border unless it is required just for greenery. It is mainly used in a mixed hedgerow or allowed to mature as a specimen tree. It is often included in wild, natural planting schemes.

Wildlife benefits In spring, the brimstone butterfly lays its eggs on the foliage, and the caterpillars eat the leaves before emerging as adults. The flowers provide early nectar for insects, particularly bees, and the berries are eaten by birds.

Closely related species Similar wildlife is attracted to common buckthorn (*R. cathartica*), which has dull green, ovate leaves with insignificant yellow-green flowers, followed by glossy black fruit. *R.* 'Tall Hedge' is often used as a screen or hedge.

Rhododendron luteum
DECIDUOUS AZALEA
Family: Ericaceae
Native: E Europe to Caucasus

R. luteum is one of the main species used in hybridization to produce many of the modern cultivars of *Azalea*. This deciduous shrub reaches from 1.5–2.5m (5–8ft) high and bears heavily scented, funnel-shaped yellow flowers in spring, and green, oblong, lance-shaped leaves with a wonderful rich autumn colour.

Cultivation Azaleas demand acid soil with plenty of organic matter to help retain moisture in dry periods, and a site in semi-shade. Propagate by seed or semi-ripe cuttings in late summer. ❀ ❀ ❀ Zone 5.

Uses Azaleas are ideal for using at the edge of a woodland, but not inside because it'll be too shady. Plant in large, bold groups for a striking effect, both in terms of flower and autumn colour. Do not under-plant because of the shallow root system.

Wildlife benefits The sweetly scented flowers are frequently visited by bees and bumblebees seeking nectar. Honey made from rhododendron nectar contains a substance called andromedotoxin, a potent toxin if ingested causing terrible vomiting.

Closely related species All rhododendron flowers are real favourites with bees. Spring-flowering species include *R. williamsianum*, an evergreen shrub reaching 1.5m (5ft) high with pink flowers, and *R. yakushimanum*, to 90cm (3ft), an evergreen, dome-shaped shrub bearing pink flowers.

Rhamnus frangula

Rhododendron luteum

Ribes nigrum

Ribes nigrum
BLACKCURRANT
Family: Grossulariaceae
Native: Europe to C Asia, the Himalayas and Russia

A wide-spreading, aromatic, deciduous shrub that grows up to 1.8m (6ft) high, grown for its round, black, edible fruit. The leaves have 3–5 lobes and a distinct aroma, especially if crushed. Hanging racemes of 4–10 flowers are produced in spring. They are small and bell-shaped, green on the outside, and red-white inside.

Cultivation Blackcurrants thrive in full sun and fertile, well-drained soil. Cut the older stems hard back, by one-third, in winter. Propagate by hardwood cuttings in winter. ❀ ❀ ❀ Zone 5.

Uses When used in a vegetable garden, expose the excess fruits for the birds when you've had your fill. Alternatively they can be planted in a shrub, mixed or herb border where the fruits can be left solely for the birds and mammals.

Wildlife benefits Honeybees and particularly bumblebees (especially at low temperatures) visit the flowers for pollen. The fruits are eaten by birds, including thrushes, tits, warblers and blackbirds. The stem structure is ideal for several species of birds to nest in.

Closely related species The redcurrant (*R. silvestre*) is also grown for its fruits that are palatable to many species of birds. It bears hanging racemes of green or red cup-shaped flowers in spring, followed by red berries.

Ribes sanguineum
FLOWERING CURRANT
Family: Grossulariaceae
Native: W North America

A wonderful ornamental plant for the wildlife garden. A medium-sized shrub reaching 1.8m (6ft) or more, it produces 3–5 lobed leaves that are dark green and slightly hairy. The rose-red, tubular flowers are borne in hanging clusters in spring. This species has produced many cultivars.

Cultivation Plant in full sun in moderately fertile, moisture-retentive, well-drained soil. Mulching aids healthy growth. Propagate by nodal hardwood cuttings in late autumn–early winter. ❀ ❀ ❀ Zone 6.

Uses An extremely useful plant for the shrub or mixed border, providing a valuable source of early nectar. Use 'Brocklebankii' if golden foliage is required, or 'Tydemans White' for bright white flowers.

Wildlife benefits The nectar is popular with bees and bumblebees, while sparrows and tits feed on visiting insects. *R. sanguineum* often fails to fruit whereas buffalo currant (*R. odoratum*) bears dark fruits eaten by songbirds and small mammals.

Closely related species *R. odoratum* is an excellent ornamental shrub for wildlife. The fragrant yellow flowers provide an early source of nectar for insects, particularly bees and butterflies, and its dense framework gives good nesting cover for birds.

Ribes sanguineum

Ribes uva-crispa

Ribes uva-crispa
GOOSEBERRY
Family: Grossulariaceae
Native: NE and C Europe

The gooseberry is a short, spreading shrub that should reach 1.2m (4ft) high, being grown for its large, green to yellow hairy fruits. The stems bear groups of thorns up to 1cm (⅓in) long, and 3–5 lobed leaves that are slightly hairy underneath. Clusters of up to three, green to pink-green, cup-shaped flowers are borne in spring.

Cultivation The gooseberry prefers well-drained garden soil in full sun, but will also grow in partial shade. Mulch to keep the roots moist. Propagate by hardwood cuttings in winter. ❀ ❀ ❀ Zone 5.

Uses It is nearly always grown in a kitchen garden for its delicious crop. When you've taken what you want for the family (and frozen some), let the wildlife take the surplus berries. Alternatively, plant in a wildlife border where all the fruit can be eaten.

Wildlife benefits The small, white, nectar-rich spring flowers are extremely popular with bees because they are borne before the main burst of spring blossom. Several birds, particularly blue tits, drink the nectar from the flowers, while the fruits are eaten by the likes of blackbirds.

Closely related species Bees and birds also like American gooseberry (*R. hirtellum*), a native of northern North America. It is a deciduous shrub that grows to 2m (6½ft) high, and produces small green flowers and round purple-black fruits in summer.

Rosa canina

Rosa canina
DOG ROSE
Family: Rosaceae
Native: Europe, SW Asia and
NW Africa

A vigorous shrub that will reach 1.5–5.5m (5–18ft) high, it bears arching stems with leaves divided into leaflets, and fierce, hooked thorns. The large, fragrant flowers are borne in summer, being followed by juicy red autumn hips. The dog rose is also called the common briar rose and dog briar rose.

Cultivation Thrives best in full sun although it will tolerate a degree of partial shade. Grow in any fertile, well-drained soil. Propagate by hardwood cuttings in early autumn. ❀ ❀ ❀ Zone 3.

Uses Dog rose is a useful plant for including in a mixed hedge with other species such as *Acer campestre*, common holly (*Ilex aquifolium*), hazel (*Corylus avellana*) and common hawthorn (*Crataegus monogyna*). It is also ideal in a wild garden where the arching stems can ramble.

Wildlife benefits The pollen-bearing flowers are a favourite with bees, bumblebees, flies and beetles. The rose hips that follow are popular with birds, small mammals and several species of gall wasps. Birds use the thorny branches as protection when nesting.

Closely related species Sweet briar (*R. rubiginosa*) bears single, pale to deep pink flowers, and can be used in borders or a mixed hedgerow. The Japanese rose (*R. rugosa*) is often used as a single-species hedge or in an ornamental border.

Rosa glauca
SHRUB ROSE
Family: Rosaceae
Native: Mountains of C and
S Europe

A tall, statuesque rose that produces small pink flowers that complement its attractive, greyish-purple foliage. The flowers are followed by spherical red hips. The almost thornless stems can reach up to 1.5–3m (5–10ft) tall and bear deciduous leaves, each one divided into 5–9 leaflets.

Cultivation Grows best in full sun and tolerates extremely low temperatures over winter. Plant in any well-drained soil. Propagate by hardwood cuttings in autumn. ❀ ❀ ❀ Zone 2.

Uses *R. glauca* is best grown as a specimen rose in a mixed or shrub border, and should be sited where the attractive foliage can be viewed easily. The pink flowers and greyish foliage mix well with purple-leaved shrubs.

Wildlife benefits Bees and hoverflies seek out pollen from the small pink flowers, and the hips are eaten by birds and small mammals. Do not prune any old growth until spring to allow the hips to be completely stripped off.

Closely related species 'Geranium' is best grown as a specimen rose and has single red flowers with a creamy centre, followed by beautiful, bright scarlet hips. *R. gallica* bears beautifully scented, single or semi-double, rose to crimson flowers.

Rosa glauca

Rubus fruticosus

Rubus fruticosus
BRAMBLE
Family: Rosaceae
Native: Unknown

A semi-deciduous shrub with arching to erect thorny stems that can grow several metres high. The leaves are dark green and deeply divided, and the flowers are white-pink. The plant *Rubus fruticosus* covers at least 14 different but closely related species, some of which may be hybrids and have become known as bramble or blackberry.

Cultivation Site in full sun to attract a large number of nectaring insects, or in semi-shade. Propagate by division of suckers in autumn or spring. ❀ ❀ ❀ Zone 6.

Uses Definitely not for the formal garden, but excellent in a wild garden. Plant on sunny banks to encourage nectar production, also enabling invertebrates to bask in the sun. A large plant will encourage birds to nest here.

Wildlife benefits The flowers are a fantastic nectar source for bees, bumblebees and many different species of butterfly. The caterpillars of the grizzled skipper and ringlet butterfly will devour the leaves, and the berries are a favourite with birds and small mammals.

Closely related species The raspberry (*R. idaeus*) is a woodland plant that can thrive in full sun or semi-shade. The white flowers are prized by bees, especially honeybees seeking nectar and particularly pollen. Small mammals and several species of birds enjoy the fruit.

Sambucus nigra
ELDERBERRY
Family: Caprifoliacae
Native: Europe, N Africa and
SW Asia

Elderberry is a fast-growing plant reaching to 10m (33ft) high, and can be classed as a shrub or small tree. Each leaf is divided into 3–9 leaflets. The stems must be two years old before they produce cream, musk-scented, summer flowers in flat-topped umbels. They are followed by round, shiny black fruits.

Cultivation   Grows best in full sun or dappled shade in rich, moist soil. Elderberry can tolerate atmospheric pollution and coastal conditions. Propagate by hardwood cuttings in winter. ❀ ❀ ❀ Zone 5.

Uses   Elderberry is too rampant for the small garden, but is ideal in large shrub or mixed borders, and in a wild garden. Do not carry out annual pruning because the plants will not flower and berry that year.

Wildlife benefits   A fantastic plant for wildlife, attracting many species of insects, including bees, flies and hoverflies, and a range of insect-eating birds. The berries are eaten by small mammals and birds, particularly finches, thrushes, starlings and garden warblers.

Closely related species   American elder (*S. canadensis*) grows to 4m (13ft) high and produces ivory flowers followed by dark fruits. Red-berried elder (*S. racemosa*) is a shrub that'll grow to 3.5m (11½ft) high, and bears green to white-yellow flowers in spring and scarlet berries.

Sambucus nigra

Skimmia japonica

Skimmia japonica
SKIMMIA
Family: Rutaceae
Native: Japan and China

An attractive, erect or low-growing evergreen shrub reaching 0.6–1.5m (2–5ft) high, grown for its flowers and berries. *S. japonica* has separate male and female plants, and both need to be grown in close proximity to produce berries. The white, female flowers are fragrant and appear in late spring, being followed by numerous red autumn berries.

Cultivation   Best grown in dappled or full shade in well-drained soil that is neutral to acidic, with plenty of organic matter. Propagate by semi-ripe cuttings in late summer. ❀ ❀ ❀ Zone 7.

Uses   Excellent for growing in a woodland garden. Plant in large groups along the side of a path to create an impressive, evergreen swathe of colour. Also grow beside rhododendrons and *Enkianthus*.

Wildlife benefits   The flowers are popular with bees and hoverflies seeking nectar. Many species of birds are attracted to the autumn fruits when insect numbers decrease. The dense, evergreen foliage provides great ground cover for insects and small mammals.

Closely related species   *S. anquetilia* is a creeping or erect shrub that grows from 30cm–1.8m (1–6ft). The evergreen leaves are strongly aromatic and it has separate male and female plants. The flowers are green to yellow and have an unpleasant smell.

Symphoricarpos albus
SNOWBERRY
Family: Caprifoliaceae
Native: W North America

A suckering, deciduous shrub that can become invasive if it is not checked. The arching stems can grow 1.2m (4ft) long and bear oval, dark green leaves and pink flowers in clusters over summer. Snow white, large round fruits follow the flowers and can persist through winter.

Cultivation   Snowberry tolerates a wide range of soil types, and will cope with urban pollution and maritime conditions. Site in sun to full shade. Propagate by softwood cuttings in summer. ❀ ❀ ❀ Zone 3.

Uses   It's probably best sited in a wild garden where it can spread freely and produce a dense stand that birds might use for nesting. In an ornamental garden it will need a large space, and will require annual pruning to keep the size of the clump in check.

Wildlife benefits   Bees, bumblebees and wasps visit the shrub seeking out the nectar-rich flowers. The leaves are occasionally eaten by the marsh fritillary butterfly and the berries are eaten by birds, especially robins, garden warblers, tits, blackbirds and finches.

Closely related species   *S.* x *chenautii* 'Hancock' provides excellent ground cover for foraging insects and small mammals. Coralberry (*S. orbiculatus*), a native to eastern North America, produces ivory-flushed pink flowers in summer followed by large, grey-white fruits.

Symphoricarpos albus

Syringa vulgaris

Ulex europaeus

Syringa vulgaris
COMMON LILAC
Family: Oleaceae
Native: SE Europe

Lilac is a beautiful, sweetly scented large shrub that can grow to 7m (23ft) high. The ovate leaves are up to 12cm (5in) long, and the flowers are borne in pyramidal, large, terminal panicles. There are many different hybrids with colours ranging from white to shades of pink, mauve and blue.

Cultivation Lilacs grow in most locations but prefer full sun with their roots in well-drained, fertile soil. Propagate by semi-ripe cuttings in late summer. ❀ ❀ ❀ Zone 5.

Uses Great for the back of a border to give height, and will also provide a blaze of colour and wonderful scent when in flower. Plant in a shrub or mixed border, though lilac is occasionally used as an informal hedge or screen.

Wildlife benefits Many insects are drawn to the flowers seeking nectar, particularly bees and butterflies. The seeds are eaten by siskins and other finches, and the dense branches are often used by blackbirds and thrushes for nesting.

Closely related species Single-flowering species lilacs are ideal for wildlife gardens. The compact, 1.5m (5ft) high *S. meyeri* is a real favourite, being well suited to the small garden or even tubs. The pink *S. villosa* grows up to 4m (13ft) high.

Ulex europaeus
GORSE
Family: Papilionaceae
Native: W Europe

Gorse is an exceptionally spiny, evergreen shrub with yellow-golden flowers that are strongly scented and smell of coconut. The

shrub can reach up to 1.8m (6ft) high, and produces extremely dense young stems. The leaves are linear or reduced to sharp spines, an excellent adaptation enabling the plant to tolerate low rainfall.

Cultivation Thrives in free-draining soil that is acidic to neutral. Best in full sun, but will tolerate dappled shade. Propagate by seed or from semi-ripe cuttings in summer. ❀ ❀ ❀ Zone 6.

Uses Gorse is ideal in a dry garden if enough space is available. It can also be used in a woodland edge or for naturalizing in a wild garden, particularly on poor, dry sandy soils or old heathland.

Wildlife benefits The long flowering period from summer to autumn makes gorse an extremely important nectar and pollen source for bees and bumblebees. The thorny stems provide excellent protection for nesting birds, such as long-tailed tits, against predators.

Closely related species Spanish gorse (*Genista hispanica*) is used more

frequently in ornamental and smaller gardens than *U. europaeus*. The stems reach up to 60cm (2ft) and produce a dense network of branches. The golden-yellow flowers appear in summer.

Viburnum x *bodnantense*
WINTER-FLOWERING VIBURNUM
Family: Caprifoliaceae
Native: Garden origin

A thicket-forming, medium-sized, upright, deciduous shrub that can grow to 3m (10ft) high. The stems bear ovate leaves from spring to autumn, and flowers that appear on naked stems from autumn to spring. The flowers are white with a strong flush of pink and appear in clusters.

Cultivation Grows well in any type of soil that is fertile and free draining. Viburnums prefer sun but will also grow in partial shade. Propagate by hardwood cuttings in autumn. ❀ ❀ ❀ Zone 7.

Uses Can be grown in an ornamental shrub or mixed border. Site next to an entrance or path because of the beautiful scent. Ideal for using in a wild garden where it is best planted in large groups, particularly if trying to encourage birds to nest.

Wildlife benefits The flowers provide a welcome source of nectar for early flying insects, especially bumblebees. The dense network of stems provides good cover for nesting songbirds. The dark blue fruits in spring are eaten by birds if insect numbers are low.

Closely related species Other *Viburnum* species that are excellent for wildlife include *V.* x *burkwoodii* and *V. lantana*. *V. tinus* flowers from late winter to early spring, and is a winner with early flying insects.

Viburnum x *bodnantense*

MIXED HEDGES

Crataegus monogyna
HAWTHORN
Family: Rosaceae
Native: Europe

Hawthorn is widely known as the May tree, being named after the month in which it flowers. It is typically thought of as a hedgerow shrub, and is named after the Saxon word for hedge. The thorns form an excellent barrier but, if left uncut, an individual hawthorn eventually develops into a strong tree with a dense crown.

Cultivation An easily cultivated plant, it thrives in a variety of soil types and a range of settings, including hedgerow, scrub, thicket and woodland. Best raised from seed. ❀ ❀ ❀ Zone 5.

Uses An excellent hedging plant that grows rapidly, is long-lived and provides abundant blossom and fruit. Prune after flowering to aid flower and fruit production next season. In natural settings it protects seedlings of other broadleaved trees, particularly oak (*Fagus*), from being grazed, and aids natural regeneration.

Wildlife benefits Hawthorn provides food for over 150 different species of insect. The spring blossom is an excellent source of nectar for bees, and the berries are eaten by mice and many birds, including finches, blue tits, starlings and thrushes. Blackbirds and finches nest in the dense branches.

Closely related species *C. aestivalis* is grown in North America for similar purposes, and Midland hawthorn (*C. laevigata*) is very similar but has pink or red blossom and is often grown as a street tree, while blackthorn is a related shrub used in hedgerows.

Crataegus monogyna

Euonymus europaeus

Euonymus europaeus
SPINDLE TREE
Family: Celastraceae
Native: E and W Asia

This deciduous shrub or small tree can grow to 5m (17ft) high, and is frequently found in hedges although it naturally inhabits the edges of forest and gentle slopes. The rather inconspicuous flowers are produced in late spring, followed by red to purple or pink fruit with orange seeds that tend to persist until late autumn.

Cultivation It tolerates a wide range of soils, although it tends to perform best on nutrient-rich, chalky and salt-poor soil. It is best raised from stratified seed sown in spring. ❀ ❀ ❀ Zone 3.

Uses The bright pink or purple capsules that contain the seeds, and the attractive autumn colouring of the foliage against the green bark, have made it a popular ornamental plant in gardens and parks. It has also been used extensively as a hedging plant, especially in cold, windswept places.

Wildlife benefits The plant provides light cover for roosting birds and the flowers, though insignificant, provide nectar for insects. The autumn fruits are eaten by birds, particularly starlings, sparrows, wood pigeons, garden warblers and finches.

Closely related species The winged spindle (*E. alatus*) is a deciduous, spreading shrub native to eastern Asia, its stems being notable for their four corky ridges or "wings". *E. fortunei* is an Asian species that is widely planted in gardens, and climbs by small rootlets on the stems.

Ilex aquifolium

Ilex aquifolium
HOLLY
Family: Aquifoliaceae
Native: S and W Europe and W Asia

With its bright red berries (found only on female plants), and shiny, evergreen leaves, the holly has been a symbol of midwinter festivals since pre-Christian times, and of Christmas. It grows as a shrub or tree with a narrow, conical crown, smooth silver-greyish bark and spiny leaves, and is often found in hedges.

Cultivation Though it tolerates shade, it grows best in full sun. It prefers neutral to slightly acid, moist, well-drained soil. Sow fresh seed in autumn, but note it can take 18 months to germinate. ❀ ❀ ❀ Zone 6.

Uses Slow-growing holly takes a number of years to form a hedge-sized plant, but is still well worth including in a mixed hedge. It increases the security aspect, and its shade-tolerance means it can be grown under the canopy of deciduous trees.

Wildlife benefits The small white spring flowers are packed with nectar that attracts many insects, including holly blue butterflies and honeybees. The holly blue butterfly caterpillars also eat the flower buds. The berries are eaten by the likes of robins and thrushes during winter.

Closely related species American holly (*I. opaca*) – native to eastern and central North America – is a small to medium evergreen tree with red berries that persist into winter. Yaupon holly (*I. vomitoria*) is an evergreen from south-east North America.

Prunus spinosa
BLACKTHORN
Family: Rosaceae
Native: Europe to Iran and
SW Siberia

Blackthorn has a long history as a hedgerow plant because of its thorns. The beautiful white blossom tends to appear early in the year before the leaves, often in a very cold period following a false spring (widely known as "blackthorn winter"). The bitter bluish-black fruits, or sloes, have a whitish bloom and contain a single, hard-shelled seed.

Cultivation An easily grown deciduous shrub that will grow in most well-drained, moisture retentive soils. Site in a sunny position for the best fruiting. Raise from seed after stratification. ❀ ❀ ❀ Zone 4.

Uses It grows very well in exposed seaside locations, although it can be rather bare in winter and does not provide very good shelter if grown as a single-species hedge. It does have early blossom, though, and the fruit (sloes) are used to flavour gin, jellies, conserves and syrups.

Wildlife benefits The flowers provide nectar and pollen for early emerging bees and other insects. The leaves are important for caterpillars of several species, including the emperor moth and brown hairstreak butterfly. Dense branches shelter nesting birds, especially nightingales. The berries are eaten by birds, particularly thrushes and starlings.

Closely related species Blackthorn is related to the plums, and the most similar is possibly the damson, an edible, cultivated variety of the plum tree, *P. domestica*, also known as the damask plum. *P. d.* subsp. *institia* is another form of the plum, often found growing in hedges.

Prunus spinosa

Ulmus glabra

Ulmus glabra
WYCH ELM
Family: Ulmaceae
Native: Europe and W Asia

This large deciduous tree was once common across its range but its susceptibility to Dutch elm disease means that it is now rare, except as suckering growth in hedges. It survives there because the elm bark beetles that transmit the disease fly at a height of 4m (13ft) in search of healthy elms. If unaffected by disease it can live for up to 500 years.

Cultivation An easily grown tree, succeeding in any moist soil, but it does not thrive if the soil is too acidic or chalky. Grow in sun or dappled shade. Propagate from ripe seed. ❀ ❀ ❀ Zone 5.

Uses Was once a common sight in hedgerows, and often grew as part of mixed woodlands. Its use has declined since the outbreak of Dutch elm disease, although it may still be used in a mixed hedge, particularly in windy locations.

Wildlife benefits The tiny red flowers that appear in spring provide pollen for bees. The leaves are eaten by the caterpillars of moths and butterfly species, including the large tortoiseshell and white hairstreak butterflies. The seeds may also be eaten by birds, including sparrows, siskins and other finches.

Closely related species Many species of elm are similarly affected by disease and are therefore rare. *U. procera* is similar but the leaves have bristly hairs on the upper surface and are generally smaller, with fewer veins.

Viburnum lanata

Viburnum lanata
WAYFARING TREE
Family: Caprifoliaceae
Native: S and C Europe to N Africa

This attractive deciduous shrub is found on chalk and limestone areas as part of woodland edges, or in hedgerows. The undersides of the leaves are covered with dense, white, silky hairs and, in midsummer, the whole bush is covered in fragrant white flowers that are followed in autumn by oblong red berries, which turn black as the season progresses.

Cultivation This bush does well in any soil, although it is best on chalk and limestone. It is wind-tolerant and grows happily in sun or partial shade. Propagate from ripe seed. ❀ ❀ ❀ Zone 3.

Uses *V. lanata* is an excellent garden specimen that can be used as a free-standing shrub, and in hedges and woodland-edge borders. The young growth and even winter twigs are covered in a woolly bloom, giving added interest to a mixed hedge throughout the season.

Wildlife benefits All viburnums are a good source of nectar for bees, and are excellent for attracting hoverflies, effective predators of aphids. The fruit is also an important food for many birds, particularly members of the thrush family, as well as a number of mammals.

Closely related species The guelder rose (*V. opulus*) is native to Europe and Asia, and is very closely related to the North American species *V. trilobum*. Possum haw (*V. acerifolium*) is also common in eastern North America.

SINGLE-SPECIES HEDGES

Berberis thunbergii
JAPANESE BARBERRY
Family: Berberidaceae
Native: Japan

Barberry is a dense, deciduous, spiny shrub that, if left untrimmed, grows 1–2m (3½–6½ft) tall. In its natural habitat or in areas where it has become naturalized, it can be found beside roads, along field margins, in hedgerows or in open woods. It has deeply grooved, brown branches with a single spine at each leaf cluster.

Cultivation Grows best in full sun or light shade on moist, loamy soil, but will also succeed on thin, dry, shallow or heavy clay ground. Sow seed as soon as it is ripe, or take cuttings of half-ripe wood. ❀ ❀ ❀ Zone 4.

Uses Makes a good medium-sized hedge because it's very tolerant of trimming and re-sprouts well from the base. Its dense, prickly nature makes an effective barrier, and since deer find the leaves unpalatable it has become a popular landscape species.

Wildlife benefits Excellent for providing shelter for a number of smaller species of nesting birds, with the thorns preventing attacks from cats and larger birds. The flowers are visited by honeybees and bumblebees seeking nectar, and the berries are eaten by birds and small mammals.

Closely related species
B. canadensis is a North American species with sharply toothed leaves and three-pronged spines. *B. vulgaris*, native to central and southern Europe, can be distinguished from *B. thunbergii* by its spiny, toothed leaves and flowers in a long raceme.

Berberis thunbergii

Buxus sempervirens

Buxus sempervirens
COMMON BOX
Family: Buxaceae
Native: W and S Europe, N Africa and W Asia

This evergreen, small tree is rather slow-growing but long-lived. It reaches a maximum height of 6m (20ft), with a trunk about 15cm (6in) in diameter, covered by rugged, greyish bark and yellowish branches. It is more familiar as a clipped, shrubby specimen, and is most commonly used as a hedging plant.

Cultivation Box naturally prefers chalk and limestone, although it tolerates a wide variety of soils and thrives in sun or part shade. Can be grown from seed or, more commonly, cuttings. ❀ ❀ ❀ Zone 5.

Uses Box is a popular ornamental plant, partly due to its small, scented flowers and deep green leaves, although it is most valued for topiary and hedging because of its dense habit and tolerance of close clipping. It is also notably resistant to honey fungus and pests in general.

Wildlife benefits If just clipped lightly and allowed to flower in early spring, the tiny blooms will attract a number of pollinators, especially any early emerging bees and flies. The dense growth makes an excellent dry hibernation site for many overwintering insects.

Closely related species Several cultivars have variegated foliage. *B. balearica*, from the Balearic Isles, is hardy to Zone 8 and *B. henryi* has a neat, vase-shaped habit. Small-leaved box (*B. microphylla*) is often used as edging.

Chamaecyparis lawsoniana

Chamaecyparis lawsoniana
LAWSON CYPRESS
Family: Cupressaceae
Native: California and Oregon

This large, coniferous, evergreen tree is also called Port Orford cedar (despite its not being a cedar) in its native range, where it can reach 60m (200ft) tall. It has blue-green, feathery foliage in flat sprays of scale-like leaves, with narrow white markings on the underside, and makes an excellent hedge.

Cultivation Thrives in neutral to slightly acid, moist, well-drained soil, prefers full sun, and is pollution-tolerant. Propagate by cuttings, taken in winter from tips of large branches of the lower crown of young trees. ❀ ❀ ❀ Zone 6.

Uses Lawson cypress is popular in gardens, and has given rise to many named cultivars. 'Elwoodii' is very popular, being suitable for both hedging and growing as a specimen tree, and is an excellent substitute.

Wildlife benefits The dense, evergreen foliage is used as either a roost or a nesting site by many bird species, such as blackbirds, starlings and greenfinches. When grown as a hedge, the base provides cool, dry shelter for many insect species, small mammals, birds, spiders, reptiles and amphibians.

Closely related species Hinoki cypress (*C. obtusa*) and *C. pisifera* (Sawara cypress) are slow-growing trees that, if left uncut, grow to 35m (115ft) tall. Both make fine specimens but are less suited for hedging. Western red cedar (*Thuya plicata*) makes an excellent hedge.

Escallonia rubra var. *macrantha*
REDCLAWS
Family: Escalloniaceae
Native: Chile

This evergreen shrub has bright, attractive, glossy green leaves and, in favourable locations, may reach 1.8m (6ft) or more. From mid- to late summer the branch tips become clothed in deep red, tubular flowers. When it's grown in warm, seaside regions, it makes an excellent windbreak, and often grows taller than specimens growing inland.

Cultivation Thrives in most well-drained soils and tolerates lime quite well. It'll establish best if planted out when young. Propagate from cuttings of short side shoots, in mid- to late summer. ❀ ❀ ❀ Zone 8.

Uses Redclaws makes an excellent informal hedge or windbreak, and can be clipped or hard-pruned to restrict the growth, although this reduces the amount of flower. It is an ideal seaside plant, tolerant of wind and salt. If cut back by frost, it'll reshoot from the base.

Wildlife benefits Good for providing nesting sites for birds and shelter for insects and small mammals, while the nectar-rich flowers are favoured by bees and some butterfly species. It also attracts aphids which, in turn, attract predators. In Australia, the white-brow hawkmoth feeds on the leaves.

Closely related species *E. rubra* has pink rather than red flowers. *E. virgata* is a deciduous shrub with slender branches, tiny leaves and tiny white flowers, but doesn't tolerate alkaline soil. *E.* 'Langleyensis' is a popular garden hybrid.

Escallonia rubra var. *macrantha*

Rosa rugosa
RAMANAS ROSE
Family: Rosaceae
Native: E Asia

This native of coastal sand dunes is a dense, vigorous, suckering shrub that forms packed thickets of thorny stems. The flowers that appear from summer to autumn are dark pink to white, sweetly scented, and are followed by large, flattened hips; the bush often simultaneously bears fruit and flowers. The leaves turn bright yellow in autumn.

Cultivation It tolerates wind and salty conditions, in shade or full sun, and thrives in poor soil provided it's well drained. Easily propagated by seed, softwood cuttings or hardwood cuttings. ❀ ❀ ❀ Zone 2.

Uses Widely used as an ornamental plant across Europe and North America, and is valued by rose breeders for its considerable resistance to rose rust and black spot. Its tolerance of salt spray makes it ideal for planting beside roads that are treated with salt.

Wildlife benefits The attractive, strongly scented flowers attract many pollinators, especially bumblebees and malachite beetles. The large, red, tomato-like hips are extremely rich in vitamin C, and are eaten by small mammals and birds, such as finches, thrushes and waxwings.

Closely related species Numerous cultivars have been selected for garden use, with flower colour varying from white to dark red-purple. The dog rose (*R. canina*) has smaller but equally nutritious hips, and the burnet or Scots rose (*R. pimpinellifolia*) is also a good choice for seaside planting.

Rosa rugosa

Taxus baccata

Taxus baccata
YEW
Family: Taxaceae
Native: Europe, NW Africa and SW Asia

Yew is a slow-growing, evergreen tree, reaching 10–20m (33–66ft) high, and can be very long-lived, with the oldest approximately 2–4,000 years old. The soft, needle-like leaves are arranged spirally around the stem, and the highly modified seed cones are surrounded by a bright red berry-like structure called an aril, the only non-poisonous part of the plant.

Cultivation An easy plant to grow, it tolerates cold and heat, sunny and shady sites, wet and dry soils, and a range of pH. Propagate from seed or cuttings of half-ripe terminal shoots. ❀ ❀ ❀ Zone 6.

Uses Yew is widely used in gardens, and there are over 200 named cultivars, the most popular of which is the upright Irish yew (*T. baccata* 'Fastigiata'). They are popular subjects for topiary, and make highly attractive, long-lived hedges that are very resistant to honey fungus.

Wildlife benefits The berry-like arils ripen over 2–3 months and are eaten by thrushes, waxwings and other birds. The foliage is toxic to most mammals, but is eaten by deer because they can break down the poisons. The larvae of some moth species, including willow beauty, also eat the leaves.

Closely related species All yews are closely related, and some botanists treat them all as the subspecies or varieties of one widespread species. Good examples include the Pacific yew (*T. brevifolia*) from north-west North America, Canada yew (*T. canadensis*) and Japanese yew (*T. cuspidata*).

TREES

Acer campestre
FIELD MAPLE
Family: Aceraceae
Native: Europe, Near East and Africa

The field maple is a relatively small tree that can sometimes be found in semi-natural woods and, most frequently, in hedgerows. Its small leaves have 3–5 lobes, are greyish-green turning to gold in autumn, while the grey to yellowish-brown bark has a rough texture. It never achieves the size of its relative, the sycamore (*A. pseudoplatanus*), but can reach a great age.

Cultivation Easily grown in full sun or partial shade, it prefers moist, well-drained soil and tolerates urban conditions much better than most maples. Sow seed as soon as it is ripe. ❀ ❀ ❀ Zone 4.

Uses Field maple makes a strong, very durable hedge thanks to its dense foliage with well-developed branches, but it can also make an attractive freestanding tree. The young foliage is initially reddish before turning dark green and then yellow in autumn.

Wildlife benefits Field maple supports over 50 species of wildlife, being the food plant for many moths including the winter moth, maple pug, mocha and small yellow wave. Nectar and pollen attract bees and other insects, and the strong, dense growth makes an ideal haven for nesting birds.

Closely related species The taller sycamore (*Acer pseudoplatanus*) is well known for its ability to make a fine specimen, and for the nuisance value of its seedlings. If space is limited, try growing the 8m (25ft) high Japanese maple (*A. palmatum*).

Acer campestre

Alnus glutinosa

Alnus glutinosa
COMMON ALDER
Family: Betulaceae
Native: Europe

Its native habitat is wet ground, and it can certainly withstand regular immersion in water. The oval leaves are distinctive, with a notch at the tip of the main vein, and the buds appear on short stalks. In winter, small, persistent, woody "cones" appear near the branch tips.

Cultivation Grows in most soils, including the waterlogged, and because it fixes nitrogen in its root nodules it can grow on quite infertile ground. Propagate by seed in late autumn. ❀ ❀ ❀ Zone 3.

Uses Its ability to withstand poor soil has made it a tree of choice for land reclamation and waterside planting. In time it makes a handsome specimen, growing 25m (85ft) high, making it best suited to large gardens.

Wildlife benefits The seeds attract finches, such as redpolls and siskins, and tits. The caterpillars of around 30 moth species, including alder kitten, brindled beauty, large emerald, and the waved carpet, feed on the leaves, as do alder sawfly and alder leaf-miners.

Closely related species There are approximately 35 species of alder, and many are quite similar to the common alder. *A. rubra* is an American species, also suited to wet ground, while the grey alder (*A. incana*) and Italian alder (*A. cordata*) are better suited to drier sites. All are useful wildlife trees.

Betula pendula

Betula pendula
SILVER BIRCH
Family: Betulaceae
Native: Europe and Asia Minor

Silver birch is a common, widely used tree that's grown for its graceful habit provided by the thin, whip-like twigs that are pendulous at the tips. Its silvery, attractive bark becomes rugged, with black patches appearing as the tree ages. A fast-growing tree (though quite short-lived with a life expectancy of around 90 years), it quickly colonizes open areas, such as unmanaged heaths and abandoned land.

Cultivation Silver birch grows in a wide range of habitats, and is incredibly tolerant of a wide-ranging soil pH, from 3.5–7. It is usually best in dry, sandy soils or harsh settings where other trees fail. Propagate by seed in late autumn. ❀ ❀ ❀ Zone 1.

Uses Often called "lady of the woods" because of its outstanding elegance, it is a wonderful landscape tree, especially when young. Despite its rapid growth rate, it rarely dominates or shades the garden too much.

Wildlife benefits Birch seeds are a food source for overwintering birds, such as tits and finches, and older trees provide nesting sites in cracked trunks for the likes of tree creepers. The leaves are a food source for well over 100 kinds of moth caterpillar, as well as birch leaf miners.

Closely related species While silver birch grows best on drier soils, the closely related downy birch (*B. pubescens*) is chiefly associated with damper soils and grows well with alder.

Carpinus betulus

Carpinus betulus
COMMON HORNBEAM
Family: Carpinaceae
Native: Europe and Asia Minor

This large, attractive forest tree closely resembles beech (*Fagus*), and has a pyramidal shape that later becomes more rounded. It produces flowers in the form of catkins, which remain on the tree until early autumn when the small "nutlets" hang in clusters of green, three-pointed, papery wings. During winter, dead leaves remain on the lower branches until spring.

Cultivation Hornbeam is especially good in chalky and clay soil, though it will tolerate wet ground, and likes both dense shade and exposed, windy sites. It is raised from seed, which remains dormant in the soil for 18 months. Propagate by seed in spring or autumn. ❊ ❊ ❊ Zone 5.

Uses Hornbeam makes an excellent hedge because of its ability to retain its withered, tan or light brown leaves until spring, a characteristic called *marcescence*. It also makes a fine specimen tree, although it's only suited to larger gardens.

Wildlife benefits Hornbeam supports many insects, including caterpillars of the small white wave and copper underwing moths. The nuts are eaten in winter by birds, such as hawfinches, while hares, rabbits and field mice eat the young leaves. It provides good bird cover when grown as a hedge.

Closely related species There are a number of species that are similar to, and as handsome as, the European hornbeam. American hornbeam (*C. caroliniana*) is a tree or large shrub from eastern North America, and the Japanese *C. japonica* is a medium-sized tree with deep, flaking, fissured bark.

Castanea sativa
SWEET CHESTNUT
Family: Fagaceae
Native: Mediterranean

It has been cultivated for over 3,000 years, and was widely spread beyond its original range by Roman legionaries who used the nuts as a staple food. It grows into a tall tree with deep, spirally fissured bark, has distinctively large, tough, serrated leaves, and slim, cream-coloured flower panicles followed, in autumn, by chestnuts held in prickly cases.

Cultivation Sweet chestnut does best on deep, moist, sandy soil and well-drained clay, and suffers if grown on very wet or lime-rich ground. It fruits best in areas with long, hot summers. Propagate by seed in autumn. ❊ ❊ ❊ Zone 5.

Uses It ultimately grows into a beautiful tree, but you'll need a huge garden. It is tolerant of drought, grows fast when young and is quite showy in bloom, making it a popular choice where space permits.

Wildlife benefits The long yellow catkins are attractive to many pollinating insects, especially bees. The nuts that follow are eaten by mammals, including squirrels, badgers and dormice. The tree is also a good nesting site for woodpeckers, nuthatches and nightingales, while waved carpet moths eat the leaves.

Closely related species The Japanese *C. crenata* and Chinese *C. mollisima* are widely planted in North America with the American chestnut (*C. dentate*) because they are blight-resistant. Note that *C. alnifolia* is a suckering, dwarf, American native just 1m (3ft) high.

Castanea sativa

Cercis siliquastrum
JUDAS TREE
Family: Caesalpiniaceae
Native: E Mediterranean

A handsome, small, deciduous, ornamental tree reaching 6m (20ft) high, it gradually develops a rounded crown and needs well-drained soil and a sunny location. In early summer, lilac pea-like flowers clothe both the branches and the main trunk, and are followed by conspicuous, purple-tinted, bean-like seed pods later in summer.

Cultivation It prefers deep, fertile, moist but well-drained soil in full sun or light shade, and needs hot summers to flower. Plant when young because it resents root disturbance. Propagate seed when ripe. ❊ ❊ ❊ Zone 6.

Uses The Judas tree makes an excellent freestanding specimen, although it can also be planted towards the back of a shrub border or trained against a wall. It is nitrogen-fixing and very drought-tolerant once established, and is notably resistant to honey fungus.

Wildlife benefits The nectar and pollen provide an excellent source of food for insects, especially bees. In the spring the flowers often appear quite early, preceding the foliage. This gives a valuable boost to early, emerging bees, and to some early flying butterfly species.

Closely related species California or Western redbud (*C. occidentalis*) is a large Californian shrub quite similar to the Judas tree, and grows well in a sunny, well-drained site. The Chinese redbud (*C. chinensis*) forms a fine specimen shrub or small tree, and bears lavender to crimson flowers.

Cercis siliquastrum

Crataegus monogyna

Crataegus monogyna
COMMON HAWTHORN
Family: Rosaceae
Native: Europe

This short, deciduous, long-lived, thorny tree is dense with leaves, and is regularly found in naturally regenerating woodland. Its reddish new shoots and leaves are most attractive in late spring or early summer when the distinctive, white, scented blossom appears. The autumn red berries are called haws.

Cultivation It occurs on a wide range of soil types, including very dry and wet ground, and isn't in the least bit fussy, being resistant to both exposure and pollution. Propagate by seed in autumn after stratification. ❀ ❀ ❀ Zone 5.

Uses Hawthorn has long been used to create stock-proof hedges, and is still widely used for this purpose. Cultivars or hybrids are often grown in the garden, but the wild species forms a fine, small specimen tree, with an attractive, deep, rounded dome shape.

Wildlife benefits Hawthorn supports many insects including the caterpillars of over 70 species of moth, and is an important nectar source for others early in the year. The berries provide vital winter food supplies for small mammals and especially birds, such as redwings, fieldfares and waxwings.

Closely related species The red-flowering Midland hawthorn (*C. laevigata*) is similar to *C. monogyna*. The south-east American *C. aestivalis* has large fruit enjoyed by birds, and Washington thorn (*C. phaenopyrum*) has fragrant blooms.

Fagus sylvatica
BEECH
Family: Fagaceae
Native: Europe

This large forest tree eventually forms a large specimen with smooth, metallic grey bark. The rounded crown is very dense and often casts such deep shade that little else can grow beneath it. The spring flowers are followed by triangular nuts with edible kernels in late summer. In autumn, the leaves turn amber and bronze.

Cultivation Beech is usually happiest on moist, alkaline soil, but is very tolerant of a wide range of soils and conditions, and will grow in quite acidic conditions. Young trees are very shade-tolerant. Propagate by seed in late autumn. ❀ ❀ ❀ Zone 5.

Uses Forms a beautiful specimen tree with smooth, grey bark and copper and russet autumn foliage, but it's too large for all but the biggest gardens. It makes a superb hedge however, retaining its foliage through winter, and is useful in a rather shady setting.

Wildlife benefits The nuts are attractive to many small mammals, including mice, voles, squirrels and badgers, with birds such as bramblings, chaffinches and parakeets also eating the seed. The leaves provide food for caterpillars of over 20 moth species, including the green silver-lines and large emerald.

Closely related species American beech (*F. grandifolia*) is also useful for wildlife, and is the only member of the genus found in North America. It makes a fine specimen with leaves initially a light blue, turning golden-bronze in autumn.

Fagus sylvatica

Larix decidua

Larix decidua
EUROPEAN LARCH
Family: Pinaceae
Native: Continental Europe

From the alpine regions of Europe, it is somewhat unusual for a conifer because it is deciduous, shedding its leaves each autumn. The foliage is also less needle-like than most conifers, being soft and light green. In spring the female, rose-coloured cones appear with the more yellowish male ones towards the end of the branches.

Cultivation Larch tends to do well in wetter, hilly districts on well-drained, acidic soil where it can withstand high winds and exposure. Propagate by seed when ripe. ❀ ❀ ❀ Zone 4.

Uses Ultimately forming a large, spreading, handsome tree, with a conical crown when young, becoming broader on maturity, it is too large for smaller gardens. The dwarf, weeping selections, such as *L. decidua* 'Puli,' are better suited to smaller gardens.

Wildlife benefits The light shade cast by larch provides good cover for birds and animals sheltering from the elements. Seed- and bud-eating birds, such as tree creepers, crested tits, redwings and fieldfares, rely on the larch, as do the caterpillars of larch pug and small engrailed moths.

Closely related species Japanese larch (*L. kaempferi*) is probably the most similar species, growing to 45m (145ft), and makes a good shelter, best for a large garden. This species attracts small finches, tits and treecreepers. The European larch (*L. x marschlinsii*) thrives on less fertile soils.

Malus sylvestris

Malus sylvestris
CRAB APPLE
Family: Rosaceae
Native: Europe and W Asia

The crab apple is a small, thorny, deciduous tree, common in oak woods and hedges, and is most highly visible in spring when its abundant blossom – pink in bud and white-pink when open – clothes the branches. The flowers are followed by small, hard fruits that are quite bitter and unpalatable to humans, but are quickly taken by wildlife.

Cultivation Grows most prolifically on chalky soils, and needs to be situated in sun to thrive. It is best planted on well-drained soil, and will grow happily even in heavy clay provided it has been opened up so that it is free-draining. ❀ ❀ ❀ Zone 4.

Uses Besides being an attractive specimen tree in its own right, the crab apple is a good pollinator for fruiting apples. While the wild form can grow up to 10m (33ft) tall, there is also a wide selection of cultivated varieties, with some for small gardens.

Wildlife benefits Crab apples support over 100 different animal species, including crevice-living insects. The caterpillars of over 20 moth species, including the eyed hawkmoth, eat the leaves while the flowers support many insects, and the fruits are eaten by birds, rodents and various insects.

Closely related species Orchard apples are very closely related to *M. sylvestris*, although the fruit is much larger and sweeter. Hall's crab apple (*M. halliana*) is a Chinese species with pink flowers and purple fruits, and the Nagasaki crab apple (*M. cerasifera*) has white flowers and red fruit.

Nothofagus antarctica
SOUTHERN OR ANTARCTIC BEECH
Family: Nothofagaceae
Native: S Chile and Argentina

This native of the temperate rainforests of South America is naturally quite variable, making tall bushes from 2–3m (6½–10ft) high in some places, and in others making 25m (85ft) high trees. It has a slender trunk with attractive, scaly bark while its branches, arranged in a herringbone formation, are covered by small, heart-shaped leaves that turn yellow in autumn.

Cultivation A fast-growing tree that does best in a sunny position on acid loam. It will not tolerate lime but is very hardy, and tolerates wind and drought once properly established. Propagate by seed in autumn. ❀ ❀ ❀ Zone 7.

Uses The large forms make a remarkably attractive tree that is too big for all but the biggest gardens. 'Puget Pillar' is a good example of the dwarf form with more upright branches, and is better suited to medium-sized gardens.

Wildlife benefits Antarctic beech is excellent at supporting wildlife, even in areas where it is not native. It is the larval food plant for many species of ghost moth, and its deep-fissured bark provides shelter for many insects, especially overwintering butterflies. The seeds are eaten by birds.

Closely related species *N. moorei*, found in Australia (and also called Antarctic beech), is somewhat less hardy than its namesake. Two other species, *N. procera* and *N. obliqua*, are also South American, from the same area as *N. antarctica*, and are large, deciduous trees.

Nothofagus antarctica

Pinus sylvestris

Pinus sylvestris

Pinus sylvestris
SCOTS PINE
Family: Pinaceae
Native: Europe

This conifer normally grows up to 25m (85ft) high, although it is variable across its range and can even reach 45m (145ft). The bark is thick, scaly and dark grey-brown on the lower trunk and changes to thin, flaky and orange higher up. The mature tree's habit is distinctive due to its long, bare, straight trunk topped by a rounded or flat-topped mass of foliage.

Cultivation Whilst Scots pine grows on a wide range of soils, it prefers light, dry sands and gravels, and tolerates poor soils, often colonizing areas of heath land. Propagation is by seed. ❀ ❀ ❀ Zone 2.

Uses Although its main use is for forestry, it makes a very attractive specimen, and is used as an accent plant because of its distinctive mature shape. It is too large for most gardens, but try cultivars 'Glauca Nana' and 'Compressa' where space is limited.

Wildlife benefits Scots pine provides nesting sites for many birds, and the seeds are the preferred food of red squirrels and crossbills. A number of moth caterpillars, including the pine beauty, pine carpet and pine hawkmoth, live on it, and the deep-fissured bark provides shelter for many insects.

Closely related species The lodge-pole pine (*P. contorta*) is from western North America where it grows on much wetter soils than Scots pine. The black pine (*P. nigra*) is a southern European relative which grows to 40m (130ft) and has many cultivars.

Prunus avium
WILD CHERRY, GEAN
Family: Rosaceae
Native: Europe, N Africa and
W Asia

The wild cherry can grow to an impressive size, sometimes reaching 30m (100ft) although 15m (50ft) is more common. The flowers appear in clusters on short shoots along the twigs of established wood in spring, and are often spectacular, but the fruits are much less conspicuous than those of cultivated varieties.

Cultivation Easily grown in most fertile soils, but it does not do well on acidic ground. Propagation is usually from seed, though it can be grown from cuttings when taken from young trees. ❀ ❀ ❀ Zone 3.

Uses A stately and very attractive tree, both when in bloom and for the rest of the year. It looks good in naturalistic, mixed planting and is an ideal back-of-the-border specimen for a woodland-edge border. Many cultivated forms are available.

Wildlife benefits During the flowering season the blossom is a good nectar source for a variety of insects, especially bees. The fruits are eaten by numerous bird species that quickly strip them from the trees almost as soon as they are ripe. Green pug moth caterpillars eat the leaves.

Closely related species Wild cherry is one of the parents of most European cultivated cherries, and is very similar to most of them. The bird cherry (*P. padus*) is a small, deciduous tree with flowers in short, branched inflorescences, followed by black, egg-shaped fruit. It prefers moist sites.

Prunus avium

Pyrus communis
COMMON PEAR
Family: Rosaceae
Native: C and E Europe and
SW Asia

A medium-sized tree that is likely to reach 10m (33ft) high but can, if conditions are ideal, double that. It has glossy, oval leaves that turn from dark green to orange and red in autumn. The conspicuous, white, star-shaped flowers with five petals appear in spring. A mass of white flowers open in April.

Cultivation Grows in full sun on most fertile, well-drained soil, although a sandy or clay loam with a pH of 5–7 is best. It has strong, vertical branches and requires little pruning. Propagate by seed in spring. ❀ ❀ ❀ Zone 4.

Uses Its narrow and rather conical form, coupled with the fact that it casts fairly light shade, means it can be grown in a lawn without badly affecting the grass. It is very attractive when flowering in spring, and the glossy, bright green leaves sometimes colour up well in autumn.

Wildlife benefits Finches may attack young shoots, and blossom and green pug moths also feed on the flowers. The open flowers are an excellent source of nectar, especially for bees. Hawkmoths feed on the leaves, and many species eat the overripe fruit in autumn.

Closely related species The European pear probably descended from two species of wild pear, *P. pyraster* and *P. caucasica*, both of which hybridize with the domestic species. Willow-leaved pear (*Pyrus salicifolia*) is grown widely as an ornamental tree.

Pyrus communis

Quercus robur

Quercus robur
ENGLISH OAK
Family: Fagaceae
Native: Europe, Asia Minor and
N Africa

A large, long-lived, deciduous tree that reaches 25–35m (85–115ft) in height, with a large, wide-spreading head of rugged branches. While it may naturally live to a few hundred years old, some coppiced oaks are known to be over 1,000 years old and the whole tree, including the deadwood, is an extremely valuable habitat for wildlife.

Cultivation The oak grows on a range of soils, including heavy clay, and has a pH tolerance ranging from 4.5–7.5. Mature trees are very robust and will tolerate flooding, even by seawater. Propagate by seed in late autumn. ❀ ❀ ❀ Zone 6.

Uses Oaks are ultimately large trees that dominate the landscape. In the garden, they need plenty of space and are only really suited to a large site. The variety 'Fastigiata' has erect branches and a narrow, pyramidal form, and is useful if you want to limit the amount of shade cast.

Wildlife benefits Mature trees can support over 300 species of insects that, in turn, feed birds such as woodpeckers, tree creepers and nuthatches. Acorns feed small mammals and the likes of jays, and the leaves are a larval food source for over 100 moth and butterfly species.

Closely related species The sessile oak (*Q. petraea*) shares much of the English oak's range, and the two often hybridize in the wild, creating *Q. x rosacea*. The white oak (*Q. alba*), from America, is very similar, but slightly taller.

Salix caprea
GOAT WILLOW
Family: Salicaceae
Native: Europe and NW Africa

Also known as the pussy willow or great sallow, this deciduous shrub or small tree reaches a height of 6–14m (20–45ft), or more rarely 20m (66ft). The leaves are broader than those of most other willows, and the spring catkins emerge before the foliage and resemble animal fur, hence the name pussy willow.

Cultivation Goat willow grows in both wet and dry ground, wherever bare soil is available. Unlike almost all other willows, goat willow does not take root readily from cuttings. Propagate by seed. ❀ ❀ ❀ Zone 5.

Uses The species is not often planted because of its somewhat unruly nature in the garden. 'Kilmarnock' is a cultivated variety with pretty catkins borne in early spring, and a weeping habit. It is normally grafted on to a rootstock to give height to what would otherwise be a small tree.

Wildlife benefits Goat willow is visited by early emerging bees that collect the abundant pollen, which also provides larval food for the poplar hawkmoth, puss moth and many other insects. Many invertebrates hide in the cracks and splits that appear in the bark and stems of older trees.

Closely related species Willow is a variable and widespread genus with many closely related species. White willow (*S. alba*), crack willow (*S. fragilis*) and bay willow (*S. pentandra*) all occur naturally in the same area as the goat willow, and introduced species readily naturalize.

Salix caprea

Sorbus aucuparia
MOUNTAIN ASH
Family: Rosaceae
Native: Europe and W Asia

This small- to medium-sized deciduous tree, also known as rowan, grows up to 20m (66ft) high but is often smaller, and is common in temperate European regions. It has divided leaves, bunches of white flowers and red, edible berries. It is very tolerant of cold, and is often found at high altitude on mountains, hence its common name.

Cultivation Grows best in humus-rich, lime-free, moderately fertile soil, provided it isn't waterlogged. It is also pollution-tolerant, although it dislikes shading. Propagate seed when ripe. ❀ ❀ ❀ Zone 2.

Uses Mountain ash is ideal for a wide variety of gardens, usually being medium height and relatively compact growing. It is ideal for birds or a forest-edge border, and is extremely decorative when adorned with blossom in spring, or autumn berries.

Wildlife benefits In early summer the abundant, small, white, nectar-rich flowers are extremely popular with bees. The berries that follow are especially liked by starlings, finches, waxwings and thrushes, with leaves being eaten by several moths, including the brimstone and orange underwing.

Closely related species Over 60 species of *Sorbus* are closely related to mountain ash, including the sargent's rowan (*S. sargentiana*) and the small-leaf rowan (*S. microphylla*), both from China, and American mountain ash (*S. americana*) and showy mountain ash (*S. decora*).

Sorbus aucuparia

Tilia cordata

Tilia cordata
SMALL-LEAVED LIME
Family: Malvaceae
Native: Europe

Lime trees are a highly variable genus, and are mostly deciduous, medium to large trees. *T. cordata* typically grows 15–18m (50–60ft) high but can reach 25–28m (85–90ft). They are pyramidal or conical when young, gradually becoming ovate when mature with a dense, compact nature consisting of upright and spreading branches.

Cultivation Lime prefers moist, deep, fertile, well-drained soil but also tolerates poor ground, drought, a range of pH and air pollution, and is easy to transplant. Propagate by seed in autumn. ❀ ❀ ❀ Zone 3.

Uses Small-leaved lime has sweet-smelling flowers and is an attractive tree that has been widely planted along roads and in parks where it can be pollarded or heavily pruned. It can also be grown as a large hedge.

Wildlife benefits Lime is an excellent nectar source, especially for bees, and unlike many large forest trees is pollinated by insects rather than the wind. Numerous moths eat the foliage, including the lime hawkmoth and orange sallow, and the seeds are taken by some birds.

Closely related species Limes hybridize very freely, with common lime being a hybrid of *T. cordata* and large-leaved lime (*T. platyphyllos*), a widely grown street tree. Small-leaved lime is widely cultivated in North America as a substitute for the American linden (*T. americana*), which has a larger leaf.

CLIMBERS

Clematis tangutica
CLEMATIS
Family: Ranunculaceae
Native: Mongolia and NW China

A vigorous, summer-to-autumn-flowering clematis that grows to 3m (10ft) high. The drooping, lantern-shaped, golden-yellow flowers are borne on new shoots, and are followed by gorgeous, decorative, fluffy, silvery seed heads. The abundant, bright green leaves are deeply divided into lance-shaped leaflets.

Cultivation Grow in shade or full sun. It prefers its roots in rich, free-draining soil in shade. Propagate by semi-ripe cuttings in summer. ❀ ❀ ❀ Zone 5.

Uses Like many other clematis, it is grown for its flowers and seed heads, and is best displayed when trained on walls and trellises. It can also be trained up trees or grown through other climbers, such as roses, to add extra interest.

Wildlife benefits Bees and bumblebees visit the flowers seeking nectar, and the flower buds are eaten by bullfinches. The seed heads are eaten by birds and used to make nests. The mass of unpruned, twining stems are ideal places for birds to secure their nests.

Closely related species Old man's beard (*C. vitalba*) is a rampant climber with small, white, nectar-rich flowers visited by bumblebees, bees, hoverflies and night-flying moths, and seeds eaten by birds. *C. montana* is used in ornamental gardens where bees visit the flowers for pollen.

Clematis tangutica

Hedera helix

Hedera helix
COMMON IVY
Family: Araliaceae
Native: Europe, Scandinavia and Russia

This vigorous, evergreen, self-clinging climber grows to 10m (33ft) high. It has two distinct phases, the juvenile and adult, the main difference being the leaf shape. The juvenile leaves are small and 5-lobed whereas the adult foliage is simple and ovate. The yellow-green flowers are borne from autumn, and are followed by black berries from winter to spring.

Cultivation Site in sun or semi- to full shade, in any well-drained, alkaline soil. Propagate by softwood cuttings of new growth in summer. ❀ ❀ ❀ Zone 5.

Uses Ivies are excellent for covering large areas, such as walls, sheds and tree stumps. They are also frequently used as ground cover in gardens where the evergreen foliage acts as a foil for the border plants, especially in winter and spring.

Wildlife benefits The flowers provide late nectar for bees, hoverflies and butterflies. The flower buds are eaten by the caterpillar of the holly blue butterfly. The berries provide valuable winter food for birds, particularly thrushes and finches. Birds, such as wrens and blackbirds, nest in the foliage.

Closely related species Persian ivy (*H. colchica*) and Irish ivy (*H. hibernica*) are two of the best species for covering large areas. *H. c.* 'Dentata Variegata' has attractive variegated, cream-yellow leaves.

Humulus lupulus
HOP
Family: Cannabaceae
Native: Northern temperate regions

This herbaceous, twining climber can reach up to 6m (20ft) each year. It displays hairy, rough stems and deeply divided, 3–5 lobed leaves. There are separate male and female plants, and it is the female that is grown ornamentally. It produces green-yellow fruits that hang in clusters from autumn.

Cultivation Thrives in full sun or semi-shade in deep, fertile, well-drained soil. Grow the golden 'Aureus' in full sun for the best foliage colour. Propagate by tip cuttings in spring. ❀ ❀ ❀ Zone 5.

Uses Hops are traditionally used to make beer, but in gardens they are brilliant for clothing a pergola or arch, and for screening a fence or wall. Grow 'Aureus' with large, purple-flowering clematis to create a striking colour combination.

Wildlife benefits The caterpillars of the comma butterfly and the buttoned snout moth (also recorded on the cultivar 'Aureus') feed on the leaves. Small birds will use the dried hop fruits as nesting material. If left uncut, the stems will harbour overwintering insects.

Closely related species Most gardeners grow 'Aureus' because of its beautiful lime-green leaves. The Japanese *H. japonicus* is normally grown as an annual in temperate climates, and 'Variegatus' has blotched and streaked white foliage.

Humulus lupulus

Jasminum officinale

Jasminum officinale
COMMON JASMINE
Family: Oleaceae
Native: Asia Minor, Himalayas and China

This semi-evergreen (sometimes deciduous) twining climber can reach up to 12m (40ft) high. The dark green leaves are deeply divided, each leaf comprising 7–9 leaflets. Clusters of white, tubular flowers are borne from summer to autumn. Common jasmine is one of the best fragrant plants.

Cultivation Plant in a sunny, sheltered position that is protected from harsh winds. Grow in moist, fertile, free-draining soil. Propagate by semi-ripe cuttings in late summer. ❀ ❀ Zone 7.

Uses Common jasmine is ideal for growing up a pergola, trellis or archway. Also plant next to a path, door or seating area because of its amazing scent. Frequently selected for a specialist moth border.

Wildlife benefits The sweetly scented flowers are excellent at attracting bees and butterflies by day, while at night the visiting moths will attract bats to the area. The dense mat of twining stems is ideal for birds to nest in, and for foraging. Roosting insects are frequent visitors.

Closely related species
J. polyanthum, to 3m (10ft) high, is an evergreen, twining climber that produces clusters of scented white flowers from late summer to winter. Winter jasmine (*J. nudiflorum*) is a deciduous arching shrub bearing bright yellow flowers in winter.

Lathyrus latifolius
PERENNIAL PEA
Family: Fabaceae
Native: C and S Europe

This herbaceous, perennial climber dies down every winter and re-emerges in spring. The stems climb by tendrils and can reach up to 3m (10ft) in a season. The pea-like, rose-pink flowers are borne from summer to autumn but aren't scented. The leaflets are borne in pairs, and are grey-green terminating in a 3-branched tendril.

Cultivation For best results, plant in full sun although it can stand partial shade, and grow in moderately fertile, well-drained soil. Propagate by seed or division in spring. ❀ ❀ ❀ Zone 5.

Uses Peas are often grown up an ornate wigwam of bamboo canes or, better still, on pollarded hazel stems. They are also ideal for covering and rambling across hot, sunny banks. Can also be planted in informal hanging baskets to cascade over the sides.

Wildlife benefits The pollen-rich flowers, complete with two large nectar glands, attract many insects including bees, bumblebees, butterflies and beetles. The leaves are eaten by the caterpillar of the long-tailed blue butterfly. Site in full sun for optimum insect visits.

Closely related species The everlasting pea (*L. grandiflorus*), to 1.5m (5ft) high, is a herbaceous perennial with pink-purple and red flowers in summer. The sweet pea (*L. odoratus*) is a hardy annual climber with large, fragrant flowers from summer to early autumn.

Lathyrus latifolius

Lonicera periclymenum

Lonicera periclymenum
COMMON HONEYSUCKLE
Family: Caprifoliaceae
Native: Europe, Asia Minor, Caucasus and W Asia

Beautiful fragrant flowers adorn this twining climber that can reach up to 4m (13ft) high. The opposite green-bluish leaves are rounded and slightly hairy. The scented, tubular flowers are red and yellow-white, and can extend to 5cm (2in) long, being followed by spherical red fruits.

Cultivation Plant in moist but well-drained soil enriched with organic matter, such as leaf mould. Grow in full sun or part shade. Propagate by semi-ripe cuttings in summer. ❀ ❀ ❀ Zone 4.

Uses Ideal for growing on a trellis, wall, pergola, fence, or over an old tree stump. Plant a honeysuckle every 3–5m (10–17ft) along a mixed hedgerow to enrich the habitat. Keep the roots in the shade and the top growth in full sun.

Wildlife benefits The nectar-rich flowers attract moths, particularly hawkmoths, in midsummer. The shiny red berries are eaten by birds, especially song thrushes, blackbirds, tits, robins and finches. Old bark is stripped off by pied flycatchers and dormice to use as nesting material.

Closely related species *L. nitida* makes an excellent hedge. *L. n.* 'Baggescens Gold' is an attractive golden-leaved cultivar. The dense foliage attracts many nesting birds. *L.* x *purpusii* is a semi-evergreen shrub with nectar-rich flowers from winter to spring, providing food for early emerging insects.

Parthenocissus quinquefolia

Parthenocissus quinquefolia
VIRGINIA CREEPER
Family: Vitaceae
Native: E North America to Mexico

A self-clinging climber that hauls itself up by tendrils and adhesive pads. The stems can reach to 30m (100ft) high, and bear deciduous, dull green leaves, each with 3–5 leaflets. The foliage produces spectacular autumn colour when it turns flashy rich crimson. The summer flowers are insignificant, but are followed by small blue fruits.

Cultivation Virginia creeper enjoys deep, moist soil with plenty of organic matter. Plant in partial shade for the best autumn colour. Propagate by sowing fresh seed. ❀ ❀ ❀ Zone 3.

Uses Ideal for growing over pergolas, walls, buildings and fences, and for growing up through trees. Only use where you have room, and where it can be trimmed regularly and prevented from snaking under and disturbing the roof tiles.

Wildlife benefits The mass of stems host a variety of wildlife, sheltering insects and nesting birds, while the leaves are eaten by the Virginia creeper sphinx moth caterpillar. The round, blue berries are eaten by birds, including mistle thrushes, blackcaps and magpies.

Closely related species *P. henryana*, which can reach up to 5m (17ft) high, is more suited to a small garden. The green-pink, veined, compound leaves are its most striking feature. Boston ivy (*P. tricuspidata*) is another rampant species that should be used with caution.

Phaseolus coccineus
SCARLET RUNNER BEAN
Family: Fabaceae
Native: Tropical America

Often just called runner bean, this is a tender, twining, perennial vine with bright red flowers. Due to its tenderness to frost, it is usually grown as an annual. The stems can reach a height of 4m (13ft) in a year, and produce edible seed pods 10–30cm (4–12in) long. The round seeds are red to purple.

Cultivation It enjoys a warm, sheltered spot in free-draining soil. Sow outdoors in mid-spring, or sow under glass and harden off before planting outside. ❀ Zone 10.

Uses Traditionally used in the vegetable garden, but why not try growing it up a wigwam of hazel stems in the ornamental garden, either in the herbaceous or mixed border, or in pots. It can also be used to clothe archways or a trellis.

Wildlife benefits Runner beans are pollinated by bees as they manoeuvre into the bright red flowers to reach the nectar. Bumblebees have been observed eating part of the flower near the nectaries to gain easy access to the sugary drink.

Closely related species An alternative, but not as good for wildlife, is the self-fertile French bean (*Phaseolus vulgaris*). Research indicates that only 8 per cent of a yield is caused by bee pollination. Beekeepers do not consider this crop an important source of nectar and pollen.

Phaseolus coccineus

Pisum sativum
GARDEN PEA
Family: Fabaceae
Native: S Europe

The garden pea is an annual grown for its edible seed pods. The climber grows to 2m (6½ft) high using its tendrils. The leaves are deeply divided into 1–4 pairs of leaflets. The pretty flowers are white, and sometimes stained with red-purple markings. The thin, oblong seed pods that follow can grow to 15cm (6in) long.

Cultivation It grows best in an open but sheltered site, and the soil should be deep and fertile. Ideally, manure or compost should have been added the previous autumn. Sow seeds outside in spring. ❀ ❀ ❀ Zone 5.

Uses Netting usually protects the garden peas, and can be lifted after cropping has finished to allow the wildlife to move in. Alternatively, grow in pots or up ornamental wigwams.

Wildlife benefits Although pea flowers produce nectar and pollen, it is rarely in large quantities, making the pea seeds the big benefit to wildlife. The seeds are eaten by birds, especially wood pigeons, blue tits, siskins, linnets, crossbills and other finches.

Closely related species The everlasting pea (*Lathyrus grandiflorus*) is a perennial reaching 2m (6½ft) high. The violet flowers are borne in summer. *L. laetiflorus*, a native to western North America, is a perennial with white-pink flowers.

Pisum sativum

Rosa banksiae

Rosa banksiae
BANKSIA ROSE
Family: Rosaceae
Native: W and C China

A strong climber, it can grow up to 12m (40ft) high. The yellow or white, fragrant flowers are borne in umbels in early summer. The flowers are usually single but occasionally double, and are followed by dull red fruits. The glossy, evergreen leaves are divided into 3–7 leaflets.

Cultivation Plant in full sun for the best results where it will tolerate a range of soils, but the ground must be free-draining. Mulch in winter to protect the roots. Propagate by hardwood cuttings in autumn. ❊ ❊ ❊ Zone 7.

Uses A tall species rose that can be used to grow up the front of large houses, fences and walls, but it will only thrive in a sunny, sheltered location. Grow a red or pink large-flowering clematis through the rose for added interest.

Wildlife benefits Bees and bumblebees are attracted to the flowers seeking pollen. The flowers are followed by hips that, when mature, are eaten by small mammals and birds. Many insects, including ladybirds and lacewings, overwinter in the stems and foliage.

Closely related species If choosing a cultivar or variety to plant, select *R. b.* var. *normalis* or the cultivar *R. b.* 'Lutescens' for their single, scented flowers. Do not select double-flowering cultivars, or varieties such as *R. banksiae* var. *banksiae* or the cultivar 'Lutea' with double yellow flowers, because these are of little use to wildlife.

Vitis vinifera
COMMON GRAPE VINE
Family: Vitaceae
Native: S and C Europe

The common grape vine is a deciduous, woody-stemmed climber that can grow up to 7m (23ft). The pale green, insignificant flowers borne in clusters from late spring to early summer are followed by bunches of green or purple fruits. The leaves are palmate with 3–5 lobes, and are slightly hairy when young.

Cultivation Thrives in fertile, free-draining, chalky soil in sun or semi-shade. Produces best fruits in full sun. Propagate by hardwood cuttings in late winter. ❊ ❊ ❊ Zone 6.

Uses A valuable plant used for clothing a pergola or planted against a sunny wall. It will give a tropical feel to a garden, especially around a seating area. A purple-leaved cultivar, such as 'Purpurea', stands out well against a white wall.

Wildlife benefits The fruits are eaten by birds, including collared doves, green woodpeckers, tits, starlings, thrushes, warblers and finches. The intricate branch work is an ideal habitat for roosting and hibernating insects, and for birds to use as nesting sites.

Closely related species *V. coignetiae* is a rampant climber that can grow to 15m (50ft) high. It is grown solely for its luscious foliage. 'Brant' has bright green leaves that turn a lovely red autumn colour, and produces green or purple fruits.

Wisteria sinensis
CHINESE WISTERIA
Family: Fabaceae
Native: China

A vigorous climber that twines anticlockwise, and reaches up to 10m (33ft) high. The deep-green leaves are deeply divided into 7–13 leaflets, and the faintly scented blue-lilac flowers are borne in hanging racemes from late spring. The flowers are followed by seed pods that can be up to 15cm (6in) long.

Cultivation Wisteria thrives in full sun and in fertile, free-draining soil. It is best to buy or propagate plants by grafting rather than from seed because the latter often have poor flowers. ❊ ❊ ❊ Zone 5.

Uses Wisteria is a beautiful climber that looks fantastic on the front of a period property. It can also look elegant on pergolas, walls and fences, but avoid planting in a restricted space because it is rampant.

Wildlife benefits Visited by insects, including bees for nectar and pollen, and several species of butterfly seeking nectar. The unruly network of stems provides excellent roosting and nesting sites for birds and many insects. Take care not to select double-flowering varieties.

Closely related species Japanese wisteria (*W. floribunda*), with clockwise-turning stems, is a deciduous, woody climber that grows to 9m (30ft) high, and produces scented, lilac flowers. *W. venusta* bears white scented flowers in early summer.

Vitis vinifera

Wisteria sinensis

POND AND BOG PLANTS

Butomus umbellatus
FLOWERING RUSH
Family: Butomaceae
Native: Eurasia

A deciduous perennial ideally suited to marginal water areas. It is grown for its colourful display of delicate pink to rose-red flowers borne in flower-packed umbels in summer. The rush-like leaves are bronze-purple when young, becoming green, narrow and twisted, and the plant can grow up to 1.5m (5ft) high.

Cultivation and uses Site in soil that is immersed in water around the pond margins, or plant in aquatic containers and grow in up to 15cm (6in) of water. Propagate by division in spring, or by seed in spring or late summer. ❀ ❀ ❀ Zone 5.

Wildlife benefits The plant attracts insect-eating birds that seek out water lily aphids, and other insects that use the leaves for cover and also visit the flowers. Birds visiting the pond for a drink use the foliage as protection.

Closely related species There are no closely related species to the flowering rush (it's a one-species genus). Bogbean (*Menyanthes trifoliate*) fills a similar niche and is very effective in bogs and shallow, marginal areas. It attracts elephant hawkmoths and bees seeking nectar.

Caltha palustris

Caltha palustris
MARSH MARIGOLD
Family: Ranunculaceae
Native: Northern temperate regions

The beautiful, single, bright golden-yellow flowers are a welcome sight in early spring. As the common name suggests, it is a marginal water plant that has a small, domed habit, and bears dark green leaves that act as an effective foil for the bright flowers. It is a compact plant, to 60cm (2ft) high.

Cultivation and uses The marsh marigold is one of the most popular marginal pond plants. Site in soil, or around the pond edges in water no deeper than 23cm (9in). It can also be grown in a bog garden in full sun or light shade. Propagate by seed in autumn, or division in autumn or early spring. ❀ ❀ ❀ Zone 3.

Wildlife benefits Being one of the first spring flowers to bloom, it offers a welcome source of early nectar for bees and butterflies emerging from hibernation. The dense foliage provides welcome shelter for small insects such as beetles, and amphibians.

Closely related species
C. leptosepala grows to 30cm (1ft) high and is a fantastic little marginal water plant with white, buttercup-like flowers. Take care not to select the double-flowering cultivars of *Caltha palustris*, such as 'Flore Pleno' or 'Monstrosa', because they are of little benefit to wildlife.

Eupatorium cannabinum
HEMP AGRIMONY
Family: Asteraceae
Native: Europe

This vigorous, herbaceous perennial sports the prettiest pink flower heads, made up of small, starry flowers in late summer. It grows up to 2m (6½ft) a season, so avoid in small spaces. The leaves are lance-shaped and up to 12cm (5in) long.

Cultivation and uses Bog gardens are ideal sites because the roots thrive in moist soil. Site in partial shade as prolonged periods of strong sunlight cause wilting and, in severe cases, permanent cell damage occurs, especially if the soil dries out. Propagate by division or seed in spring. ❀ ❀ ❀ Zone 5.

Wildlife benefits One of the best plants for a wildlife garden because the flowers are always heaving with insects, particularly the small tortoiseshell, red admiral and peacock butterflies. Bees are also frequent visitors searching for pollen and nectar.

Closely related species 'Album' bears soft white flowers, but avoid the double flowers of 'Flore Pleno' because it will not provide the insects with sufficient nectar. The North American Joe Pye weed (*E. maculatum*) is also suited to bog gardens.

Butomus umbellatus

Eupatorium cannabinum

Filipendula ulmaria

Filipendula ulmaria
MEADOW SWEET
Family: Rosaceae
Native: W Asia and Europe

Meadow sweet bears clusters of creamy white flowers with a sweet almond scent in midsummer. The stems bear deeply divided, feathery foliage (which also has a slight fragrance), and grow to 90cm (3ft) high. Small, shiny seeds appear in autumn, and are taken by several species of birds and small mammals.

Cultivation and uses Best grown in a bog garden where the roots will be moist but not waterlogged. It is also suited to a woodland garden if the soil holds plenty of moisture. Plant in full sun or semi-shade, but it must be an open area so that bats can capture the moths taking the nectar in the evening. Propagate by division in autumn or winter. ❀ ❀ ❀ Zone 2.

Wildlife benefits The plants attract many summer insects, especially the bees, hoverflies and moths attracted to the scented flowers, and they in turn attract insectivorous birds. The seeds are again eaten by birds, especially finches, and the foliage provides good cover.

Closely related species Queen of the prairie (*F. rubra*), a native of eastern North America, is an excellent plant for the bog garden. It is an erect, vigorous perennial bearing large, soft pink flower heads in summer, and can reach up to 2m (6½ft) high.

Geum rivale
WATER AVENS
Family: Rosaceae
Native: Europe

This herbaceous perennial naturally occurs at the side of ponds and streams. It bears small clusters of pendent, white to dull purplish-pink, cup-shaped flowers from late spring to summer. The long sepals are reddish-brown and the oblong leaves dark green.

Cultivation and uses Grow at the front of a bog garden where the flowers and foliage soften the edge of the area. It can also be used in wildflower meadows and naturalistic plantings provided the soil is moisture-retentive. Site in full sun for best results. Propagate by seed in autumn, or division in spring or autumn. ❀ ❀ ❀ Zone 3.

Wildlife benefits The flowers are popular with bees seeking pollen. If planted in small or large groups, the foliage will provide cover for amphibians and invertebrates and create a moist, shady place that is essential in hot summer weather for frogs and toads.

Closely related species Many cultivars of *Geum rivale* are available. 'Album' sports delightful white flowers with light green leaves and 'Leonardii', formerly 'Leonard's Variety', has gorgeous copper-pink-tinted orange flowers. Do not select *G. rivale* 'Leonardii Double' because the number of petals on each flower will greatly affect the amount of pollen produced.

Geum rivale

Iris pseudacorus

Iris pseudacorus
YELLOW FLAG IRIS
Family: Iridaceae
Native: Europe to W Siberia, Turkey, Iran and N Africa

A robust, rhizomatous, beardless iris that can easily grow to 2m (6½ft) high. From early to midsummer each branched stem produces from 4–12 yellow-golden flowers with brown or violet veins, and a blotch of deeper yellow. The dull green leaves are broad and ridged, and display a prominent mid-rib. The foliage forms a dense thicket for wildlife to hide in.

Cultivation and uses Use as a marginal pond plant as it will grow in water up to 15cm (6in) deep, or it can also be planted in a bog garden. It thrives in full sun or semi-shade. Propagate by division of clumps in early autumn or mid-spring. ❀ ❀ ❀ Zone 5.

Wildlife benefits In summer, bees and hoverflies visit the flowers seeking nectar. Dragonfly larvae will also use the tall leaves to climb out of the water and pupate on, before emerging and flying off as adults. The dense foliage provides cover for birds visiting nearby water, and amphibians are often seen sheltering between the leaves.

Closely related species 'Variegata' has yellow- and green-striped foliage in spring, but can turn all-green later in the season. Japanese flag (*I. ensata*), with red-purple flowers, is ideal for marginal or bog gardens.

Lychnis flos-cuculi

Lychnis flos-cuculi
RAGGED ROBIN
Family: Caryophyllaceae
Native: Europe, Caucasus
and Siberia

Ragged robin sports pale to bright pink-purple, large flowers with deeply divided petals, giving it a ragged look. They are borne from late spring to early summer and measure 5cm (2in) across, which is large considering that the plant is 45cm (18in) tall. The basal leaves are green and lance-shaped.

Cultivation and uses Ragged robin naturally grows in water meadows and is ideally suited to damp areas of grassland. Alternatively it can be planted in a bog garden where the soil is not waterlogged permanently, but holds moisture all year round. Best grown in full sun, but it will tolerate semi-shade. Propagate by seed or division in autumn or spring. ✿ ✿ ✿ Zone 6.

Wildlife benefits The nectar-rich flowers attract many species of insect, including hoverflies, bees, several species of long-tongued bee and butterflies, from late spring onwards. In Europe the caterpillars of the campion and lychnis moths feed on the flower buds.

Closely related species The single-flowering white form, *L. f.* 'Alba', is an excellent choice, but avoid any cultivar with 'Plena' in the name because it means double flowering (as in 'Alba Plena' or 'Rosea Plena'). Too many petals inhibit creatures seeking the nectar.

Lythrum salicaria
PURPLE LOOSESTRIFE
Family: Lythraceae
Native: NE North America

A "must" when planting a pond. Tall spikes of bright reddish-purple flowers are produced from midsummer to early autumn, and extend up to 1.2m (4ft) high. The mid-green leaves are lance-like, and are usually opposite each other.

Cultivation and uses An ideal candidate for a marginal pond area or a bog garden because the roots thrive in soil that is moist or wet. Purple loosestrife is also suited to a dappled shady area in a woodland garden, provided plenty of organic matter has been incorporated to increase the moisture content of the soil. Site in full sun, though it will tolerate semi-shade. Propagate by division of clumps in autumn or by seed in spring. ✿ ✿ ✿ Zone 3.

Wildlife benefits The flowers attract bees and butterflies, and the leaves are eaten by the caterpillars of hawkmoths. Leave the stems uncut over winter to allow beneficial insects to hibernate in the dead foliage during the dormant season.

Closely related species *L. virgatum* is a clump-forming perennial, and is less vigorous than *L. salicaria*. *L. v.* 'Rose Queen' sports light pink flowers and reaches 90cm (3ft) high, and *L. v.* 'The Rocket', again to 90cm (3ft) high, produces a mass of rose-red flowers in summer.

Lythrum salicaria

Mentha aquatica
WATER MINT
Family: Lamiaceae
Native: Eurasia

In amongst the rampant stem growth of water mint, the most dainty, delicate, lilac-pink flowers can be found in late summer. The round flower heads are numerous, and start to flower from the bottom of the reddish-purple stems upwards. The stems can reach to 90cm (3ft) high, and bear scented, dark green leaves tinged purple.

Cultivation and uses Water mint is a marginal plant that is normally sited around the peripheral area of a pond. It can be grown in slightly deeper water if it is no more than 15cm (6in) above the roots. Site in full sun or semi-shade. Because water mint can become invasive, regularly check its growth after flowering. Not recommended for a small pond. Propagate by removing and replanting the rhizomes in spring. ✿ ✿ ✿ Zone 6.

Wildlife benefits The nectar-rich flowers are often covered with bees and butterflies. The foliage is eaten by caterpillars of moths, including water ermine and large ranunculus. The leaves and stems soon make dense cover and offer shelter to amphibians and insects.

Closely related species Try the dwarf form, *M. aquatica* var. *crispa*, which is more suited to a small pond. This ornamental cultivar has crinkled, curled, scented leaves.

Mentha aquatica

Myosotis palustris

Myosotis palustris
WATER FORGET-ME-NOT
Family: Boraginaceae
Native: Europe, Asia and
N America

A deciduous, herbaceous perennial, it forms neat, spreading mounds and produces narrow, mid-green leaves that complement the pretty, powder-blue summer flowers.

Cultivation and uses Ideal for very shallow marginal pond areas or a bog garden because the roots need permanently wet soil to grow successfully. Also effective along a straight edge of a pond to soften the boundary. Place in full sun or semi-shade. Propagate by seed in autumn. ❄ ❄ ❄ Zone 4.

Wildlife benefits The flowers are visited by bees and bumblebees seeking nectar and pollen, and by butterflies after the nectar. The tiny seeds produced are loved by the likes of finches, while many small invertebrates and amphibians hide out in the dense foliage.

Closely related species
M. scorpioides and *M. laxa* also like shallow water or bog gardens. The former has bright blue flowers and reaches 1m (3ft) high, while the latter is less vigorous, growing to 50cm (20in) high, again bearing bright blue flowers.

Nymphaea alba
WHITE WATER LILY
Family: Nymphaeaceae
Native: Eurasia and N Africa

The flowers of water lilies are exquisite. The summer blooms produce semi-double, pure white flowers with beautiful golden centres and can grow up to 10cm (4in) wide. The abundance of shiny, dark green, rounded leaves, up to 30cm (1ft) wide, set off the pale-coloured flowers. They are red when young, and tend to hug the water surface.

Cultivation and uses Water lilies enjoy an open, sunny position in still, deep water, the depth depending on the species. *N. alba* thrives when planted at a depth of 60cm (2ft). Propagate by dividing and replanting the roots, which are tuber-like rhizomes, every 3–4 years. ❄ ❄ ❄ Zone 5.

Wildlife benefits The flowers are visited by insects, including beetles. The dense foliage is used by basking frogs and dragonflies, and by foraging water birds. Water invertebrates hide in the shade of the leaves during the hot summer months.

Closely related species *N. citrina* has open, yellow, scented flowers and is a good choice for small ponds. *N.* 'Mexicana' is similar to *N. citrina*, with a slightly smaller flower. *N. odorata*, from eastern North America, bears fragrant white flowers.

Typha minima
MINIATURE REED MACE
Family: Typhaceae
Native: Eurasia

Miniature reed mace is grown for its decorative, poker-like, cylindrical seed heads that appear in late summer. The rounded leaves can reach up to 45–60cm (18–24in) high, and the roots bear needle-like tips that can easily pierce pond liners. Care should be taken when selecting reed mace for your pond.

Cultivation and uses Use miniature reed mace in marginal areas of a pond,

Typha minima

either planted in soil or in a basket. Place it on a pond shelf at a maximum of 30cm (1ft) of water. Site in sun or part-shade. Due to the intricate root system it can be used as a soil stabilizer on banks of soil. Propagate by seed or by division of the rootstock in spring. ❄ ❄ ❄ Zone 6.

Wildlife benefits The fluffy seed heads are often used by birds for nesting material. The intricate root system collects pond silt and debris, making it a rich breeding ground for pond invertebrates and overwintering amphibians.

Closely related species *T. latifolia* is a large, herbaceous perennial that can grow to 2.5m (8ft) high, but can be invasive in a small pond. It produces spikes of light brown flowers in late summer, followed by decorative, dark brown, cylindrical seed heads in autumn.

Nymphaea alba

FUNGI AND DECOMPOSERS

Agaricus campestris
FIELD MUSHROOM
Family: Agaricaceae
Native: Eurasia and America
This common wild mushroom is closely related to the cultivated mushroom *A. bisporus*, one of the most important of all edible mushroom crops. *A. campestris* is most frequently encountered in meadows, but also grows in gardens.
Appearance The mushroom is 3–10cm (1¼–4in) in diameter, with a creamy white cap, sometimes developing small scales as it matures. The cap margin is down-turned when fully expanded.
Role in garden habitats The field mushroom is a decomposing organism, with the mushroom cap being only part of the fungus. The rest – a mass of white threads called *mycelium* – remains beneath the soil, breaking down organic matter and recycling nutrients.
Wildlife benefits Rather surprisingly, and in spite of its edibility for humans, the field mushroom is actually eaten by comparatively few garden creatures, although the caps often become heavily infested with maggots. On the whole, though, its benefits are mostly as a decomposer and recycler.
Closely related species There are several other similar species, including some poisonous mushrooms with which it can easily be confused. The yellow staining mushroom (*A. xanthodermus*) can cause serious stomach upsets, and is distinguished by the fact that it turns yellow when cut or bruised.

Agaricus campestris

Amanita muscaria

Amanita muscaria
FLY AGARIC
Family: Amanitaceae
Native: Northern Hemisphere
This distinctive fungus, native to birch (*Betula*), pine (*Pinus*), spruce (*Picea*) and fir woodlands of the Northern Hemisphere and high elevations of central North America, is generally encountered in autumn. The common name is thought to derive from its European use as a crude insecticide, when sprinkled in milk.
Appearance Fly agaric is a large, imposing, white-gilled, white-spotted, red mushroom, making it one of the most recognizable of any fungus. It features in many folk- and fairytales.
Role in garden habitats Fly agaric is a type of fungus called a *mycorrhiza*, and is important because a plant's roots and the fungus form a mutual association. The plant supplies the fungus with food (sugars) and, in return, the fungus helps the root absorb mineral nutrients from the soil.
Wildlife benefits While fly agaric is poisonous and therefore eaten by very few species of wildlife, its benefit as a *mycorrhiza* on the roots of some trees is extremely important to the trees' long-term health. It is therefore an important part of the soil and wider garden ecology.
Closely related species *A. muscaria* is very variable and can be mistaken for other species, such as the edible Mexican *A. basii*, and *A. caesarea* of Europe.

Armillaria mellea

Armillaria mellea
HONEY FUNGUS
Family: Marasmiaceae
Native: Worldwide
Honey fungi are parasitic, living on trees and woody shrubs. They are long-lived organisms and include some of the largest living organisms in the world, with *A. ostoyae* said to be thousands of years old and covering more than 8.9sq km (3.4sq miles). They are a serious pest and can affect ornamental trees.
Appearance The yellow-brown coloured mushrooms that appear at, or just above, the base of the infected plant have caps from 3–15cm (1¼–6in) across, and are covered with small, dark scales.
Role in garden habitats Although honey fungus is a naturally occurring species, it is disliked by most gardeners because of its ability to kill otherwise apparently healthy trees and shrubs. Once present, it can easily spread to other neighbouring woody plants, but it does not affect herbaceous specimens.
Wildlife benefits Honey fungus generally has limited importance to other species of wildlife, despite its edibility. Some flies lay eggs in the caps of the mushrooms but, on the whole, its benefits are limited.
Closely related species The *Armillaria* genus includes about 10 species that were formerly lumped together as *A. mellea*. They are all quite similar and occur widely throughout the world.

Ganoderma adspersum

Ganoderma adspersum
ARTIST'S FUNGUS
Family: Ganodermataceae
Native: Europe and America

This bracket fungus is widespread and parasitic on deciduous trees. *G. adspersum* is one of the commonest species and is called artist's fungus because it is possible to make pictures or drawings on the white pore surface.

Appearance The large, brown brackets have a white underside and develop a new layer each year, resulting in a heavily ridged upper surface as the annual growth remains visible and becomes a permanent structure.

Role in garden habitats It is generally thought of as an unwelcome guest in the garden because its long-lived brackets often grow one above the other, on the lower part of tree trunks. They gradually weaken the woody tissue, and the trunks can snap in high winds.

Wildlife benefits The fungus is an important element of forest habitats. Though it can be devastating for an individual tree, it often results in large amounts of deadwood that is consumed by other species, and helps maintain diversity.

Closely related species The closely related *G. resinaceum* has large brackets with an upper surface that starts out yellow, before maturing to a chestnut or blackish colour. The surface is covered with a glossy, resinous layer, and the white underside turns pale brown or cinnamon with age.

Marasmius oreades
FAIRY RING CHAMPIGNON
Family: Marasmiaceae
Native: Widely distributed, especially in temperate Northern Hemisphere

There are a number of fungi that make "fairy rings", i.e. a ring or arc of mushrooms. In time these rings may grow over 10m (33ft) in diameter, although they are usually most evident when much smaller than this. This species forms conspicuous "toadstools" between late spring and early autumn in a dead circle of grass.

Appearance They are most apparent when the pale brown toadstools appear, although the bare ring, just inside a ring of dark green grass, is visible in turf all year round.

Role in garden habitats There are two types of fairy ring fungus. One type is found in woods, being formed by *mycorrhiza* living on tree roots in a mutually beneficial partnership (see fly agaric). The meadow fairy rings live on decaying material but do not form an association with another plant.

Wildlife benefits Fairy ring champignon generally has a limited importance to other species of wildlife, despite its edibility. Some flies do lay eggs in the caps of the toadstools but, on the whole, its benefits seem to be as a decomposer.

Closely related species Most *Marasmius* species are small, nondescript brown mushrooms that do not form rings. There are somewhere in the region of 40–60 mostly unrelated species however, which do form fairy rings, although many of them only really become apparent once the toadstools appear.

Marasmius oreades

Slime mould

Various species
SLIME MOULD
Family: Many related groups
Native: Worldwide

Slime moulds are extraordinary organisms that show some features of fungus, and some of protozoa. They were formerly though to be a fungus but are now classed as a group on their own, and should not be confused with true moulds that are actually fungi. Although cosmopolitan in distribution, they are mostly small and rarely noticed.

Appearance Slime moulds form a resting organ consisting of a stalk and a head of spores that may, in some cases, be brightly coloured.

Role in garden habitats Slime moulds are naturally found in damp, shady habitats, such as dark forest floors, where they tend to grow over rotted wood after it has rained. They occur widely, with the most visible species occasionally prominent on lawns where they live among dead grass.

Wildlife benefits They are generally of limited importance to other species of wildlife because few other species feed on them. They feed mostly on bacteria, and are usually very beneficial in helping to break down decaying plant remains and other organic matter in the garden.

Closely related species There are several different groups of slime mould, all of which differ in their complex life cycles. While some can easily be seen, some – such as clubroot disease (*Plasmodiophora brassicae*) of cabbages – cannot.

CALENDAR OF CARE

WINTER

EARLY WINTER

- Make bird boxes when work in the garden is quiet, and erect them in suitable places. The birds will get used to them before nesting in spring.
- Place a little bedding, such as dry straw or moss, in new nest boxes to encourage birds to use them.
- Reposition any boxes that have not been used for two years or more.
- Continue feeding resident birds, and introduce high-energy foods, such as fat balls, to help birds through the forthcoming cold weather.
- Provide food from now onwards, until warmer weather arrives for non-hibernating mammals.
- Dig over the soil in the vegetable patch if it is not too wet, and leave for the frost to break it down. Resident birds will search the overturned ground for grubs and insects.
- The compost heap can be emptied and the contents incorporated into the vegetable patch with single or double digging.
- Start to plant out deciduous shrubs and bare-root trees.

MIDWINTER

- If water in the birdbath freezes, thaw it out with boiling water because birds still have to drink and bathe in cold weather.
- Float a rubber ball on a pond or birdbath to prevent the water freezing over.
- Purchase seeds of annuals and herbs for growing next spring.
- Continue to plant out deciduous shrubs and bare-root trees.
- Winter, as well as autumn, is an ideal time to plant out containerized plants because they will grow new roots deeper into the soil before the winter rains cease. If you plant in a dry spring, containerized stock will struggle to find adequate moisture, and the growth will be checked.
- Prune fruit bushes and trees, such as blackcurrants and apples, because the plants are now dormant. This can be continued into late winter.
- Take hardwood cuttings and layers of deciduous shrubs.
- Be sure to feed resident birds at this time, as the coldest weather and dwindling natural foods make life hard for them.

LATE WINTER

- Clean and remove old nesting material from bird boxes because lice and fleas will overwinter and infect new chicks next spring.
- Do not clean out ponds because newts, toads and other creatures will start to migrate here from their winter sites to breed.
- Mulch around shrub borders on a warm day when the soil is still damp.
- Trim one side of the hedge before birds begin to nest, and leave the other side to be pruned next year. This will ensure flowers and fruits every year.
- Plant climbers, such as honeysuckle (*Lonicera*) and clematis, in an established hedgerow to provide a rich nectar source in summer.
- An ideal time for planting a deciduous mixed hedge if the soil is dry enough to work on. This task can be carried out any time during winter.
- Remove any fish from a pond to stop them eating tiny young frogs, toads and newts in spring.
- Under glass, start to sow annuals, such as trailing lobelia and petunias, for summer bedding. Vegetables can also be started off indoors.

SPRING

EARLY SPRING

- Continue sowing annuals and vegetables under glass.
- Cut back herbaceous plants towards the end of this period to provide the maximum shelter for overwintering insects.
- Compost old herbaceous stems. Cut them into small pieces so that they decompose quickly.
- After pruning, mulch herbaceous borders with light material, such as old compost or bark. Mulching with manure can often rot a plant's crown.
- Lift and divide established herbaceous plants every 5–6 years. Compost any dead material, often found in the centre of old clumps.
- Do not put out whole peanuts on the bird table because they may choke chicks. Feeding whole peanuts can recommence after the nesting season is over.
- Put out protein-rich live food, such as mealworms, for birds to feed their chicks.
- Hedgehogs emerging from hibernation will benefit from a bowl of cat food or specialist hedgehog food, which is sold at many garden centres.
- Commence mowing.

MID-SPRING

- Scarify a lawn, and then make a moss ball out of all the debris collected. Hang the ball up in a tree for birds to collect for nesting material.
- Top dress lawns after scarification to encourage beneficial soil organisms, such as worms, into an area of short grass.
- Construct a new pond for planting up next month. Make a list of all the plants needed, and order from a supplier.
- Sow a wildflower meadow mix after preparing the soil. This will entail removing the topsoil to reduce fertility. This can also be carried out in autumn.
- Sow seeds of hardy vegetables outdoors. Cloches may be needed to warm up the soil and provide protection.
- Seedlings of summer-flowering annuals and vegetables grown indoors can be moved to cold frames for hardening off, before planting out.
- Make solitary bee boxes and hang them in a sheltered, sunny position.
- Start weeding, and don't let up.

LATE SPRING

- Plant up hanging baskets and containers to encourage wildlife, and put outside at the end of spring.
- Plant out summer bedding plants, such as nicotiana and verbena, after hardening them off.
- Plant up a new pond when the water starts to warm up and the plants are ready to burst into new growth.
- Sow seeds of hardy annuals, for example sunflowers (*Helianthus annuus*), directly into annual or mixed borders.
- Sow seeds of hardy vegetables outdoors; no protection is needed.
- Remove tree stakes that have been supporting trees for over 1 year.
- Feed containers and hanging baskets with a weak, organic liquid feed to encourage flowers and attract pollinators.
- Record all wildlife present, to help you plan your future projects.
- Carry on weeding throughout the growing season, especially around seedlings. Where possible, mulch borders with old compost.

Feed the birds with high-energy fat balls

Take hardwood cuttings of deciduous shrubs

Plant a deciduous mixed hedge

Lift and divide herbaceous plants

Hang up butterfly boxes in a sunny position

Remove year-old tree stakes

SUMMER

EARLY SUMMER

- Prune out the old growth from spring-flowering shrubs, such as forsythia and flowering currants (*Ribes*).
- Sow seeds of spring-flowering bedding, e.g. wallflowers (*Erysimum*) and forget-me-nots (*Myosotis*).
- Deadhead early spring-flowering herbaceous plants to encourage a second flush of flowers.
- Protect fruit crops from birds. After harvesting, remove nets and allow the birds to forage on the excess fruits.
- Start to water hanging baskets and containers if they dry out, and continue to feed on a weekly or fortnightly basis.
- Make a bird hide for you and the children. Use binoculars to watch the activity in and around garden nest boxes and feeders.
- Butterfly spotting becomes easy as the new broods emerge. Buy an identification guide to name the different species.
- This is also a good time to go pond dipping with children.

MIDSUMMER

- Continue weeding. Remember to compost each time, separating perennial weeds into a separate bag.
- Continue grass cutting. When composting, mix it with brown material, such as dead leaves, to prevent the compost heap from turning slimy.
- Lightly trim hedges after flowering to encourage dense growth for winter.
- Turn the compost heap every two weeks, and water it during dry weather. Take care not to disturb snakes and bumblebee nests.
- Keep birdbaths and ponds topped up with stored rainwater because tap water can be very alkaline, and to avoid wasting mains water.
- Do not use pesticides during summer when infestations of aphids can be troublesome. Let beneficial insects tackle the problem. Use organic plant oils and soft soap to reduce pest numbers until this happens.
- Note how beneficial insect numbers are quickly increasing, provided no chemicals have been used.

LATE SUMMER

- Clear out overgrown ponds.
- Leave the hauled-out vegetation and soil from the pond at the side for a few days to allow inhabitants to return to the water. After this duration of time, recycle the plant material on the compost heap.
- Only clear out up to one-third of a pond at any one time.
- Trim the nectar-rich, summer-flowering herbaceous plants to encourage a second flush of flowers.
- Site a hedgehog box under a hedge or log pile to enable wildlife to get used to it before it is used in autumn. Add some bedding.
- Fill bird boxes that are no longer in use with straw to provide hibernation sites for bumblebee queens and other insects.
- Take semi-ripe cuttings of many species of shrubs.
- Cut down about a third of a nettle patch to promote new growth. Late-flying butterflies will prefer laying their eggs on new leaves.
- Put out hibernation boxes for beneficial insects, such as ladybirds.

AUTUMN

EARLY AUTUMN

- Put netting over a pond to stop leaves falling in. The leaves can be used to make leaf mould.
- Collect seeds from garden plants to sow next year. They should be stored in a paper bag to allow the seeds to breathe and prevent mould.
- Build a "habitat stack", log pile or drystone wall to provide overwintering and hibernation sites for a variety of animals.
- Leave any annual herbs, such as dill, or vegetables (carrots and lettuce) to flower to boost the nectar supplies for autumn insects.
- Start to plant out bulbs that will flower the following spring.
- Sow a wildflower meadow mix while the ground is warm – the seeds will germinate quickly. In the preparation, remove the soil for best results.
- Now or in mid-autumn, remove the summer-flowering plants in a hanging basket and replace with spring-flowering plants.
- Create piles of leaves and small twigs under vegetation, as these make ideal hibernation spots for small mammals.

MID-AUTUMN

- Do not cut down old herbaceous stems in autumn because insects will overwinter in the crevices and hollow stems.
- Leave seed heads of oil-rich species, such as lavender and evening primrose, for seed-eating birds.
- Assess all the garden plants for their wildlife value.
- If redesigning part of the garden, make sure that any new plants are wildlife-friendly, providing berries, nectar, pollen and nesting material.
- Plant out spring bedding plants for flowering next year. Use plants such as single-flowering wallflowers (*Erysimum*) and forget-me-nots (*Myosotis*).
- If the soil is not dry, plant new containerized shrubs, climbers and trees.
- Plant out potted wildflowers, such as cowslips (*Primula*), in areas of grass.
- Pick ripe berries off bushes, e.g. hawthorn (*Crataegus*), and remove the fleshy covering before sowing.
- Lift and divide herbaceous perennials before the ground becomes too wet.

LATE AUTUMN

- Clean out the greenhouse from top to bottom to eradicate any pests and diseases, and to allow maximum light penetration over the winter months, especially if plants are being grown in it.
- Find out which bird species are resident in your area, and buy the appropriate feeders and food.
- Build a bird-feeding station close to shrub or tree cover.
- Start to feed the birds over the cold winter period. Feed with a variety of foods to encourage different species into the garden.
- If you intend using live food feeders, be prepared to continue this through the whole winter to ensure the wellbeing of carnivorous birds.
- Continue to plant out containerized shrubs, trees and herbaceous plants.
- Begin winter pruning of deciduous shrubs and trees. Save larger prunings to create log piles around the garden.
- Shred smaller twigs and make hibernation piles using branches and fallen leaves. Create a leaf-mould compost heap.

Make a bird hide for you and the children

Turn the compost every two weeks

Site hedgehog boxes under shelter

Build a habitat stack for various wildlife

Pick ripe berries off bushes to sow

Shred twigs to make wood chips

SUPPLIERS

UNITED KINGDOM

Field guides
Field Studies Council Publications
The Annexe
Preston Montford Lane
Shrewsbury
Shropshire SY4 1DU
Tel: 01743 852 140
Email: publications@field-studies-council.org

Organizations
Field Studies Council
Head Office
Montford Bridge
Preston Montford
Shrewsbury
Shropshire SY4 1HW
Tel: 01743 852 100
Email: enquiries@field-studies-council.org
www.field-studies-council.org

The Wildlife Trusts
The Kiln
Waterside
Mather Road
Newark
Nottinghamshire NG24 1WT
Tel: 0870 036 7711
Email: enquiry@wildlifetrusts.org
www.wildlifetrusts.org

Information on growing native plants
Flora locale
Denford Manor
Hungerford, Berkshire RG17 0UN
Tel: 01488 680 457
Email: info@floralocale.org
www.floralocale.org

Habitat and nesting boxes, feed and food supplements
Wiggly Wigglers
Lower Blakemere Farm
Blakemere, Herefordshire HR2 9PX
Tel: 01981 500 391
www.wigglywigglers.co.uk

CJ WildBird Foods Ltd
The Rea
Upton Magna
Shrewsbury SY4 4UR
Tel: 01743 709 545
www.birdfood.co.uk

The Specialist Bird Food Company
Gravel Hill Road
Holt Pound
Farnham, Surrey GU10 4LG
Tel: 01420 23986
www.wild-bird-food.co.uk

Plants and seeds
Emorsgate Seeds
Limes Farm, Tilney All Saints
King's Lynn, Norfolk PE34 4RT
Tel: 01553 829 028
Email: enquiries@emorsgate-seeds.co.uk
www.wildseed.co.uk

British Wildflower Plants
Burlingham Gardens
North Burlingham, Norwich NR13 4TA
Tel: 01603 716 615
Email: paul@wildflowers.co.uk

John Chambers Wild Flower Seeds
15 Westleigh Road, Barton Seagrave
Kettering, Northamptonshire NN15 5AJ
Tel: 01933 652 562

UNITED STATES

Field guides
Audubon Field Guides
Knopf Publishing Group
201 East 50th Street
New York, NY 10022
Tel: (800) 733-3000
www.audubon.org

Organizations
National Wildlife Federation
11100 Wildlife Center Drive
Reston, VA 20190
Tel: (800) 822-9919
www.nwf.org

Information on growing native plants
Lady Bird Johnson Wildflower Center
4801 La Crosse Avenue
Austin, TX 78739
Tel: (512) 232-0100
www.wildflower.org

Habitat and nesting boxes, feed and food supplements
Rachel's Robin
GregRobert Enterprises, LLC
PO Box 3152
Farmington Hills, MI 48333
www.rachelsrobin.com

Backyard Wildlife Refuge
9463 Hwy 377 South
Suite 146
Benbrook, TX 76126
www.backyardwildlife.com

Woodland Habitat
Gayle Pille
3495 Feeley Road
Burlington, KY 41005
Tel: (859) 586-0077
Email: gaylepille@yahoo.com
www.woodlandhabitat.com

Plants and seeds
Easyliving Wildflowers
PO Box 522
Willow Springs, MO 65793
Tel: (417) 469-2611
Email: john@easywildflowers.com
www.easywildflowers.com

The Wildflower Seed Company
PO Box 406
St. Helena, CA 94574
Tel: (800) 456-3359
Email: sales@wildflower-seed.com
www.wildflower-seed.com

Prairie Frontier
W281 S3606 Pheasant Run
Waukesha, WI 53189
Tel: (414) 544-6708
Email: wildflower@prairiefrontier.com
www.prairiefrontier.com

CANADA

Field guides
Audubon Field Guides
Knopf Publishing Group
201 East 50th Street
New York, NY 10022
Tel: (800) 733-3000
www.audubon.org

Nature Study Guild Publishers
PO Box 10489
Rochester, NY 14610-0489
Tel: (800) 954-2984
Email: naturebooks@worldnet.att.net
www.naturestudy.com

Organizations
Canadian Wildlife Federation
350 Michael Cowpland Drive
Kanata, Ontario K2M 2W1
Tel: 1-800-563-WILD or (613) 599-9594
www.cwf-fcf.org

Information on growing native plants
North American Native Plant Society
(formerly the Canadian Wildflower Society)
NANPS, PO Box 84, Station D
Etobicoke, Ontario M9A 4X1
Tel: (416) 631-4438
Email: nanps@nanps.org
www.nanps.org

Habitat and nesting boxes, feed and food supplements
Bird Feeders Direct
Editor, Bird Feeders Direct
Geosign Technologies Inc.
503 Imperial Road North, Units 5–9
Guelph, Ontario N1H6T9
Tel: (866) 436-7446, ext. 2295
Fax: (519) 837-1288

The Wildbird Habitat Store
8810-C Young Road
Chilliwack, British Columbia V2P 4P5
Tel: (604) 792-1239
Fax: (604) 792-3436
Email: jasono@imag.net
www.wildbirdstore.com

Plants and seeds
Prairie Habitats Inc.
Box 1, Argyle, Manitoba R0C 0B0
Tel: (204) 467-9371
Fax: (204) 467-5004
Email: jpmorgan@mb.sympatico.ca
www.prairiehabitats.com

Nature's Garden Seed Co.
PO Box 32105, 3651 Shelbourne Street
Victoria, British Columbia V8P 5S2
Tel: (250) 595-2062 or 1-877-302-7333
Email: mail@naturesgardenseed.com
www.naturesgardenseed.com

AUSTRALIA

Field guides and gardening
CSIRO Publishing
PO Box 1139
(150 Oxford Street)
Collingwood
VIC 3066
Tel: (03) 9662 7500
Email: publishing@csiro.au
www.publish.csiro.au

Organizations
Wildlife Preservation Society of Australia Inc.
PO Box 42
Brighton Le Sands
NSW 2216
Tel: (02) 9556 1537
Email: wildlifepreservation@optusnet.com.au
www.wpsa.org.au

Information on growing native plants
Australian National Botanic Garden
GPO Box 1777
Canberra, ACT 2601
Tel: (02) 6250 9540
Email: anbg-info@anbg.gov.au
www.anbg.gov.au/anbg

Habitat and nesting boxes, feed and food supplements
Melbourne Wildlife Sanctuary
La Trobe University
VIC 3086
Tel: (03) 9479 1206
Email: wildlife@latrobe.edu.au
www.latrobe.edu.au/wildlife

Hollow Log Homes
PO Box 144
Kenilworth
QLD 4574
Tel: (07) 5472 3142
www.hollowloghomes.net

Plants and seeds
Native Growth Holdings
6/15 Marine Parade
St Kilda
VIC 3182
Tel: (03) 9593 9665
Email: tim@nativenursery.com.au
nativegrowth.c3.ixwebhosting.com

Australian Seed Company
PO Box 67
Hazelbrook, NSW 2779
Tel: (02) 4758 6132

Nindethana Seed Service
PO Box 2121
Albany, WA 6330
Tel: (08) 9844 3533
Email: nindseed@iinet.net.au
www.nindethana.iinet.net.au

NEW ZEALAND

Field guides
Mobil New Zealand Nature Series
Reed Publishing (NZ)

Organizations
Royal Forest and Bird Protection Society
of New Zealand
Wellington Central Office
Level One
90 Ghuznee Street
PO Box 631
Wellington
Tel: (04) 385 7374
www.forestandbird.org.nz

Information on growing native plants
New Zealand Plant Conservation Network
PO Box 16-102
Wellington
Email: info@nzpcn.org.nz
www.nzpcn.org.nz

New Zealand Gardens Online
www.gardens.co.nz

Plants and seeds
Oriata Native Plant Nursery
625 West Coast Road
Oratia
Auckland
Tel: (09) 818 6467
www.oratianatives.co.nz

Country Cottage Nursery
205 A Godley Road
Titirangi
Auckland
Tel: (09) 817 7806
homepages.ihug.co.nz/~shrubs

New Zealand Tree Seeds
PO Box 435
Rangiora 8254
Tel: (03) 312 1635
www.nzseeds.co.nz

INDEX

PLANT HARDINESS ZONES

HARDINESS SYMBOLS

✸ = half-hardy (down to 0°C)
✸ ✸ = frost hardy (down to -5°C)
✸ ✸ ✸ = fully hardy (down to -15°C)

ZONE ENTRIES

Plant entries in the directory of this book have been given zone numbers, and these zones relate to their hardiness. The zonal system used, shown below, was developed by the Agricultural Research Service of the

U.S. Dept of Agriculture. According to this system, there are 11 zones in total, based on the average annual minimum temperature in a particular geographical zone. When a range of zones is given for a plant, the smaller number indicates the northernmost zone in which a plant can survive the winter, and the higher number gives the most southerly area in which it will perform consistently before suffering from an adverse heat-stress reaction.

This is not a hard and fast system, but simply a rough indicator, as many factors other than temperature also play an important part where hardiness is concerned. These factors include altitude, wind exposure, proximity to water, soil type, the presence of snow or shade, night temperature, and the amount of water received by a plant. This kind of factor can easily alter a plant's hardiness by as much as two zones.

KEY TO ZONES

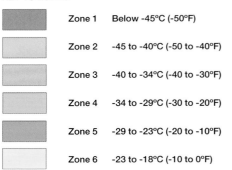
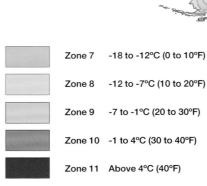

Zone 1	Below -45°C (-50°F)
Zone 2	-45 to -40°C (-50 to -40°F)
Zone 3	-40 to -34°C (-40 to -30°F)
Zone 4	-34 to -29°C (-30 to -20°F)
Zone 5	-29 to -23°C (-20 to -10°F)
Zone 6	-23 to -18°C (-10 to 0°F)
Zone 7	-18 to -12°C (0 to 10°F)
Zone 8	-12 to -7°C (10 to 20°F)
Zone 9	-7 to -1°C (20 to 30°F)
Zone 10	-1 to 4°C (30 to 40°F)
Zone 11	Above 4°C (40°F)

ACKNOWLEDGEMENTS

AUTHORS' ACKNOWLEDGEMENTS

Thank you to Writtle College and their staff for allowing the use of their grounds and glasshouses to take many of the photographs.

Thank you also to the following people who worked as models for the photography: Edward Anderson; Peter Anderson; Lin Blunt; Dave Campbell; Benjamin Crosby; Jane Dobson; Felicity Forster; Simon Grundy; Lucy and Florence Kedman-Watts; Denis Lloyd; Gemma, Oliver and Oscar Mackman; Christine and Luca Mailbaum; Rachel and George Nutton;

Charlotte, Olivia and James Power; Donna Sheringham; Chris Streward; Graham Thompstone; Mary Venables; Jackie Wright.

We would also like to thank Ben Wincott for his garden design advice and drawings.

PUBLISHER'S ACKNOWLEDGEMENTS

The publisher would like to thank the following for kindly allowing photography to take place in their gardens: Jane Dobson, Chelmsford; Debbie Hart, Bocking; Stuart and Maj Jackson-Carter; Kew Gardens; Christine and Michael Lavelle; Pam Lewis, Sticky Wicket; RHS Hyde Hall; RHS Rosemoor, Devon; RHS Wisley, Surrey; Writtle College, Chelmsford.

The publisher would also like to thank the following for allowing their photographs to be reproduced in the book (t=top, b=bottom, l=left, r=right, c=centre, f=far):
Alamy: 167 panel 2nd from l, 167 panel fr, 247b.
Steve Austin/papiliophotos.com: 23br, 40br, 46t, 47tl, 47tr, 56t, 58t, 101 panel 3rd from bl,

104t, 108t, 109 panel tc, 109 panel tr, 117tl, 117b, 130t, 136t, 140t, 141t, 142t, 143br, 145m, 150br.
Dave Bevan: 18t, 35bl, 61cr, 88 panel fl, 119 panel 8th from b, 170b, 171b, 194tl, 201b, 223bl, 224tl, 245tl, 246b.
Corbis: 91 panel fl, 151 panel 2nd from r, 167 panel 2nd from r, 169 panel tl.
Frank Blackburn/Ecoscene: 74t, 76t.
Lucy Doncaster: 93c.
Felicity Forster: 20.
Garden Picture Library: 206tl, 207br.
Garden World Images: 151 panel fl, 151 panel 2nd from l, 163 panel bl, 167 panel fl, 169 panel cl, 183t, 184tr, 188b, 191tr, 191b, 193br, 194tr, 195bl, 196bl, 200t, 202tl, 203br, 205t, 216bl, 218bl, 220bl, 221b, 222b, 226br, 229tr.
iStockphoto: 6 panel tr.
Michael Lavelle: 125b, 141br, 195br.
Charles Lightfoot: 11bl, 13c, 139tr.
NHPA: 139tl, 143bl, 172c, 172bl.